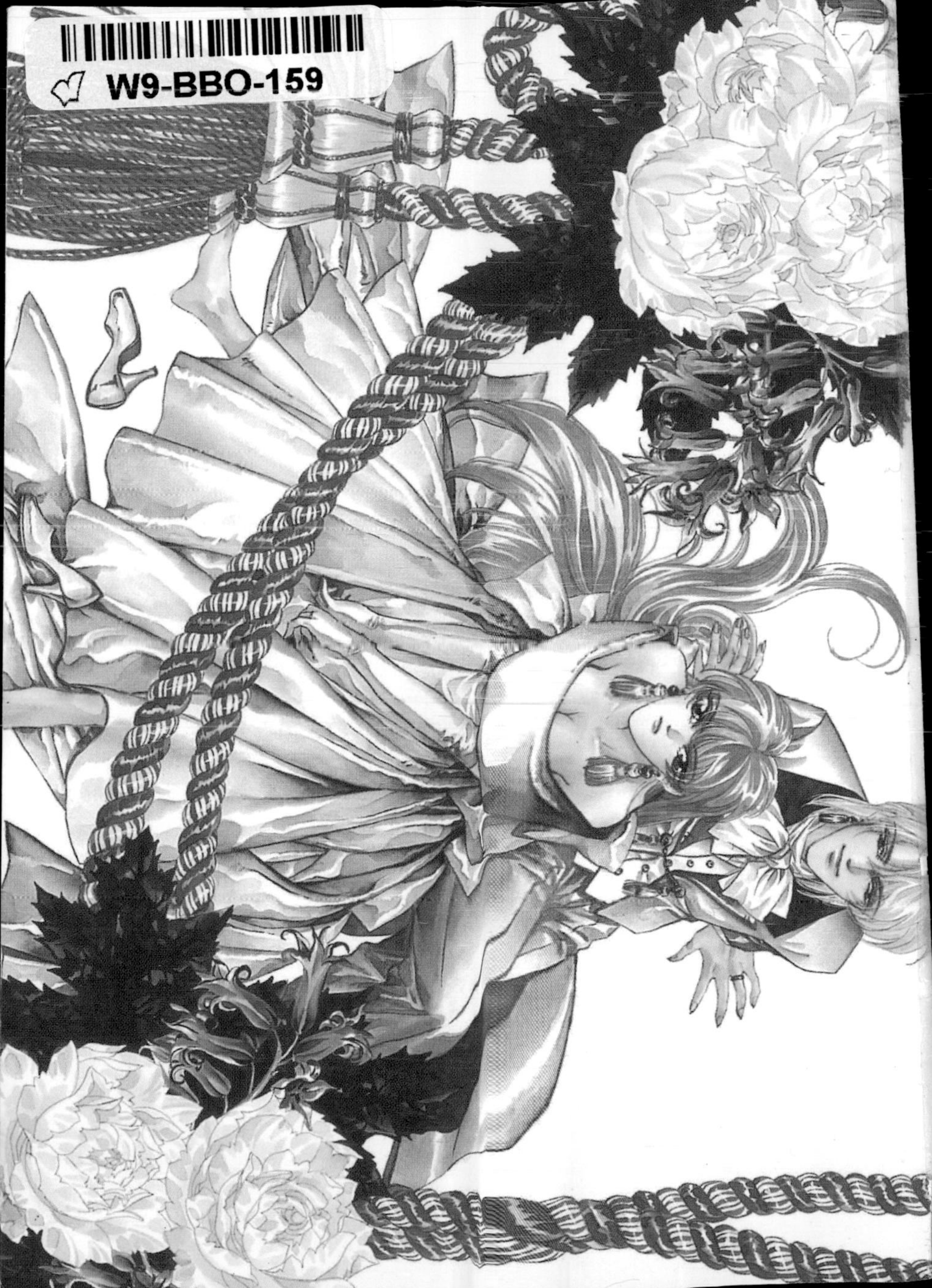

Other titles available from Broccoli Books

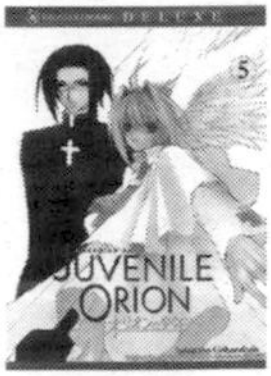
5
JUVENILE
ORION

Aquarian Age – Juvenile Orion

Sixteen-year-old Mana returns to her hometown and reunites with her childhood friend Kaname after 7 years. But he seems to have changed during their years apart. They soon discover that they are part of the Aquarian Age—a secret war raging for thousands of years—and Mana just might hold the key to end it!

Story & Art by Sakurako Gokurakuin

Suggested Retail Price: $9.99

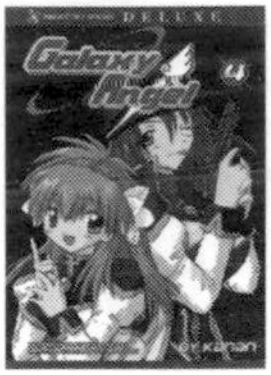
Galaxy Angel
4
Kanan

Galaxy Angel

The Angel Troupe has one mission; they must protect Prince Shiva, the sole survivor of the royal family decimated by a coup d'état. Milfeulle, Ranpha, Mint, Forte, and Vanilla each possess special gifts, making them ideal for the job at hand. Takuto finds himself leading the mission, getting caught between the five unique Angels and...space whales!?

Story & Art by Kanan

Suggested Retail Price: $9.99

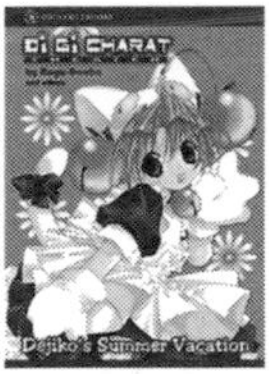
Di Gi Charat
Dejiko's Summer Vacation

Di Gi Charat Theater – Dejiko's Summer Vacation & Piyoko is Number One!

Join Dejiko and the gang as they hit the beach, switch bodies, blow up the Black Gema Gema Gang, and discover the secret of Hokke Mirin and her cat corp! And watch out Dejiko! Piyoko and her gang attempt to steal the show with their very own book!

Story & Art by Koge-Donbo and others

Suggested Retail Price: $9.99 each

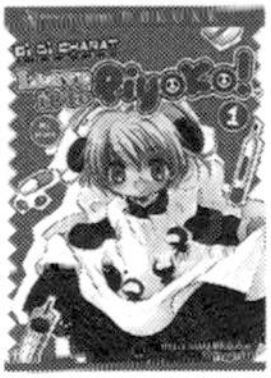
Di Gi Charat
Piyoko!
1

Di Gi Charat Theater – Leave it to Piyoko!

Follow the daily adventures of the Black Gema Gema Gang, as they continue their road to evil.

Story & Art by Hina.

Suggested Retail Price: $9.99

Volume 2 Coming Soon!

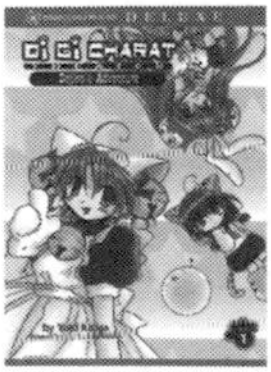
Di Gi Charat

Di Gi Charat Theater – Dejiko's Adventure

Dejiko has destroyed the Gamers retail store! Now it's up to her and the rest of the gang as they search for the secret treasure that will save Gamers.

Story & Art by Yuki Kiriga

Suggested Retail Price: $9.99

Volumes 2-3 Coming Soon!

For more information about Broccoli Books titles,
check out **bro-usa.com!**

Until the FULL Moon II

by Sanami Matoh

brought to you by
BROCCOLI BOOKS
A DIVISION OF BROCCOLI INTERNATIONAL USA

Until the Full Moon Volume 2

English Adaptation Staff
Translation: Rie Hagihara
English Adaptation: Elizabeth Hanel
Touch-Up & Lettering: Fawn "tails" Lau
Cover & Graphic Supervision: Chris McDougall

Editor: Dietrich Seto
Sales Manager: Ardith D. Santiago
Managing Editor: Shizuki Yamashita
Publisher: Hideki Uchino

Email: editor@broccolibooks.com
Website: www.bro-usa.com

A (**B**) BROCCOLI BOOKS Manga
Broccoli Books is a division of Broccoli International USA, Inc.
12211 W. Washington Blvd, Suite 110, Los Angeles CA 90066

FULLMOON ni sasayaite II © Sanami Matoh 1998
Originally published in Japan in 1998 by BIBLOS Co, Ltd.

ISBN: 1-932480-89-7

Published by Broccoli International USA, Inc.
First printing, February 2005

www.bro-usa.com

10 9 8 7 6 5 4 3 2 1
Printed in the United States

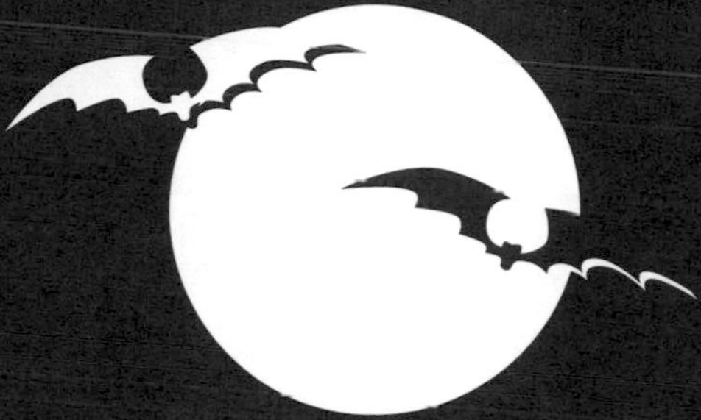

TABLE OF CONTEN

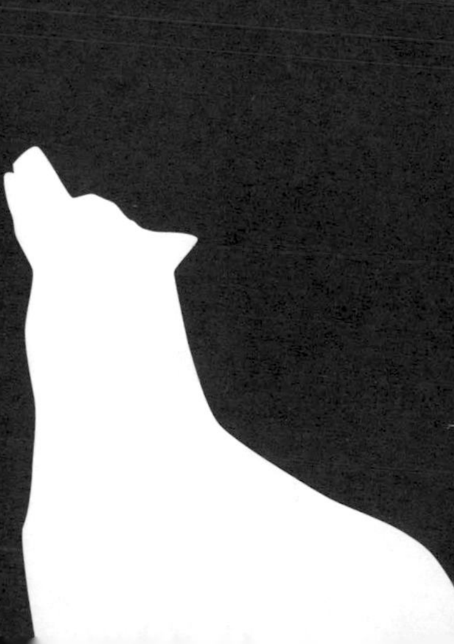

CHARACTERS

Marlo Vincent
Half-werewolf, half-vampire.
Changes into a woman during
the full moon.

Marlo Vincent
Marlo's female form.

David Vincent
Marlo's childhood friend. He's
also a vampire and a womanizer.

Arnet Vincent
David's father. A vampire
and famous doctor.

Kim
Arnet and David's servant.
He's a lower level demon.

6

Georgio Vincent
Marlo's father. He's a vampire who married a werewolf.

Mira
Marlo's mother. She's a werewolf who married Georgio, a vampire.

Claudia Beaufort
David's ex-girlfriend from when Marlo was in America.

Louis du Flenne
A vampire and pharmacist. Claudia's caretaker when she was younger.

Holly Argent
David's deceased mother. She was a human whom Arnet fell in love with.

Jennifer
Arnet's former fiancée whom he left because of his love for Holly.

Katelyn
Jennifer's daughter. She knows some witchcraft.

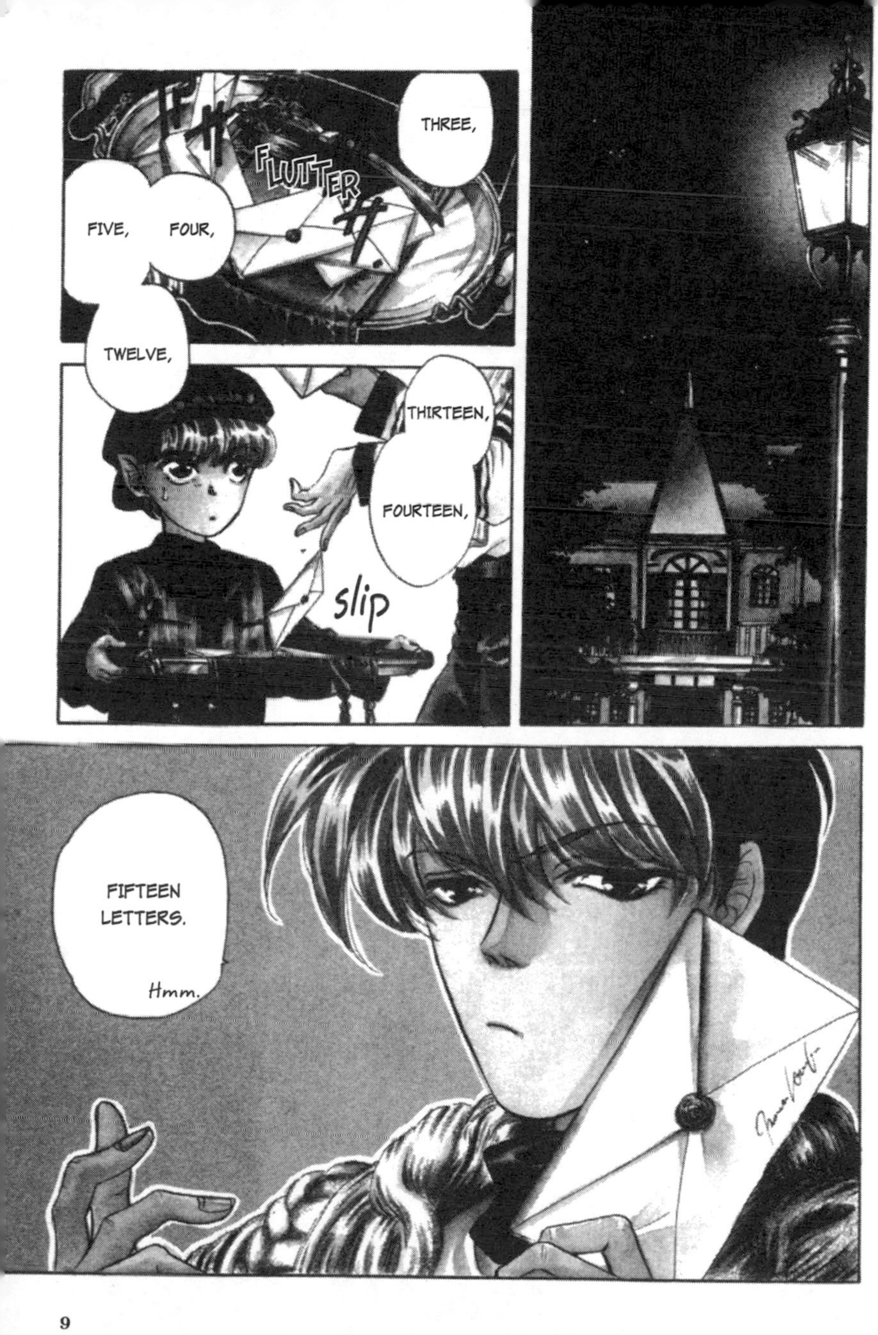
THREE,
FLUTTER
FOUR,
FIVE,
TWELVE,
THIRTEEN,
FOURTEEN,
slip
FIFTEEN LETTERS.
Hmm.

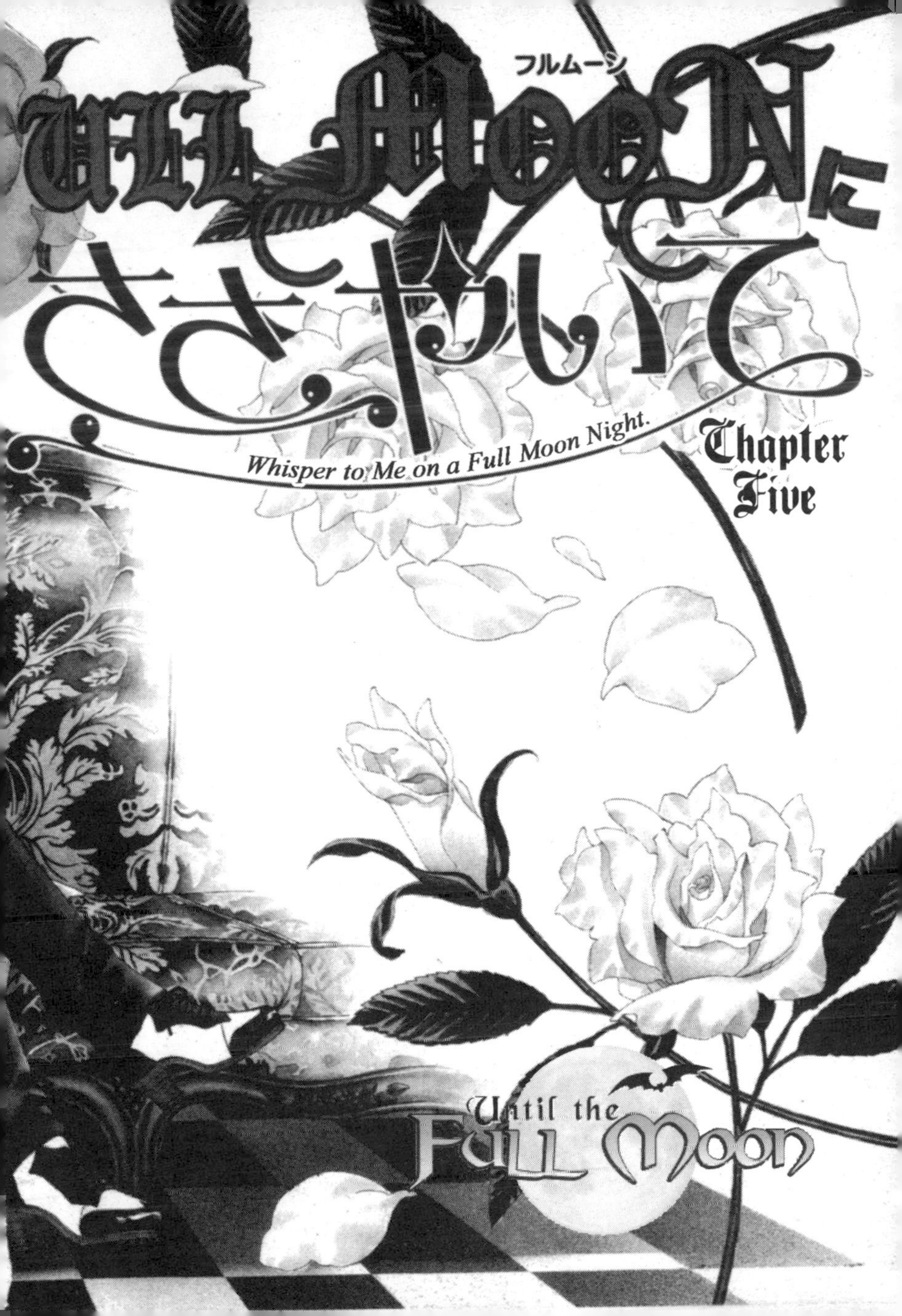
フルムーン
Whisper to Me on a Full Moon Night.
Chapter Five
Until the Full Moon

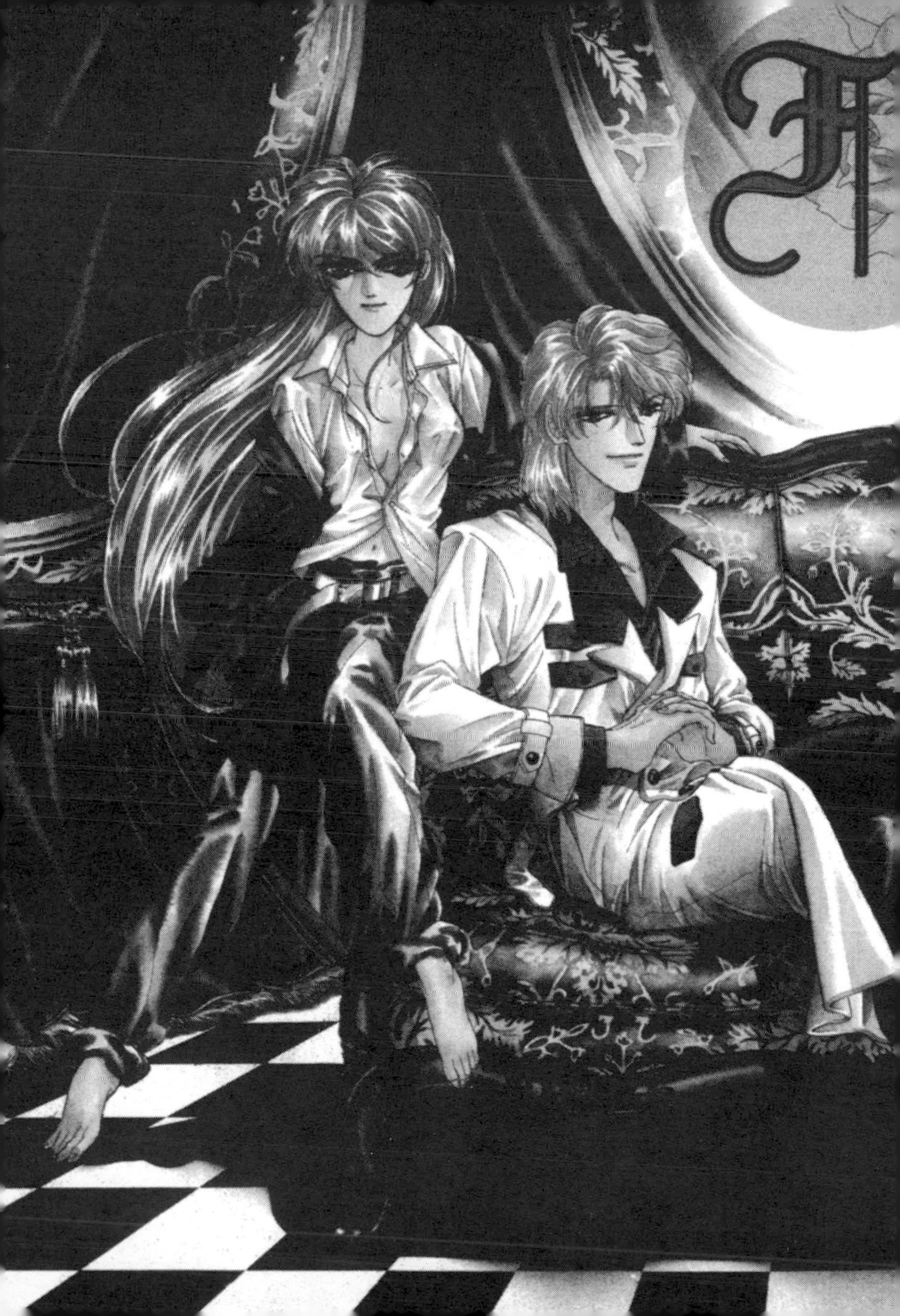

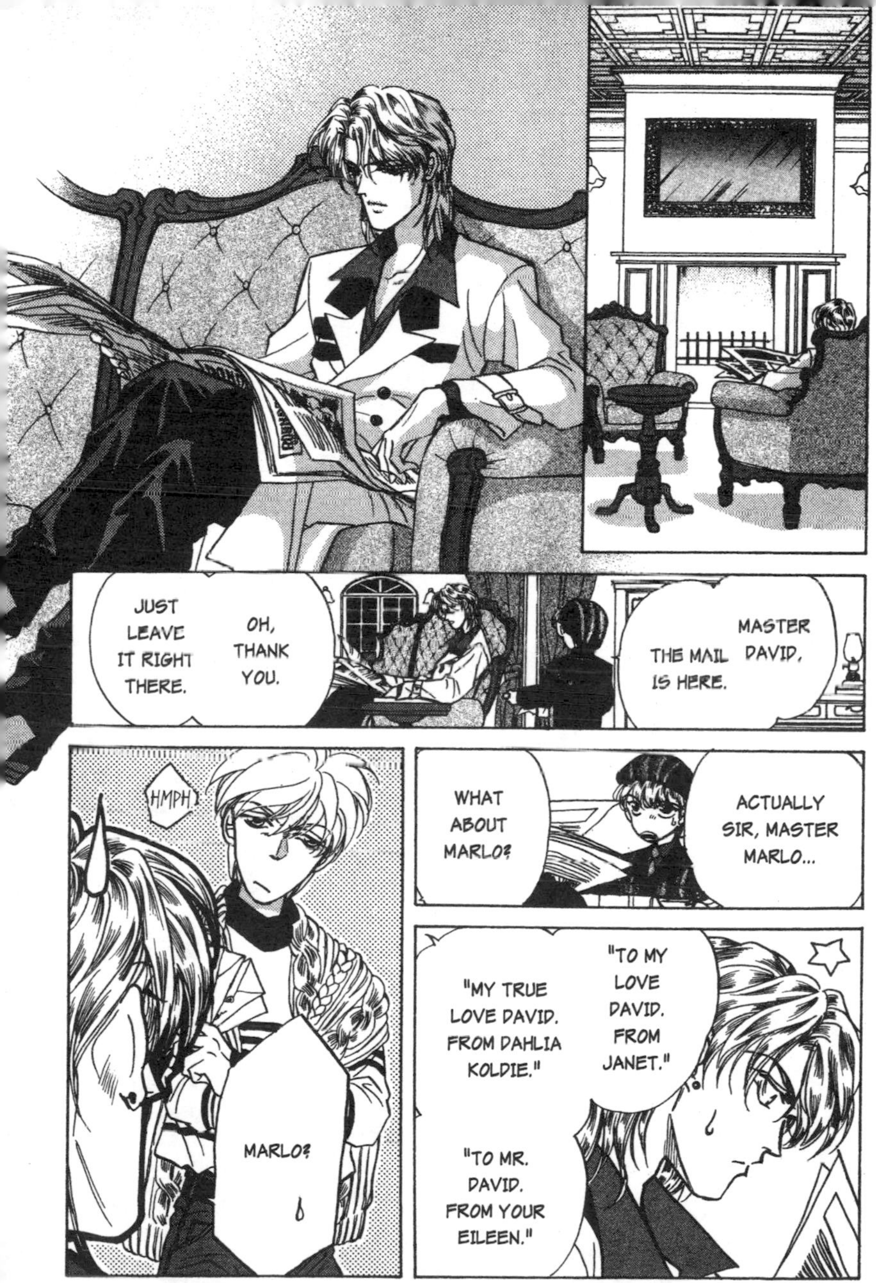
MASTER DAVID, THE MAIL IS HERE.
OH, THANK YOU.
JUST LEAVE IT RIGHT THERE.
ACTUALLY SIR, MASTER MARLO...
WHAT ABOUT MARLO?
"TO MY LOVE DAVID. FROM JANET."
"MY TRUE LOVE DAVID. FROM DAHLIA KOLDIE."
"TO MR. DAVID. FROM YOUR EILEEN."
HMPH
MARLO?

*David's father is a doctor.

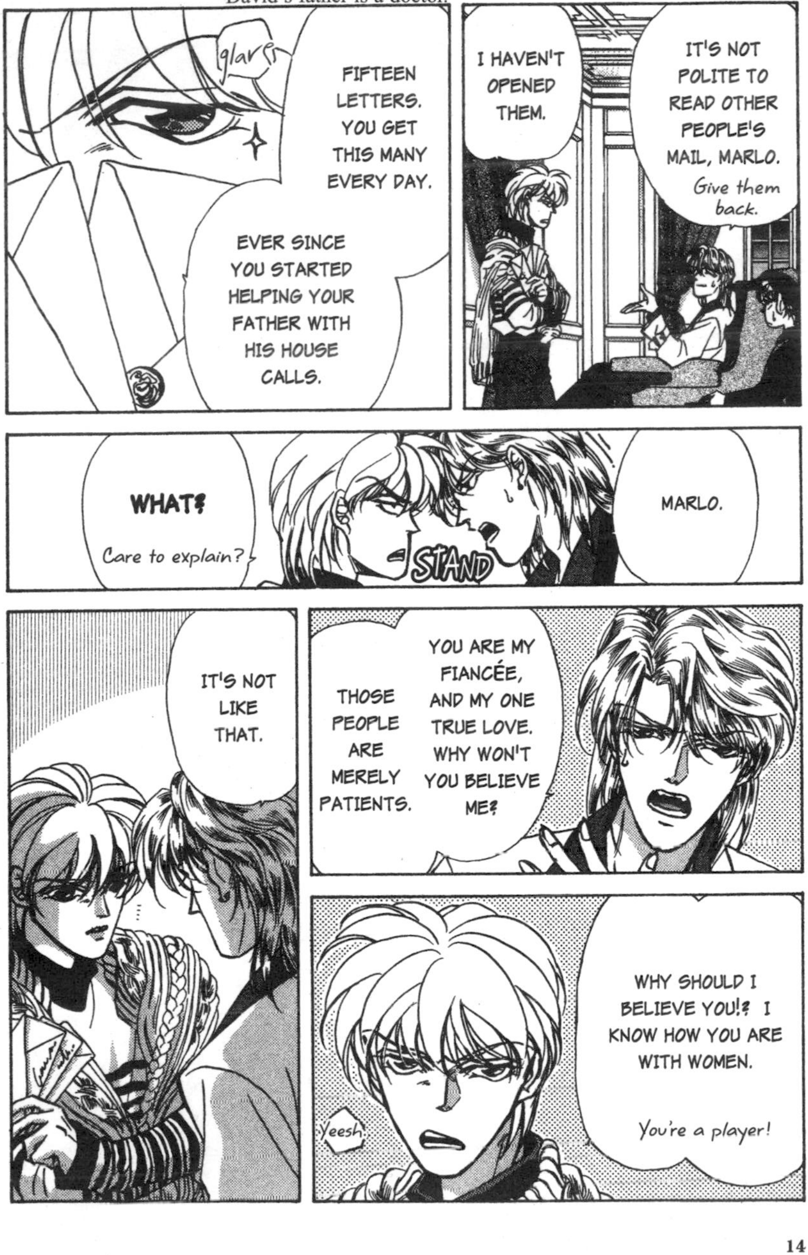
IT'S NOT POLITE TO READ OTHER PEOPLE'S MAIL, MARLO.
Give them back.
I HAVEN'T OPENED THEM.
glare
FIFTEEN LETTERS. YOU GET THIS MANY EVERY DAY.
EVER SINCE YOU STARTED HELPING YOUR FATHER WITH HIS HOUSE CALLS.
MARLO.
STAND
WHAT?
Care to explain?
YOU ARE MY FIANCÉE, AND MY ONE TRUE LOVE. WHY WON'T YOU BELIEVE ME?
THOSE PEOPLE ARE MERELY PATIENTS.
WHY SHOULD I BELIEVE YOU!? I KNOW HOW YOU ARE WITH WOMEN.
You're a player!
Yeesh
IT'S NOT LIKE THAT.

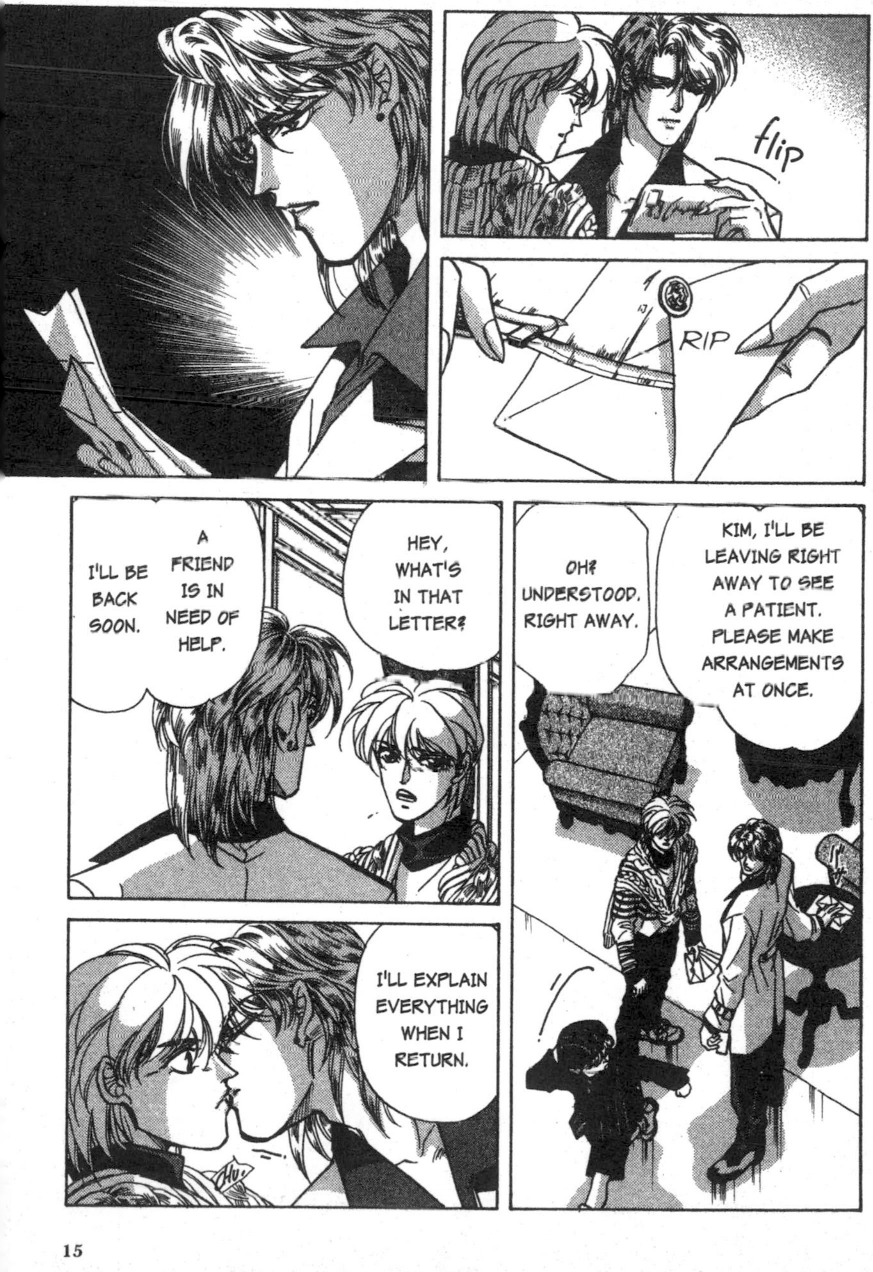
flip
RIP
KIM, I'LL BE LEAVING RIGHT AWAY TO SEE A PATIENT. PLEASE MAKE ARRANGEMENTS AT ONCE.
OH? UNDERSTOOD. RIGHT AWAY.
HEY, WHAT'S IN THAT LETTER?
A FRIEND IS IN NEED OF HELP.
I'LL BE BACK SOON.
I'LL EXPLAIN EVERYTHING WHEN I RETURN.

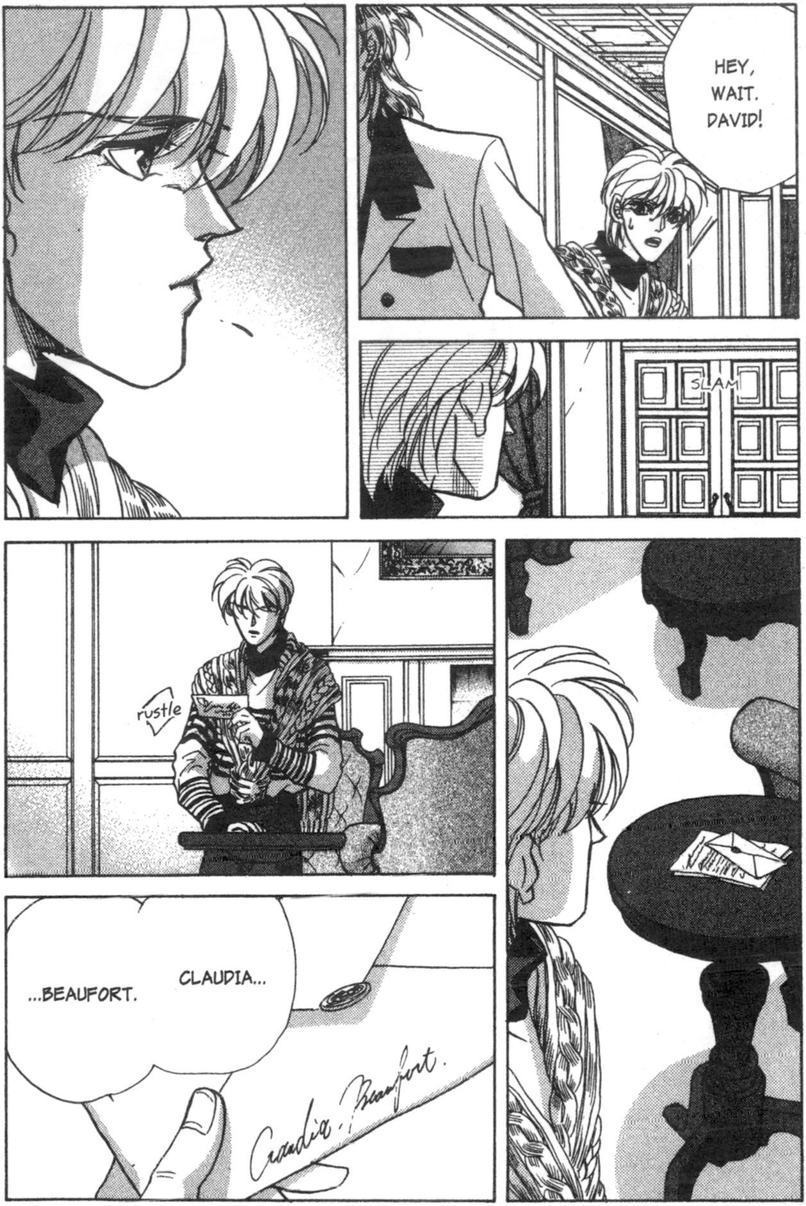
HEY, WAIT. DAVID!
SLAM
rustle
CLAUDIA...
...BEAUFORT.
Claudia. Beaufort.

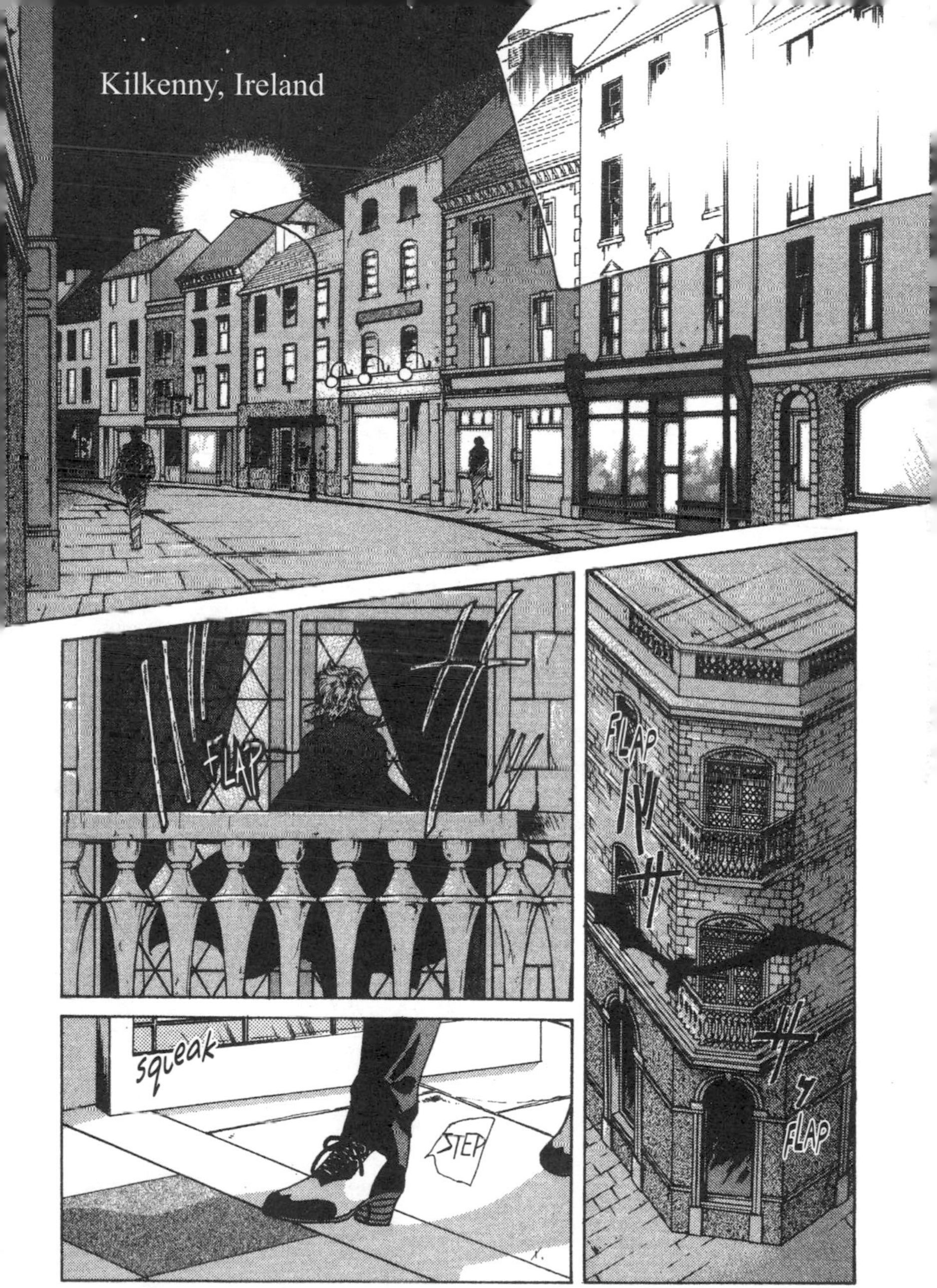
Kilkenny, Ireland
FLAP
FLAP
FLAP
squeak
STEP

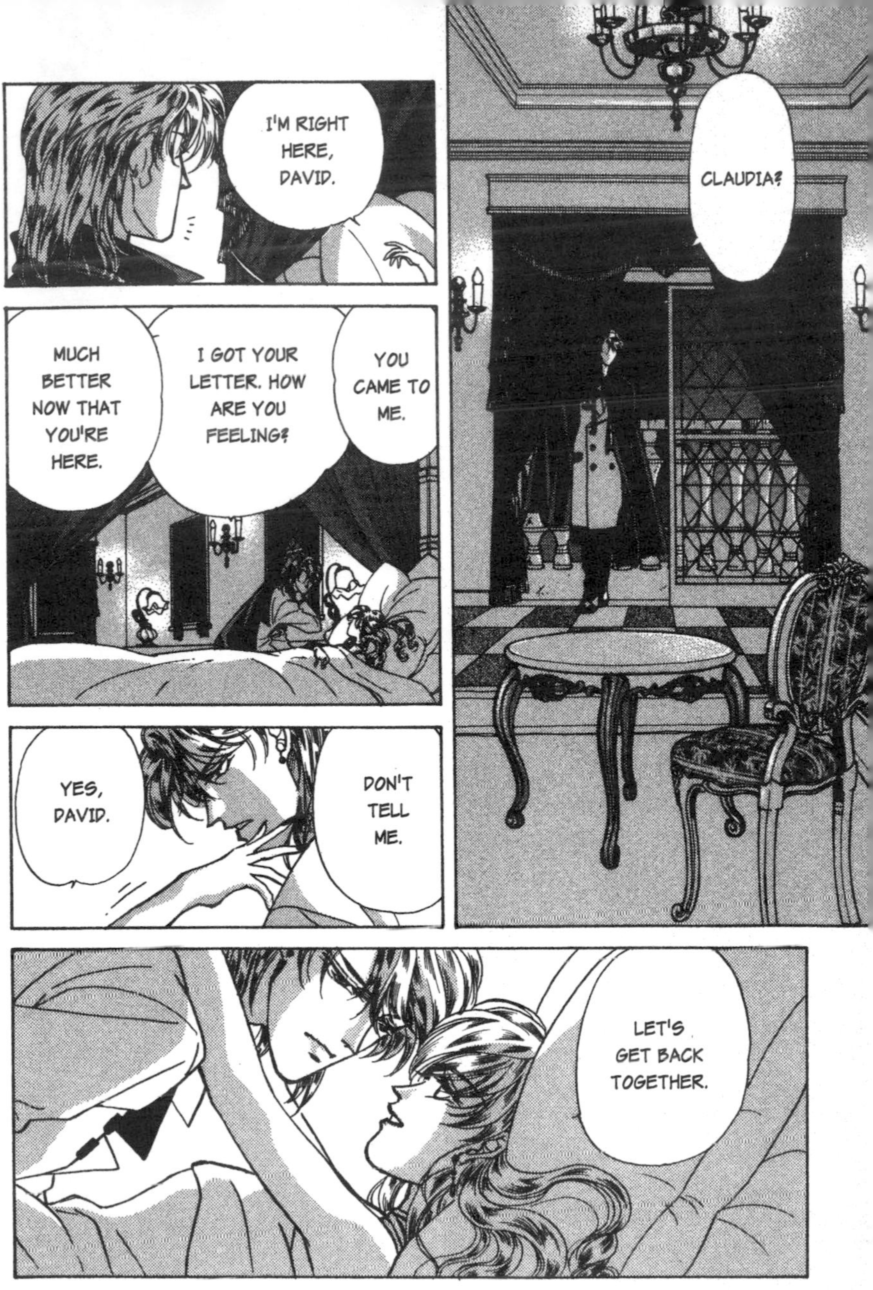
CLAUDIA?
I'M RIGHT HERE, DAVID.
YOU CAME TO ME.
I GOT YOUR LETTER. HOW ARE YOU FEELING?
MUCH BETTER NOW THAT YOU'RE HERE.
DON'T TELL ME.
YES, DAVID.
LET'S GET BACK TOGETHER.

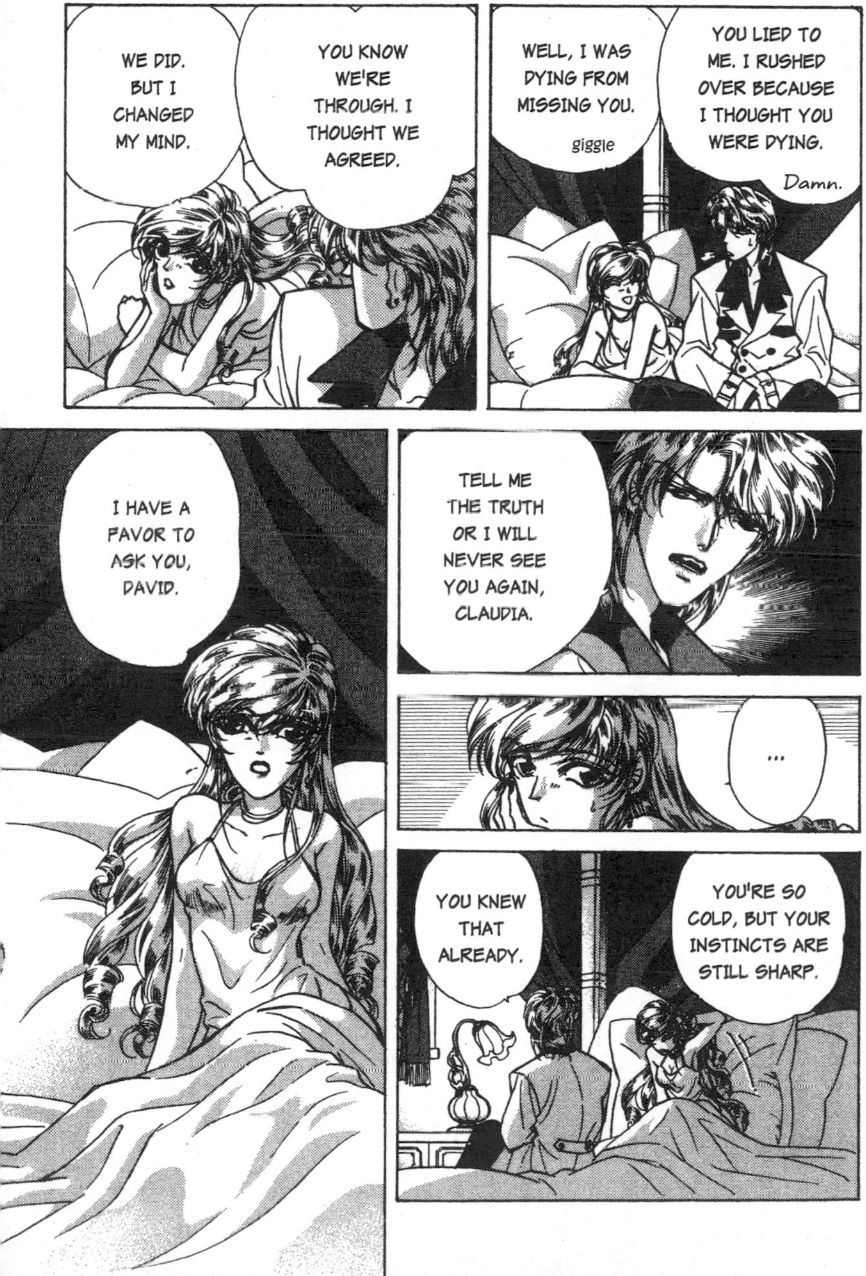
YOU LIED TO ME. I RUSHED OVER BECAUSE I THOUGHT YOU WERE DYING.
Damn.
WELL, I WAS DYING FROM MISSING YOU.
giggle
YOU KNOW WE'RE THROUGH. I THOUGHT WE AGREED.
WE DID. BUT I CHANGED MY MIND.
TELL ME THE TRUTH OR I WILL NEVER SEE YOU AGAIN, CLAUDIA.
...
YOU'RE SO COLD, BUT YOUR INSTINCTS ARE STILL SHARP.
YOU KNEW THAT ALREADY.
I HAVE A FAVOR TO ASK YOU, DAVID.

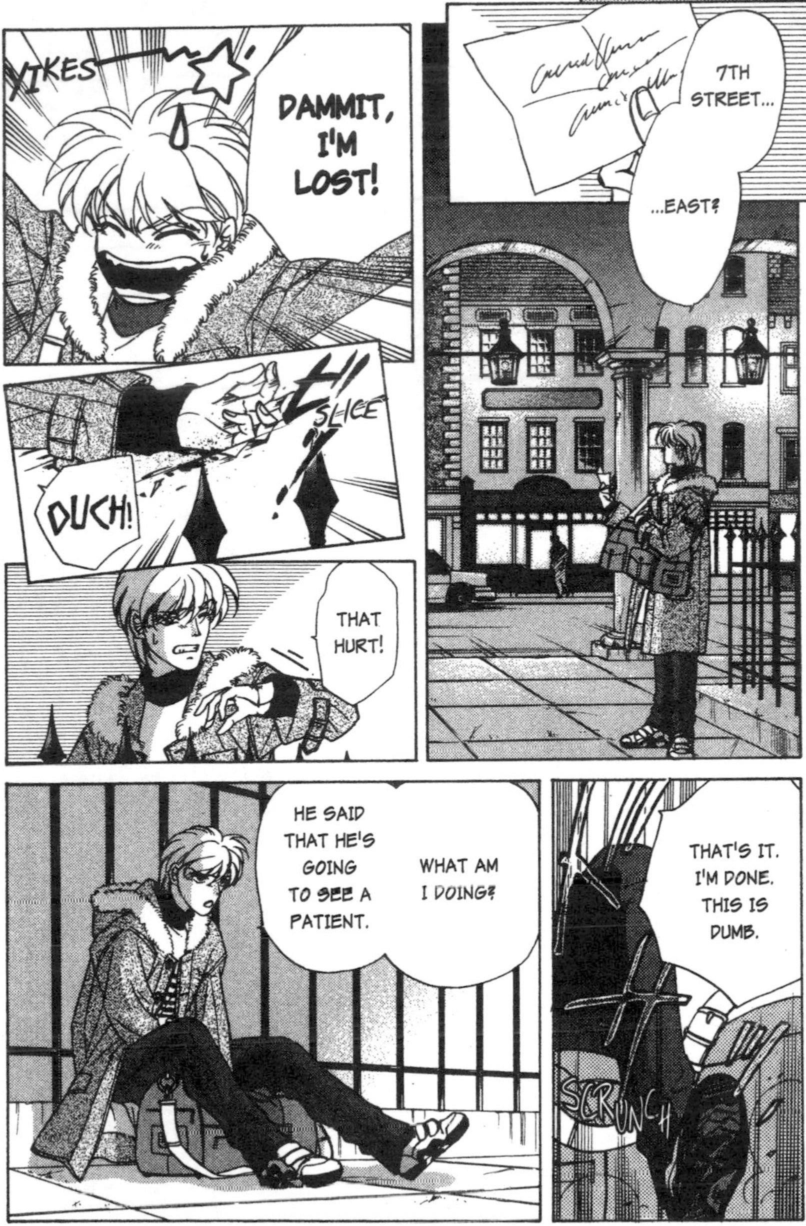
7TH STREET...
...EAST?
YIKES
DAMMIT, I'M LOST!
SLICE
OUCH!
THAT HURT!
THAT'S IT. I'M DONE. THIS IS DUMB.
SCRUNCH
HE SAID THAT HE'S GOING TO SEE A PATIENT.
WHAT AM I DOING?

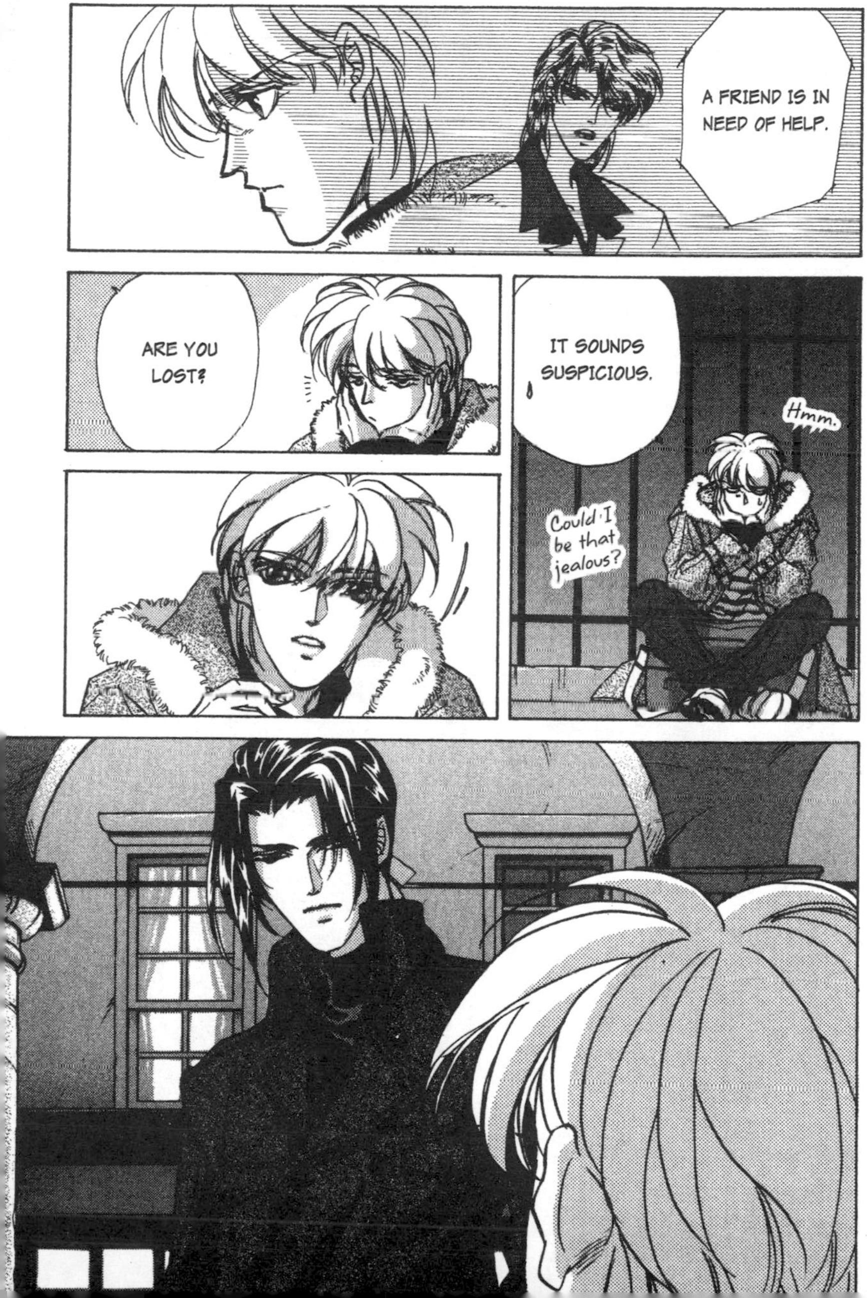
A FRIEND IS IN NEED OF HELP.
IT SOUNDS SUSPICIOUS.
Hmm.
Could I be that jealous?
ARE YOU LOST?

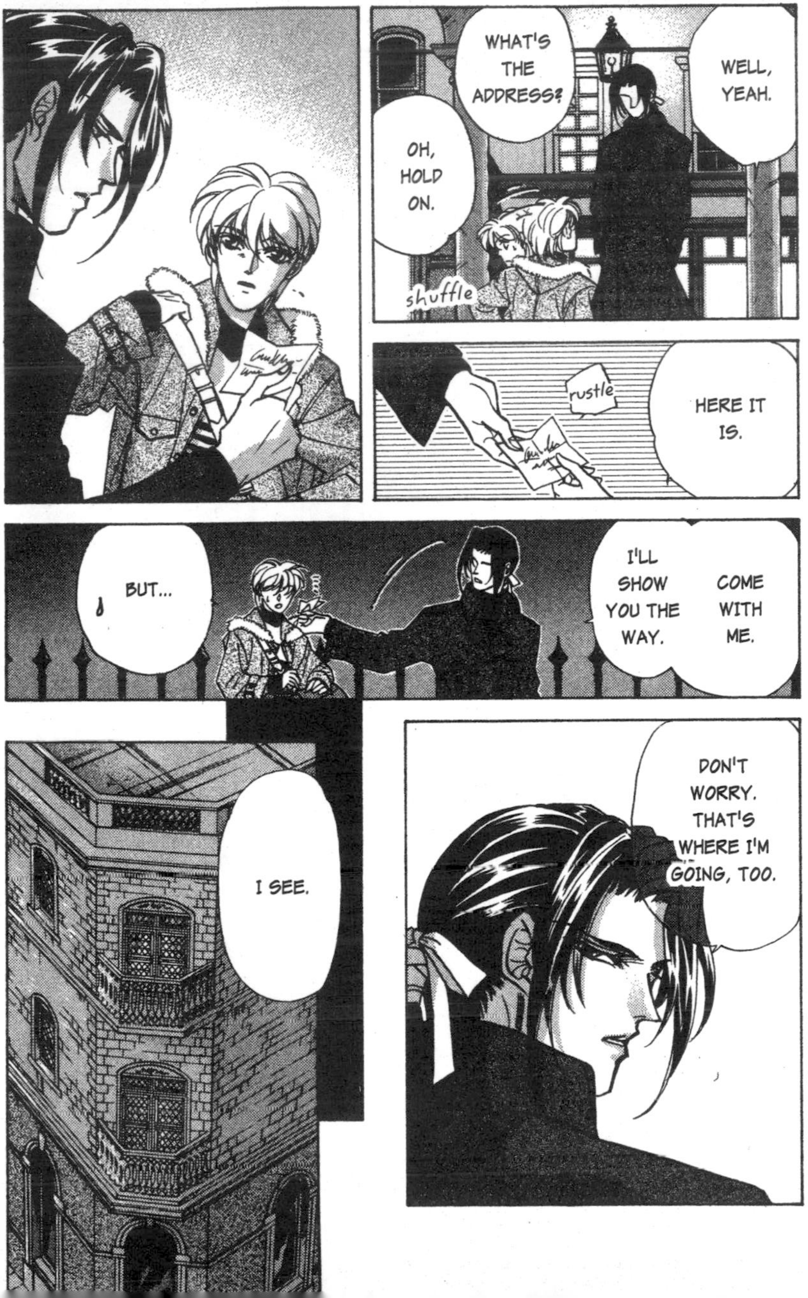
WELL, YEAH.
WHAT'S THE ADDRESS?
OH, HOLD ON.
shuffle
rustle
HERE IT IS.
COME WITH ME.
I'LL SHOW YOU THE WAY.
BUT...
DON'T WORRY. THAT'S WHERE I'M GOING, TOO.
I SEE.

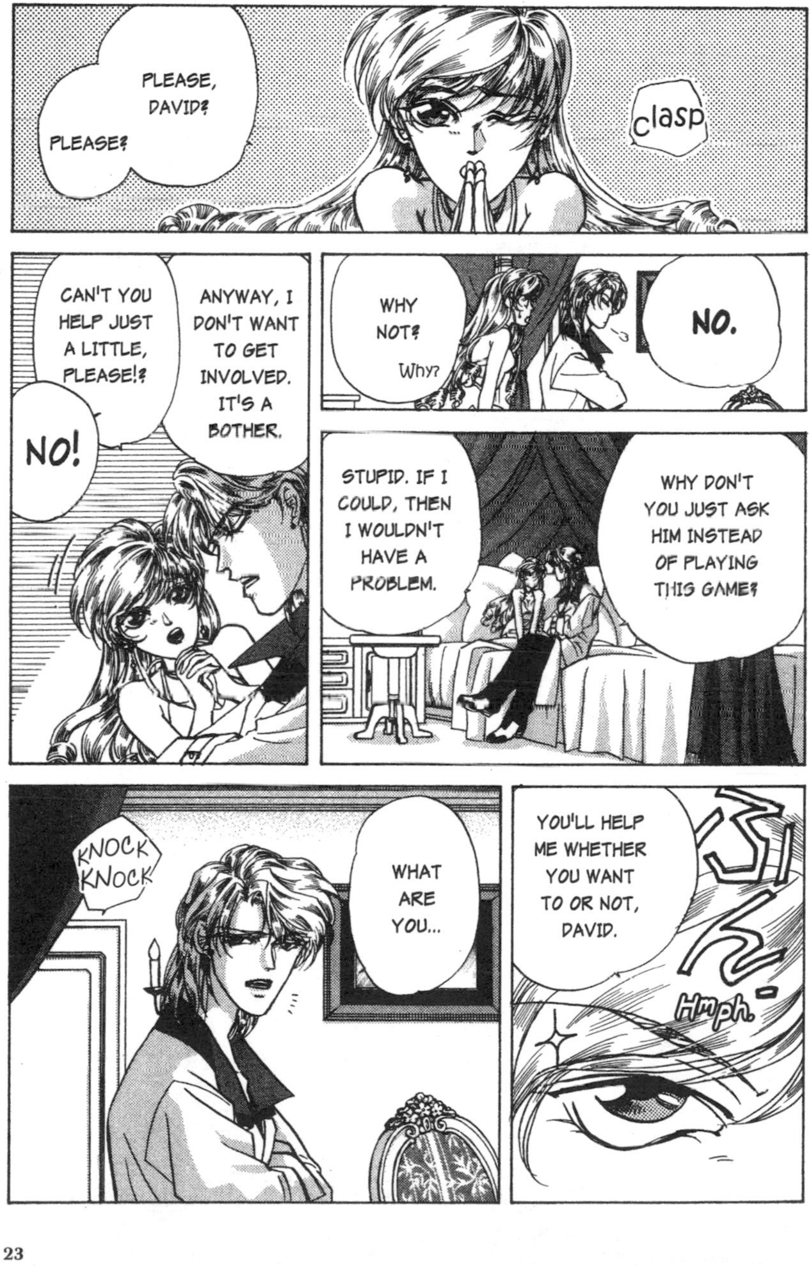
clasp
PLEASE, DAVID? PLEASE?
NO.
WHY NOT? Why?
WHY DON'T YOU JUST ASK HIM INSTEAD OF PLAYING THIS GAME?
STUPID. IF I COULD, THEN I WOULDN'T HAVE A PROBLEM.
ANYWAY, I DON'T WANT TO GET INVOLVED. IT'S A BOTHER.
CAN'T YOU HELP JUST A LITTLE, PLEASE!?
NO!
ふん
Hmph.
YOU'LL HELP ME WHETHER YOU WANT TO OR NOT, DAVID.
WHAT ARE YOU...
KNOCK KNOCK

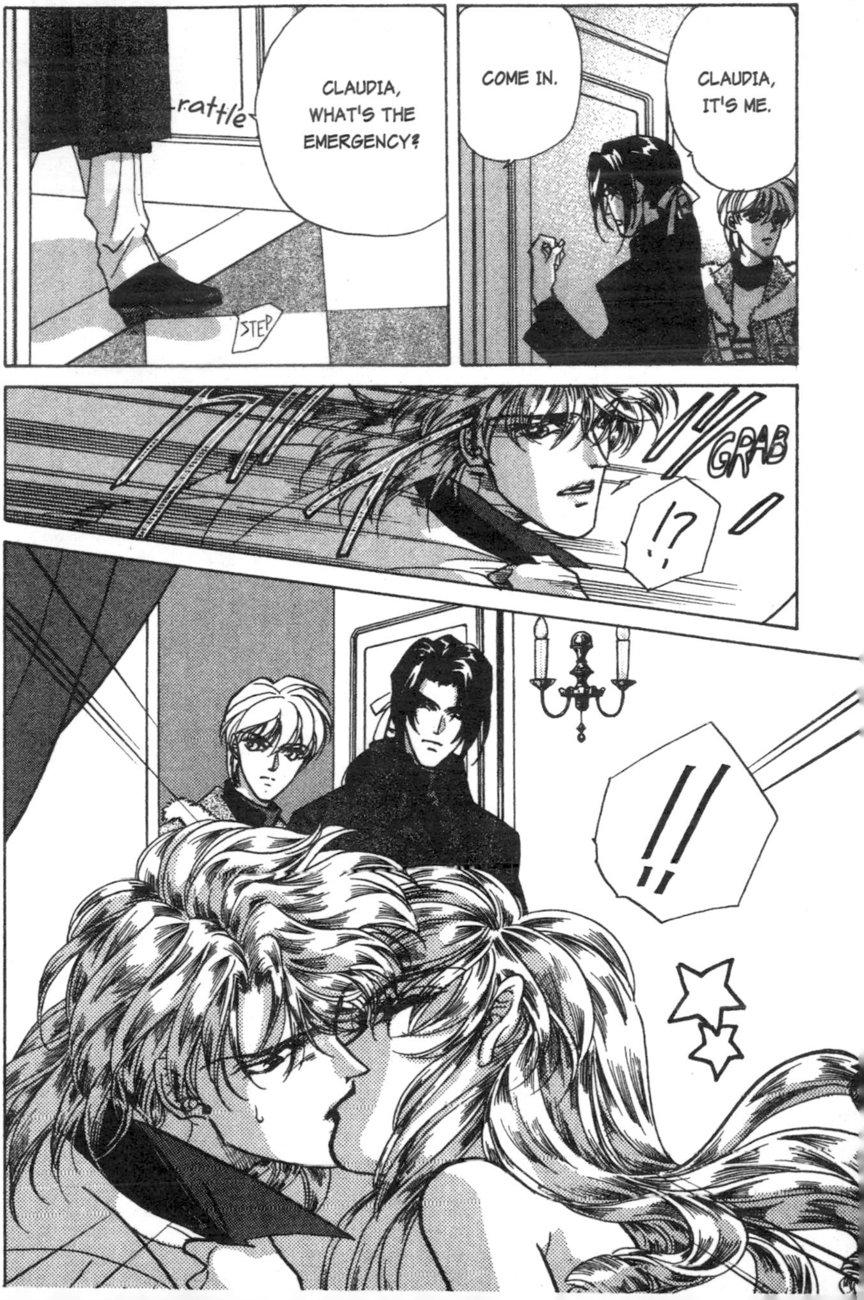
CLAUDIA, IT'S ME.
COME IN.
CLAUDIA, WHAT'S THE EMERGENCY?
rattle
STEP
GRAB
!?
!!

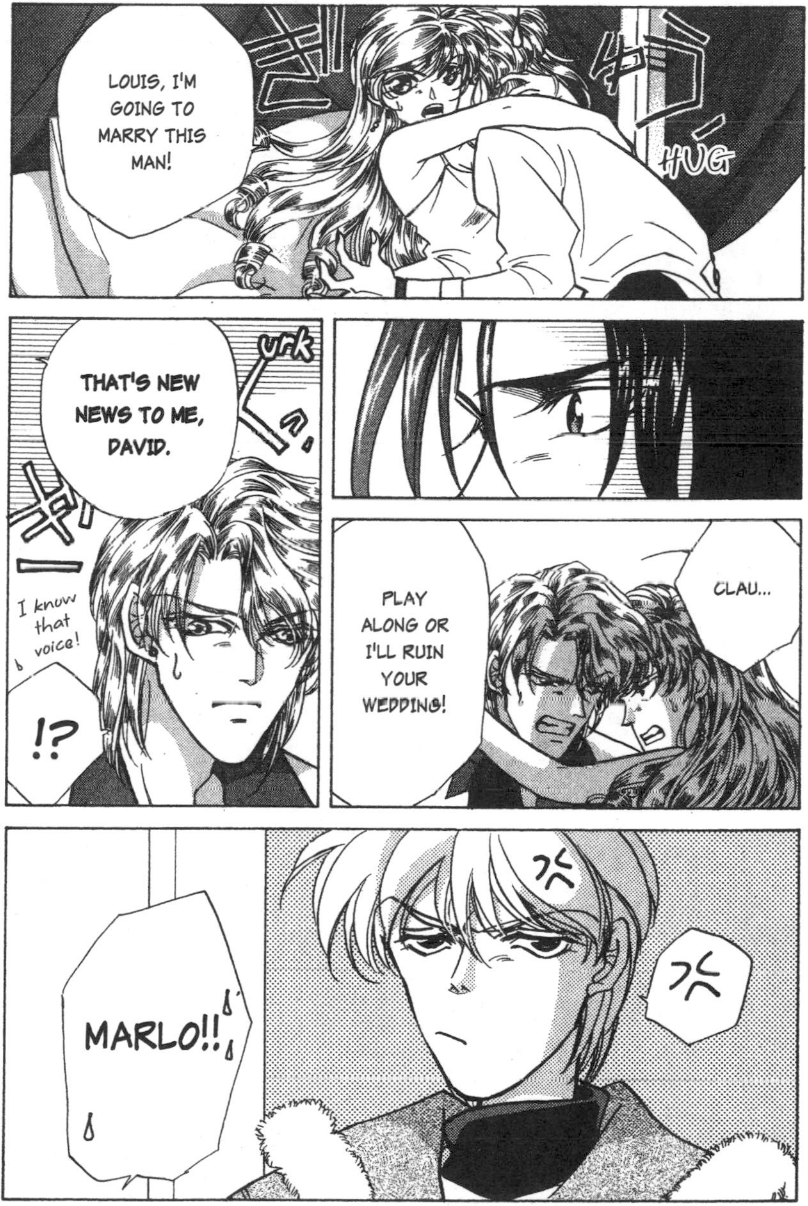
HÚG
LOUIS, I'M GOING TO MARRY THIS MAN!
CLAU...
PLAY ALONG OR I'LL RUIN YOUR WEDDING!
urk
THAT'S NEW NEWS TO ME, DAVID.
I know that voice!
!?
MARLO!!

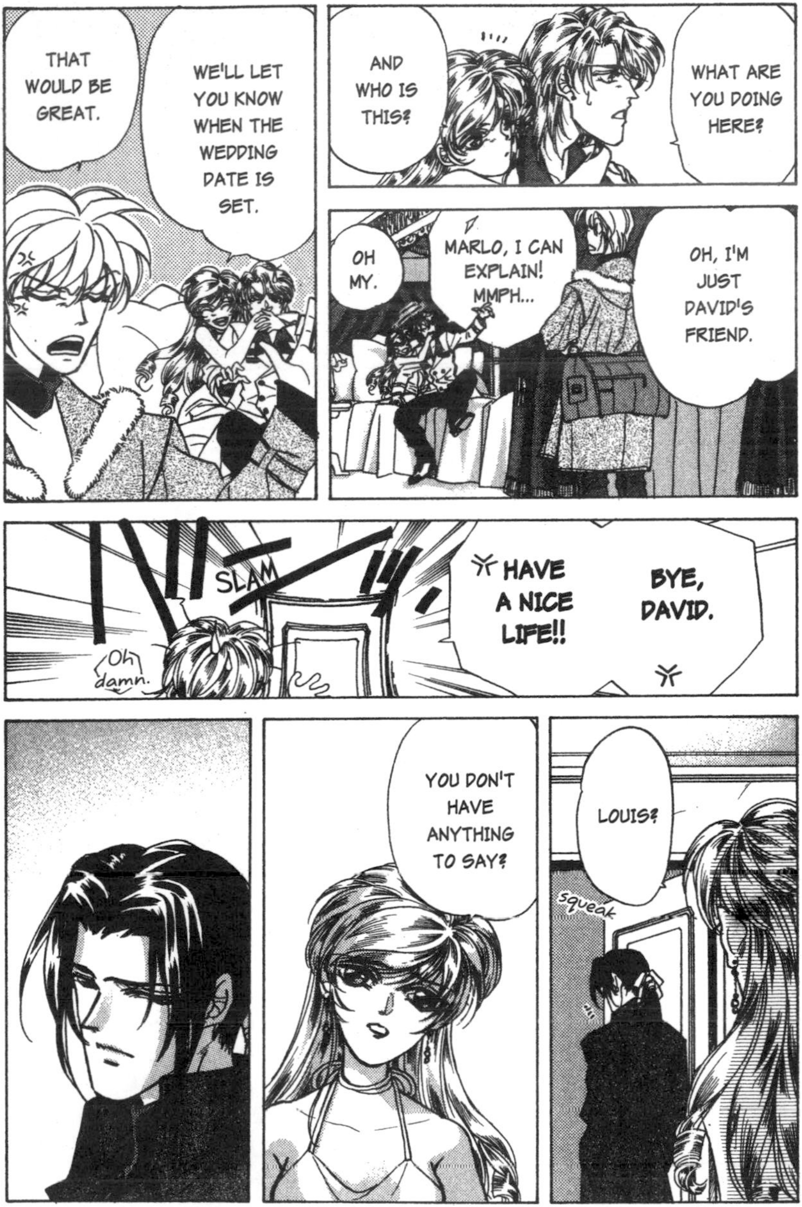
WHAT ARE YOU DOING HERE?
AND WHO IS THIS?
OH, I'M JUST DAVID'S FRIEND.
MARLO, I CAN EXPLAIN! MMPH...
OH MY.
WE'LL LET YOU KNOW WHEN THE WEDDING DATE IS SET.
THAT WOULD BE GREAT.
BYE, DAVID.
HAVE A NICE LIFE!!
SLAM
Oh damn.
LOUIS?
squeak
YOU DON'T HAVE ANYTHING TO SAY?

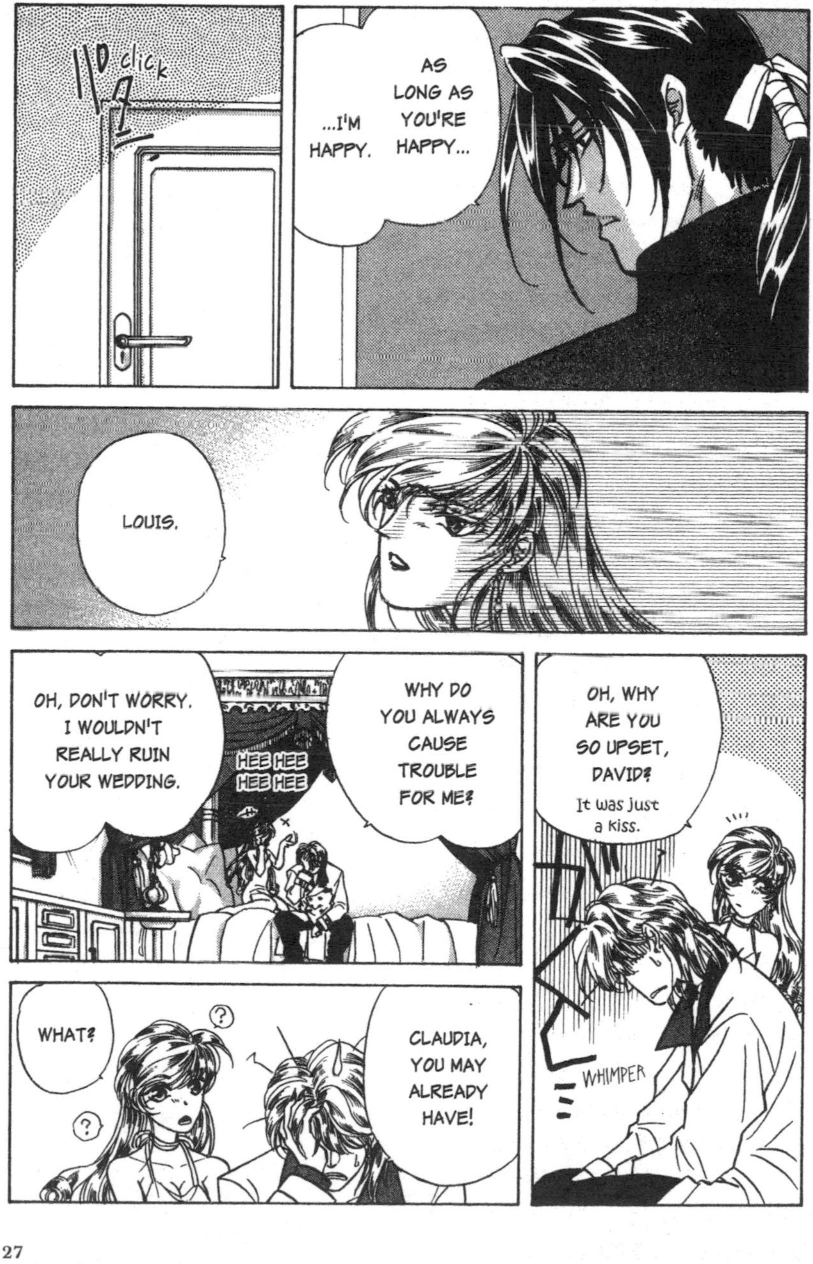
AS LONG AS YOU'RE HAPPY...
...I'M HAPPY.
click
LOUIS.
OH, WHY ARE YOU SO UPSET, DAVID?
It was just a kiss.
WHIMPER
WHY DO YOU ALWAYS CAUSE TROUBLE FOR ME?
HEE HEE HEE HEE
OH, DON'T WORRY. I WOULDN'T REALLY RUIN YOUR WEDDING.
CLAUDIA, YOU MAY ALREADY HAVE!
WHAT?

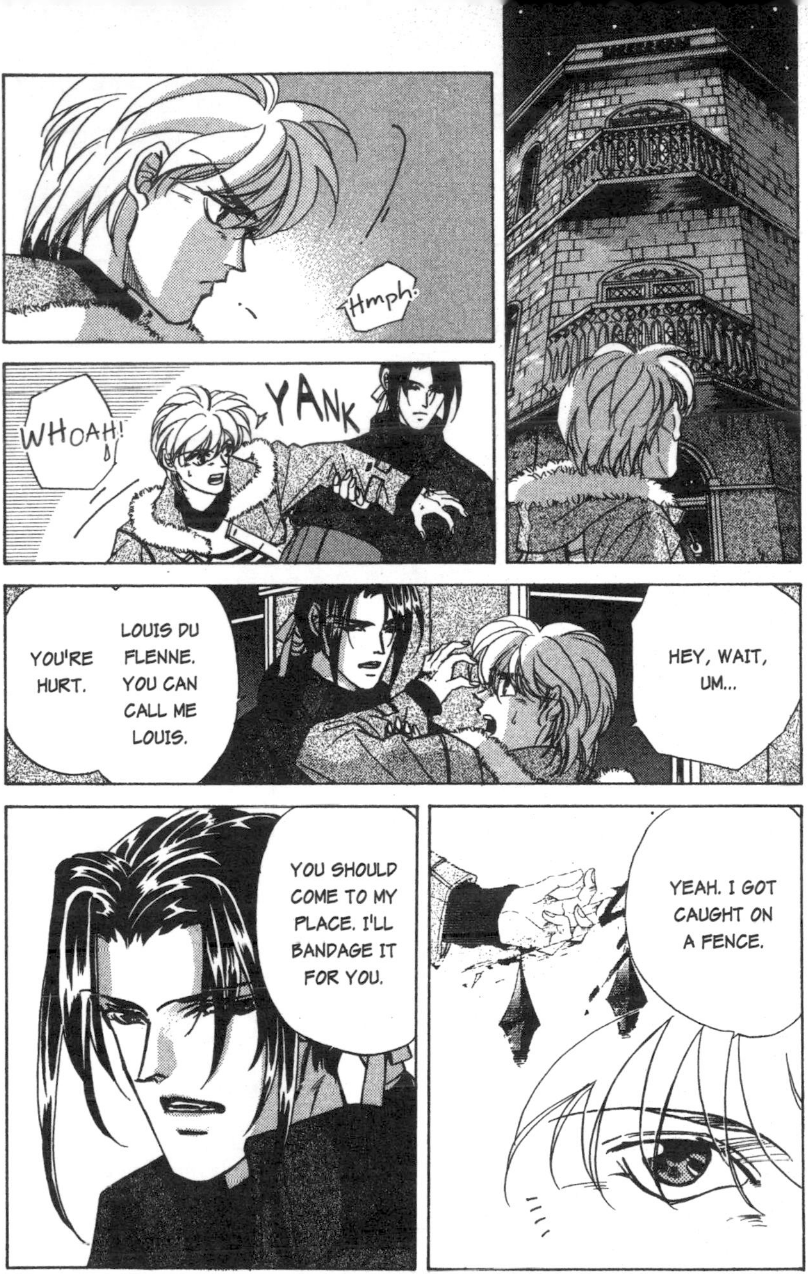
Hmph.
YANK
WHOAH!
HEY, WAIT, UM...
LOUIS DU FLENNE. YOU CAN CALL ME LOUIS.
YOU'RE HURT.
YEAH. I GOT CAUGHT ON A FENCE.
YOU SHOULD COME TO MY PLACE. I'LL BANDAGE IT FOR YOU.

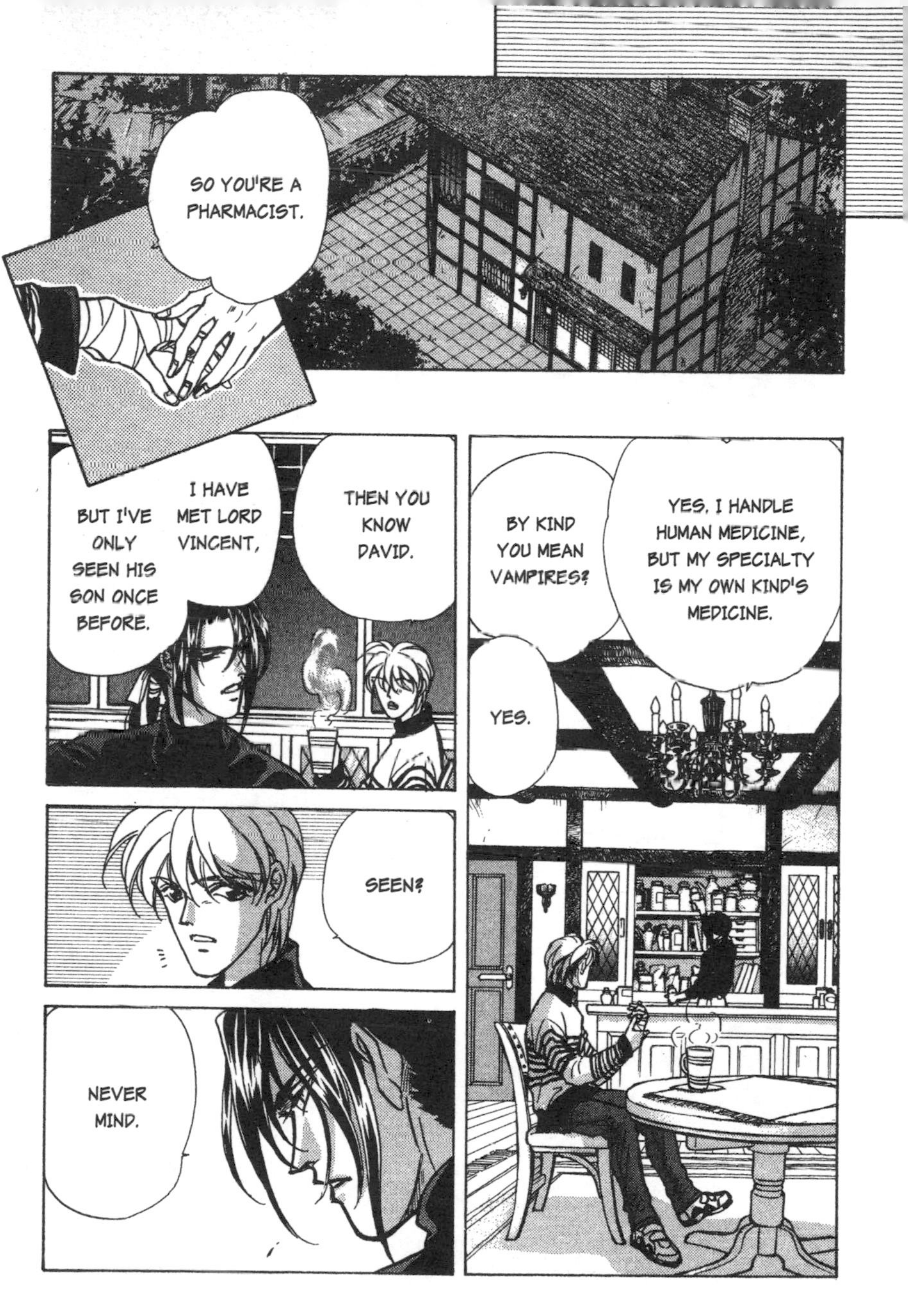
SO YOU'RE A PHARMACIST.
YES, I HANDLE HUMAN MEDICINE, BUT MY SPECIALTY IS MY OWN KIND'S MEDICINE.
BY KIND YOU MEAN VAMPIRES?
YES.
THEN YOU KNOW DAVID.
I HAVE MET LORD VINCENT,
BUT I'VE ONLY SEEN HIS SON ONCE BEFORE.
SEEN?
NEVER MIND.

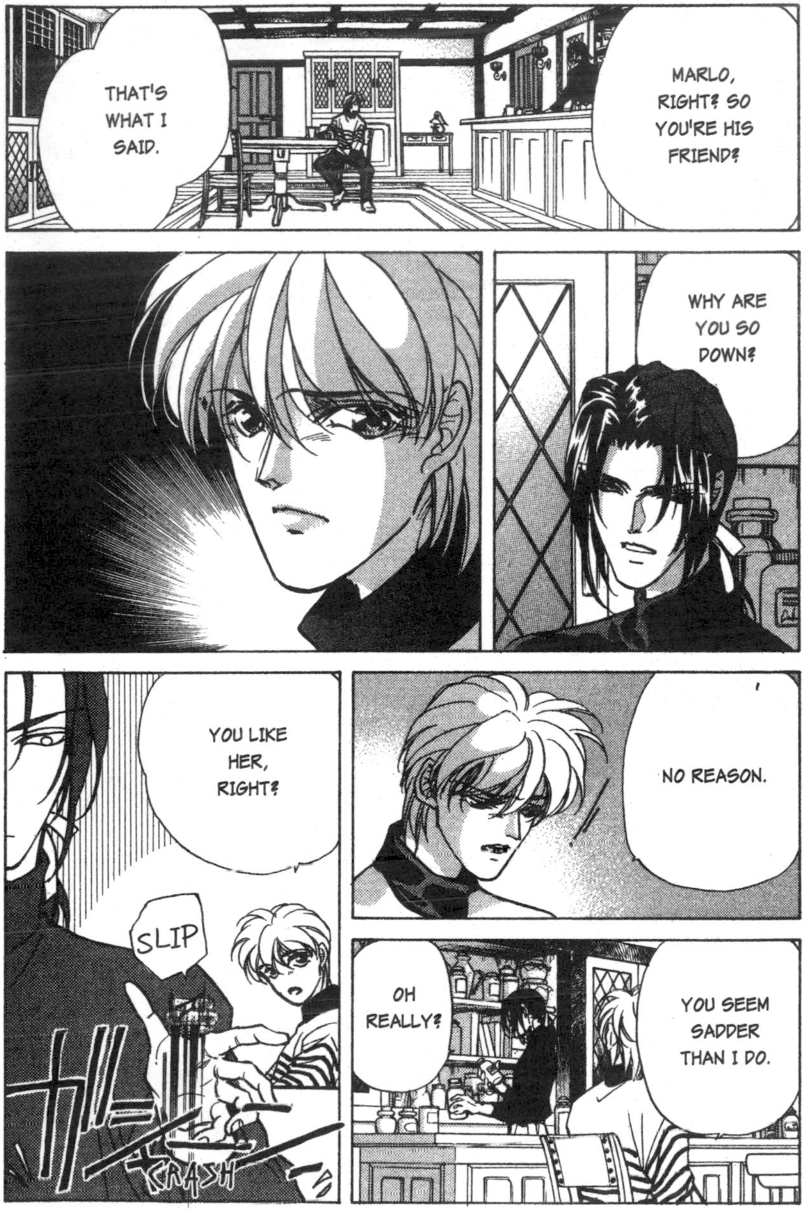
MARLO, RIGHT? SO YOU'RE HIS FRIEND?
THAT'S WHAT I SAID.
WHY ARE YOU SO DOWN?
NO REASON.
YOU SEEM SADDER THAN I DO.
OH REALLY?
YOU LIKE HER, RIGHT?
SLIP
CRASH

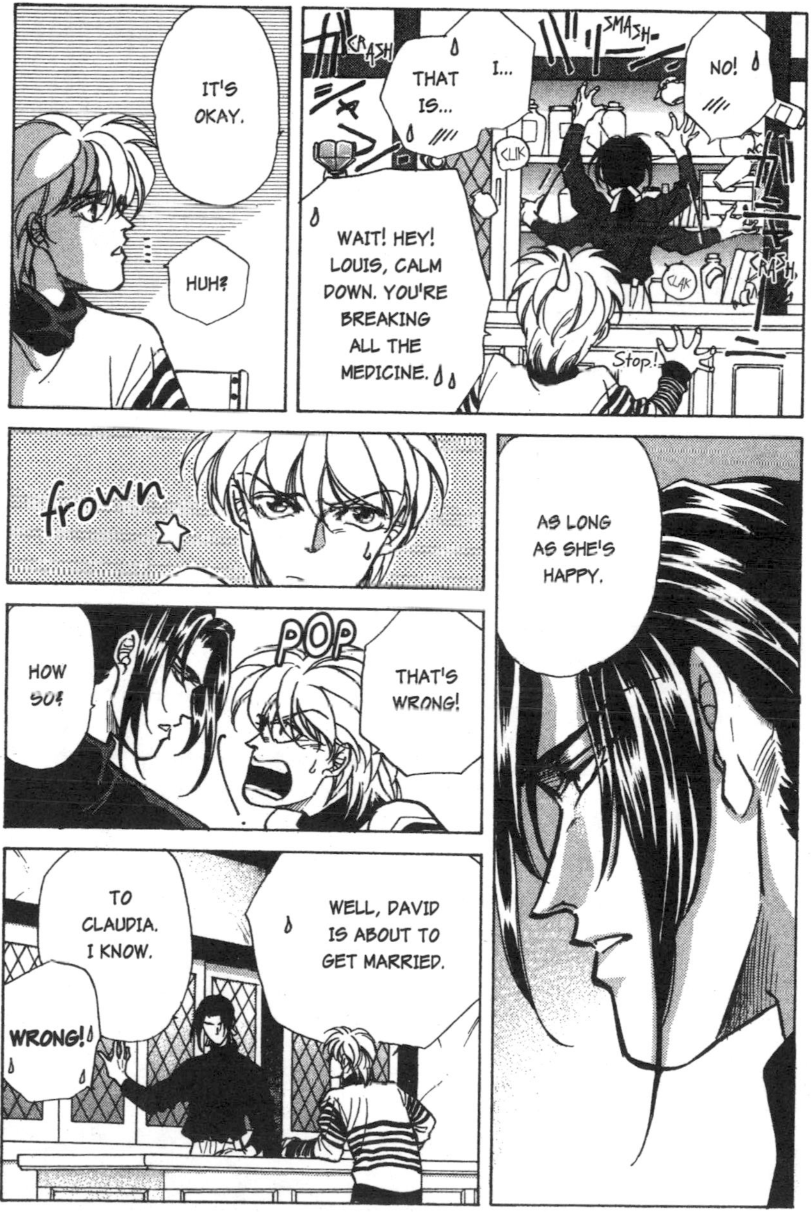
SMASH
NO!
I...
CRASH
THAT IS...
CLIK
WAIT! HEY! LOUIS, CALM DOWN. YOU'RE BREAKING ALL THE MEDICINE.
CLAK
CRASH
Stop!
IT'S OKAY.
HUH?
AS LONG AS SHE'S HAPPY.
frown
POP
THAT'S WRONG!
HOW SO?
WELL, DAVID IS ABOUT TO GET MARRIED.
TO CLAUDIA. I KNOW.
WRONG!

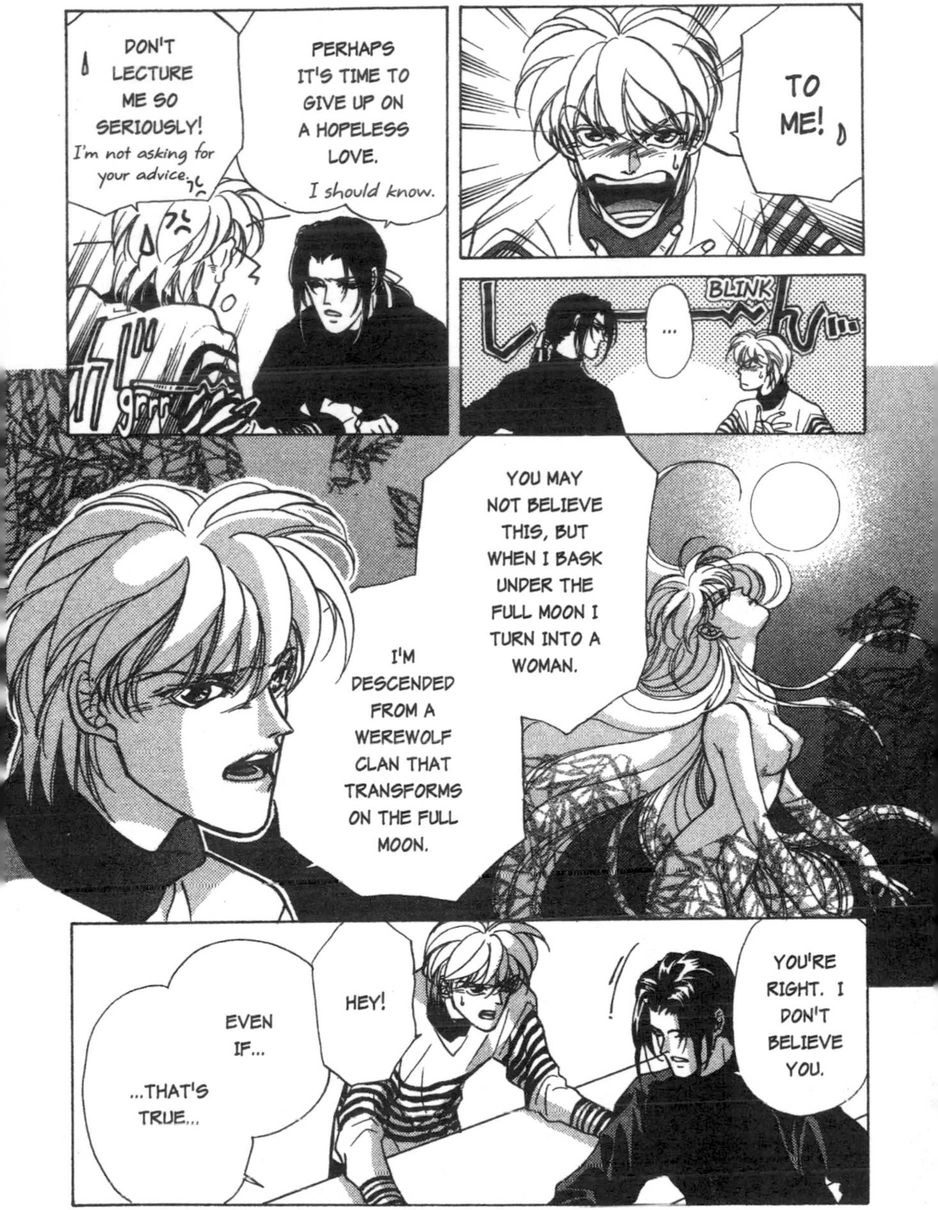
TO ME!
BLINK
...
PERHAPS IT'S TIME TO GIVE UP ON A HOPELESS LOVE.
I should know.
DON'T LECTURE ME SO SERIOUSLY!
I'm not asking for your advice.
grrr
YOU MAY NOT BELIEVE THIS, BUT WHEN I BASK UNDER THE FULL MOON I TURN INTO A WOMAN.
I'M DESCENDED FROM A WEREWOLF CLAN THAT TRANSFORMS ON THE FULL MOON.
YOU'RE RIGHT. I DON'T BELIEVE YOU.
HEY!
EVEN IF...
...THAT'S TRUE...

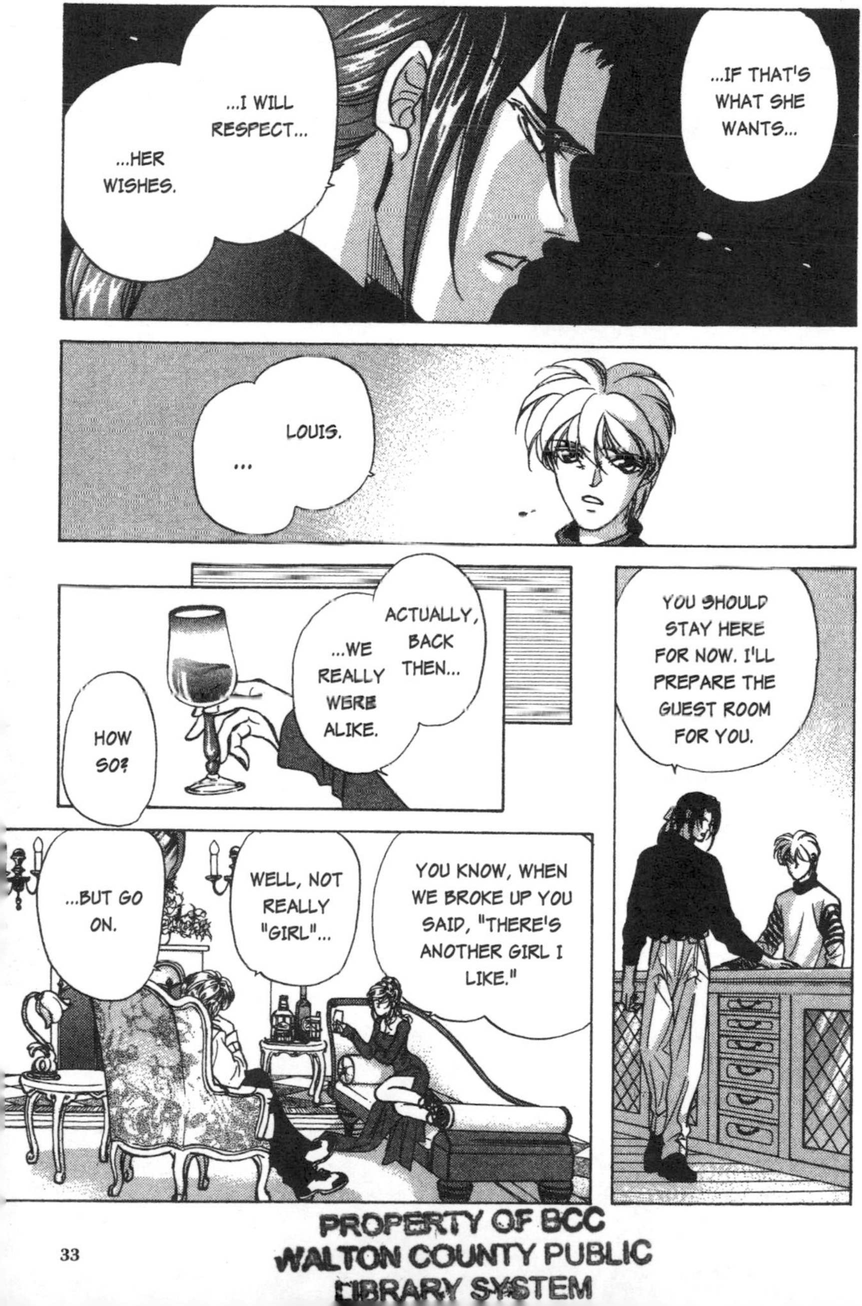
...IF THAT'S WHAT SHE WANTS...
...I WILL RESPECT...
...HER WISHES.
LOUIS. ...
YOU SHOULD STAY HERE FOR NOW. I'LL PREPARE THE GUEST ROOM FOR YOU.
ACTUALLY, BACK THEN...
...WE REALLY WERE ALIKE.
HOW SO?
YOU KNOW, WHEN WE BROKE UP YOU SAID, "THERE'S ANOTHER GIRL I LIKE."
WELL, NOT REALLY "GIRL"...
...BUT GO ON.

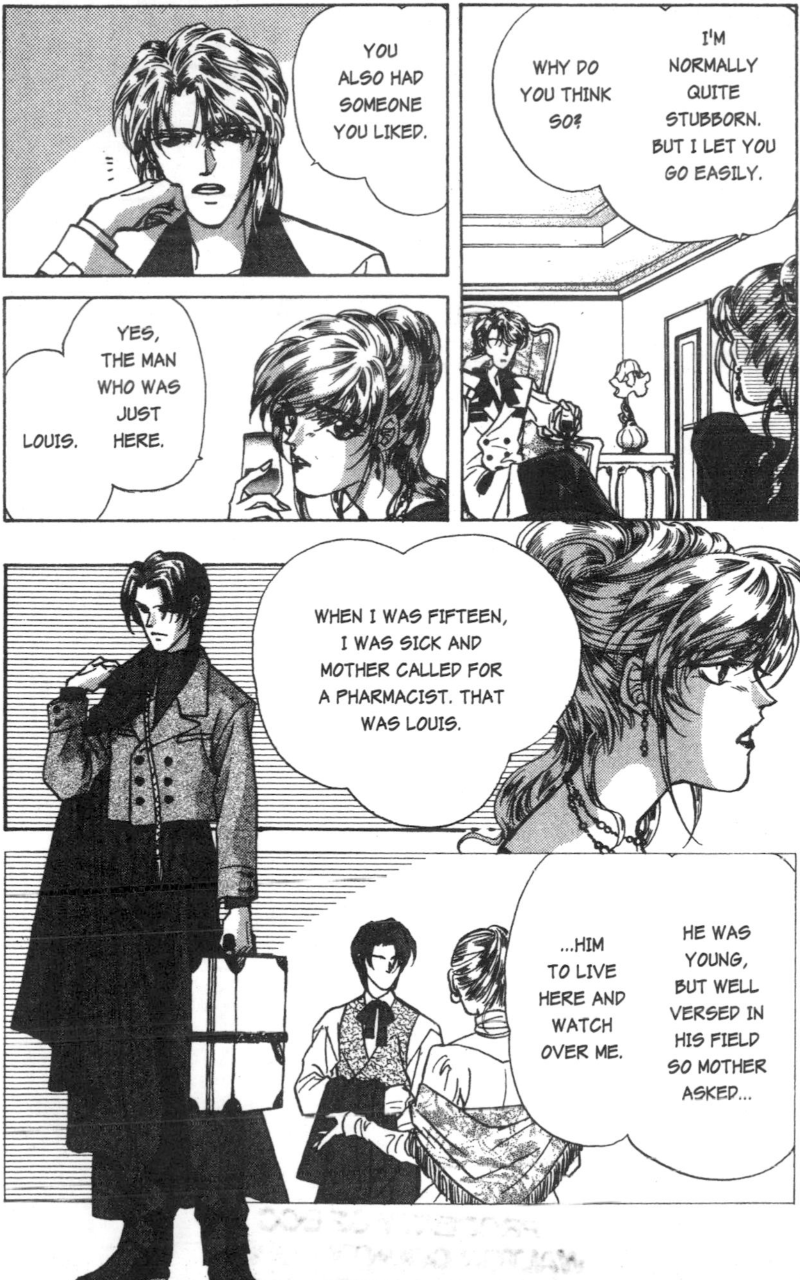
I'M NORMALLY QUITE STUBBORN. BUT I LET YOU GO EASILY.
WHY DO YOU THINK SO?
YOU ALSO HAD SOMEONE YOU LIKED.
YES, THE MAN WHO WAS JUST HERE.
LOUIS.
WHEN I WAS FIFTEEN, I WAS SICK AND MOTHER CALLED FOR A PHARMACIST. THAT WAS LOUIS.
HE WAS YOUNG, BUT WELL VERSED IN HIS FIELD SO MOTHER ASKED...
...HIM TO LIVE HERE AND WATCH OVER ME.

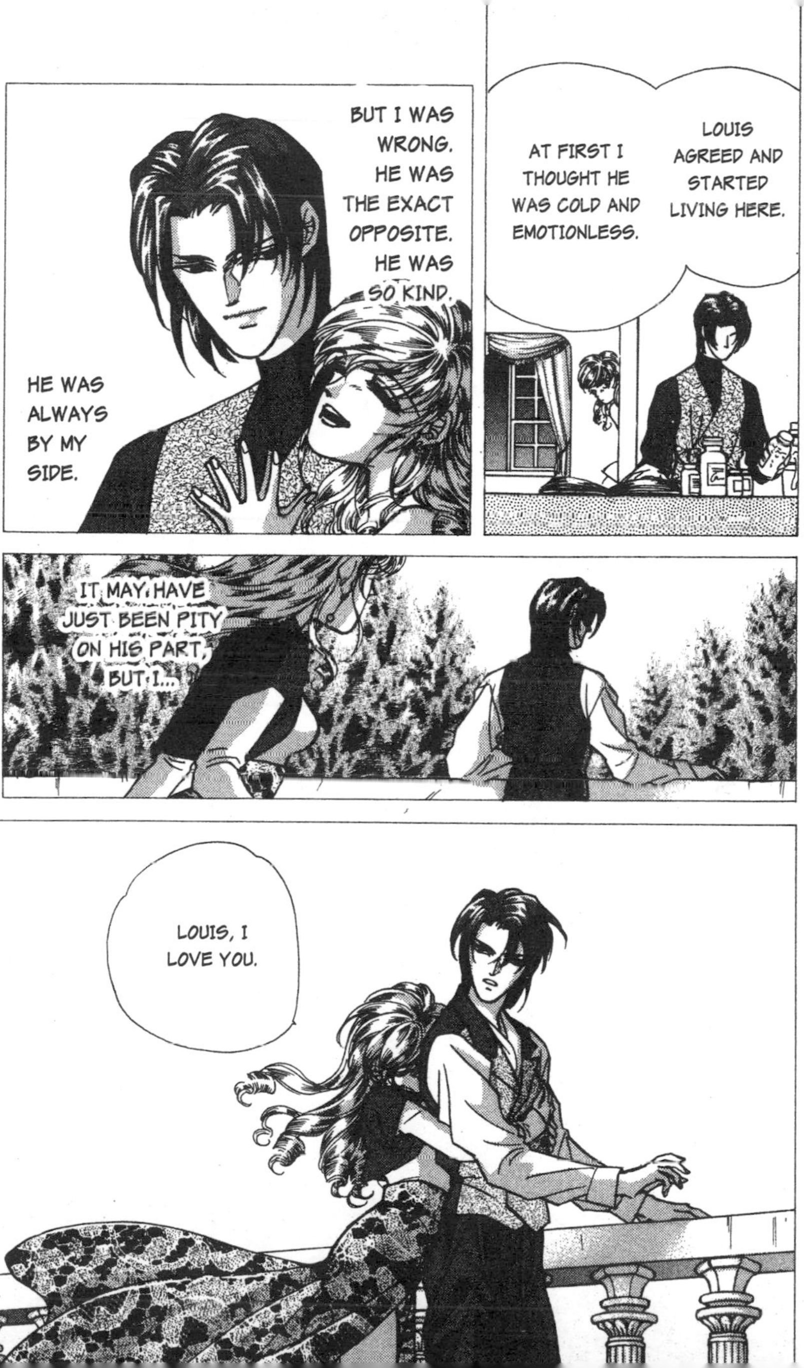
LOUIS AGREED AND STARTED LIVING HERE.
AT FIRST I THOUGHT HE WAS COLD AND EMOTIONLESS.
BUT I WAS WRONG. HE WAS THE EXACT OPPOSITE. HE WAS SO KIND.
HE WAS ALWAYS BY MY SIDE.
IT MAY HAVE JUST BEEN PITY ON HIS PART, BUT I...
LOUIS, I LOVE YOU.

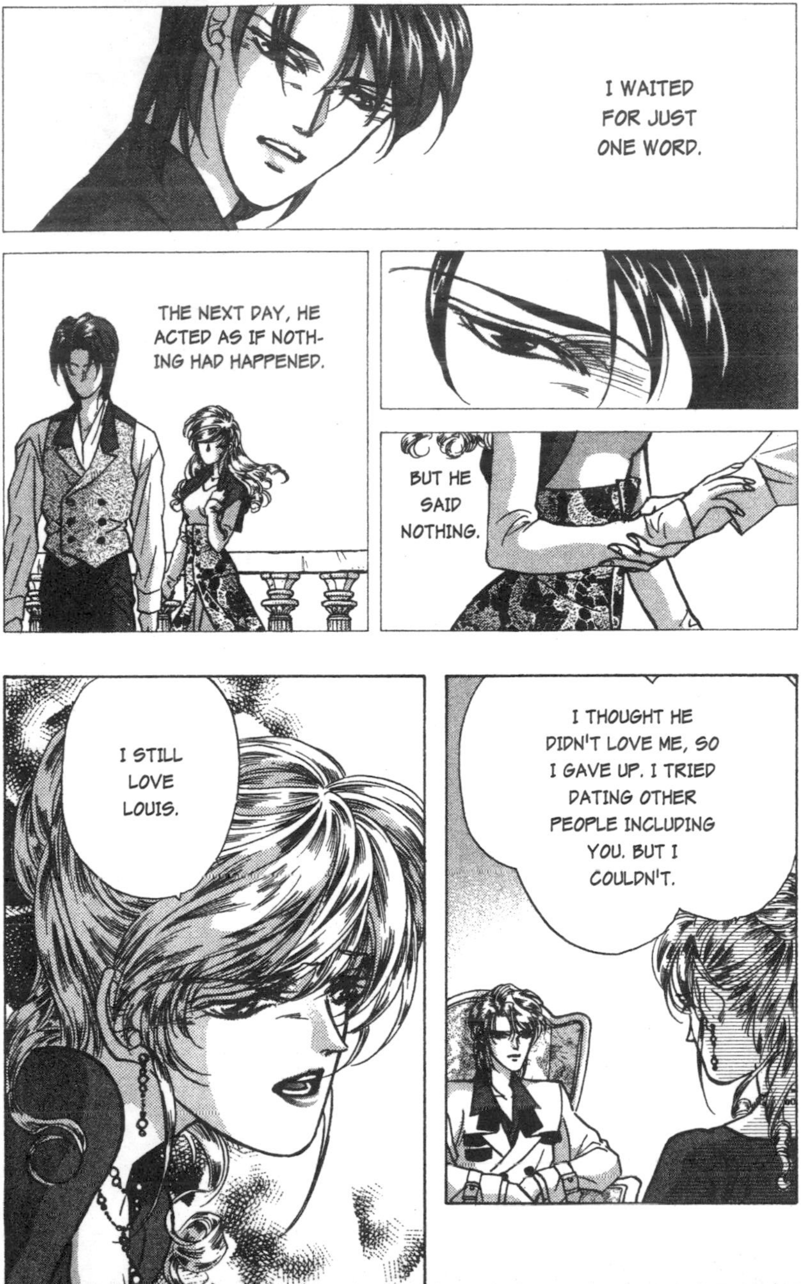
I WAITED FOR JUST ONE WORD.
BUT HE SAID NOTHING.
THE NEXT DAY, HE ACTED AS IF NOTHING HAD HAPPENED.
I THOUGHT HE DIDN'T LOVE ME, SO I GAVE UP. I TRIED DATING OTHER PEOPLE INCLUDING YOU. BUT I COULDN'T.
I STILL LOVE LOUIS.

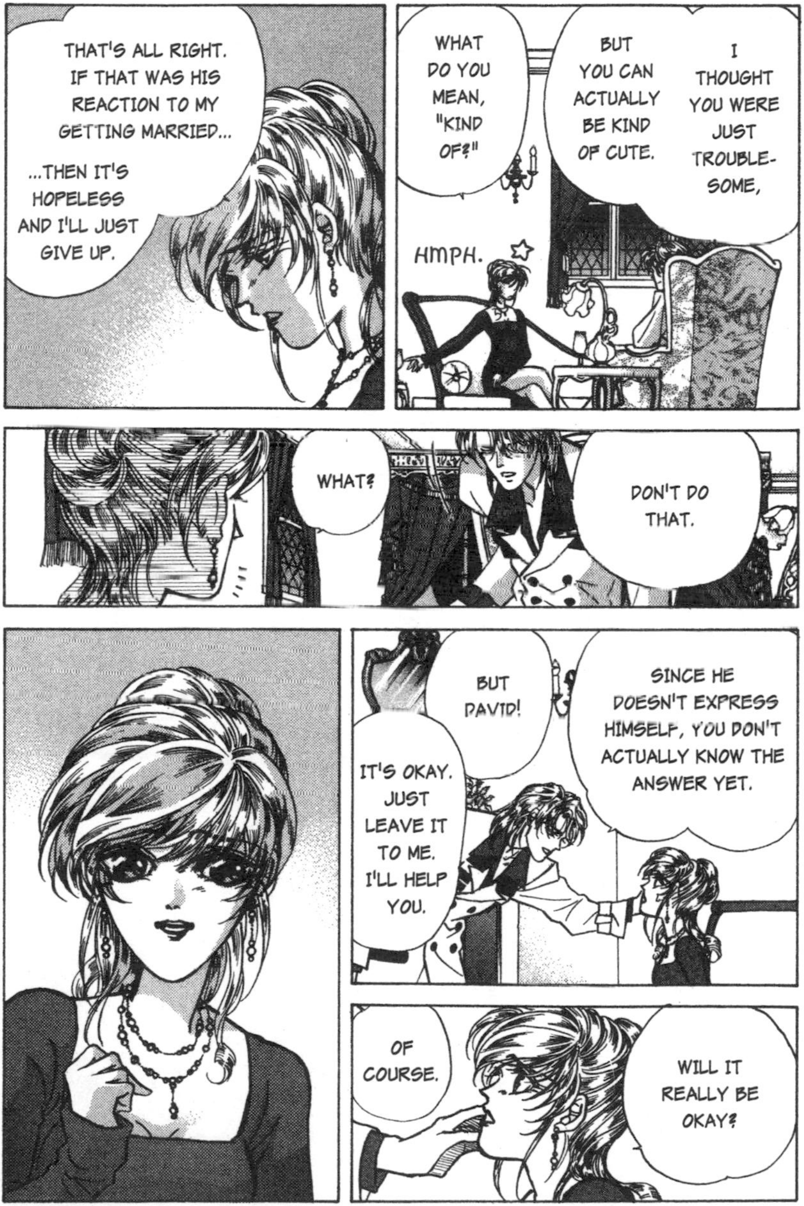
I THOUGHT YOU WERE JUST TROUBLE-SOME,
BUT YOU CAN ACTUALLY BE KIND OF CUTE.
WHAT DO YOU MEAN, "KIND OF?"
HMPH.
THAT'S ALL RIGHT. IF THAT WAS HIS REACTION TO MY GETTING MARRIED...
...THEN IT'S HOPELESS AND I'LL JUST GIVE UP.
DON'T DO THAT.
WHAT?
SINCE HE DOESN'T EXPRESS HIMSELF, YOU DON'T ACTUALLY KNOW THE ANSWER YET.
BUT DAVID!
IT'S OKAY. JUST LEAVE IT TO ME. I'LL HELP YOU.
WILL IT REALLY BE OKAY?
OF COURSE.

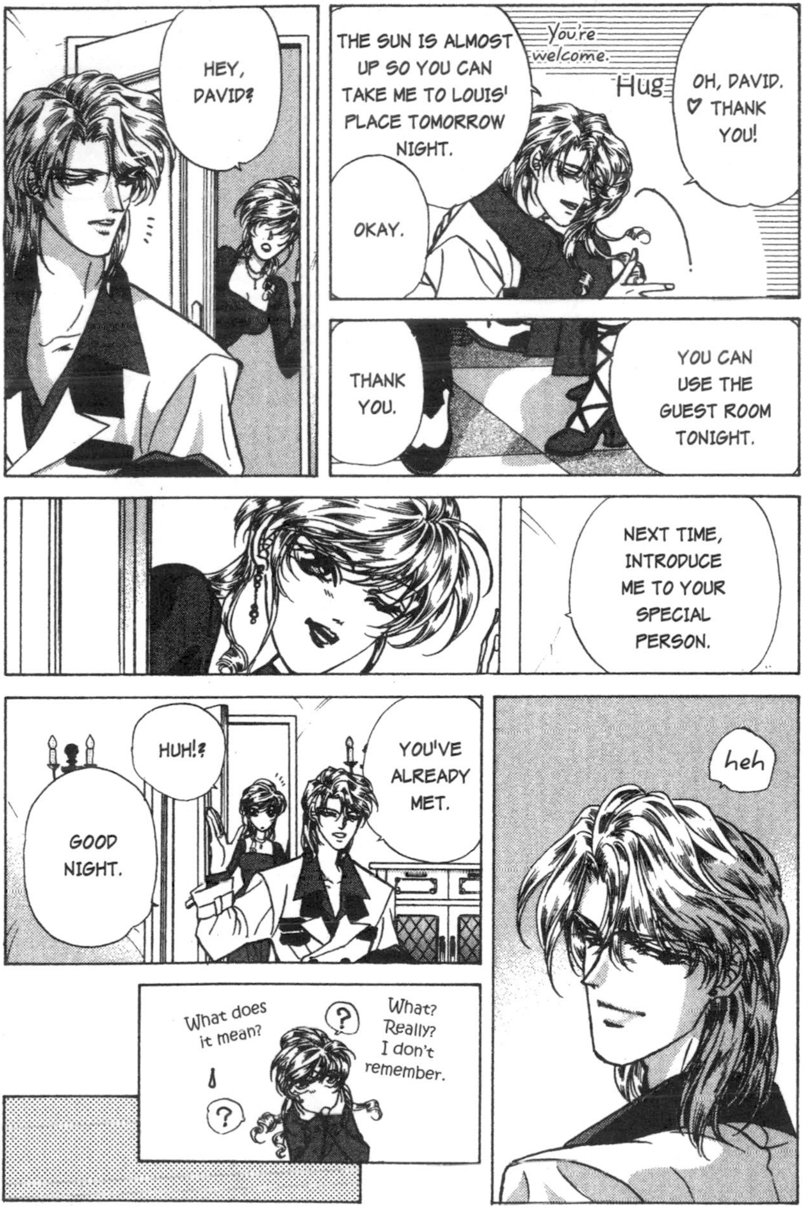
OH, DAVID. ♡ THANK YOU!
Hug
You're welcome.
THE SUN IS ALMOST UP SO YOU CAN TAKE ME TO LOUIS' PLACE TOMORROW NIGHT.
OKAY.
YOU CAN USE THE GUEST ROOM TONIGHT.
THANK YOU.
HEY, DAVID?
NEXT TIME, INTRODUCE ME TO YOUR SPECIAL PERSON.
heh
YOU'VE ALREADY MET.
HUH!?
GOOD NIGHT.
What? Really? I don't remember.
What does it mean?

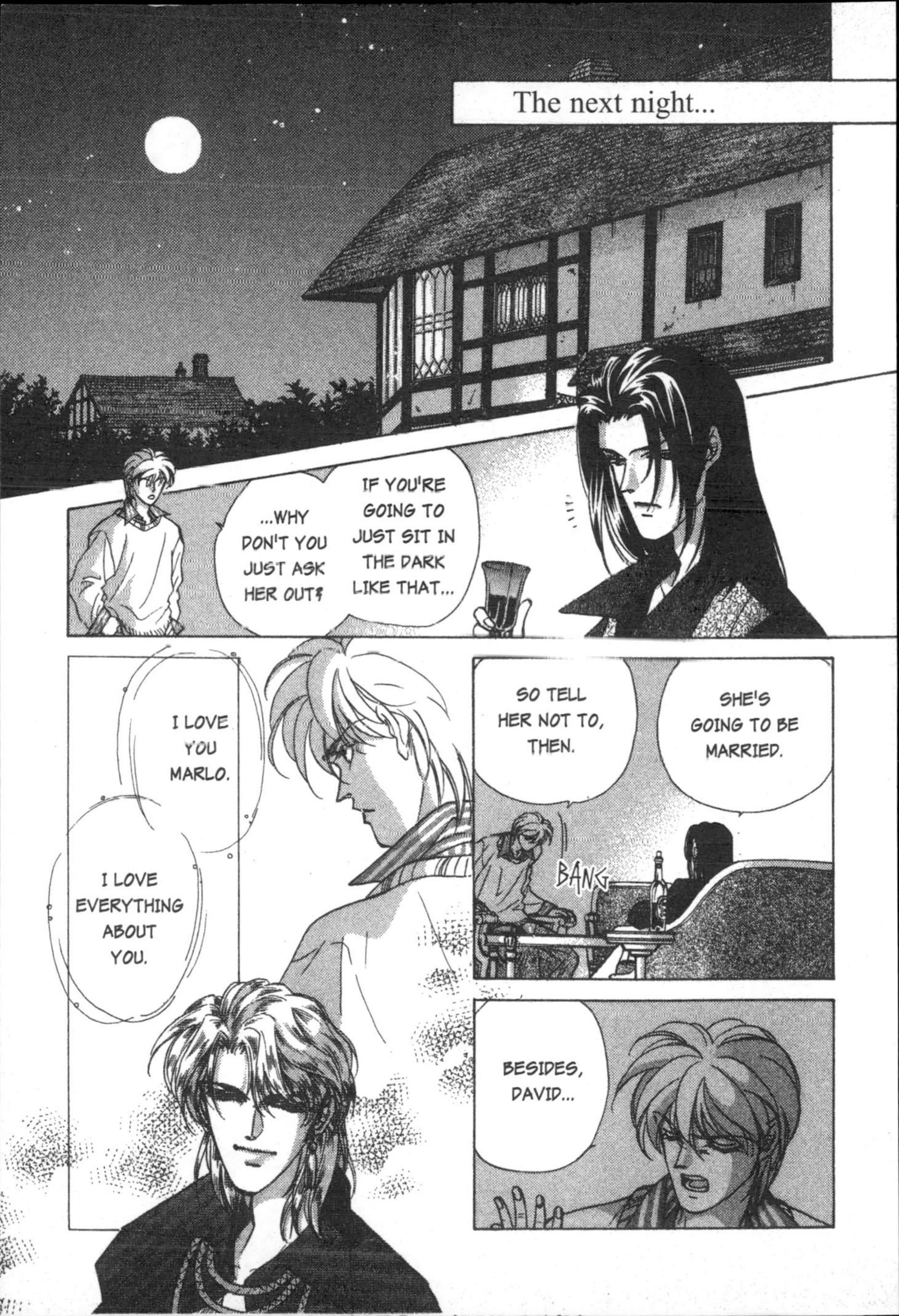
The next night...
IF YOU'RE GOING TO JUST SIT IN THE DARK LIKE THAT...
...WHY DON'T YOU JUST ASK HER OUT?
SHE'S GOING TO BE MARRIED.
SO TELL HER NOT TO, THEN.
BANG
BESIDES, DAVID...
I LOVE YOU MARLO.
I LOVE EVERYTHING ABOUT YOU.

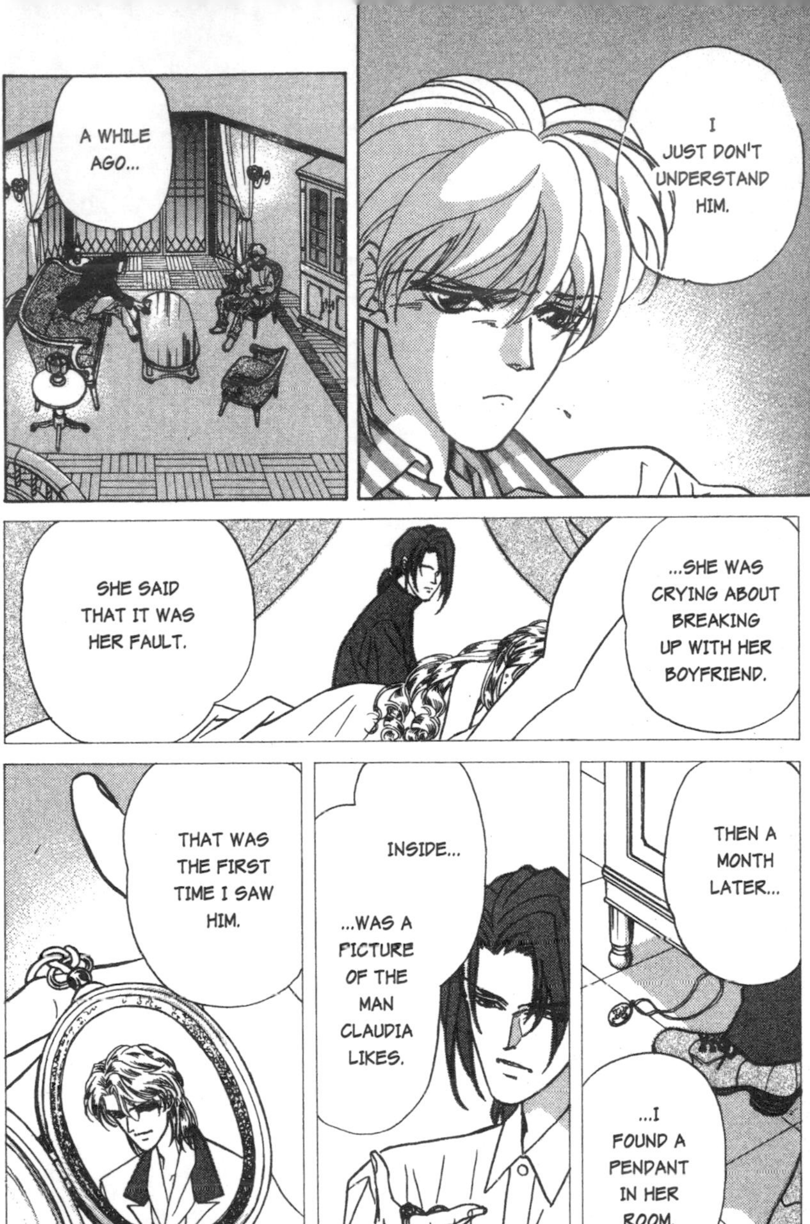
I JUST DON'T UNDERSTAND HIM.
A WHILE AGO...
...SHE WAS CRYING ABOUT BREAKING UP WITH HER BOYFRIEND.
SHE SAID THAT IT WAS HER FAULT.
THEN A MONTH LATER...
...I FOUND A PENDANT IN HER ROOM.
INSIDE...
...WAS A PICTURE OF THE MAN CLAUDIA LIKES.
THAT WAS THE FIRST TIME I SAW HIM.

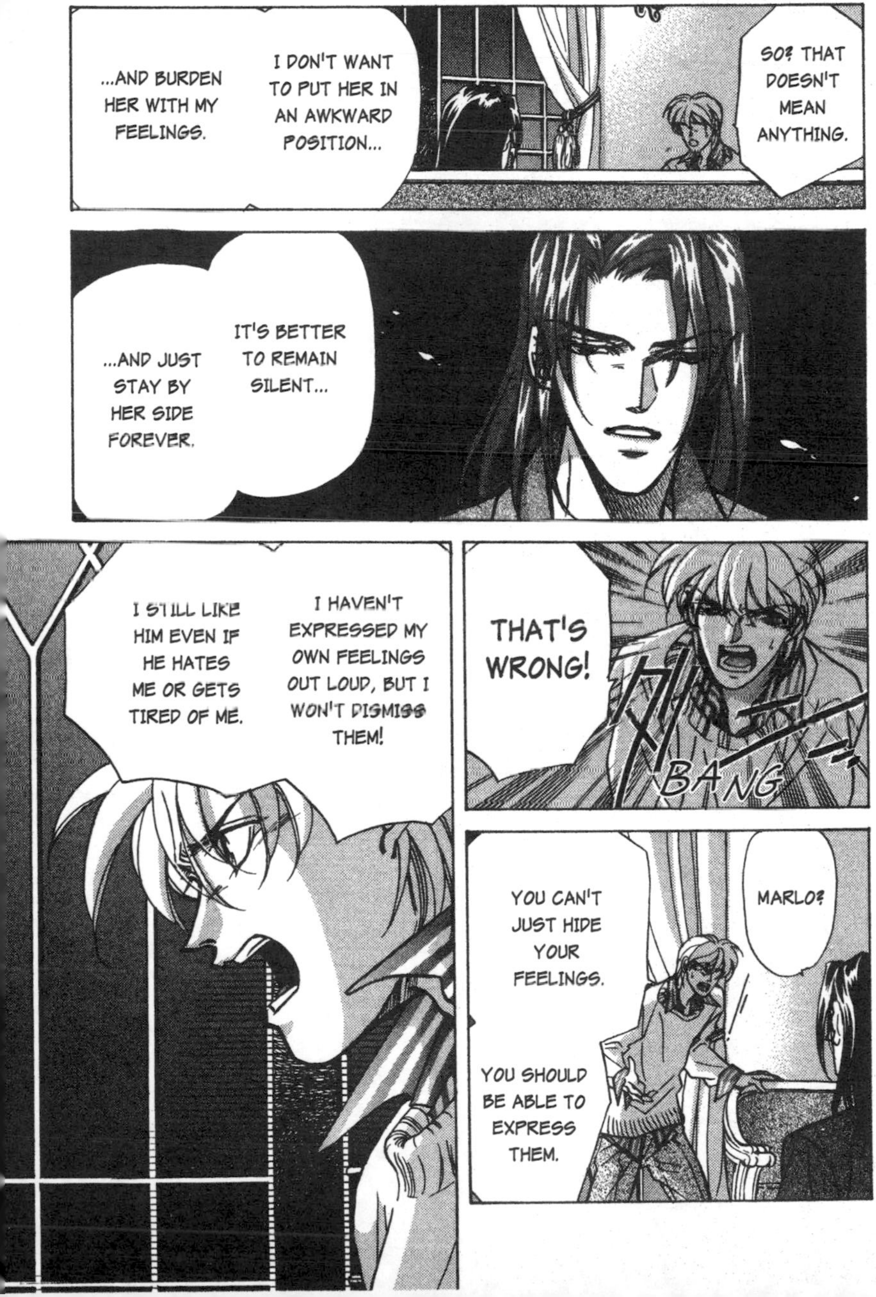
SO? THAT DOESN'T MEAN ANYTHING.
I DON'T WANT TO PUT HER IN AN AWKWARD POSITION...
...AND BURDEN HER WITH MY FEELINGS.
IT'S BETTER TO REMAIN SILENT...
...AND JUST STAY BY HER SIDE FOREVER.
THAT'S WRONG!
BANG
MARLO?
YOU CAN'T JUST HIDE YOUR FEELINGS.
YOU SHOULD BE ABLE TO EXPRESS THEM.
I HAVEN'T EXPRESSED MY OWN FEELINGS OUT LOUD, BUT I WON'T DISMISS THEM!
I STILL LIKE HIM EVEN IF HE HATES ME OR GETS TIRED OF ME.

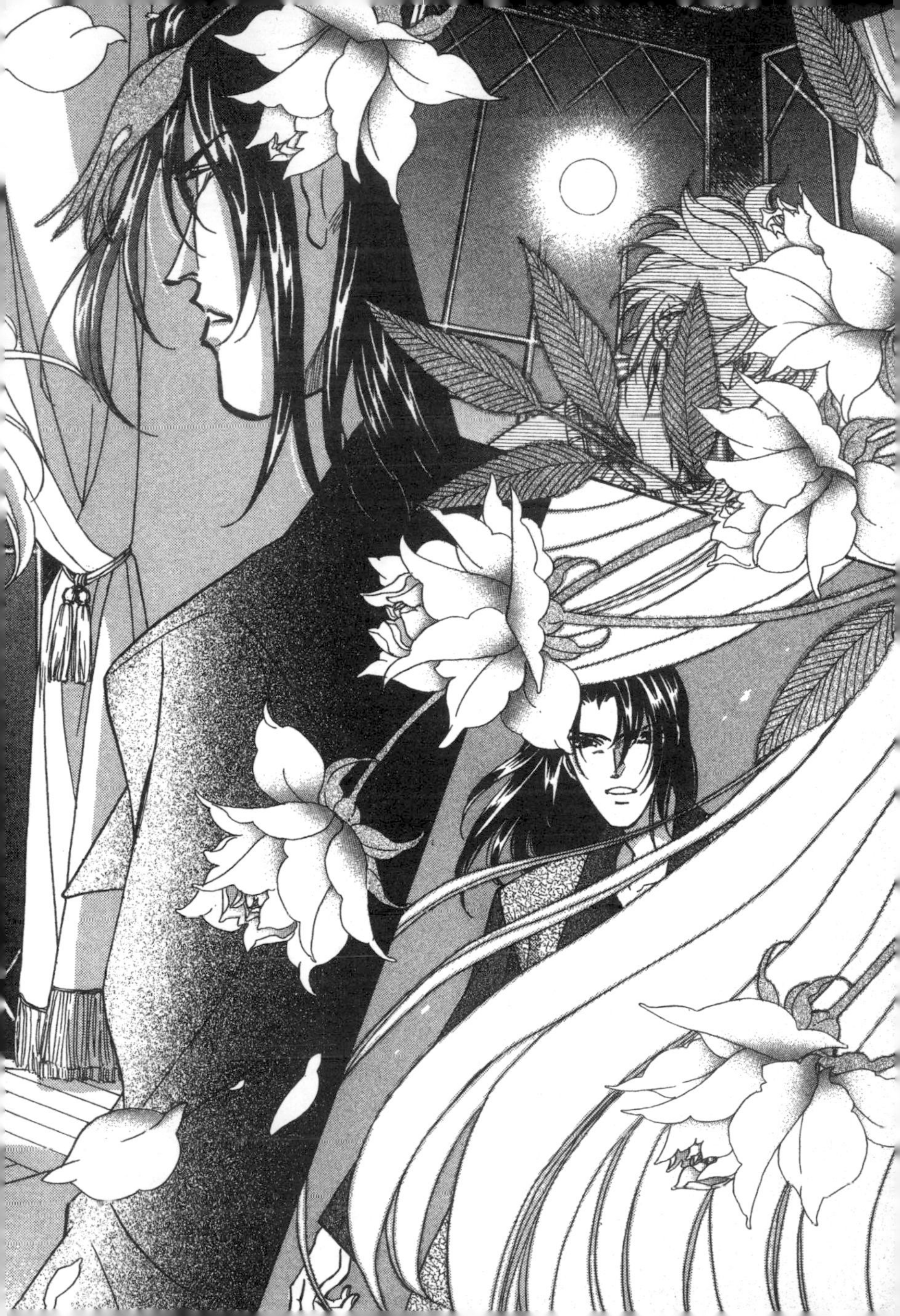

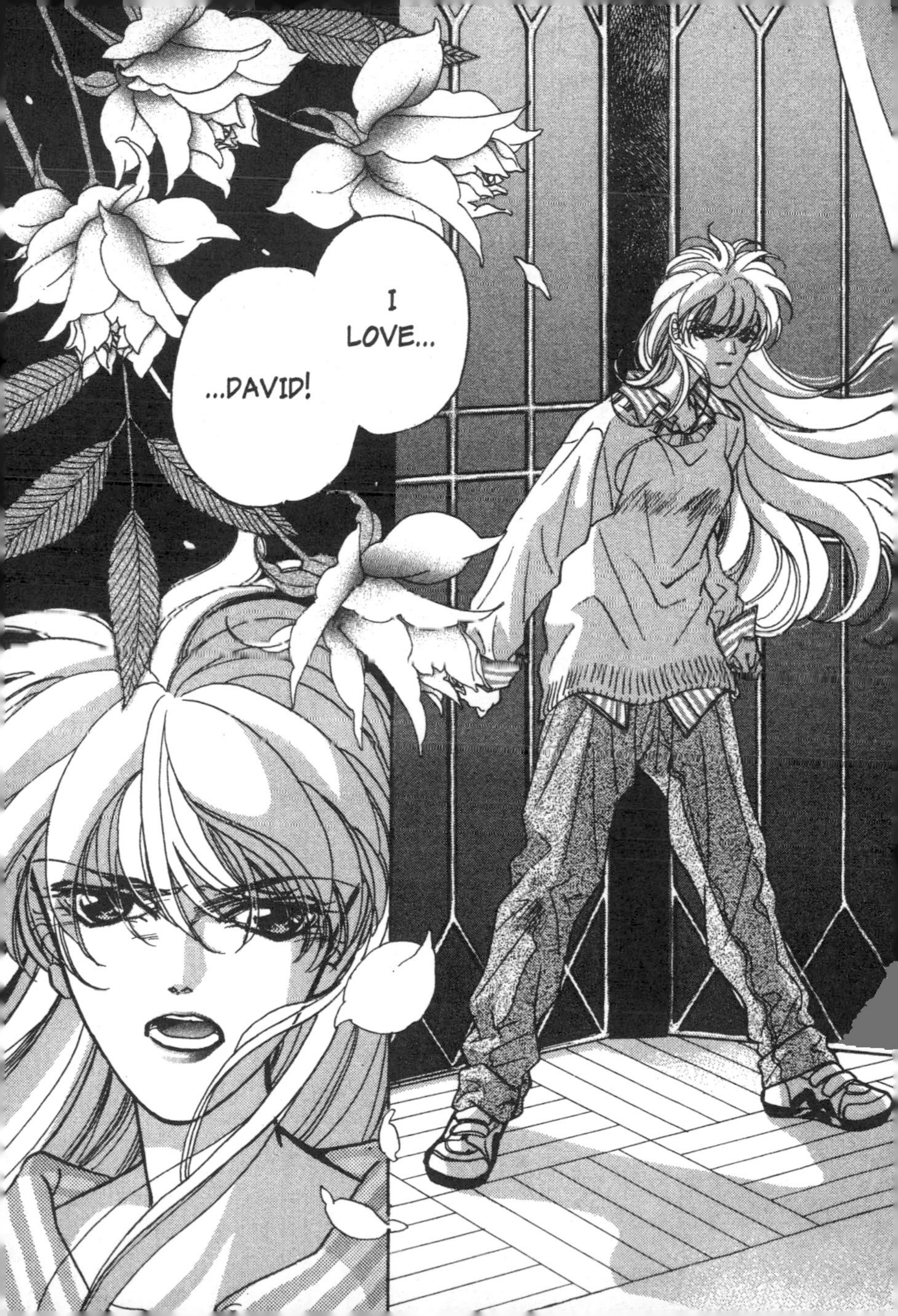
I LOVE...
...DAVID!

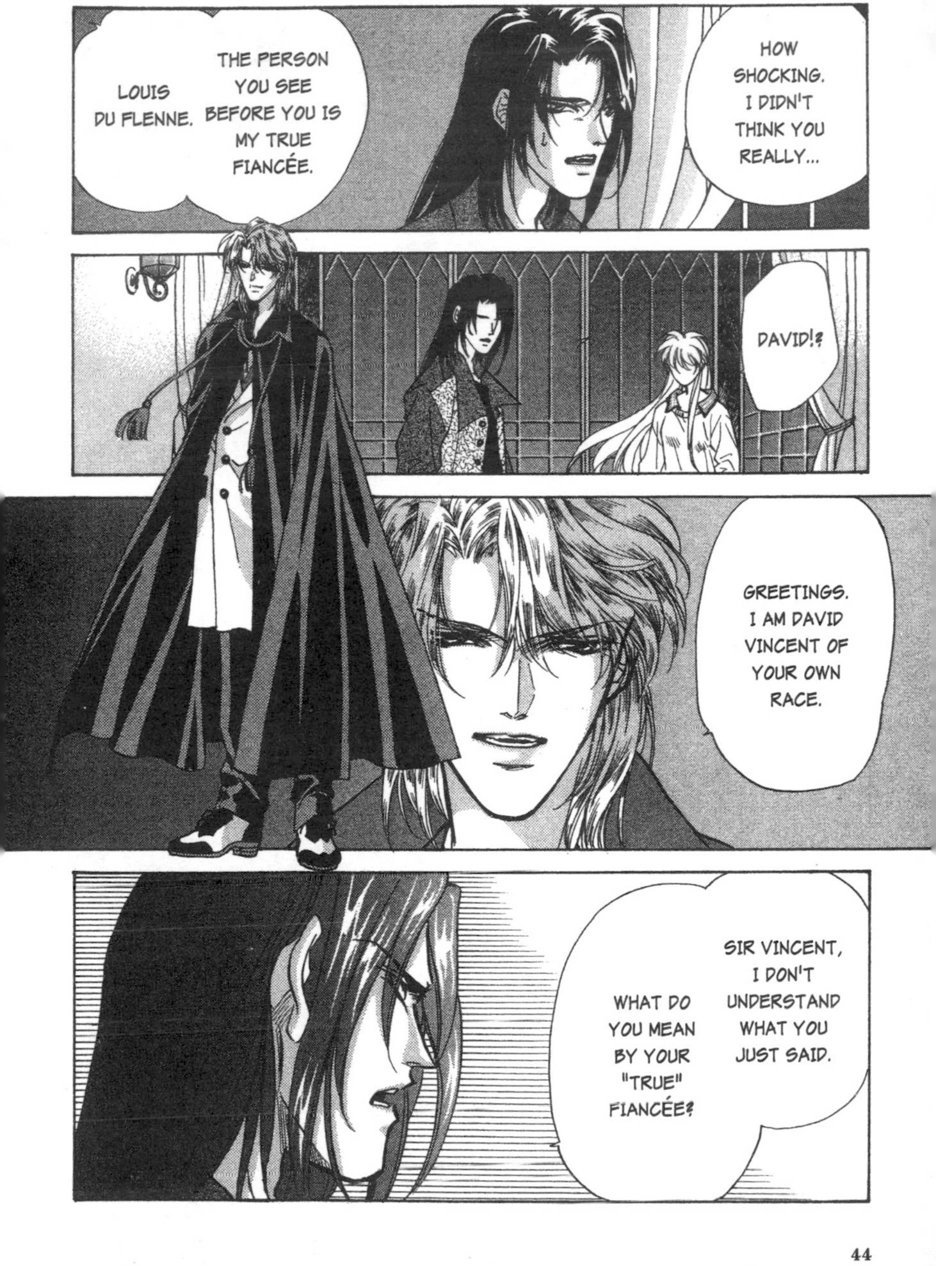
HOW SHOCKING. I DIDN'T THINK YOU REALLY...
THE PERSON YOU SEE BEFORE YOU IS MY TRUE FIANCÉE.
LOUIS DU FLENNE.
DAVID!?
GREETINGS. I AM DAVID VINCENT OF YOUR OWN RACE.
SIR VINCENT, I DON'T UNDERSTAND WHAT YOU JUST SAID.
WHAT DO YOU MEAN BY YOUR "TRUE" FIANCÉE?

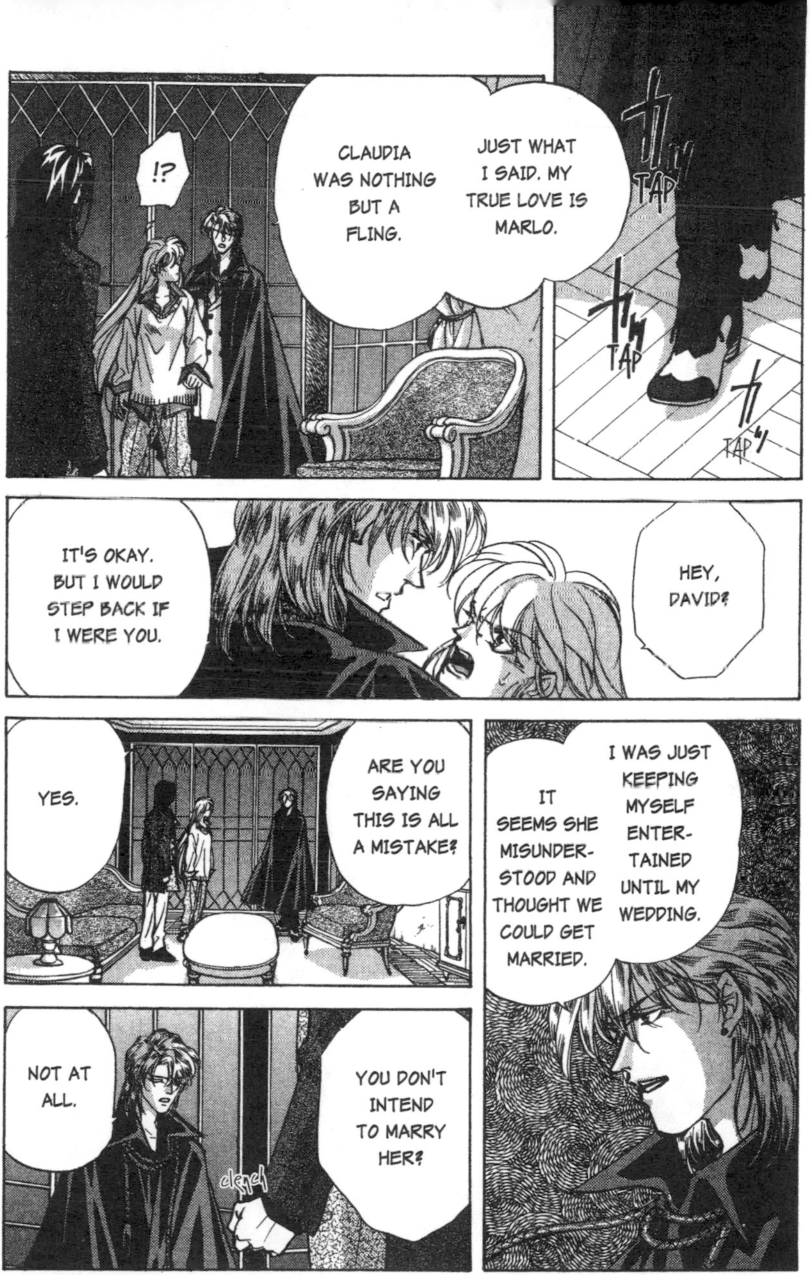
TAP
TAP
TAP
JUST WHAT I SAID. MY TRUE LOVE IS MARLO.
CLAUDIA WAS NOTHING BUT A FLING.
!?
HEY, DAVID?
IT'S OKAY. BUT I WOULD STEP BACK IF I WERE YOU.
I WAS JUST KEEPING MYSELF ENTER-TAINED UNTIL MY WEDDING.
IT SEEMS SHE MISUNDER-STOOD AND THOUGHT WE COULD GET MARRIED.
ARE YOU SAYING THIS IS ALL A MISTAKE?
YES.
YOU DON'T INTEND TO MARRY HER?
clench
NOT AT ALL.

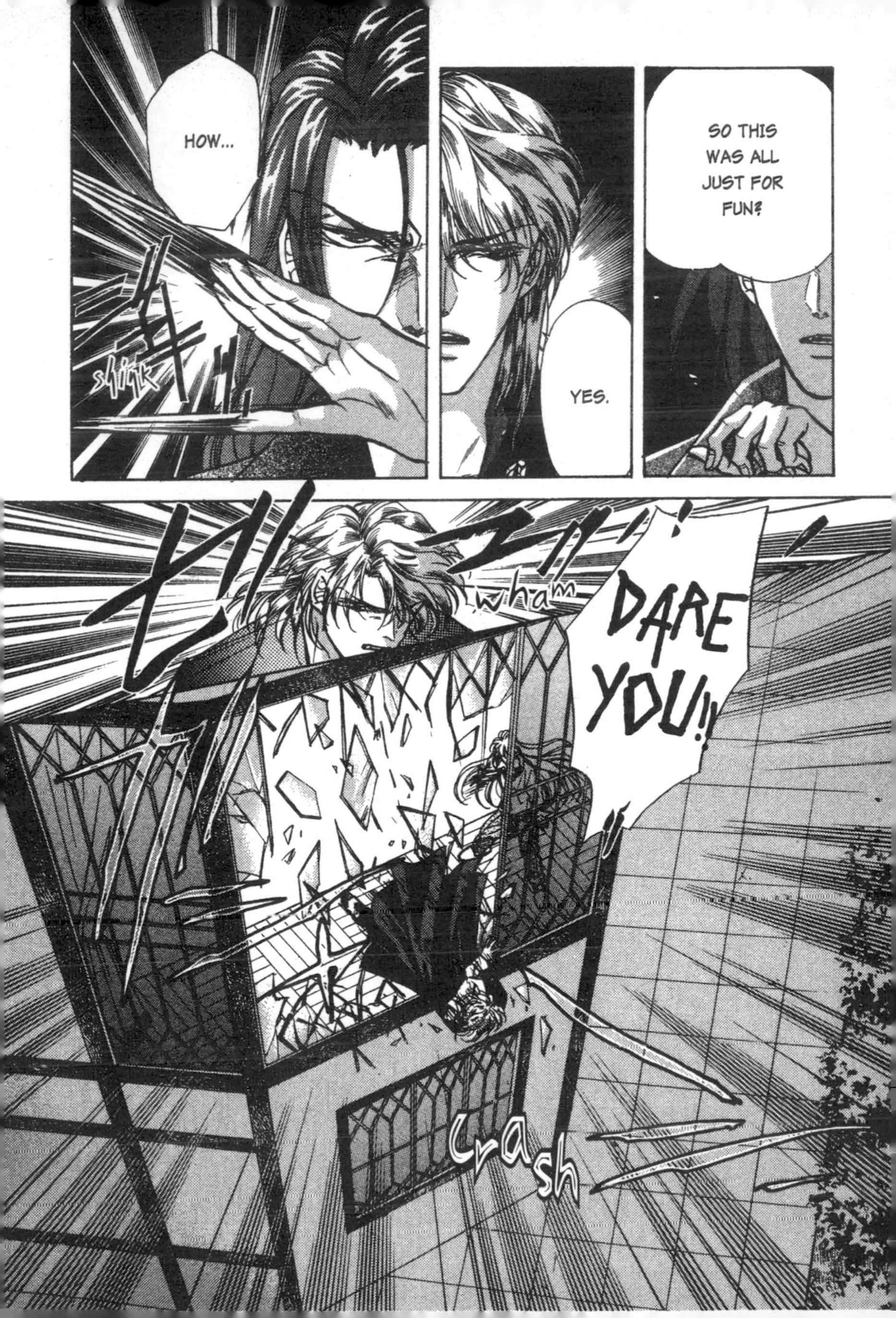
SO THIS WAS ALL JUST FOR FUN?
YES.
HOW...
shink
DARE YOU!!
wham
crash

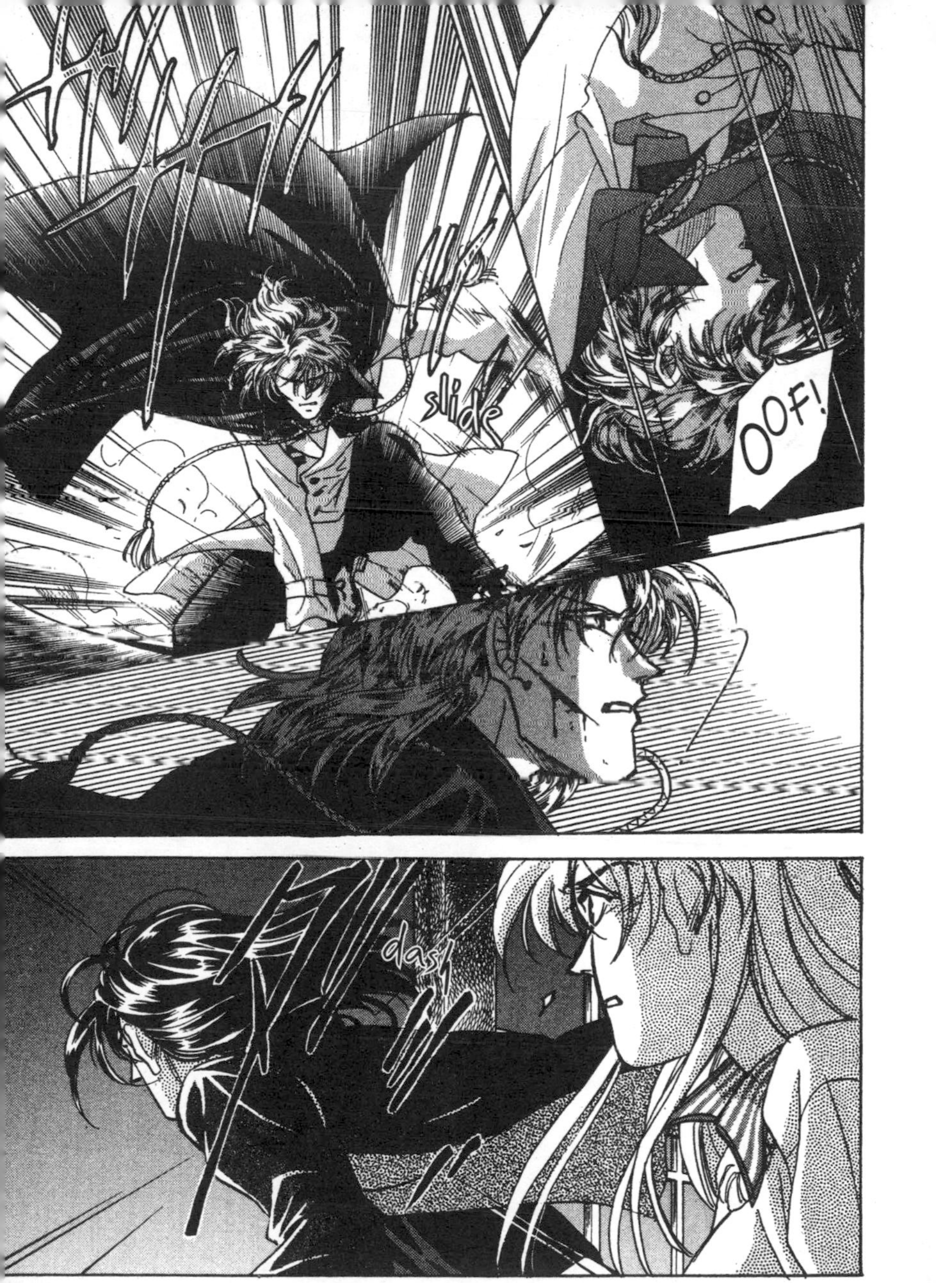
OOF!
slide
dash

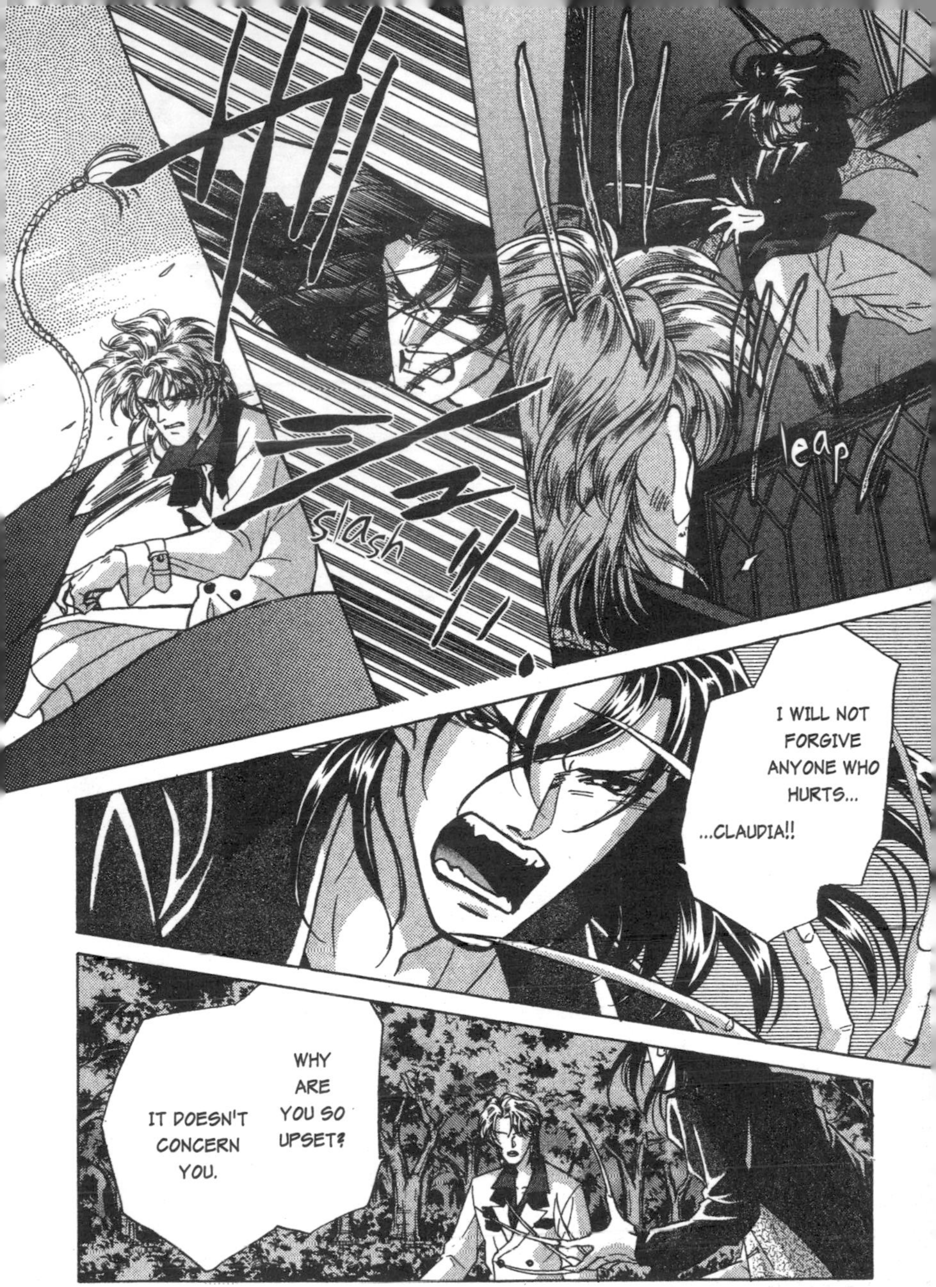
leap
slash
I WILL NOT FORGIVE ANYONE WHO HURTS...
...CLAUDIA!!
WHY ARE YOU SO UPSET?
IT DOESN'T CONCERN YOU.

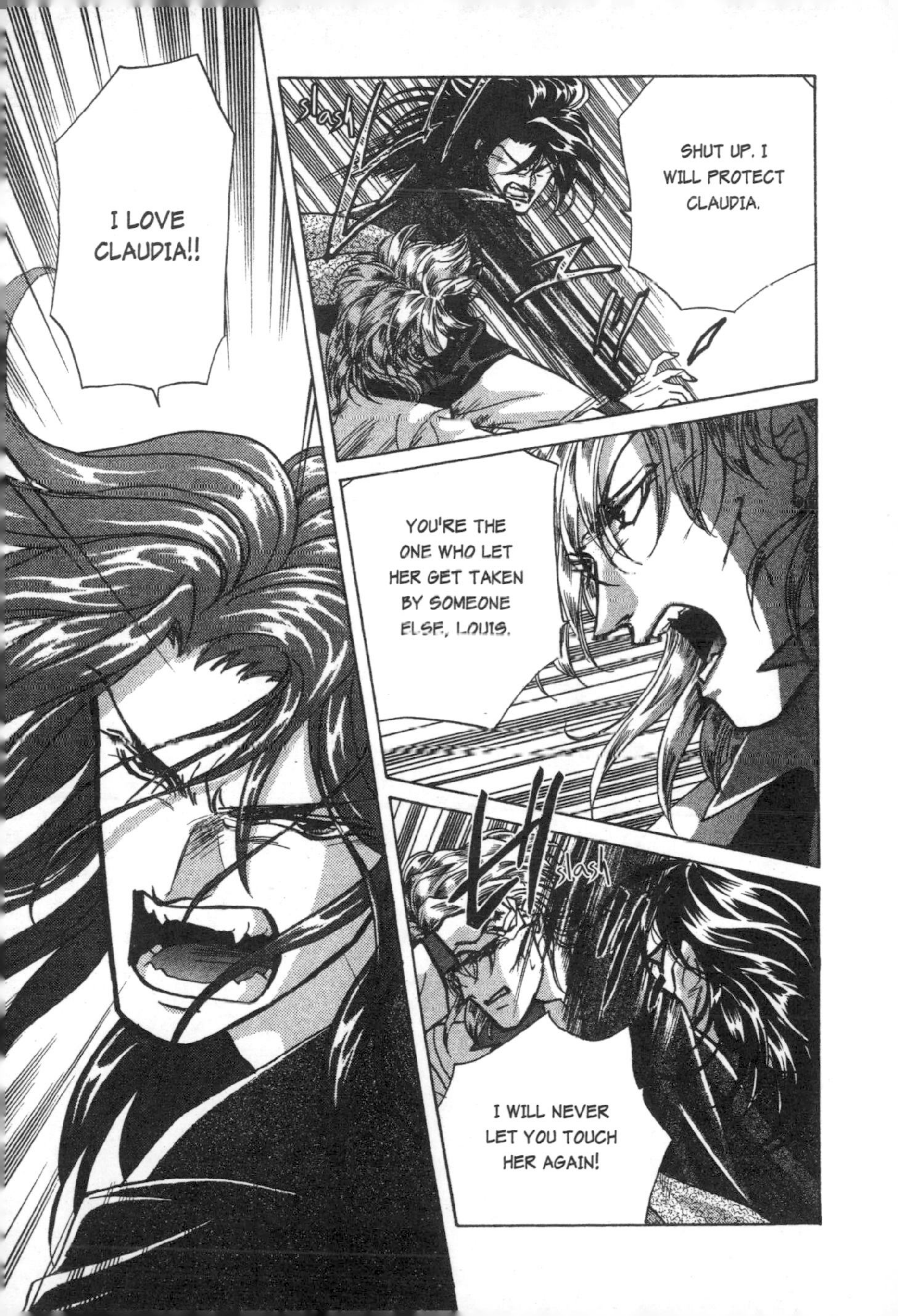
slash
SHUT UP. I WILL PROTECT CLAUDIA.
YOU'RE THE ONE WHO LET HER GET TAKEN BY SOMEONE ELSE, LOUIS.
slash
I WILL NEVER LET YOU TOUCH HER AGAIN!
I LOVE CLAUDIA!!

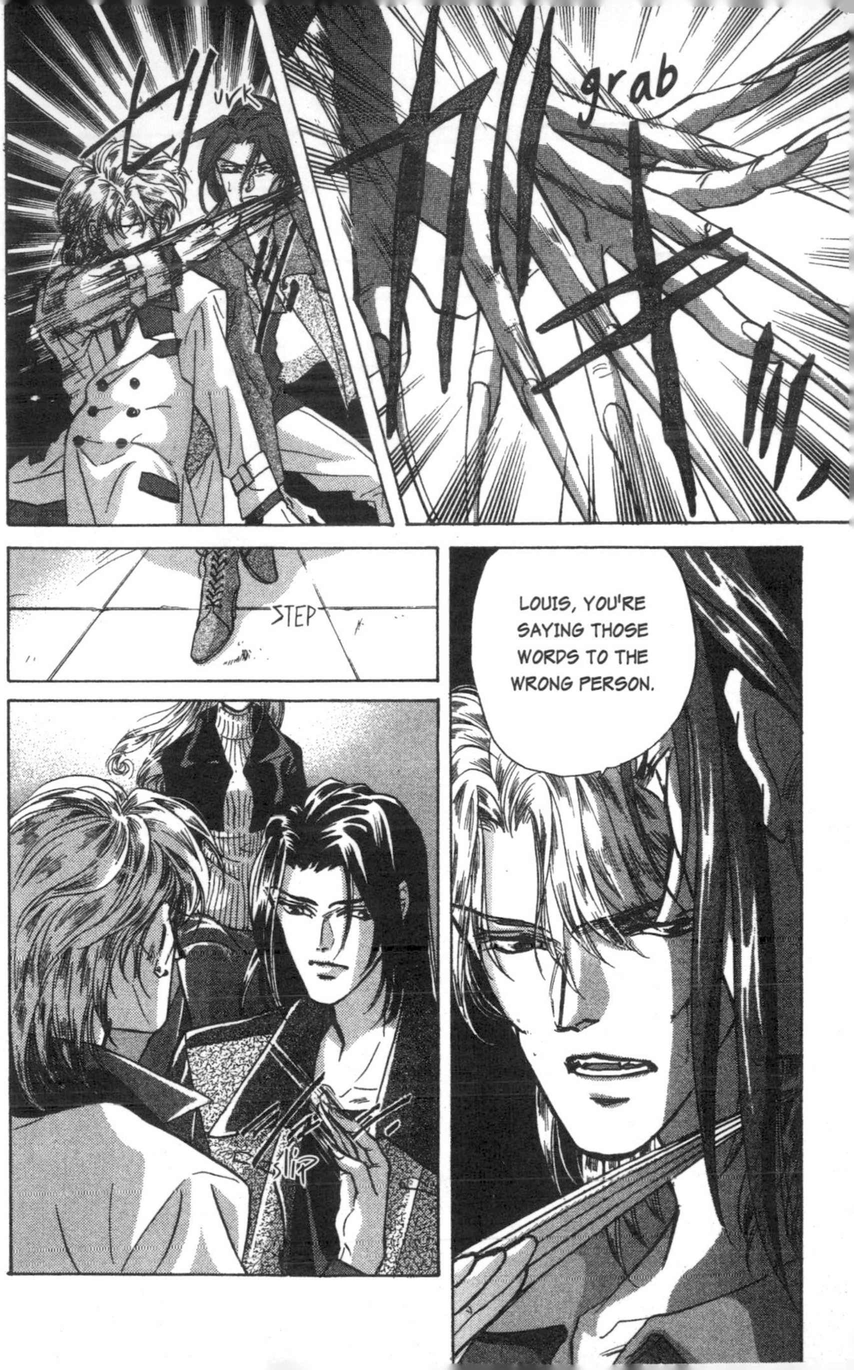
grab
Hurk
LOUIS, YOU'RE SAYING THOSE WORDS TO THE WRONG PERSON.
STEP
slip

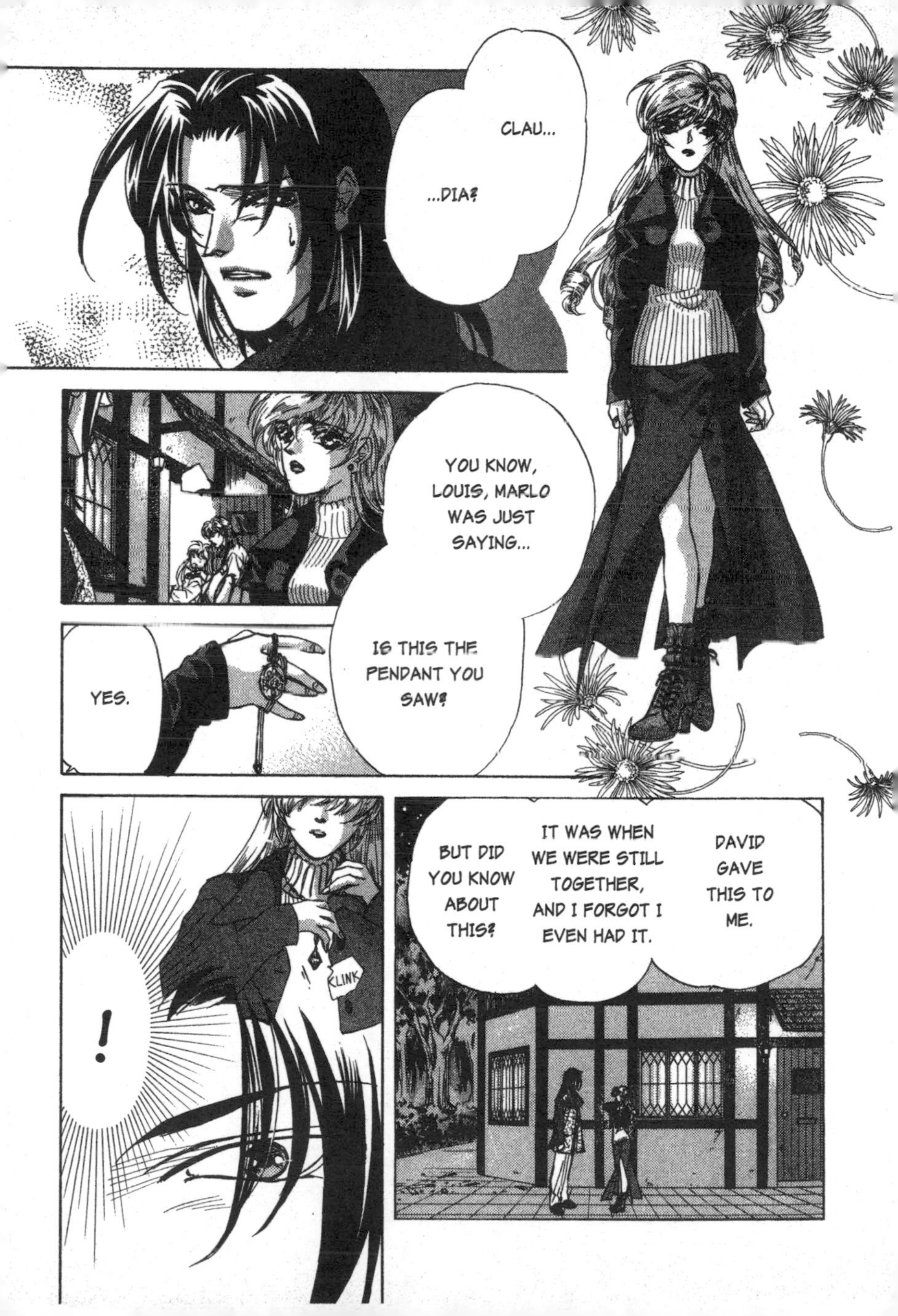
CLAU...
...DIA?
YOU KNOW, LOUIS, MARLO WAS JUST SAYING...
IS THIS THE PENDANT YOU SAW?
YES.
DAVID GAVE THIS TO ME.
IT WAS WHEN WE WERE STILL TOGETHER, AND I FORGOT I EVEN HAD IT.
BUT DID YOU KNOW ABOUT THIS?
KLINK
!

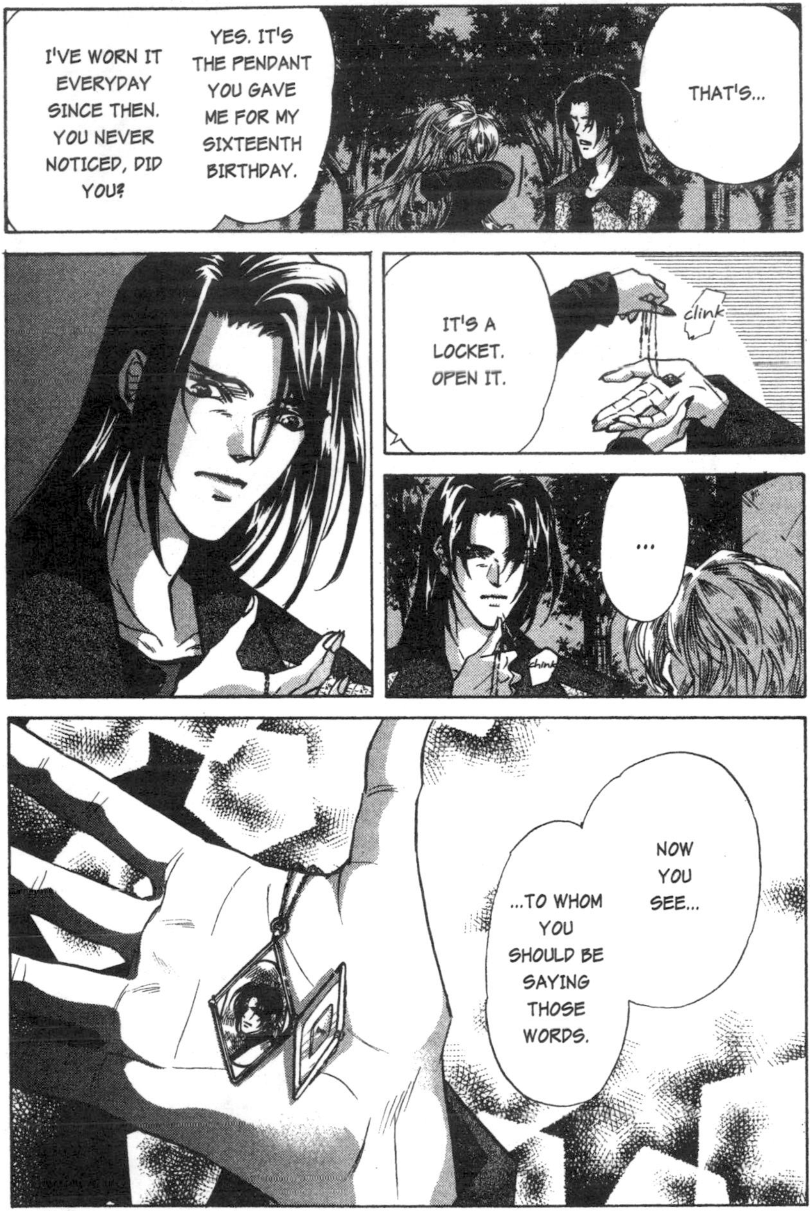
THAT'S...
YES. IT'S THE PENDANT YOU GAVE ME FOR MY SIXTEENTH BIRTHDAY.
I'VE WORN IT EVERYDAY SINCE THEN. YOU NEVER NOTICED, DID YOU?
IT'S A LOCKET. OPEN IT.
clink
...
clink
NOW YOU SEE...
...TO WHOM YOU SHOULD BE SAYING THOSE WORDS.

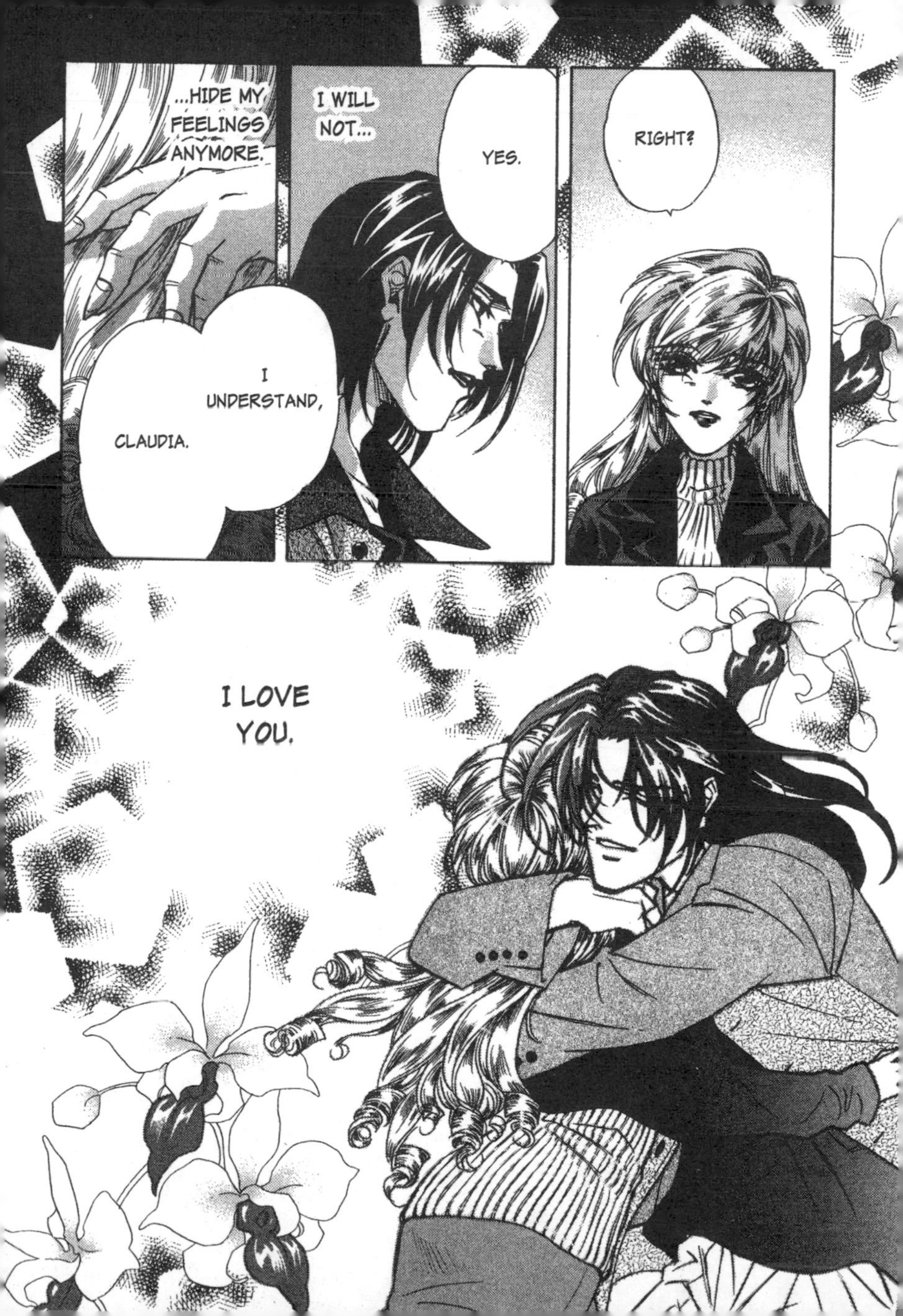
RIGHT?
YES.
I UNDERSTAND, CLAUDIA.
I WILL NOT...
...HIDE MY FEELINGS ANYMORE.
I LOVE YOU.

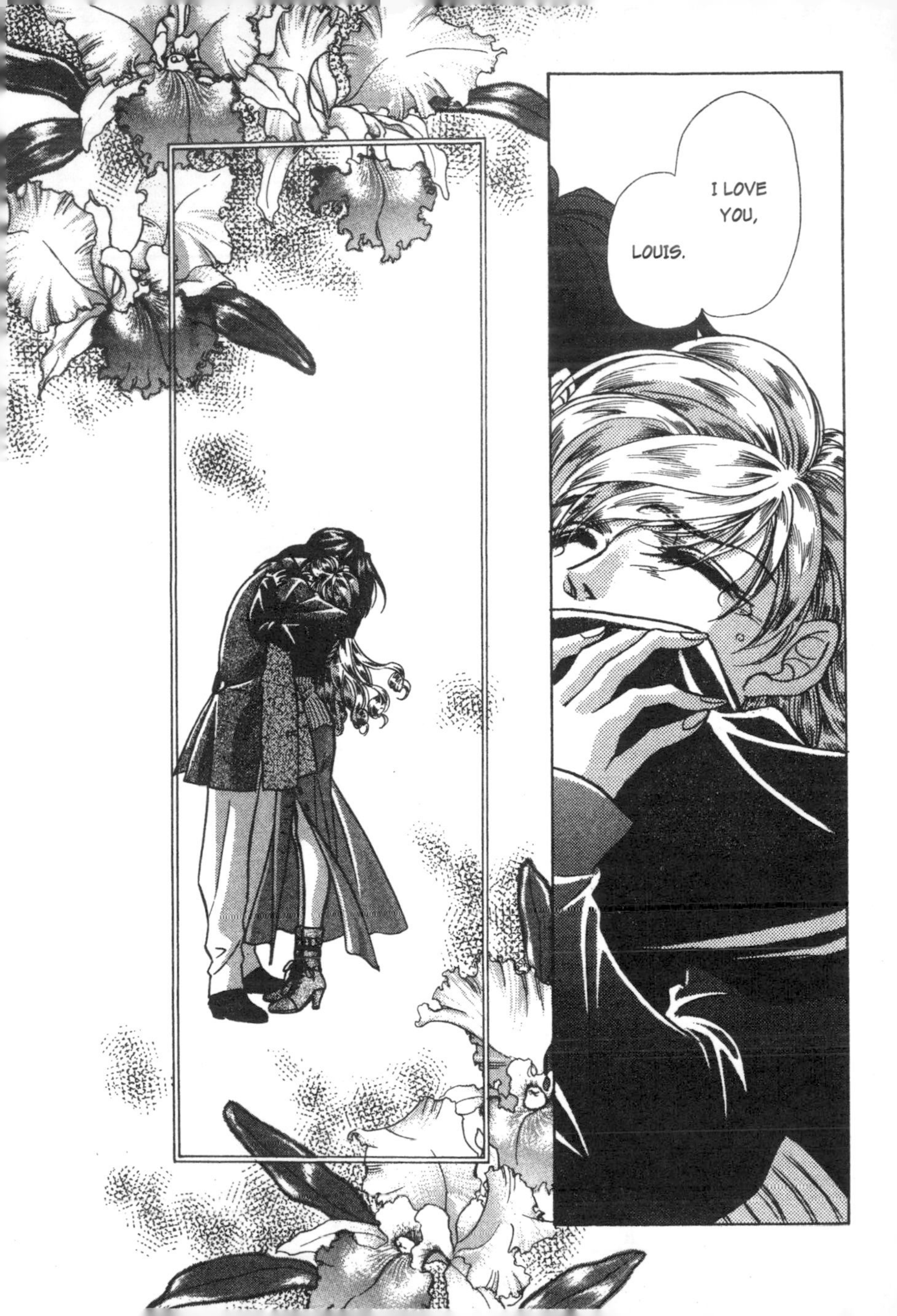
I LOVE YOU, LOUIS.

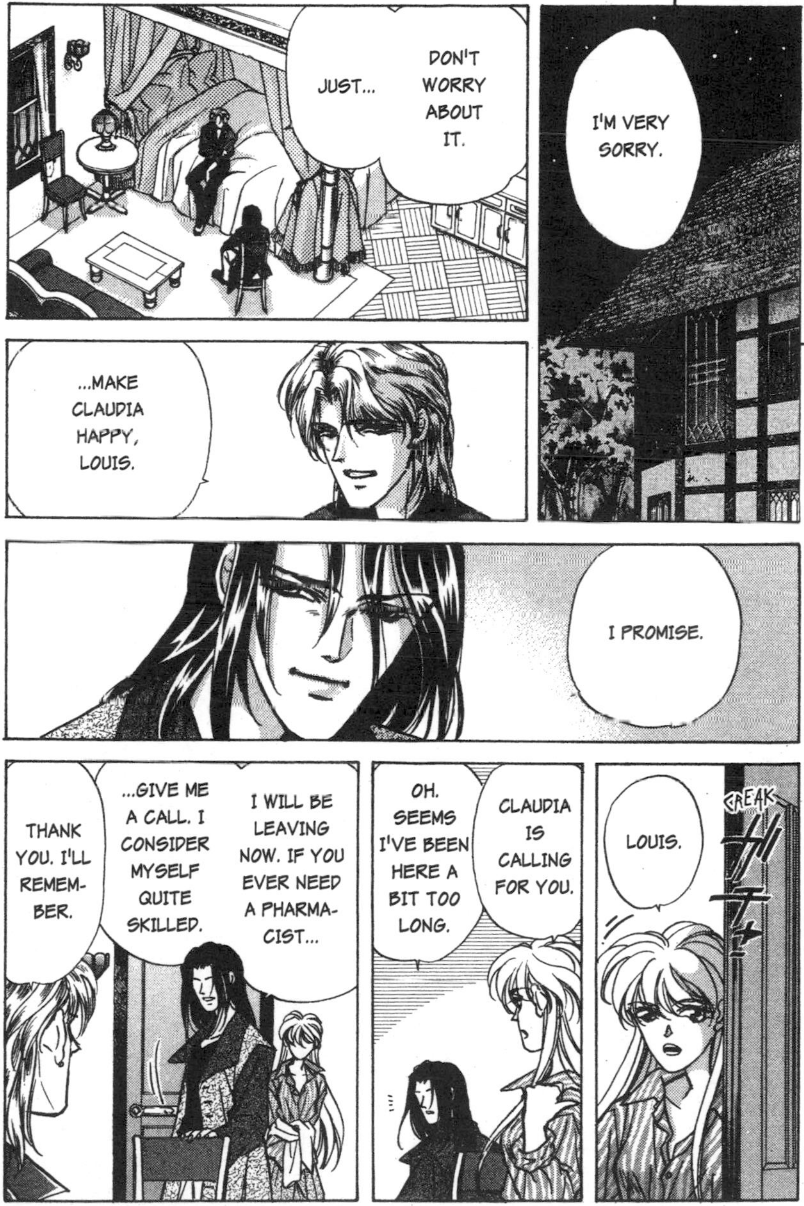
I'M VERY SORRY.
DON'T WORRY ABOUT IT.
JUST...
...MAKE CLAUDIA HAPPY, LOUIS.
I PROMISE.
CREAK
LOUIS.
CLAUDIA IS CALLING FOR YOU.
OH. SEEMS I'VE BEEN HERE A BIT TOO LONG.
I WILL BE LEAVING NOW. IF YOU EVER NEED A PHARMA-CIST...
...GIVE ME A CALL. I CONSIDER MYSELF QUITE SKILLED.
THANK YOU. I'LL REMEM-BER.

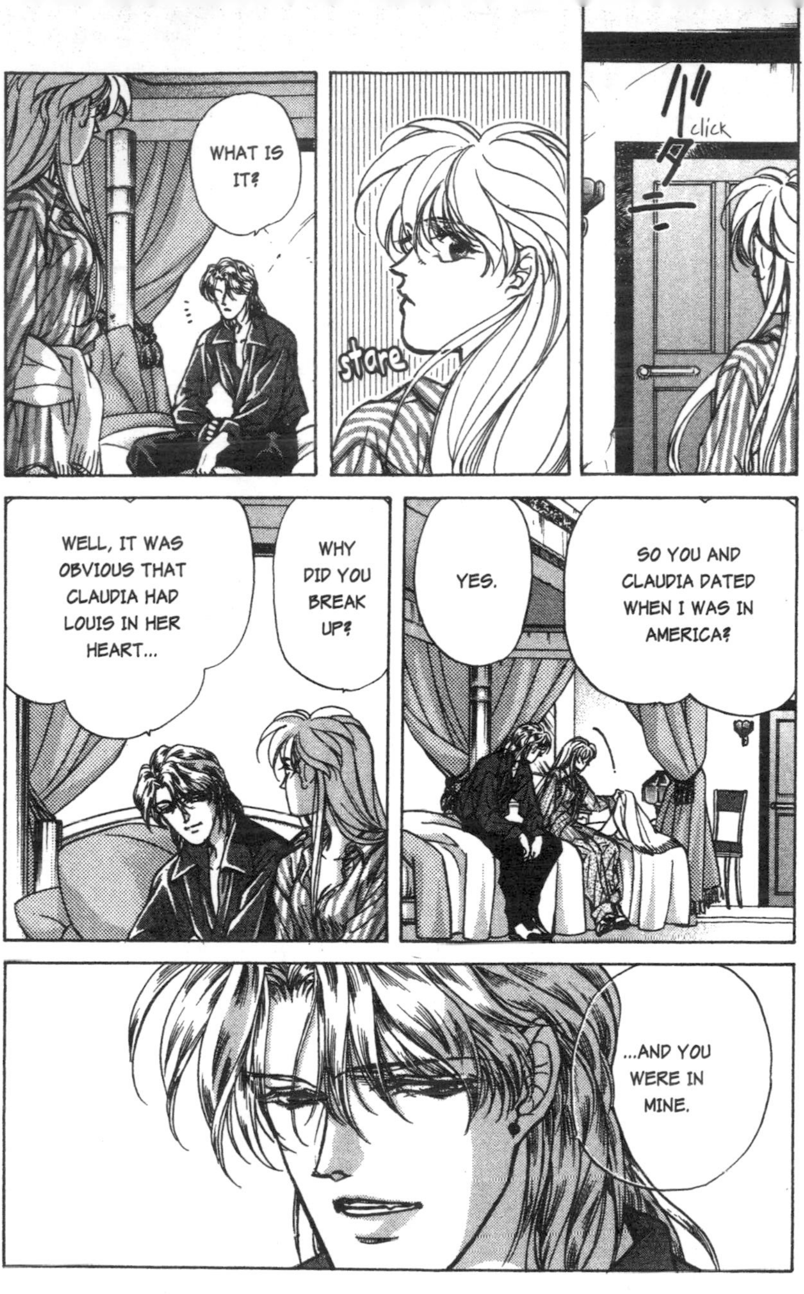
click
stare
WHAT IS IT?
SO YOU AND CLAUDIA DATED WHEN I WAS IN AMERICA?
YES.
WHY DID YOU BREAK UP?
WELL, IT WAS OBVIOUS THAT CLAUDIA HAD LOUIS IN HER HEART...
...AND YOU WERE IN MINE.

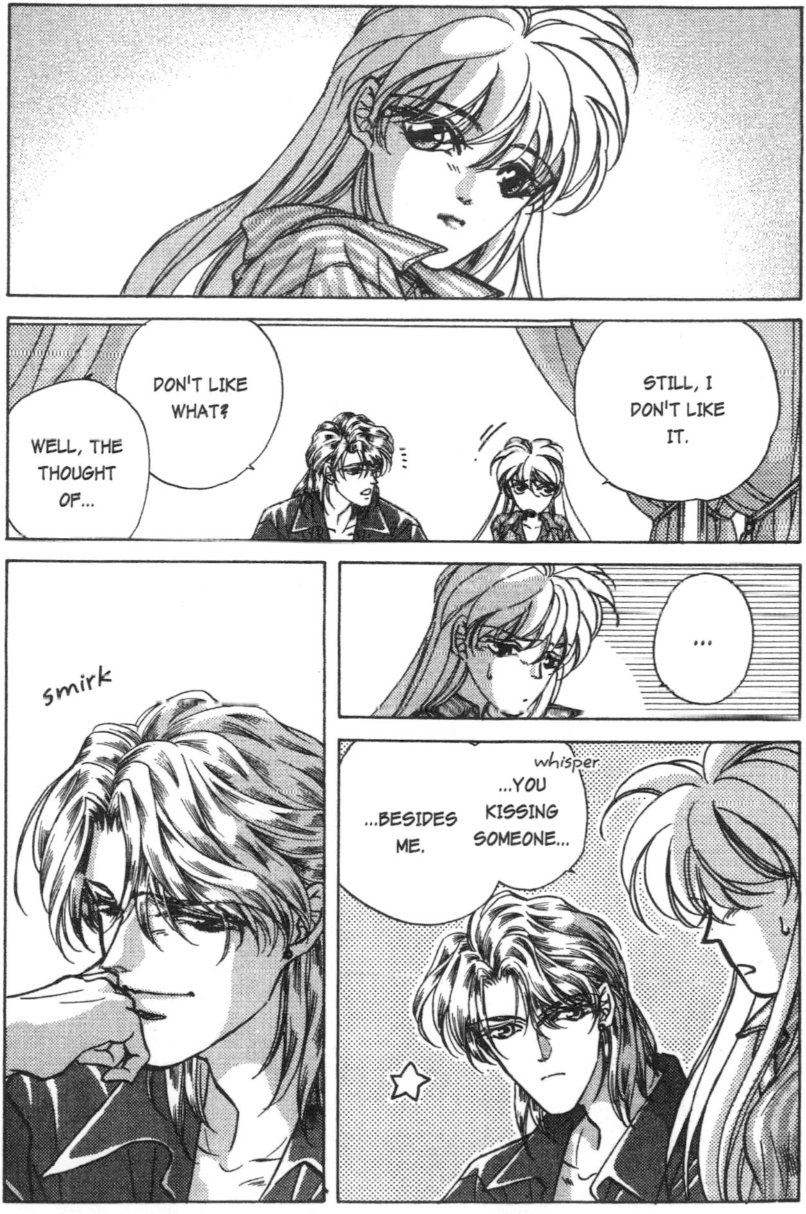
STILL, I DON'T LIKE IT.
DON'T LIKE WHAT?
WELL, THE THOUGHT OF...
...
whisper
...YOU KISSING SOMEONE...
...BESIDES ME.
smirk

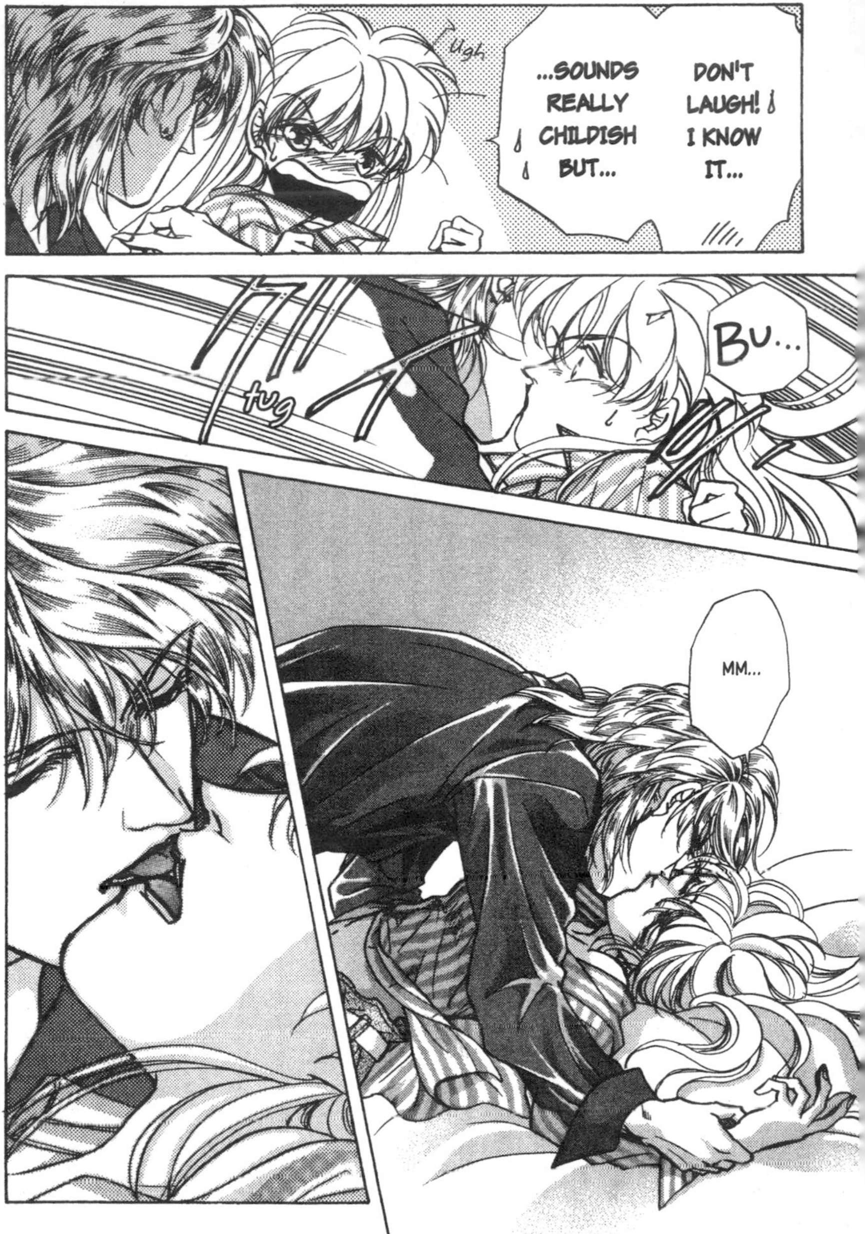
DON'T LAUGH! I KNOW IT...
...SOUNDS REALLY CHILDISH BUT...
Ugh
Bu...
tug
MM...

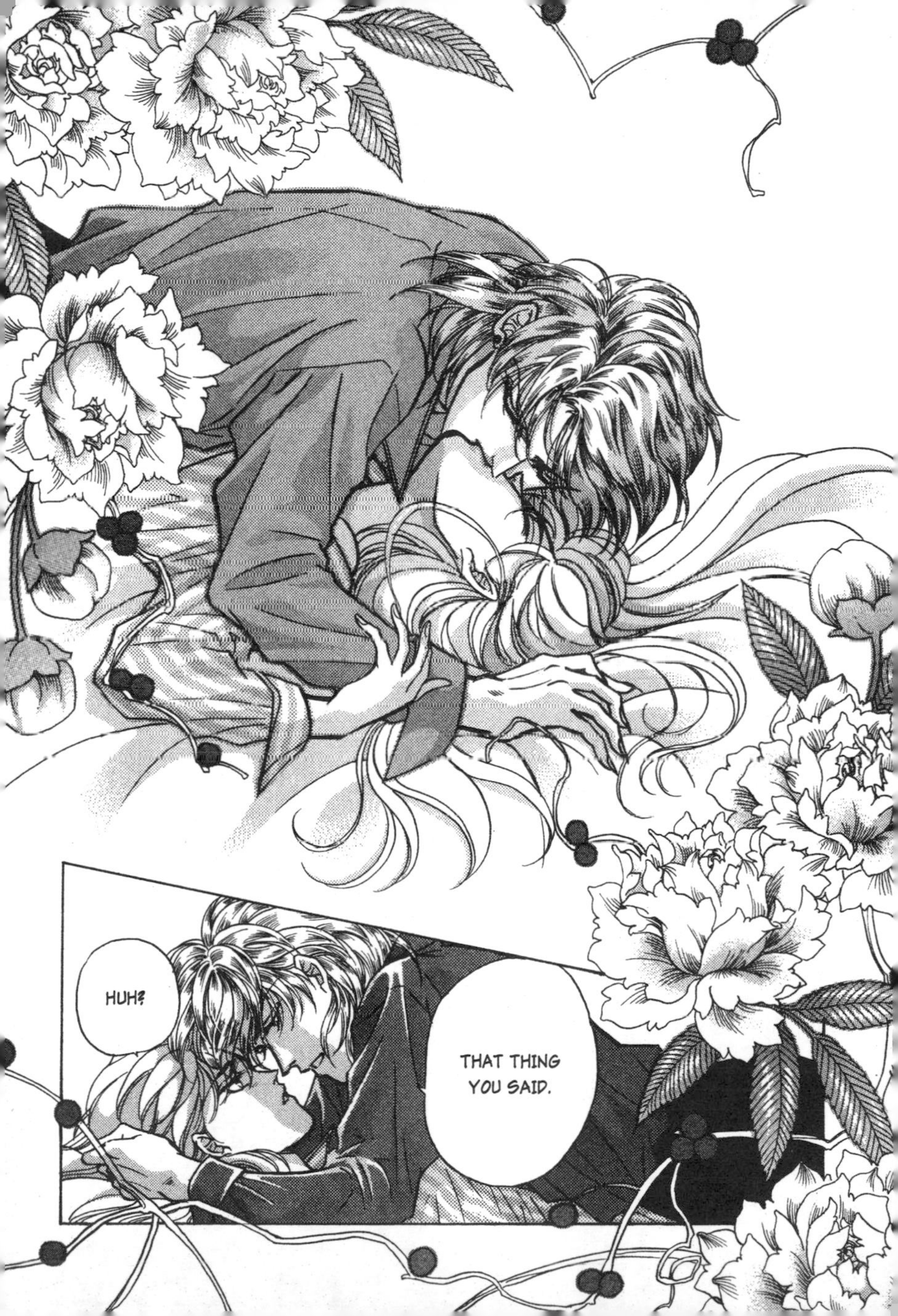
THAT THING YOU SAID.
HUH?

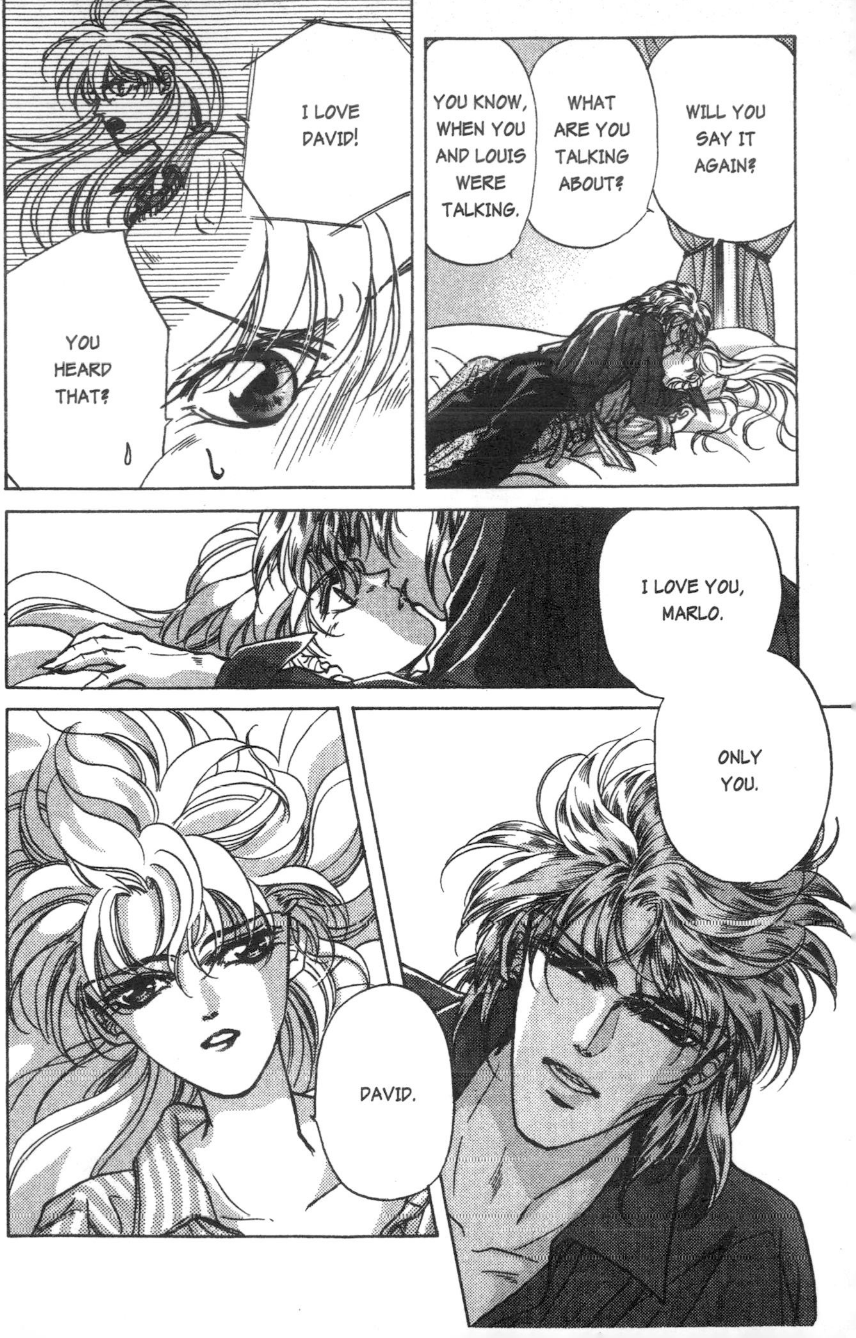
WILL YOU SAY IT AGAIN?
WHAT ARE YOU TALKING ABOUT?
YOU KNOW, WHEN YOU AND LOUIS WERE TALKING.
I LOVE DAVID!
YOU HEARD THAT?
I LOVE YOU, MARLO.
ONLY YOU.
DAVID.

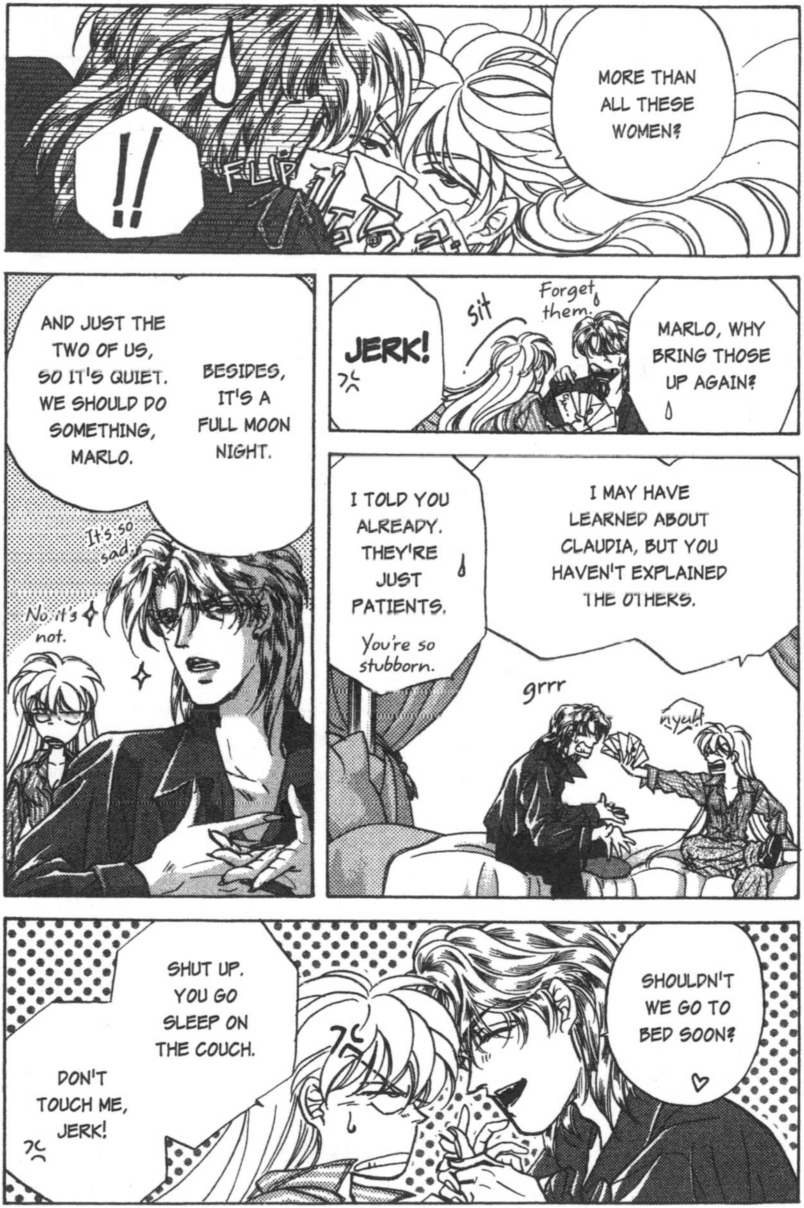
MORE THAN ALL THESE WOMEN?
!!
FLIP
MARLO, WHY BRING THOSE UP AGAIN?
Forget them.
sit
JERK!
I MAY HAVE LEARNED ABOUT CLAUDIA, BUT YOU HAVEN'T EXPLAINED THE OTHERS.
I TOLD YOU ALREADY. THEY'RE JUST PATIENTS.
You're so stubborn.
grrr
BESIDES, IT'S A FULL MOON NIGHT.
AND JUST THE TWO OF US, SO IT'S QUIET. WE SHOULD DO SOMETHING, MARLO.
It's so sad.
No it's not.
SHOULDN'T WE GO TO BED SOON?
SHUT UP. YOU GO SLEEP ON THE COUCH.
DON'T TOUCH ME, JERK!

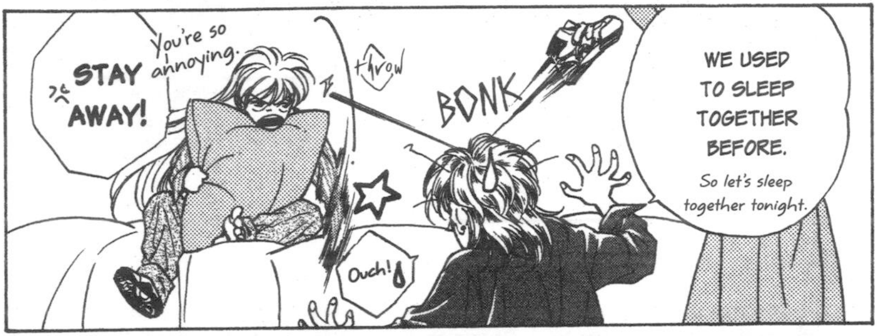
WE USED TO SLEEP TOGETHER BEFORE.
So let's sleep together tonight.
BONK
throw
You're so annoying.
STAY AWAY!
Ouch!

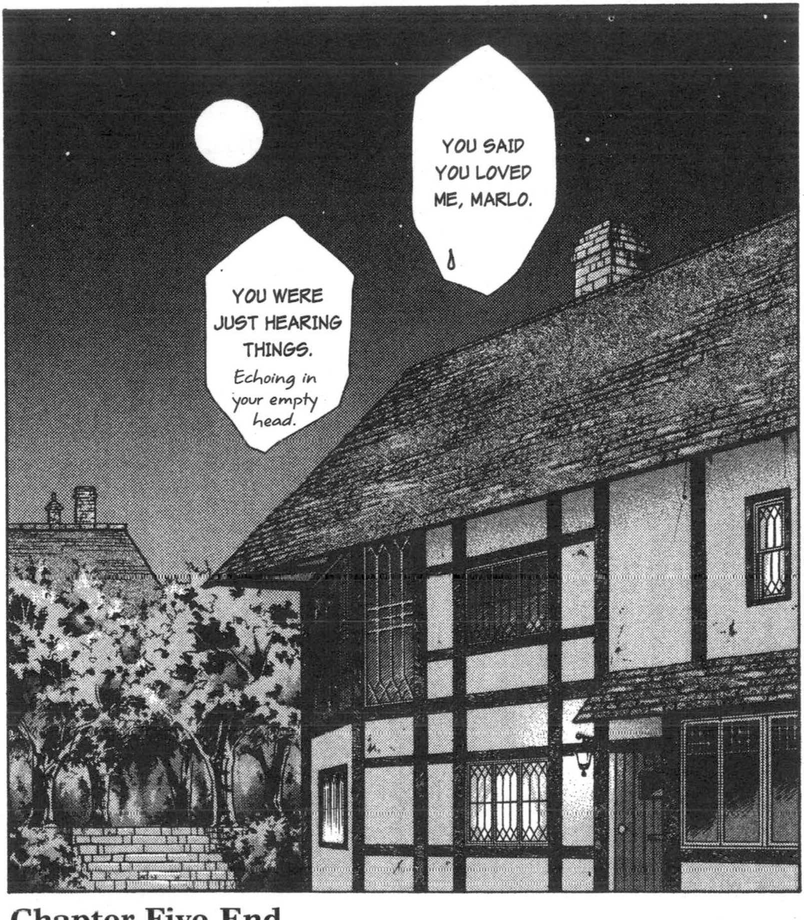
YOU SAID YOU LOVED ME, MARLO.
YOU WERE JUST HEARING THINGS.
Echoing in your empty head.

Chapter Five End

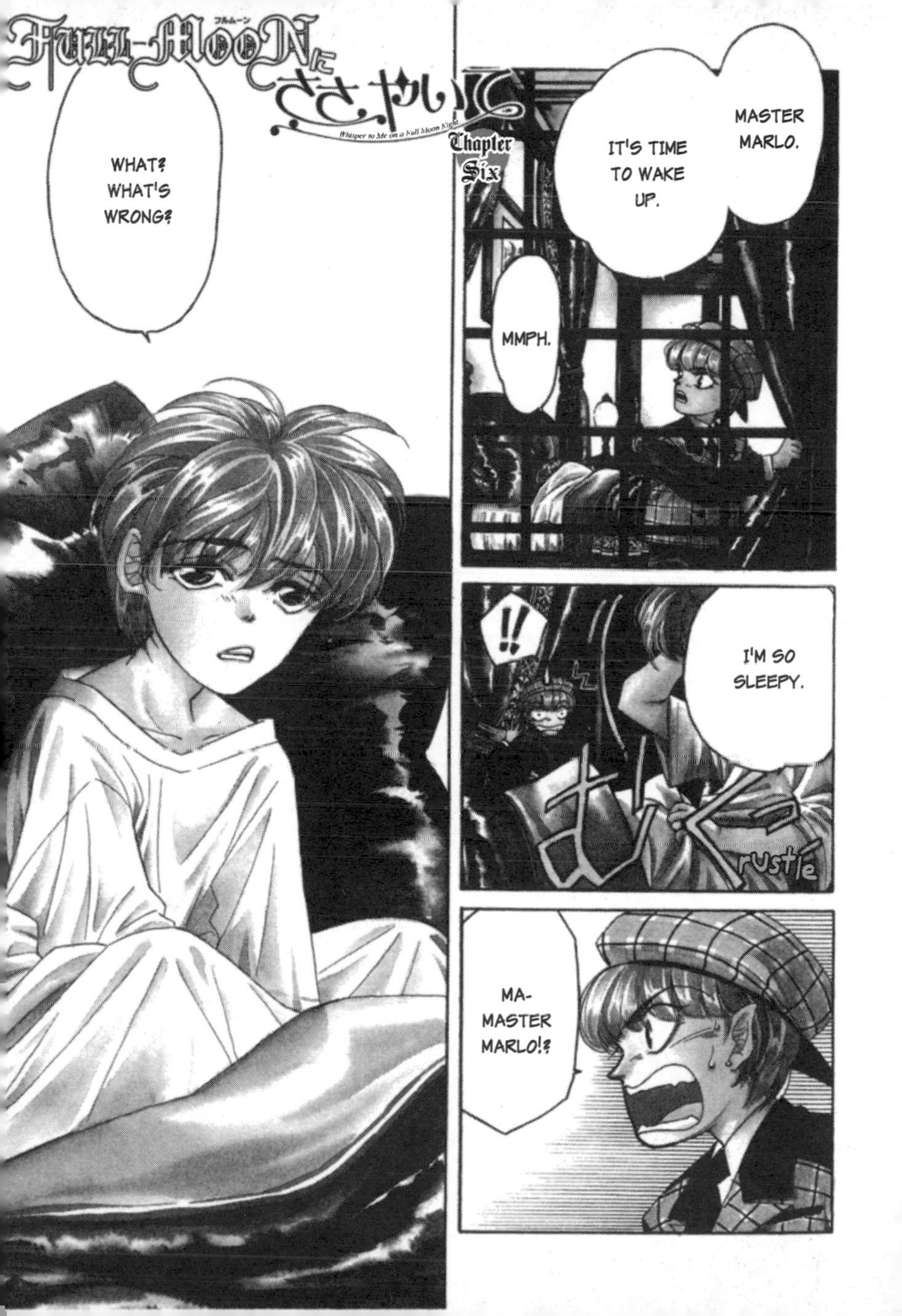

FULL-MOON にささやいて
Whisper to Me on a Full Moon Night
Chapter Six
MASTER MARLO.
IT'S TIME TO WAKE UP.
MMPH.
!!
I'M SO SLEEPY.
rustle
MA- MASTER MARLO!?
WHAT? WHAT'S WRONG?

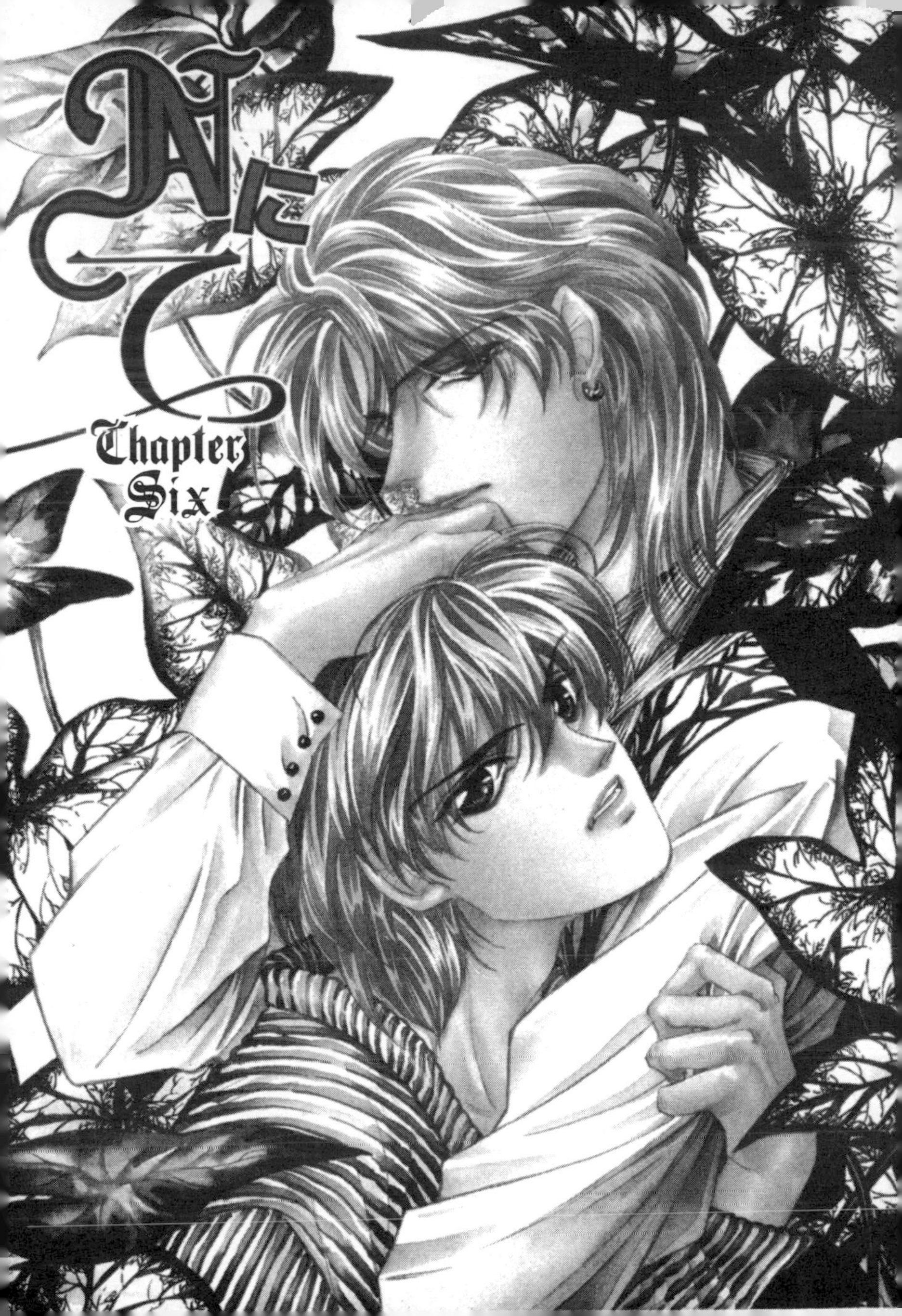
Chapter Six

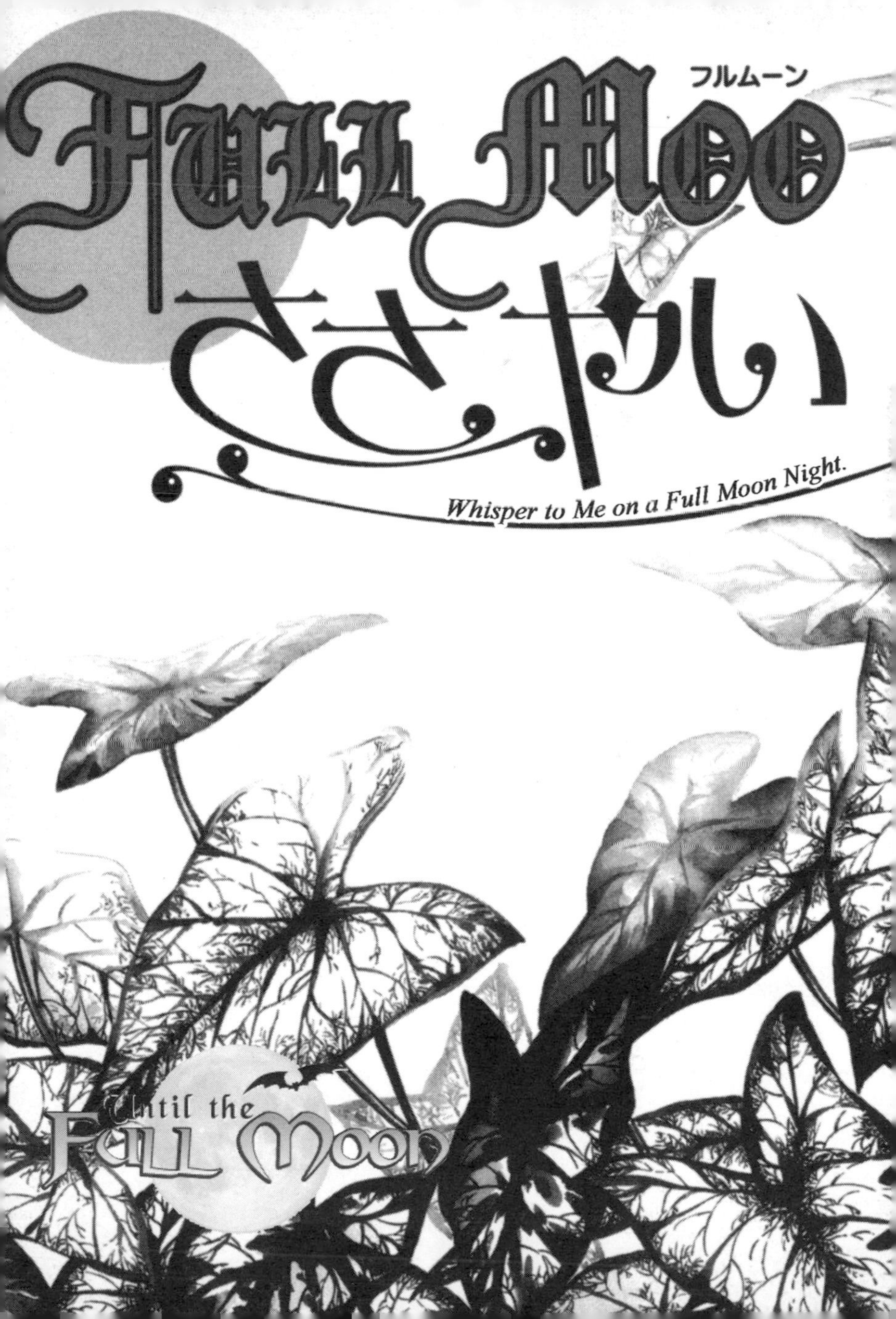
FULL MOO
フルムーン
ささやい
Whisper to Me on a Full Moon Night.
Until the FULL MOON

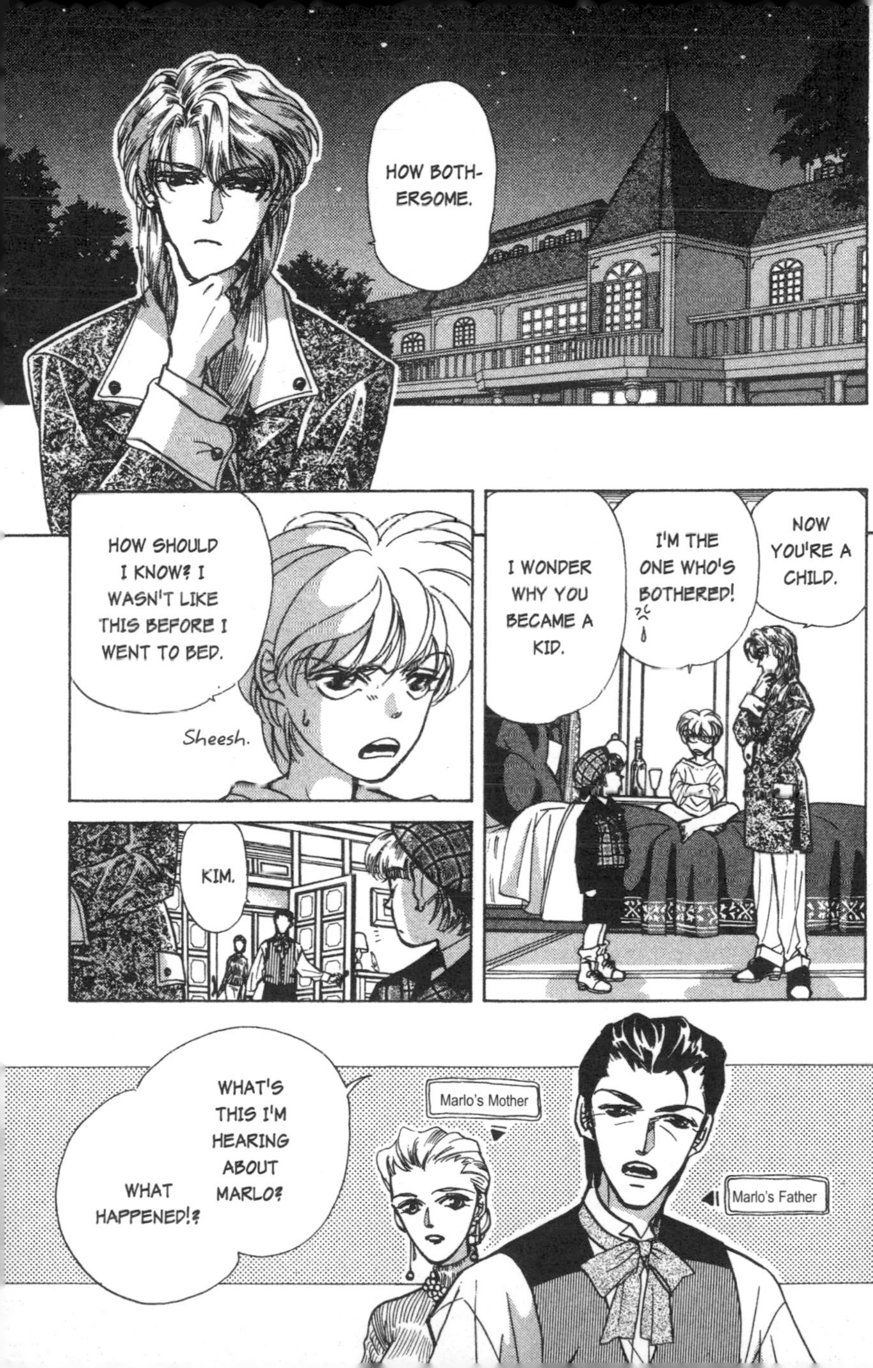
HOW BOTH-ERSOME.
NOW YOU'RE A CHILD.
I'M THE ONE WHO'S BOTHERED!
I WONDER WHY YOU BECAME A KID.
HOW SHOULD I KNOW? I WASN'T LIKE THIS BEFORE I WENT TO BED.
Sheesh.
KIM.
Marlo's Father
Marlo's Mother
WHAT'S THIS I'M HEARING ABOUT MARLO?
WHAT HAPPENED!?

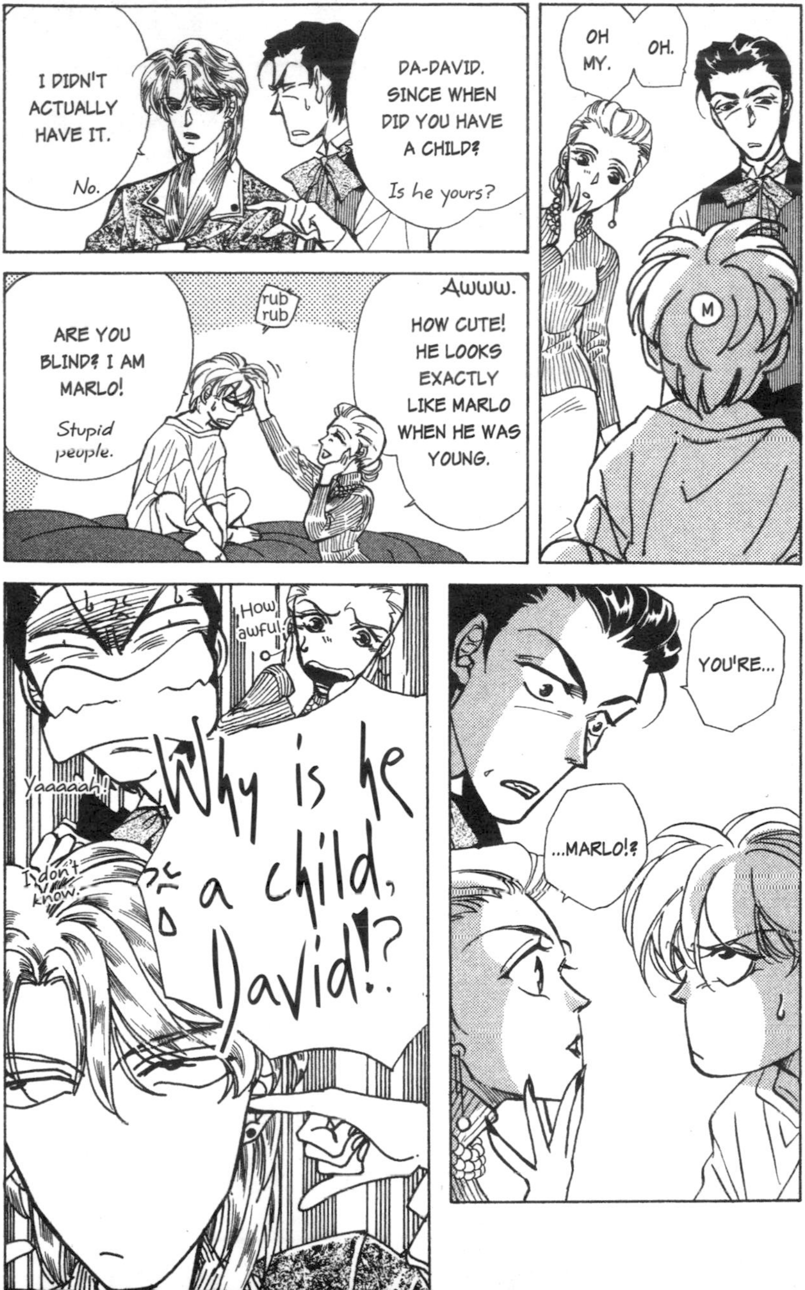
OH.
OH MY.
DA-DAVID. SINCE WHEN DID YOU HAVE A CHILD?
Is he yours?
I DIDN'T ACTUALLY HAVE IT.
No.
Awww.
HOW CUTE! HE LOOKS EXACTLY LIKE MARLO WHEN HE WAS YOUNG.
rub rub
ARE YOU BLIND? I AM MARLO!
Stupid people.
YOU'RE...
...MARLO!?
How awful!
Why is he a child, David!?
Yaaaaah!
I don't know.

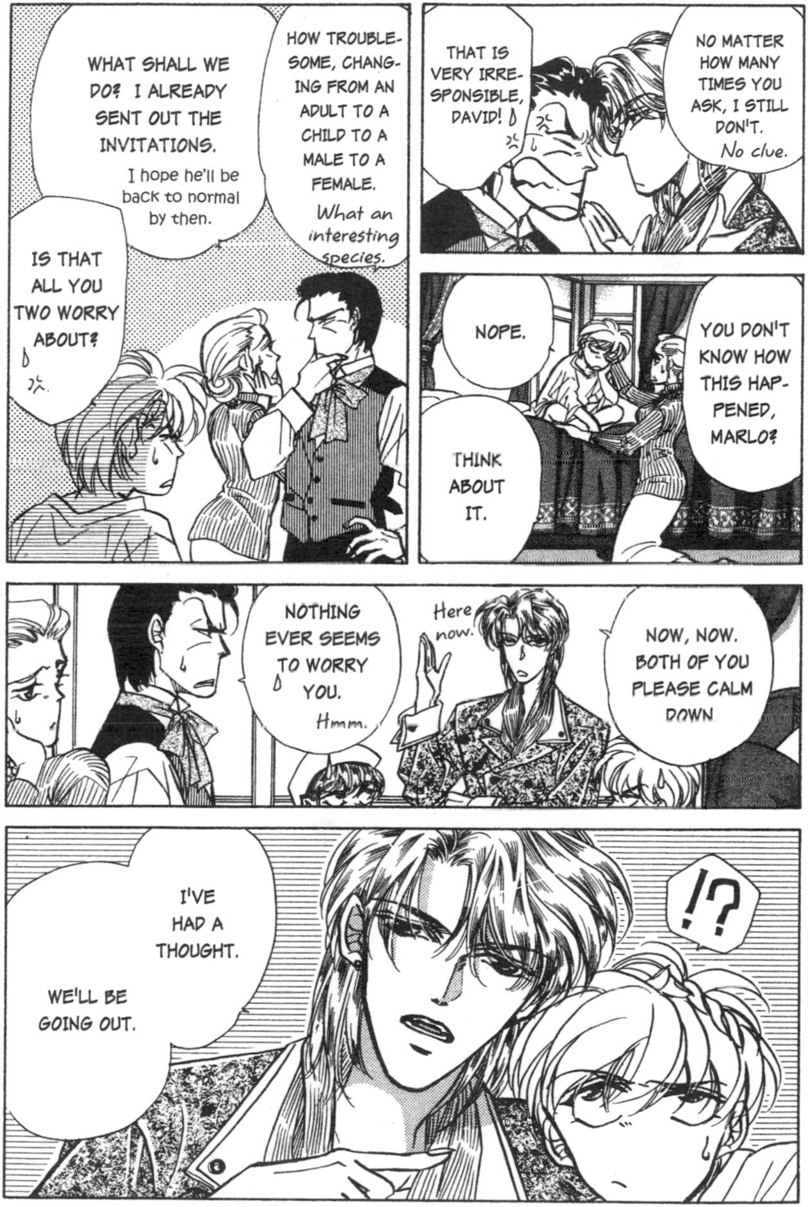
WHAT SHALL WE DO? I ALREADY SENT OUT THE INVITATIONS.
I hope he'll be back to normal by then.
HOW TROUBLE-SOME, CHANG-ING FROM AN ADULT TO A CHILD TO A MALE TO A FEMALE.
What an interesting species.
IS THAT ALL YOU TWO WORRY ABOUT?
THAT IS VERY IRRE-SPONSIBLE, DAVID!
NO MATTER HOW MANY TIMES YOU ASK, I STILL DON'T.
No clue.
YOU DON'T KNOW HOW THIS HAP-PENED, MARLO?
NOPE.
THINK ABOUT IT.
NOTHING EVER SEEMS TO WORRY YOU.
Hmm.
Here now.
NOW, NOW. BOTH OF YOU PLEASE CALM DOWN
I'VE HAD A THOUGHT.
WE'LL BE GOING OUT.
!?

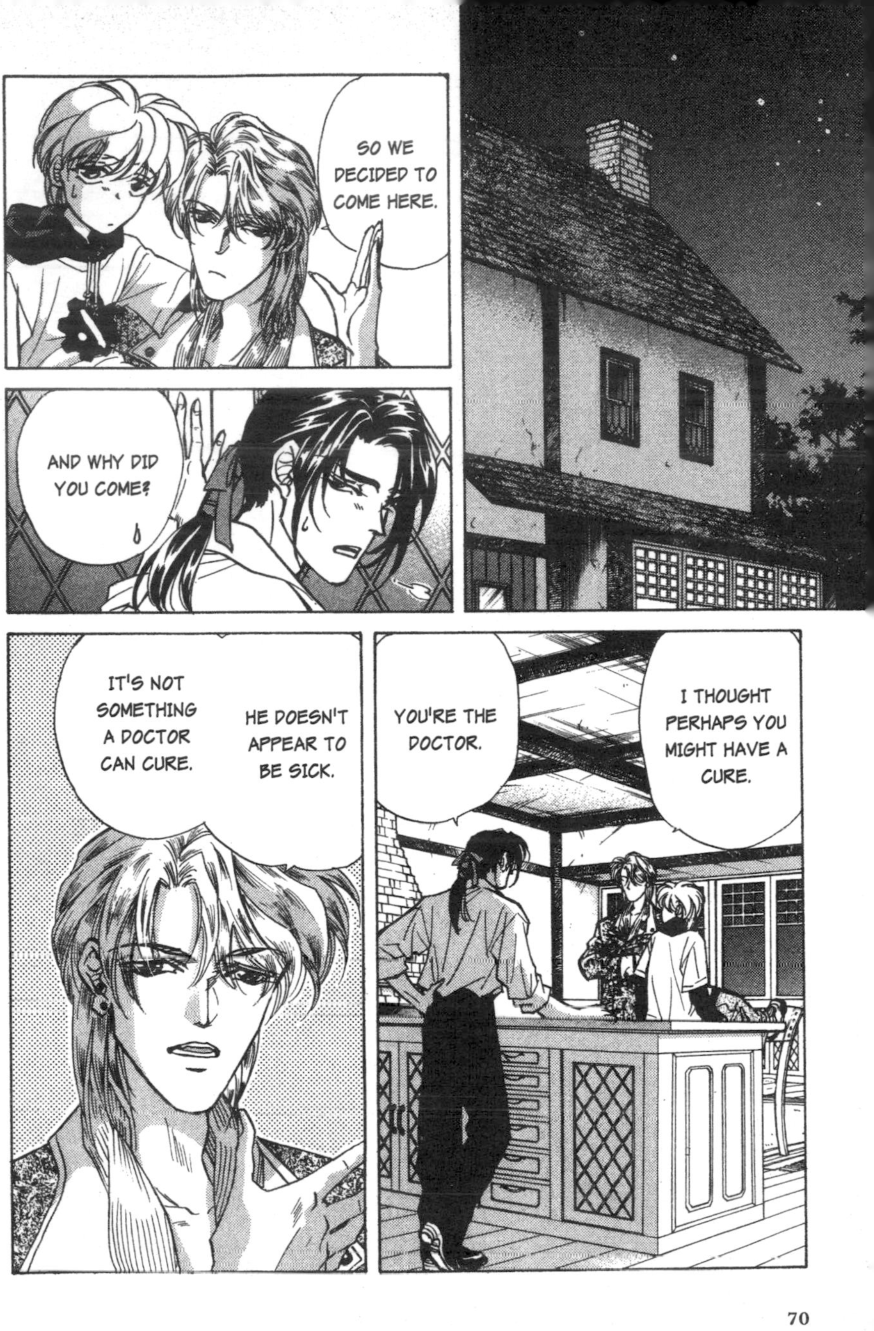
SO WE DECIDED TO COME HERE.
AND WHY DID YOU COME?
I THOUGHT PERHAPS YOU MIGHT HAVE A CURE.
YOU'RE THE DOCTOR.
HE DOESN'T APPEAR TO BE SICK.
IT'S NOT SOMETHING A DOCTOR CAN CURE.

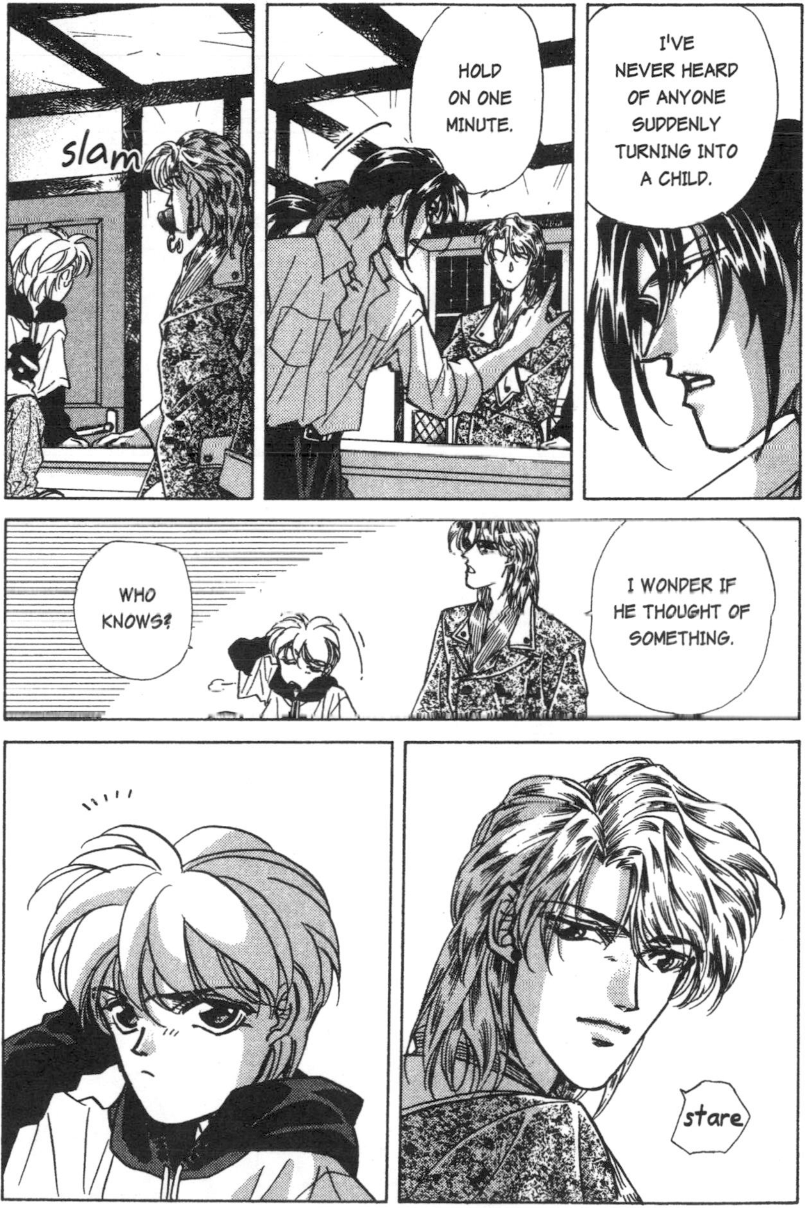
I'VE NEVER HEARD OF ANYONE SUDDENLY TURNING INTO A CHILD.
HOLD ON ONE MINUTE.
slam
I WONDER IF HE THOUGHT OF SOMETHING.
WHO KNOWS?
stare

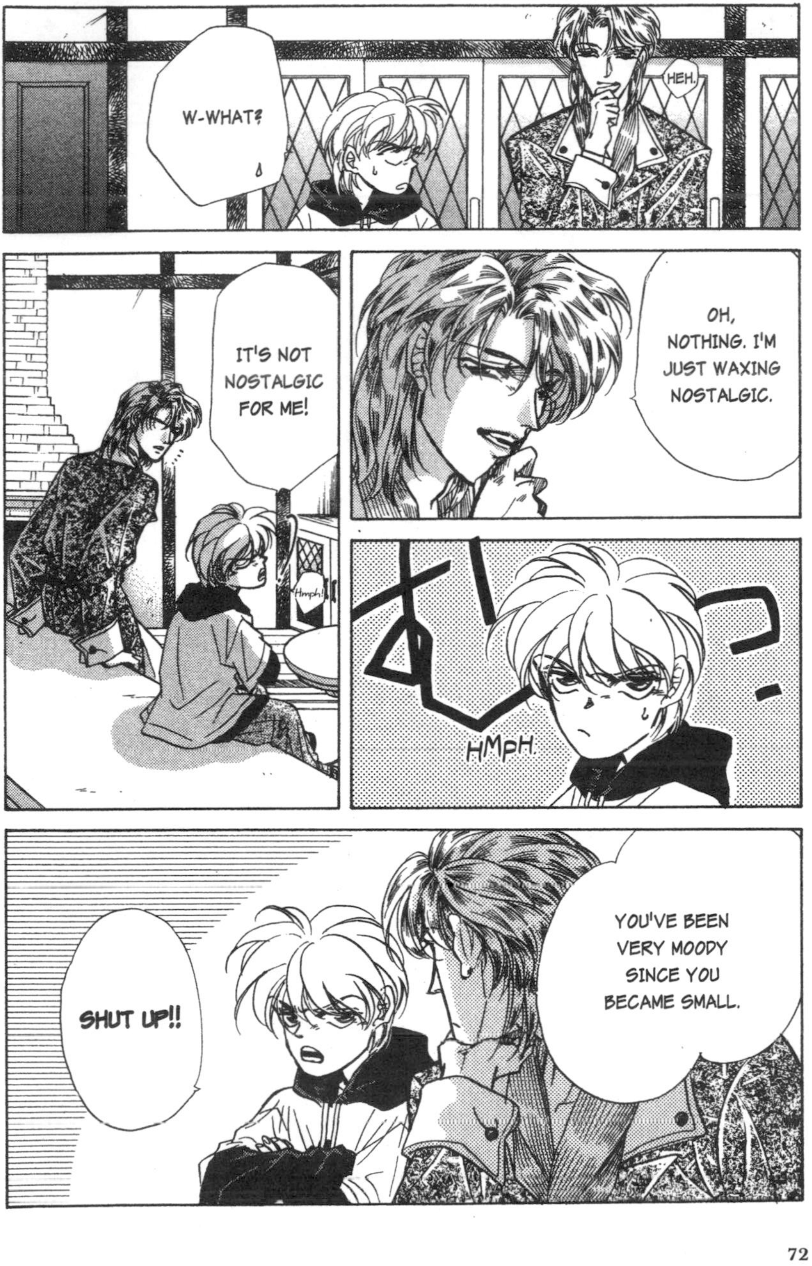
HEH.
W-WHAT?
OH, NOTHING. I'M JUST WAXING NOSTALGIC.
HMPH
IT'S NOT NOSTALGIC FOR ME!
Hmph!
YOU'VE BEEN VERY MOODY SINCE YOU BECAME SMALL.
SHUT UP!!

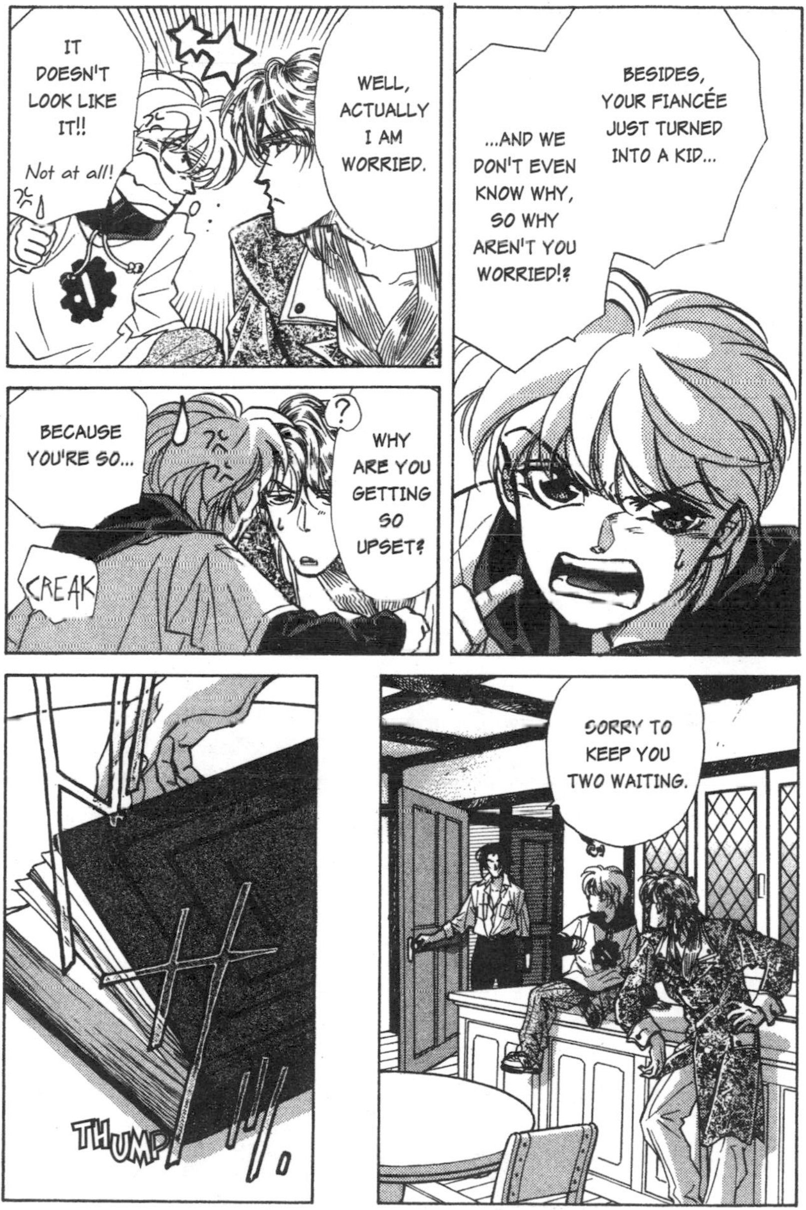
BESIDES, YOUR FIANCÉE JUST TURNED INTO A KID...
...AND WE DON'T EVEN KNOW WHY, SO WHY AREN'T YOU WORRIED!?
WELL, ACTUALLY I AM WORRIED.
IT DOESN'T LOOK LIKE IT!!
Not at all!
WHY ARE YOU GETTING SO UPSET?
BECAUSE YOU'RE SO...
CREAK
SORRY TO KEEP YOU TWO WAITING.
THUMP

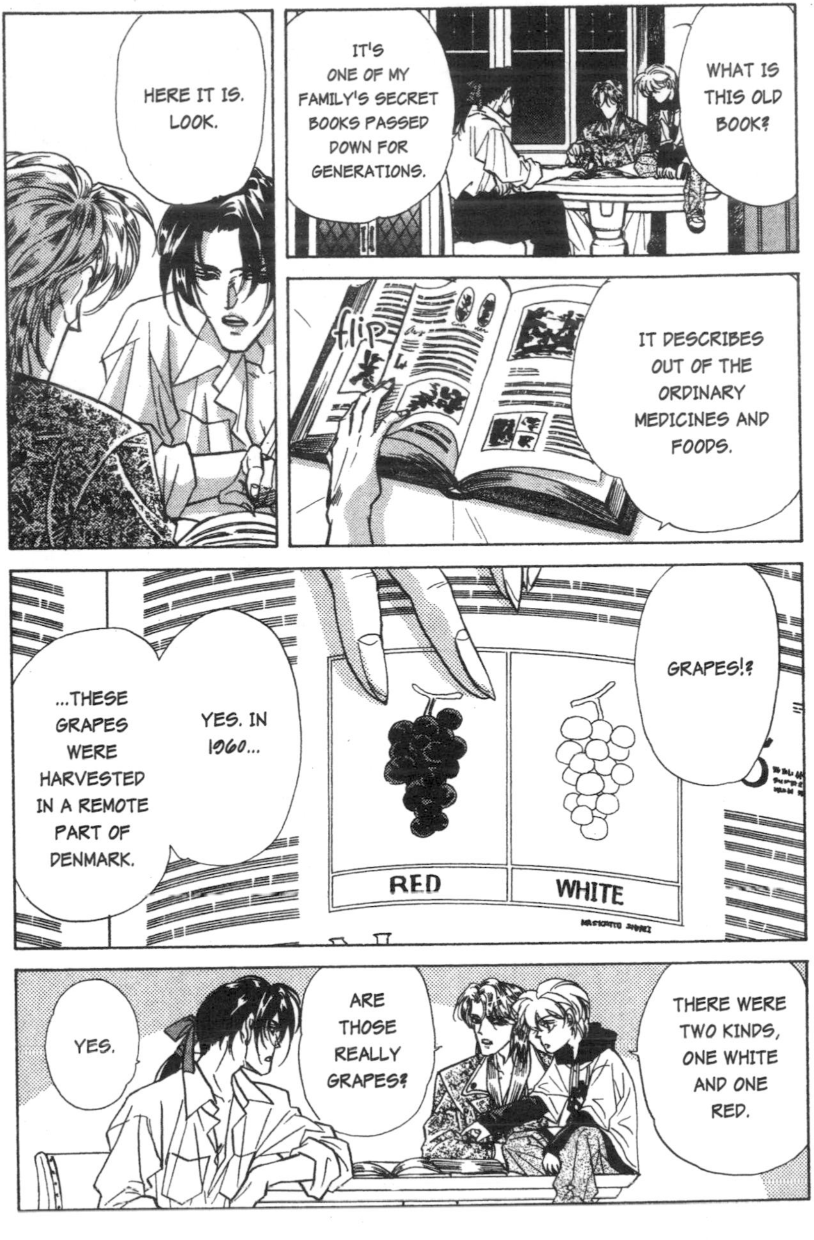
WHAT IS THIS OLD BOOK?
IT'S ONE OF MY FAMILY'S SECRET BOOKS PASSED DOWN FOR GENERATIONS.
IT DESCRIBES OUT OF THE ORDINARY MEDICINES AND FOODS.
flip
HERE IT IS. LOOK.
GRAPES!?
YES. IN 1960...
...THESE GRAPES WERE HARVESTED IN A REMOTE PART OF DENMARK.
RED
WHITE
THERE WERE TWO KINDS, ONE WHITE AND ONE RED.
ARE THOSE REALLY GRAPES?
YES.

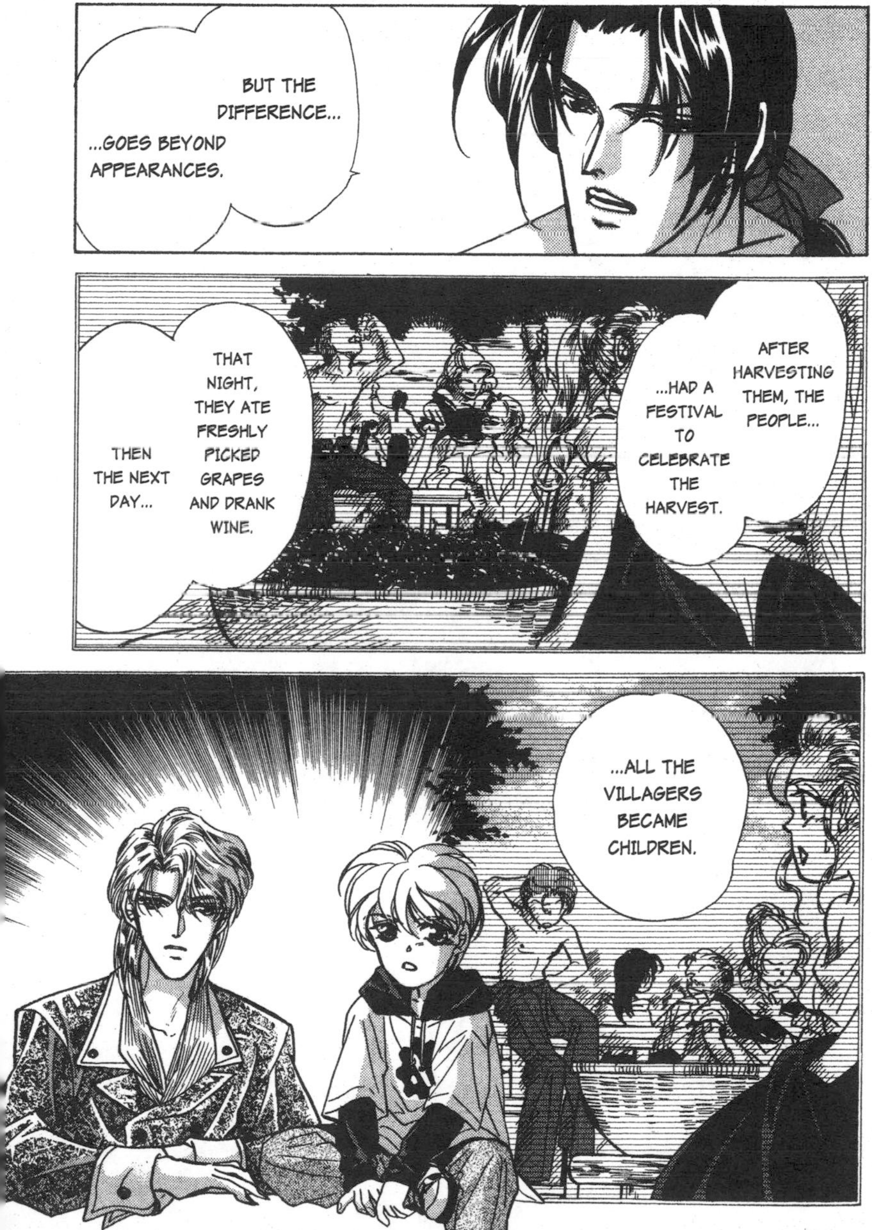
BUT THE DIFFERENCE...
...GOES BEYOND APPEARANCES.
AFTER HARVESTING THEM, THE PEOPLE...
...HAD A FESTIVAL TO CELEBRATE THE HARVEST.
THAT NIGHT, THEY ATE FRESHLY PICKED GRAPES AND DRANK WINE.
THEN THE NEXT DAY...
...ALL THE VILLAGERS BECAME CHILDREN.

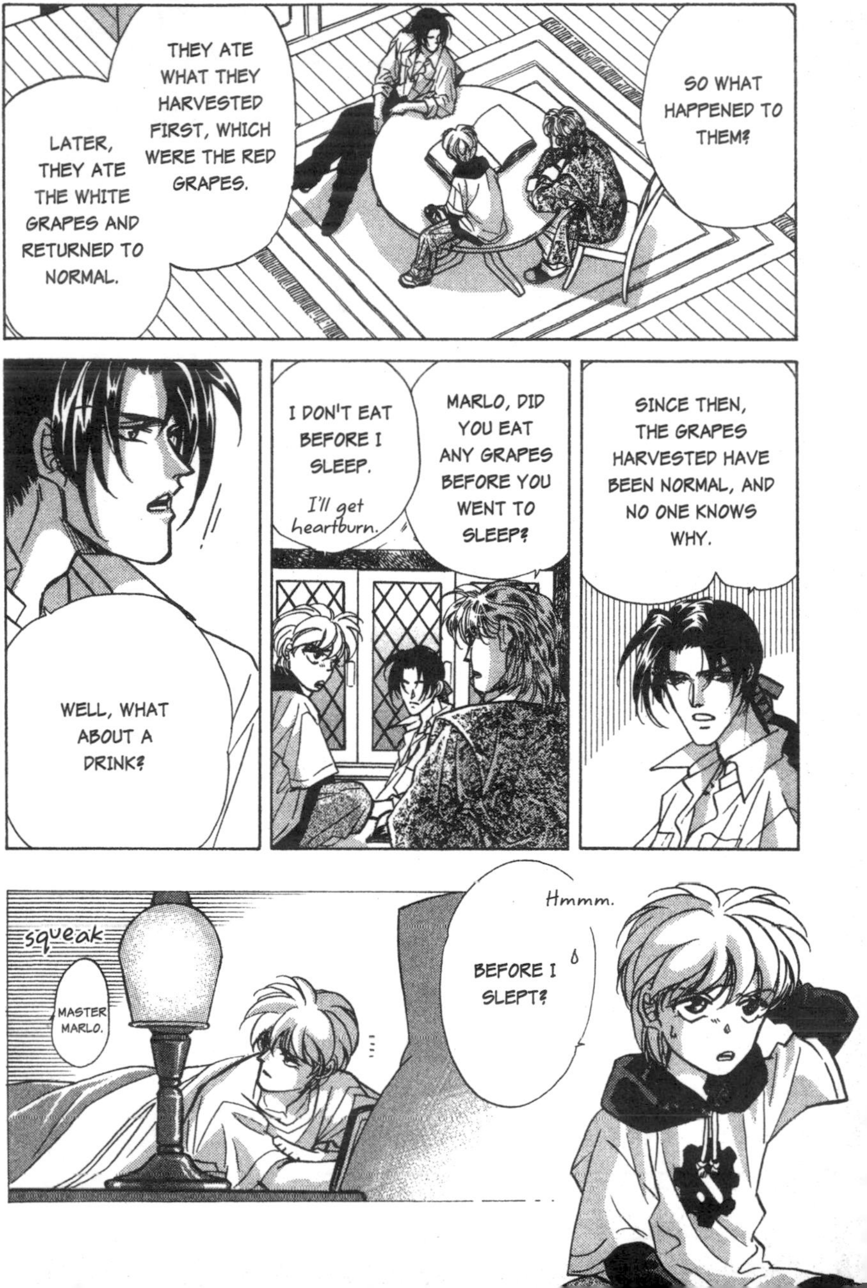
SO WHAT HAPPENED TO THEM?
THEY ATE WHAT THEY HARVESTED FIRST, WHICH WERE THE RED GRAPES.
LATER, THEY ATE THE WHITE GRAPES AND RETURNED TO NORMAL.
SINCE THEN, THE GRAPES HARVESTED HAVE BEEN NORMAL, AND NO ONE KNOWS WHY.
MARLO, DID YOU EAT ANY GRAPES BEFORE YOU WENT TO SLEEP?
I DON'T EAT BEFORE I SLEEP.
I'll get heartburn.
WELL, WHAT ABOUT A DRINK?
Hmmm.
BEFORE I SLEPT?
squeak
MASTER MARLO.

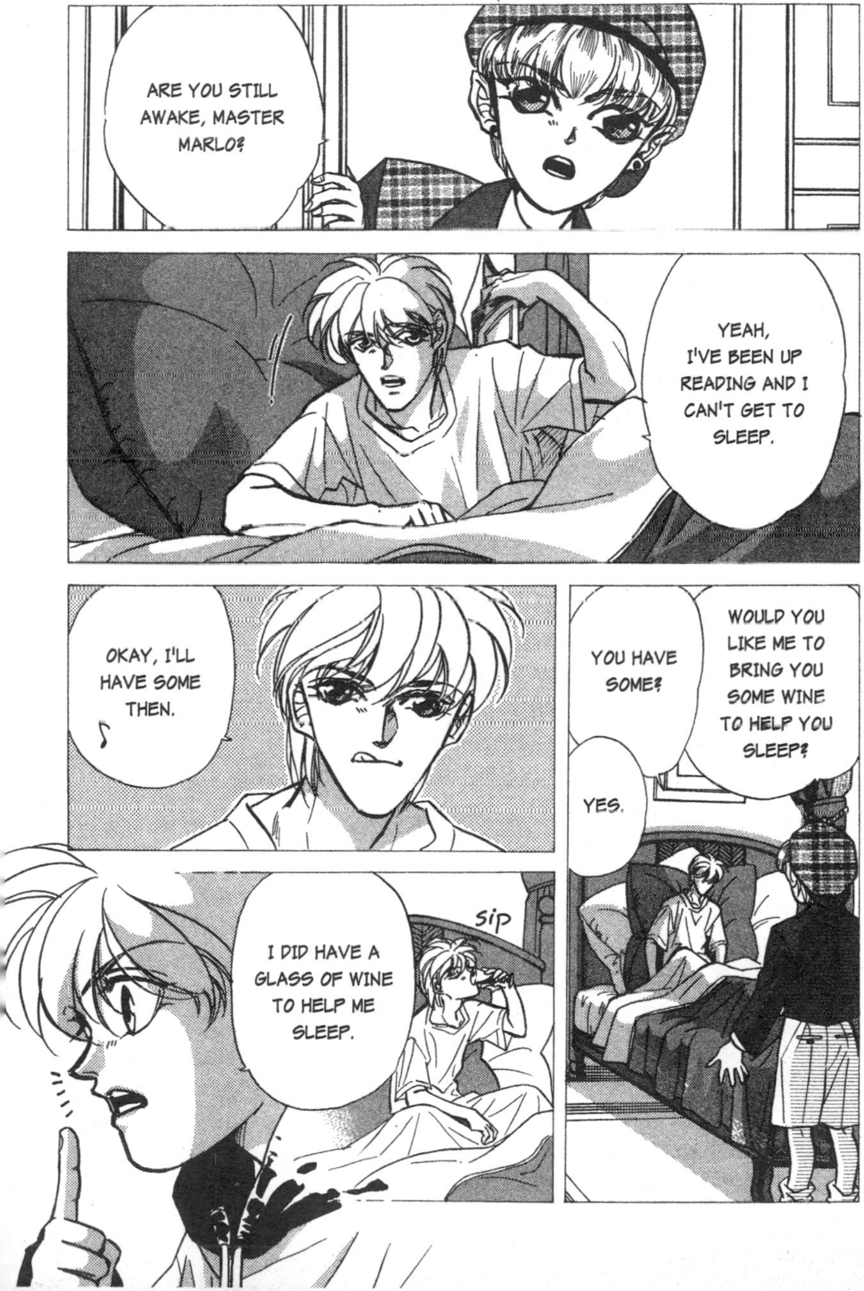
ARE YOU STILL AWAKE, MASTER MARLO?
YEAH, I'VE BEEN UP READING AND I CAN'T GET TO SLEEP.
WOULD YOU LIKE ME TO BRING YOU SOME WINE TO HELP YOU SLEEP?
YOU HAVE SOME?
YES.
OKAY, I'LL HAVE SOME THEN.
sip
I DID HAVE A GLASS OF WINE TO HELP ME SLEEP.

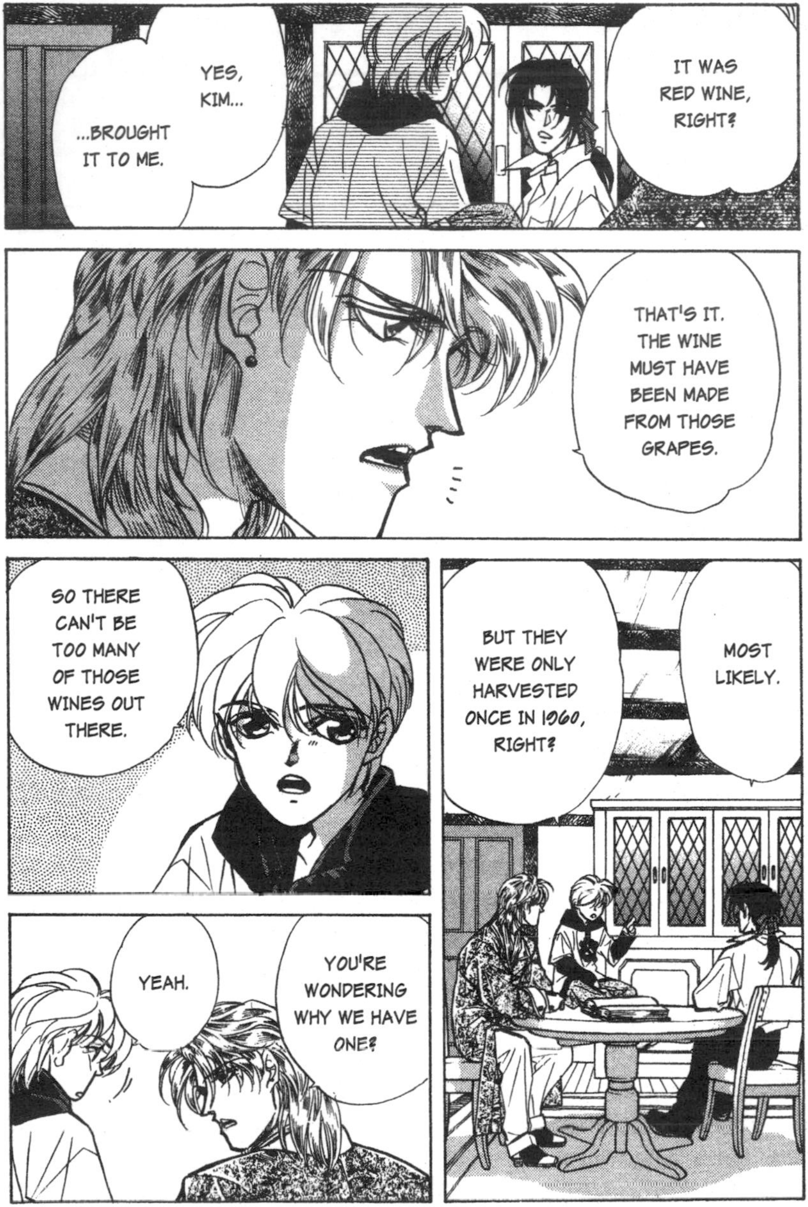
IT WAS RED WINE, RIGHT?
YES, KIM...
...BROUGHT IT TO ME.
THAT'S IT. THE WINE MUST HAVE BEEN MADE FROM THOSE GRAPES.
MOST LIKELY.
BUT THEY WERE ONLY HARVESTED ONCE IN 1960, RIGHT?
SO THERE CAN'T BE TOO MANY OF THOSE WINES OUT THERE.
YOU'RE WONDERING WHY WE HAVE ONE?
YEAH.

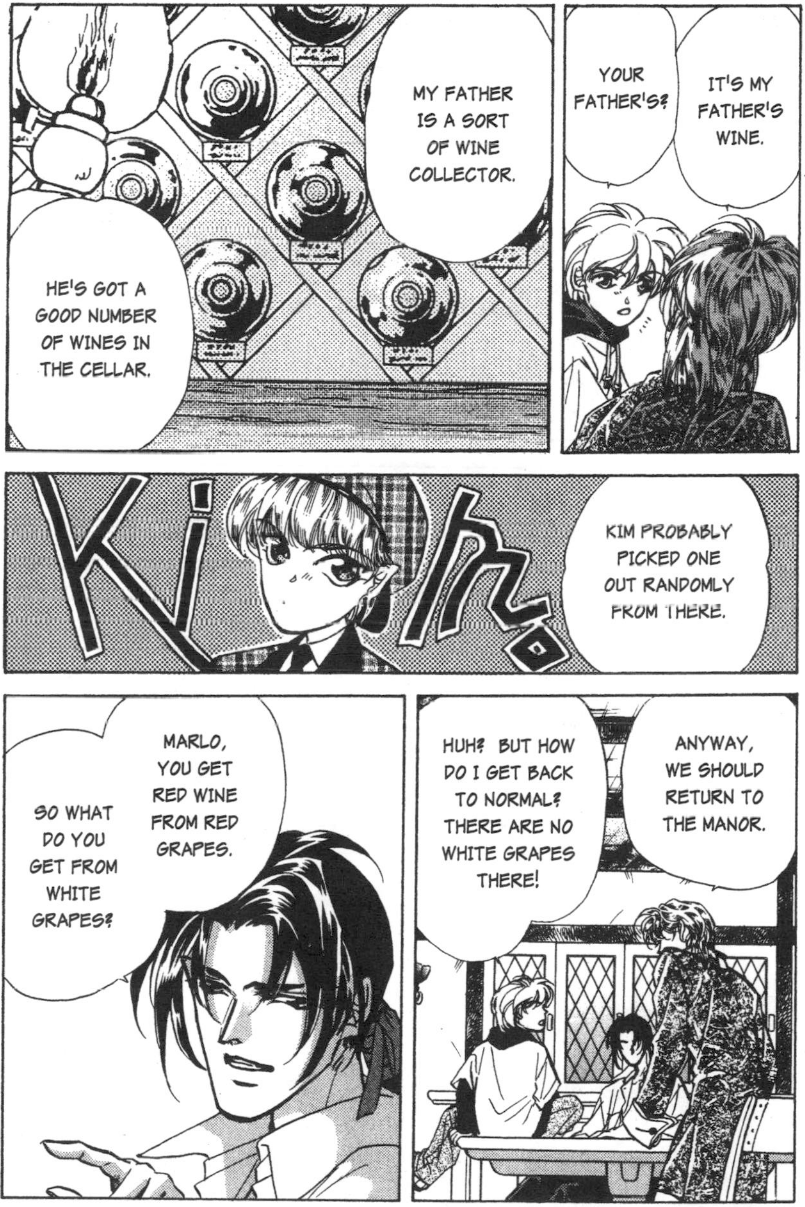
IT'S MY FATHER'S WINE.
YOUR FATHER'S?
MY FATHER IS A SORT OF WINE COLLECTOR.
HE'S GOT A GOOD NUMBER OF WINES IN THE CELLAR.
KIM PROBABLY PICKED ONE OUT RANDOMLY FROM THERE.
Kim.
ANYWAY, WE SHOULD RETURN TO THE MANOR.
HUH? BUT HOW DO I GET BACK TO NORMAL? THERE ARE NO WHITE GRAPES THERE!
MARLO, YOU GET RED WINE FROM RED GRAPES.
SO WHAT DO YOU GET FROM WHITE GRAPES?

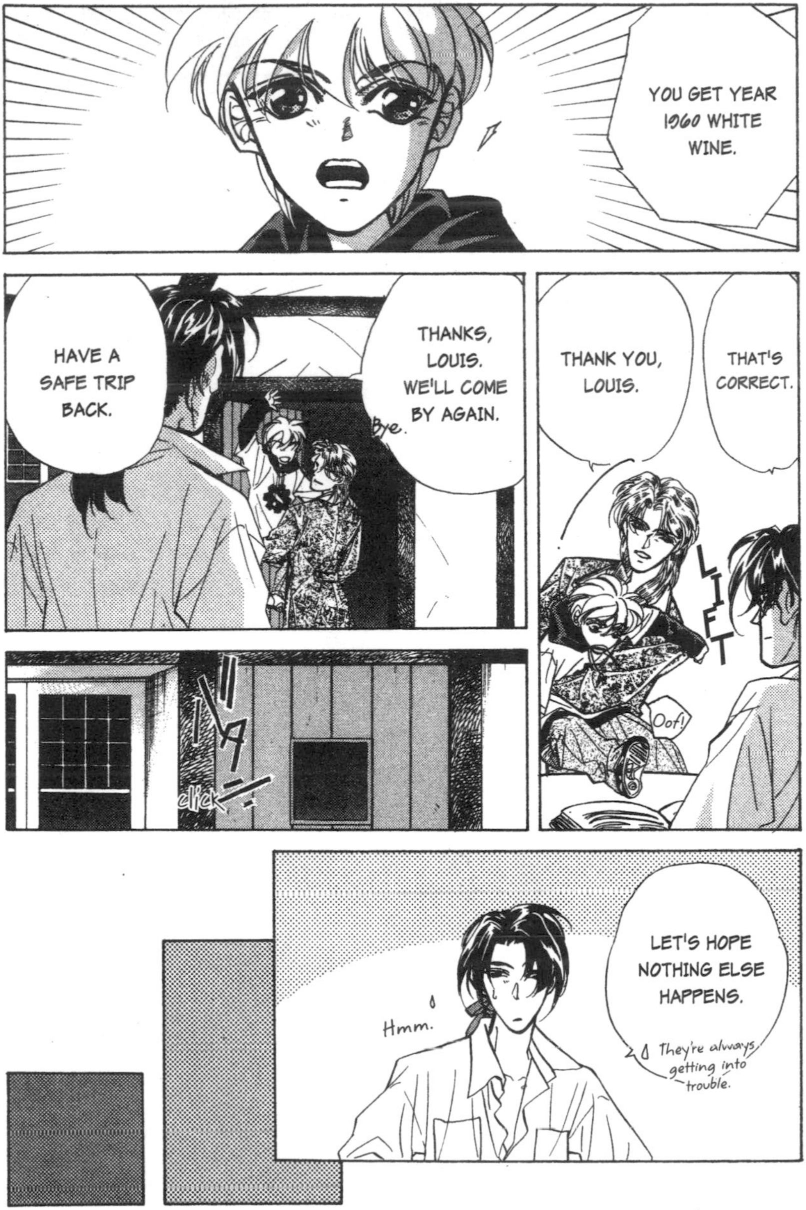
YOU GET YEAR 1960 WHITE WINE.
THAT'S CORRECT.
THANK YOU, LOUIS.
LIFT
Oof!
THANKS, LOUIS. WE'LL COME BY AGAIN.
Bye.
HAVE A SAFE TRIP BACK.
click
LET'S HOPE NOTHING ELSE HAPPENS.
They're always getting into trouble.
Hmm.

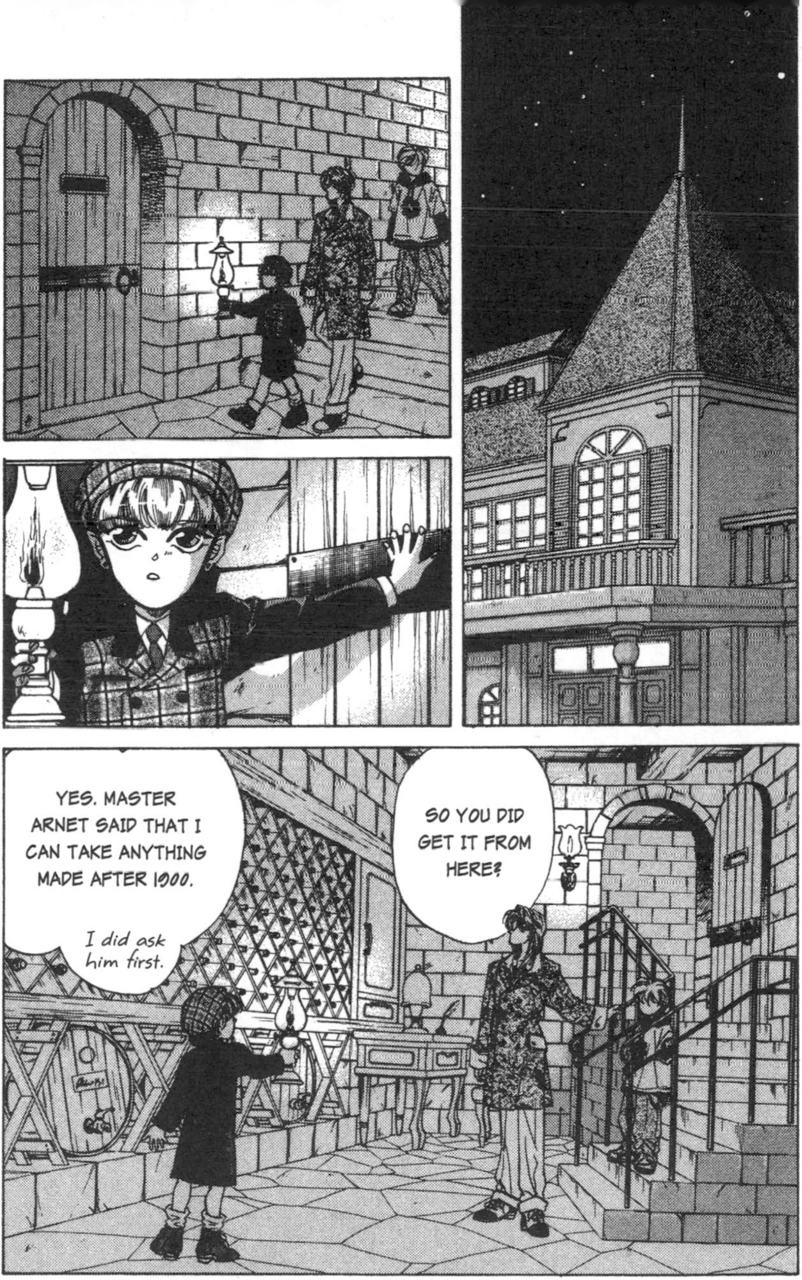
SO YOU DID GET IT FROM HERE?
YES. MASTER ARNET SAID THAT I CAN TAKE ANYTHING MADE AFTER 1900.
I did ask him first.

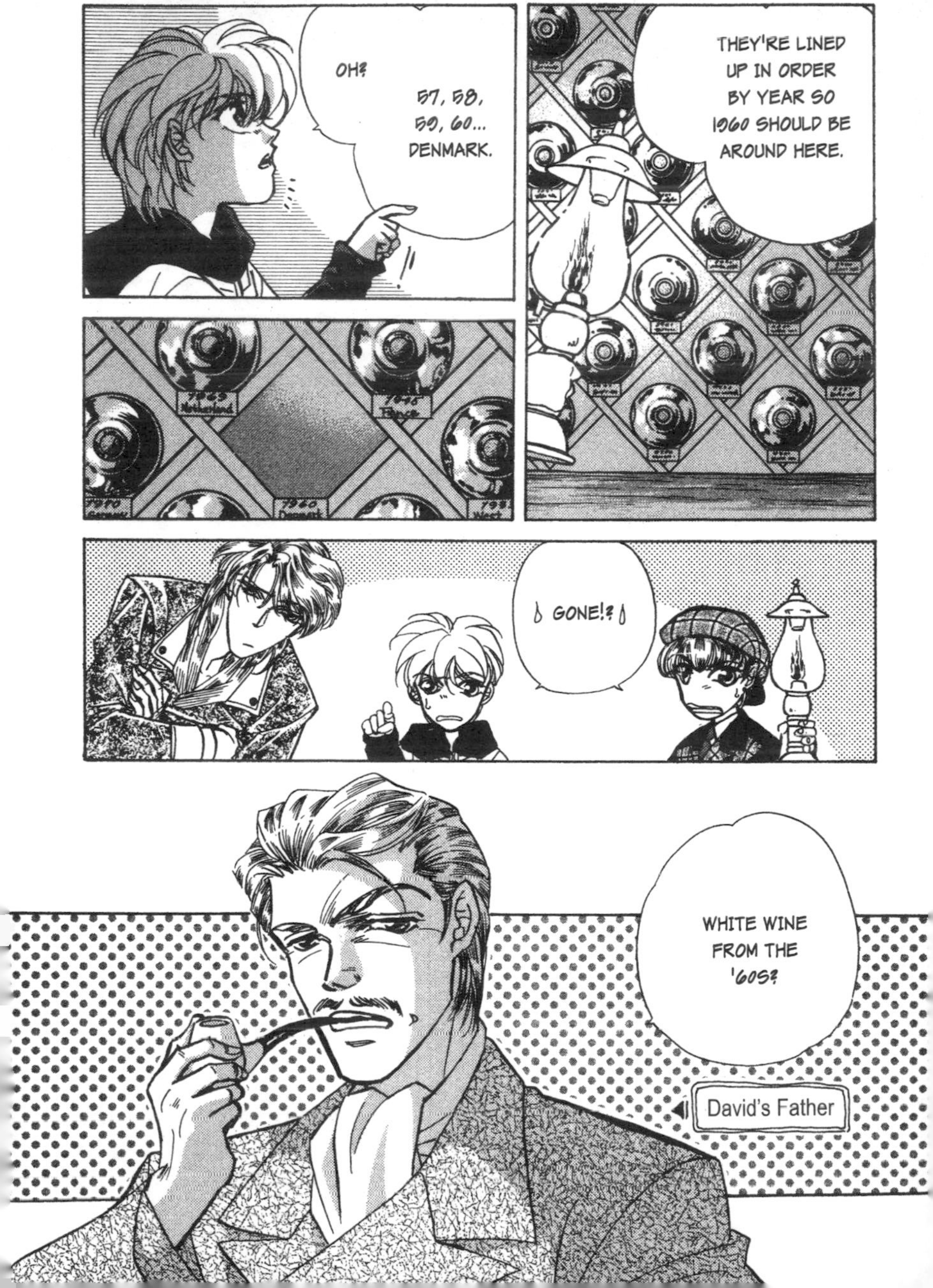
THEY'RE LINED UP IN ORDER BY YEAR SO 1960 SHOULD BE AROUND HERE.
OH?
57, 58, 59, 60... DENMARK.
GONE!?
WHITE WINE FROM THE '60S?
David's Father

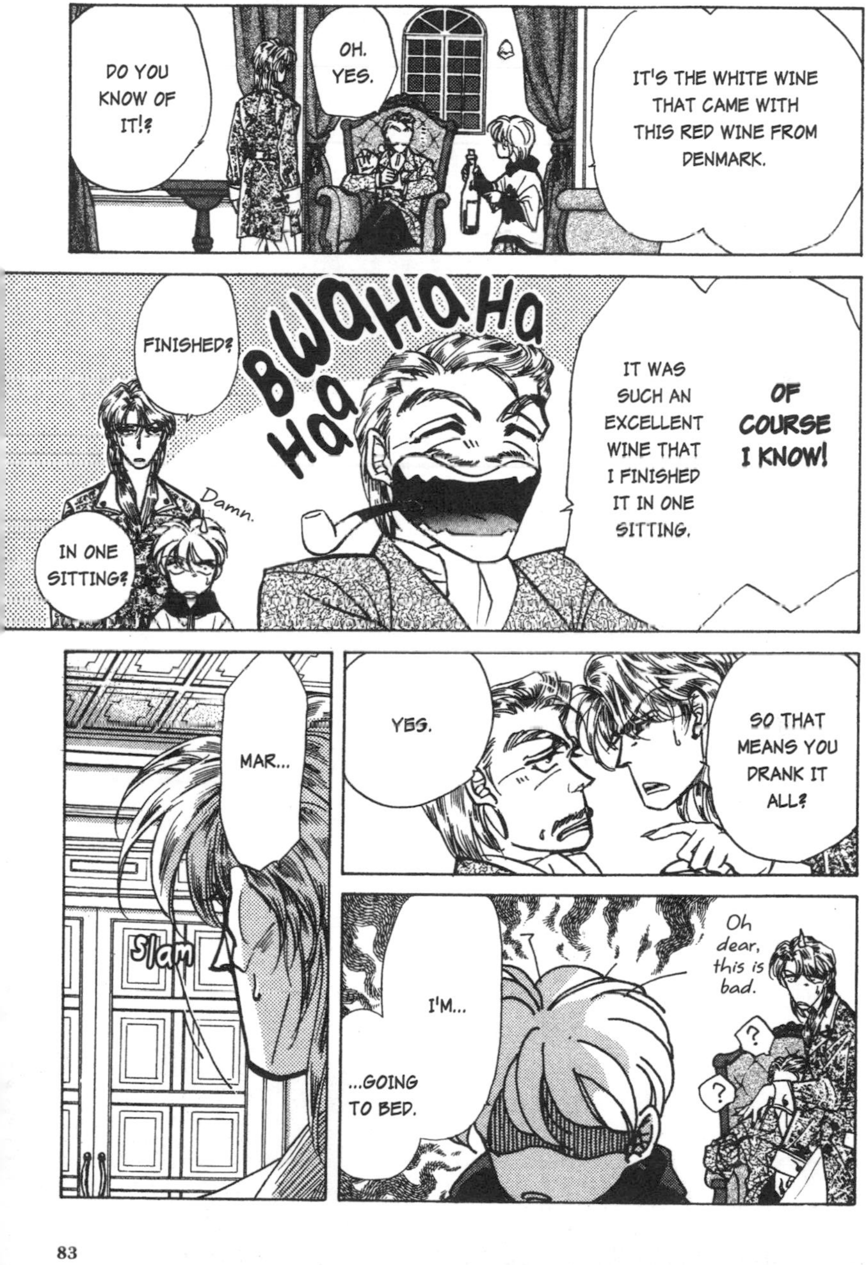
IT'S THE WHITE WINE THAT CAME WITH THIS RED WINE FROM DENMARK.
OH. YES.
DO YOU KNOW OF IT!?
OF COURSE I KNOW!
IT WAS SUCH AN EXCELLENT WINE THAT I FINISHED IT IN ONE SITTING.
BWAHAHA Ha Ha
FINISHED?
Damn.
IN ONE SITTING?
SO THAT MEANS YOU DRANK IT ALL?
YES.
Oh dear, this is bad.
?
?
I'M...
...GOING TO BED.
MAR...
Slam

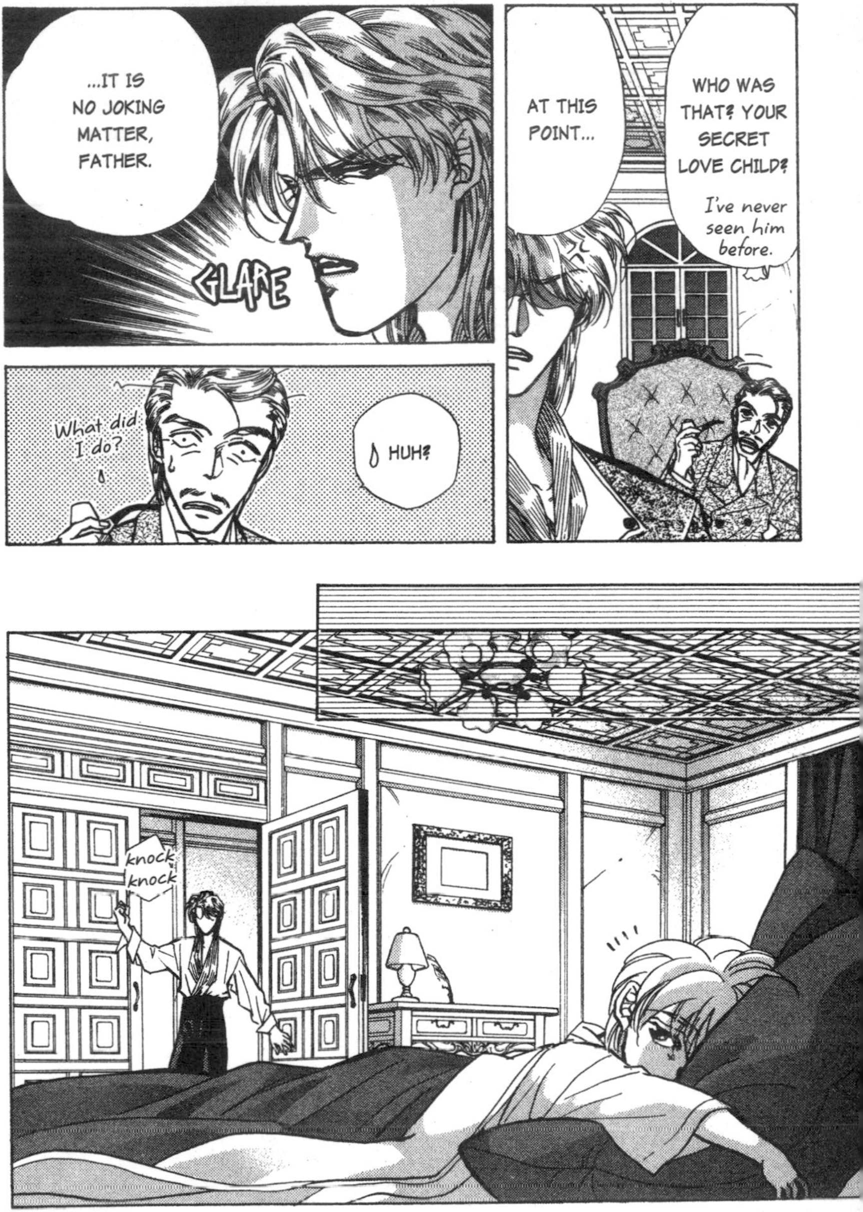
WHO WAS THAT? YOUR SECRET LOVE CHILD?
I've never seen him before.
AT THIS POINT...
...IT IS NO JOKING MATTER, FATHER.
GLARE
HUH?
What did I do?
knock knock

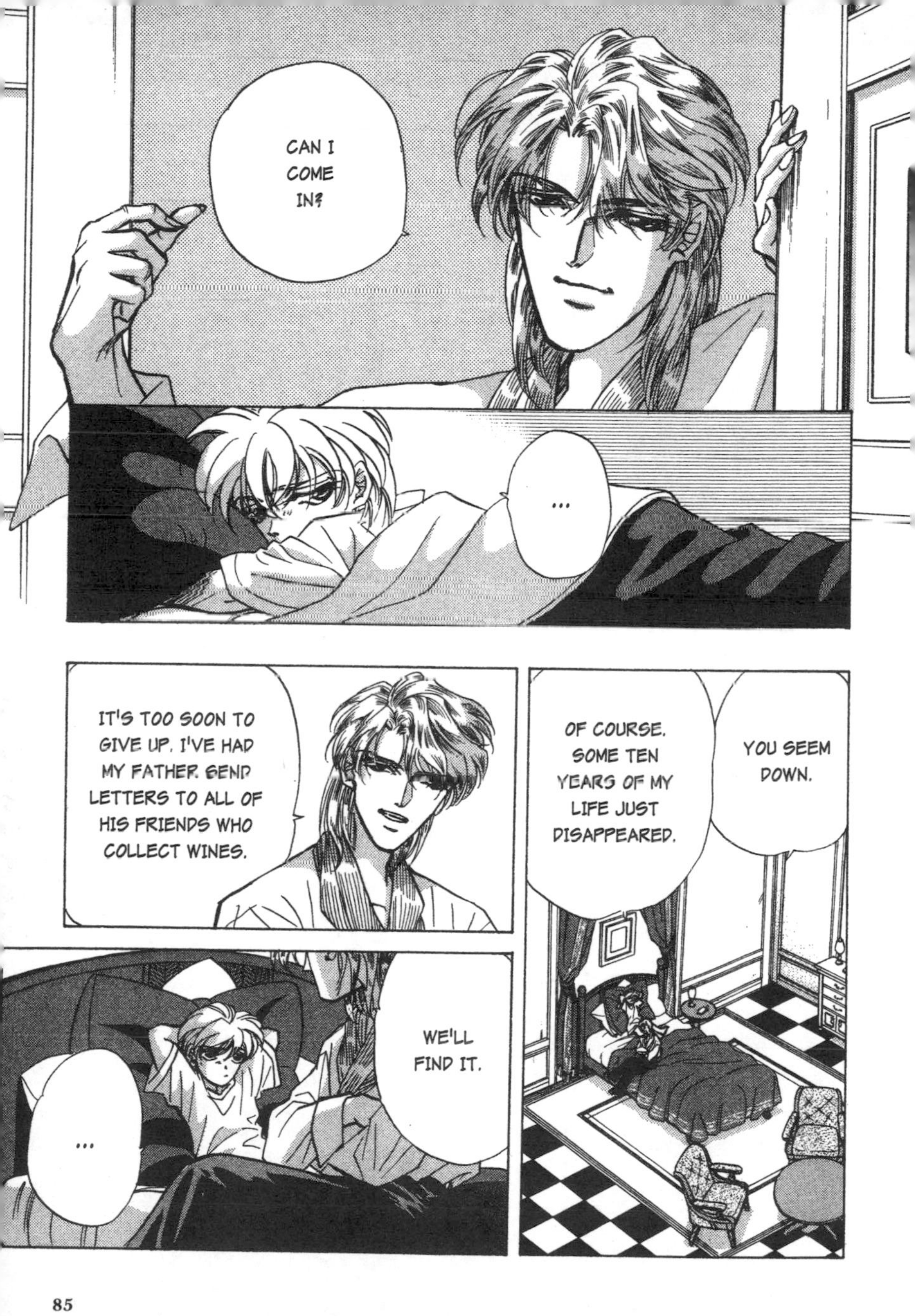
CAN I COME IN?
...
YOU SEEM DOWN.
OF COURSE. SOME TEN YEARS OF MY LIFE JUST DISAPPEARED.
IT'S TOO SOON TO GIVE UP. I'VE HAD MY FATHER SEND LETTERS TO ALL OF HIS FRIENDS WHO COLLECT WINES.
WE'LL FIND IT.
...

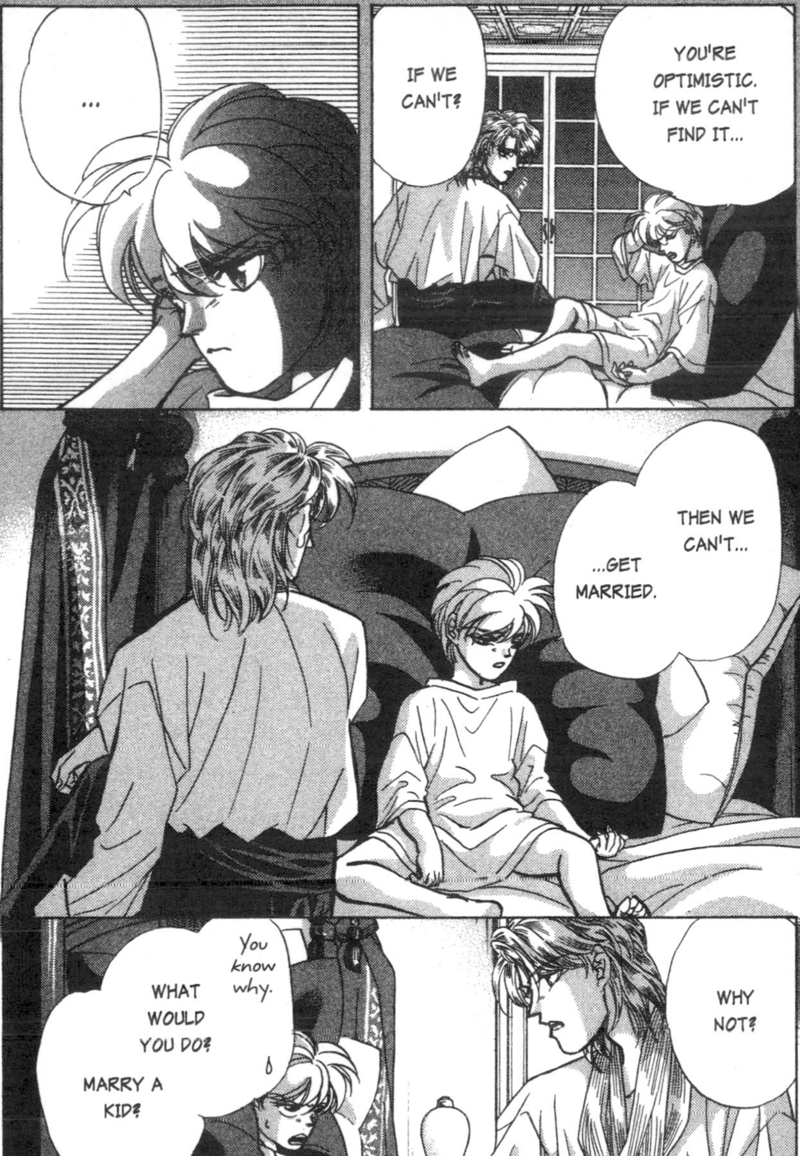
YOU'RE OPTIMISTIC. IF WE CAN'T FIND IT...
IF WE CAN'T?
...
THEN WE CAN'T...
...GET MARRIED.
WHY NOT?
You know why.
WHAT WOULD YOU DO?
MARRY A KID?

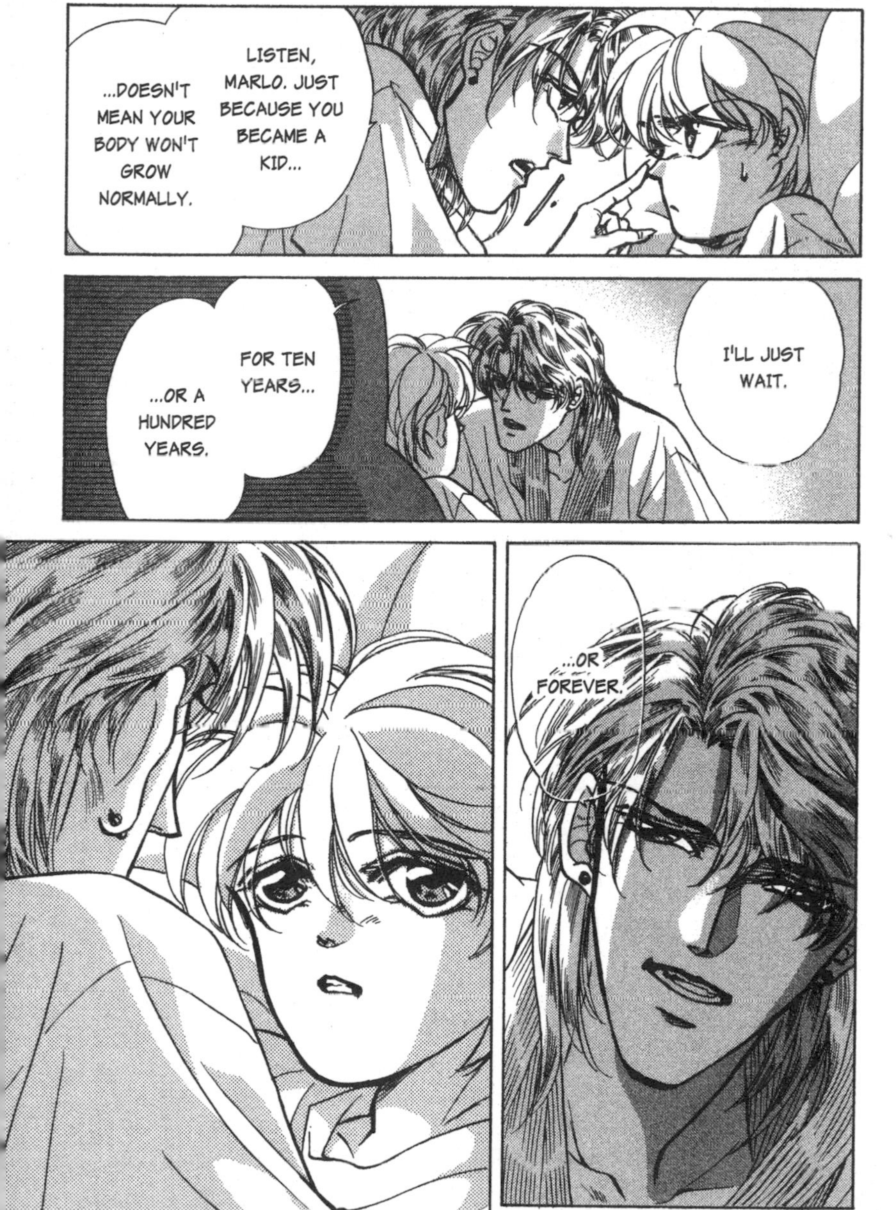
LISTEN, MARLO. JUST BECAUSE YOU BECAME A KID...
...DOESN'T MEAN YOUR BODY WON'T GROW NORMALLY.
I'LL JUST WAIT.
FOR TEN YEARS...
...OR A HUNDRED YEARS.
...OR FOREVER.

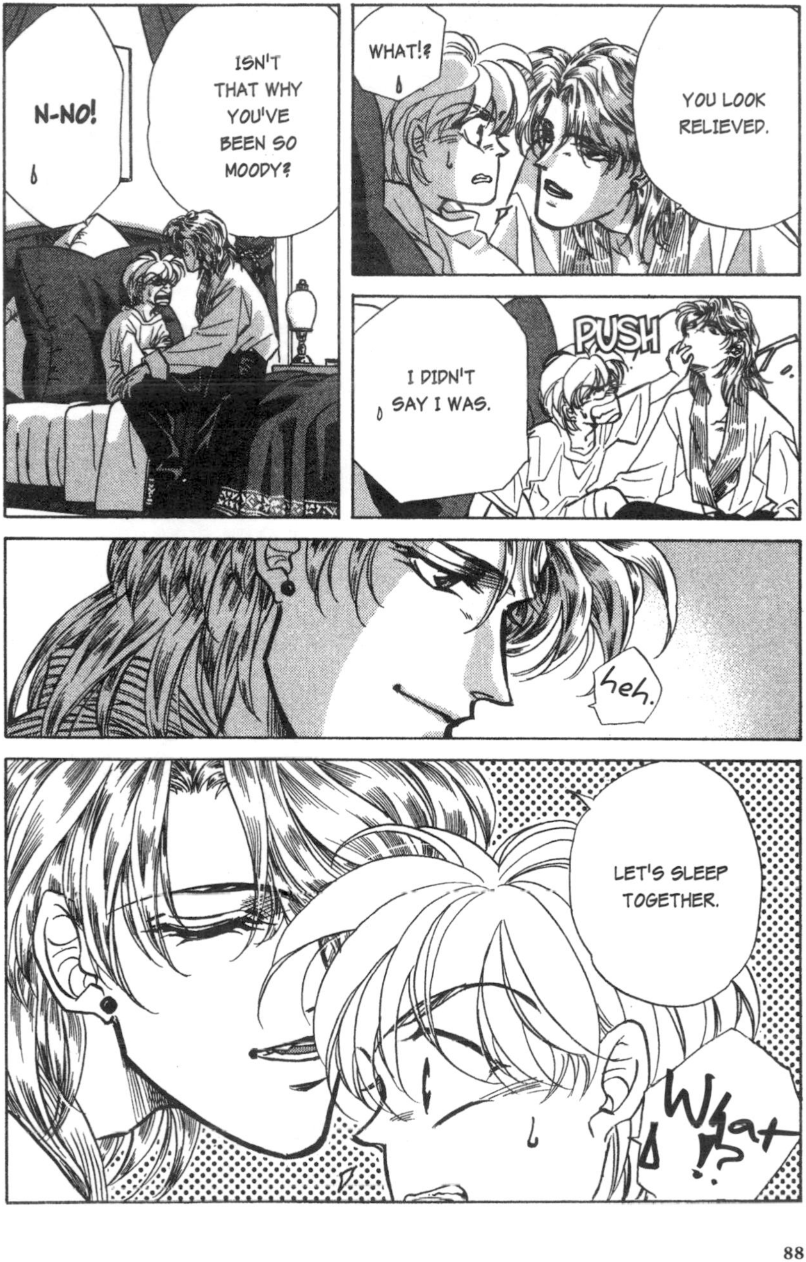
YOU LOOK RELIEVED.
WHAT!?
PUSH
I DIDN'T SAY I WAS.
ISN'T THAT WHY YOU'VE BEEN SO MOODY?
N-NO!
heh.
LET'S SLEEP TOGETHER.
What!?

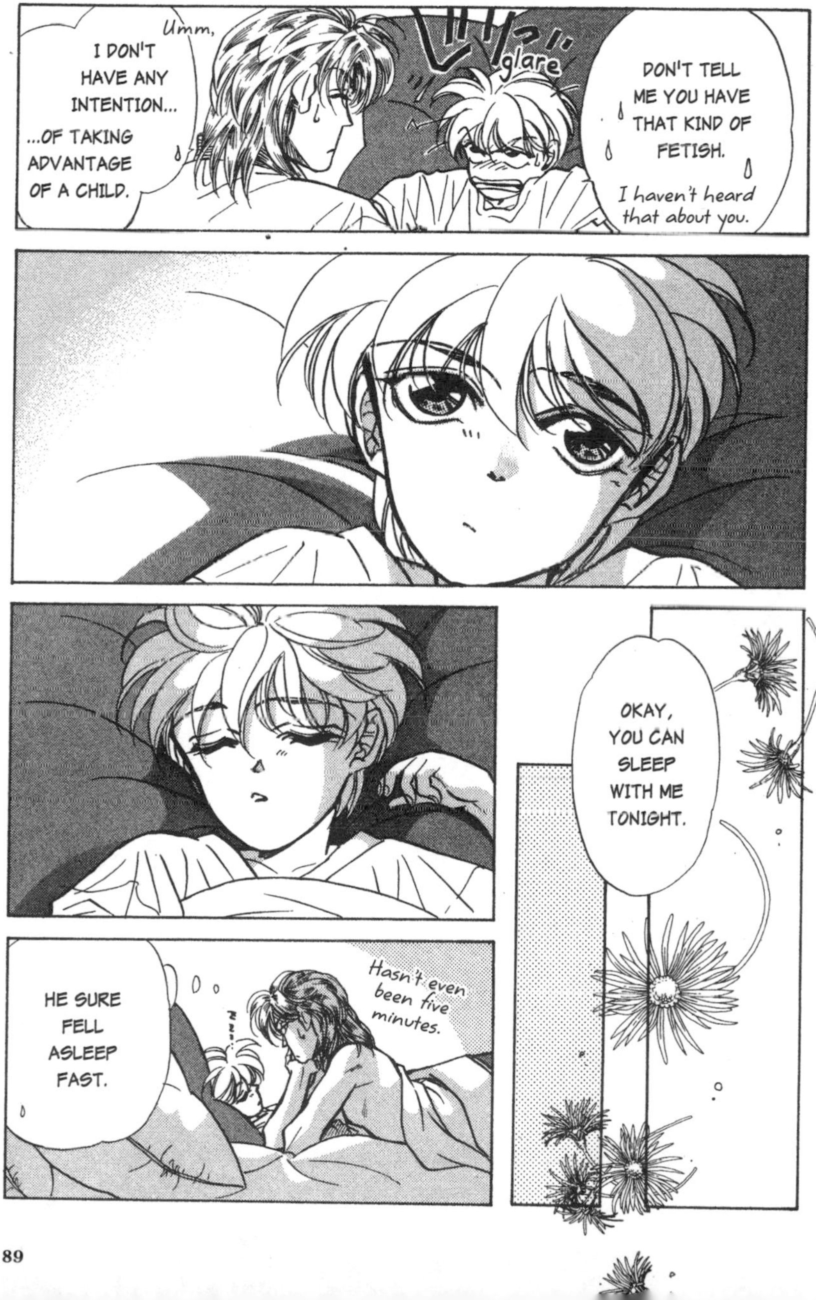
DON'T TELL ME YOU HAVE THAT KIND OF FETISH.
I haven't heard that about you.
glare
Umm,
I DON'T HAVE ANY INTENTION...
...OF TAKING ADVANTAGE OF A CHILD.
OKAY, YOU CAN SLEEP WITH ME TONIGHT.
Hasn't even been five minutes.
HE SURE FELL ASLEEP FAST.

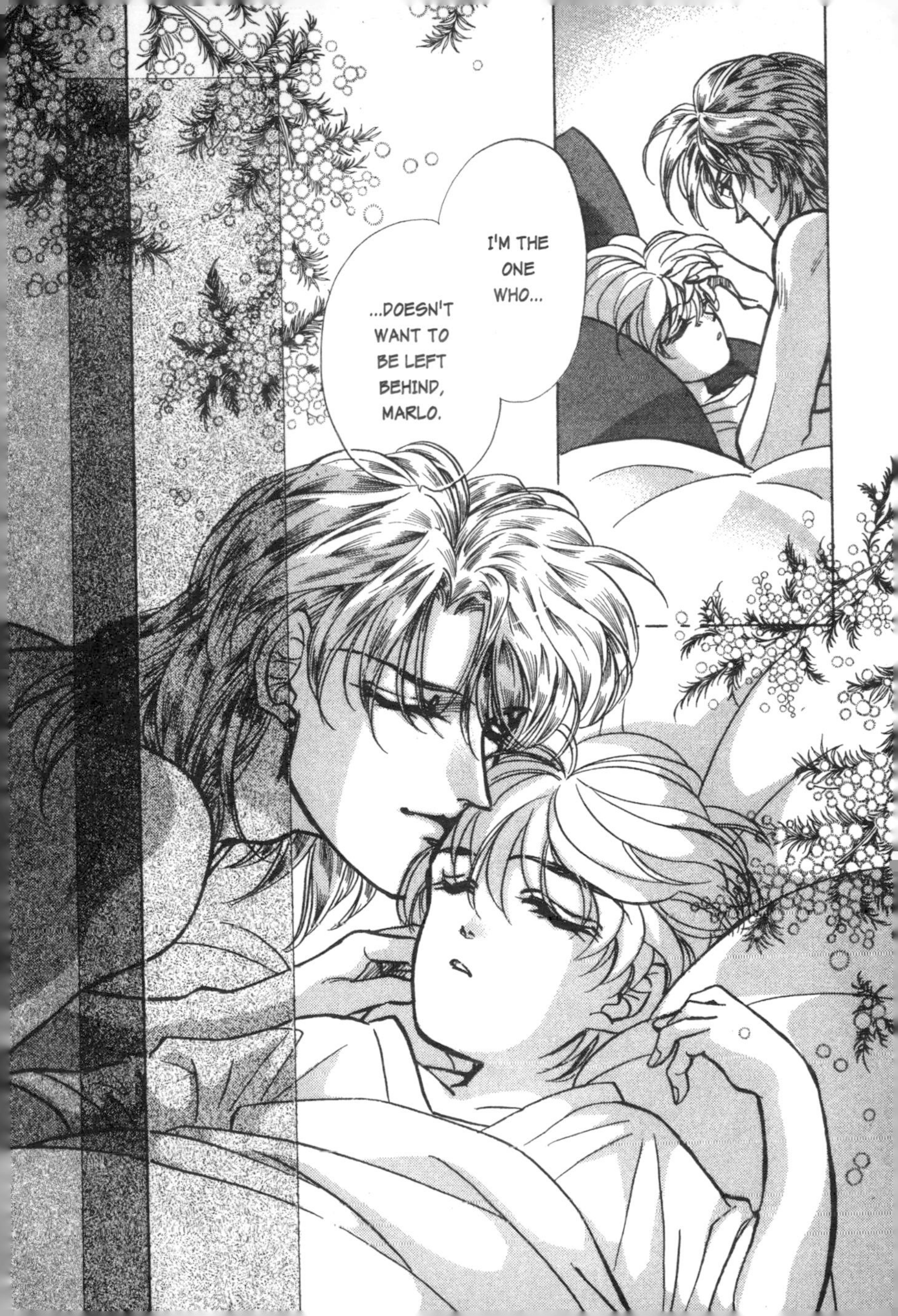
I'M THE ONE WHO...
...DOESN'T WANT TO BE LEFT BEHIND, MARLO.

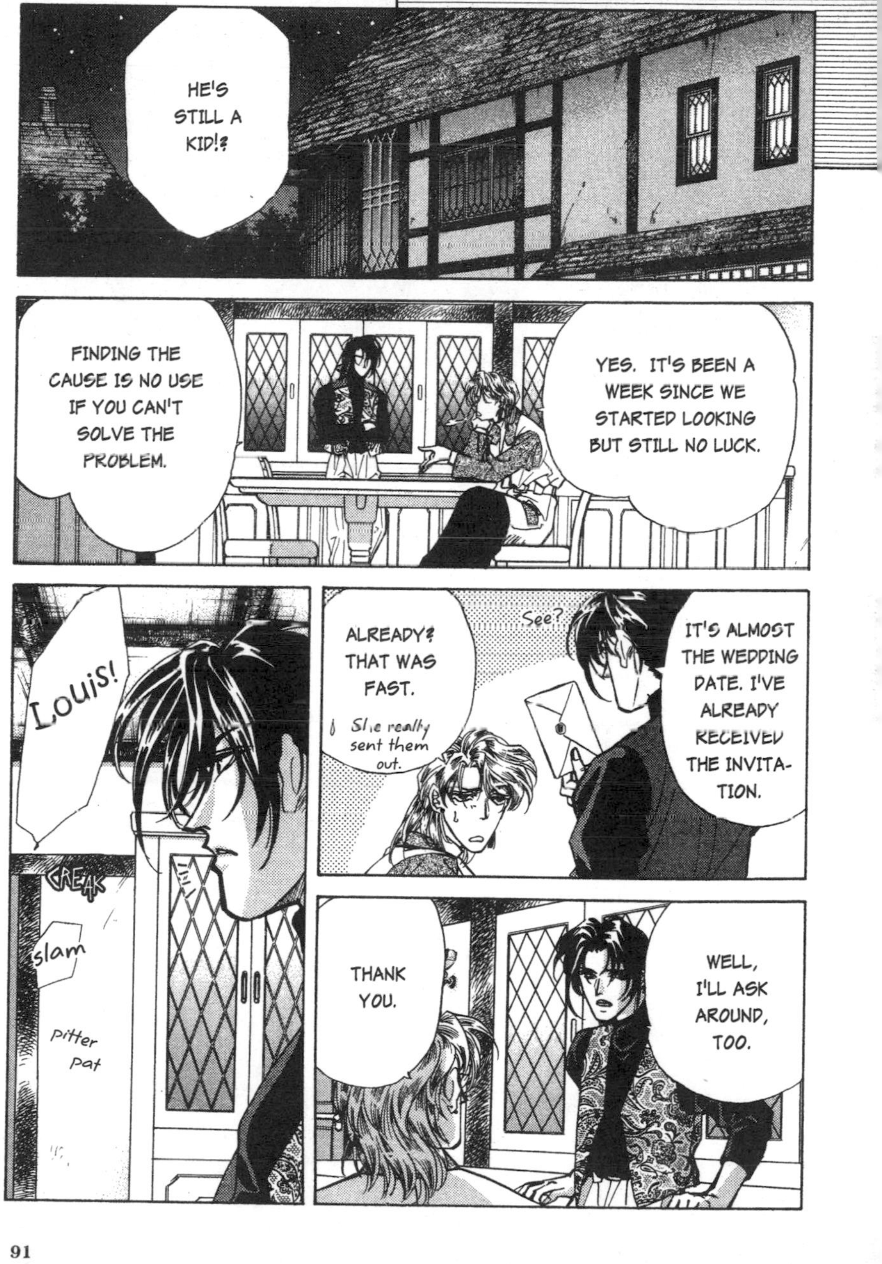
HE'S STILL A KID!?
YES. IT'S BEEN A WEEK SINCE WE STARTED LOOKING BUT STILL NO LUCK.
FINDING THE CAUSE IS NO USE IF YOU CAN'T SOLVE THE PROBLEM.
IT'S ALMOST THE WEDDING DATE. I'VE ALREADY RECEIVED THE INVITATION.
See?
ALREADY? THAT WAS FAST.
She really sent them out.
WELL, I'LL ASK AROUND, TOO.
THANK YOU.
Louis!
CREAK
slam
pitter pat

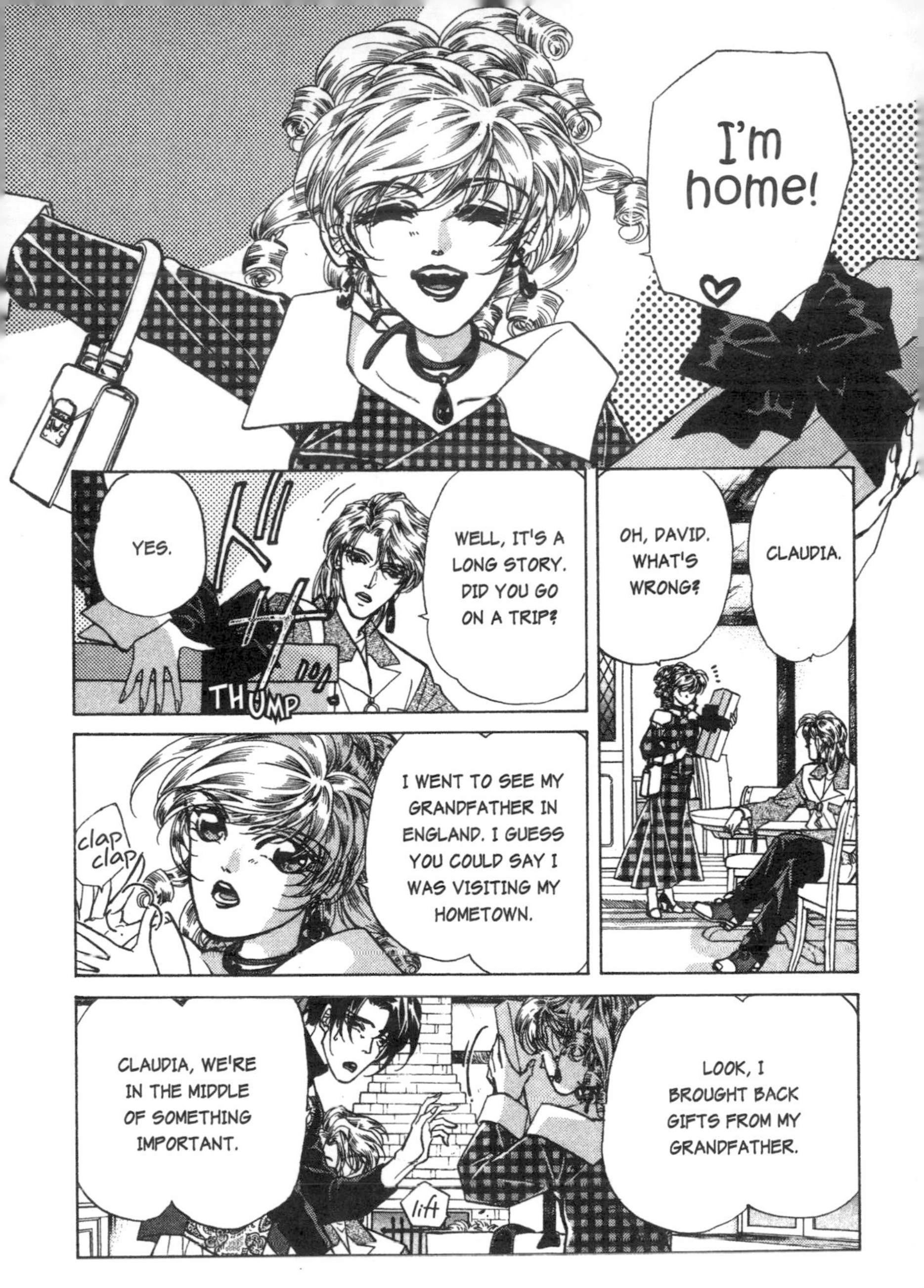
I'm home!
CLAUDIA.
OH, DAVID. WHAT'S WRONG?
WELL, IT'S A LONG STORY. DID YOU GO ON A TRIP?
YES.
THUMP
I WENT TO SEE MY GRANDFATHER IN ENGLAND. I GUESS YOU COULD SAY I WAS VISITING MY HOMETOWN.
clap clap
LOOK, I BROUGHT BACK GIFTS FROM MY GRANDFATHER.
CLAUDIA, WE'RE IN THE MIDDLE OF SOMETHING IMPORTANT.
lift

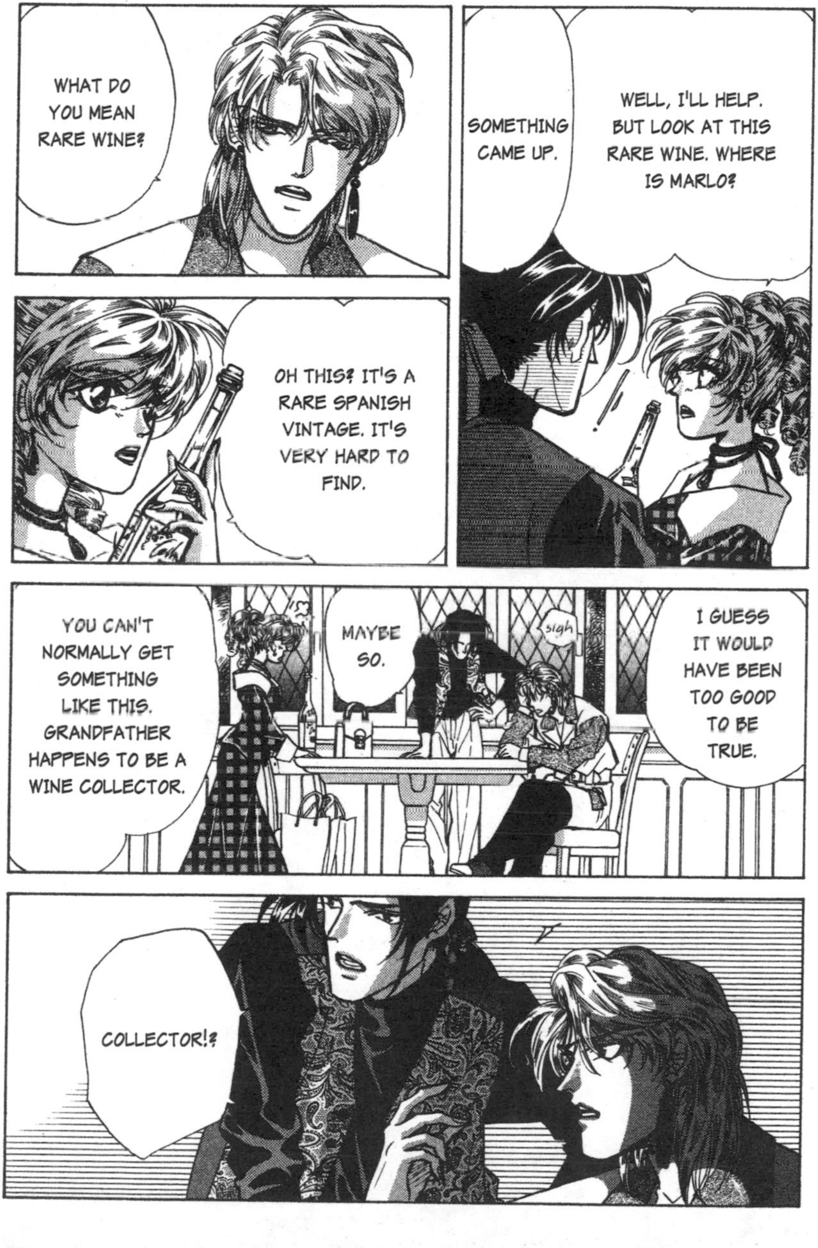
WELL, I'LL HELP. BUT LOOK AT THIS RARE WINE. WHERE IS MARLO?
SOMETHING CAME UP.
WHAT DO YOU MEAN RARE WINE?
OH THIS? IT'S A RARE SPANISH VINTAGE. IT'S VERY HARD TO FIND.
I GUESS IT WOULD HAVE BEEN TOO GOOD TO BE TRUE.
sigh
MAYBE SO.
YOU CAN'T NORMALLY GET SOMETHING LIKE THIS. GRANDFATHER HAPPENS TO BE A WINE COLLECTOR.
COLLECTOR!?

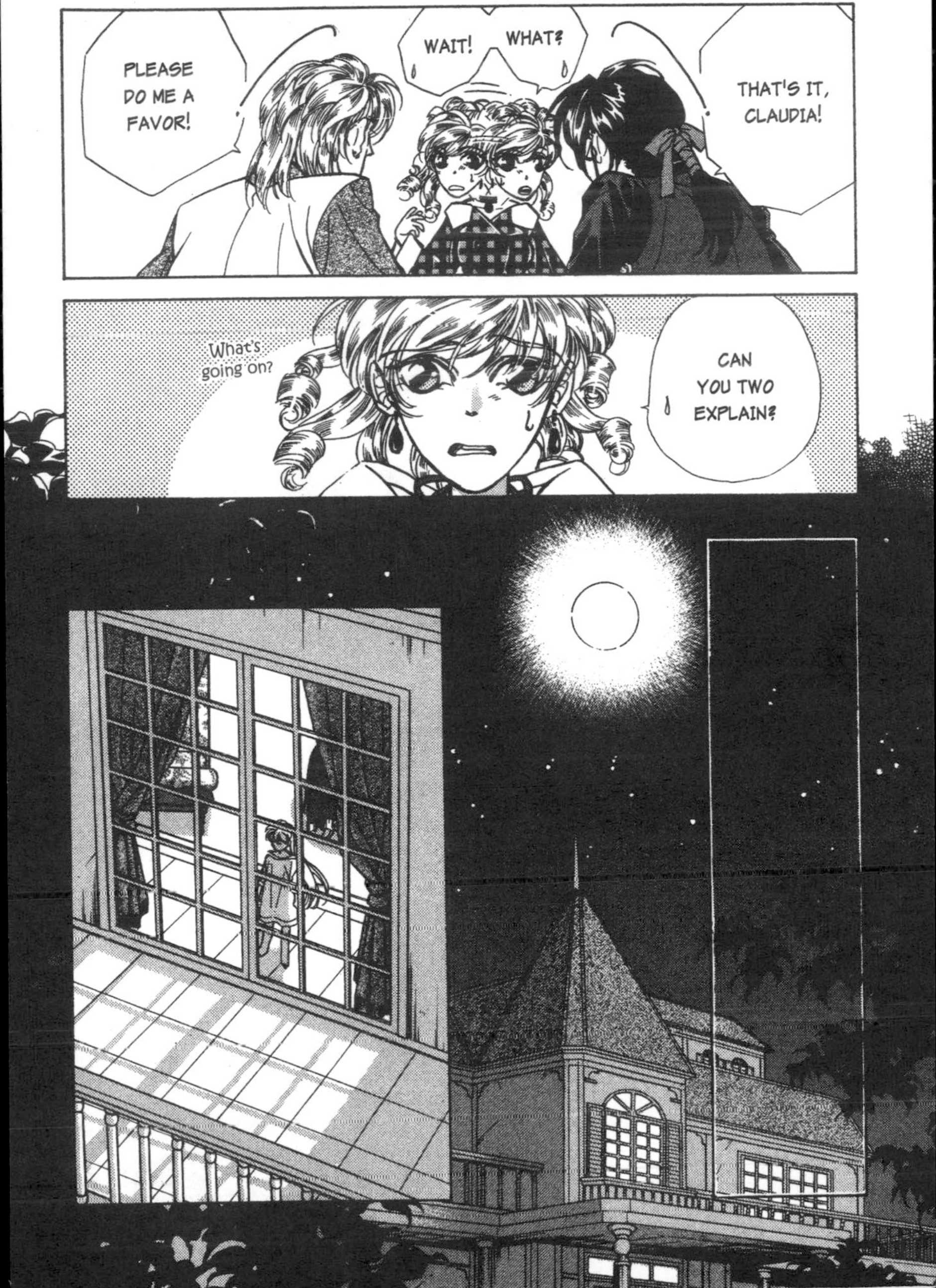
THAT'S IT, CLAUDIA!
WHAT?
WAIT!
PLEASE DO ME A FAVOR!
CAN YOU TWO EXPLAIN?
What's going on?

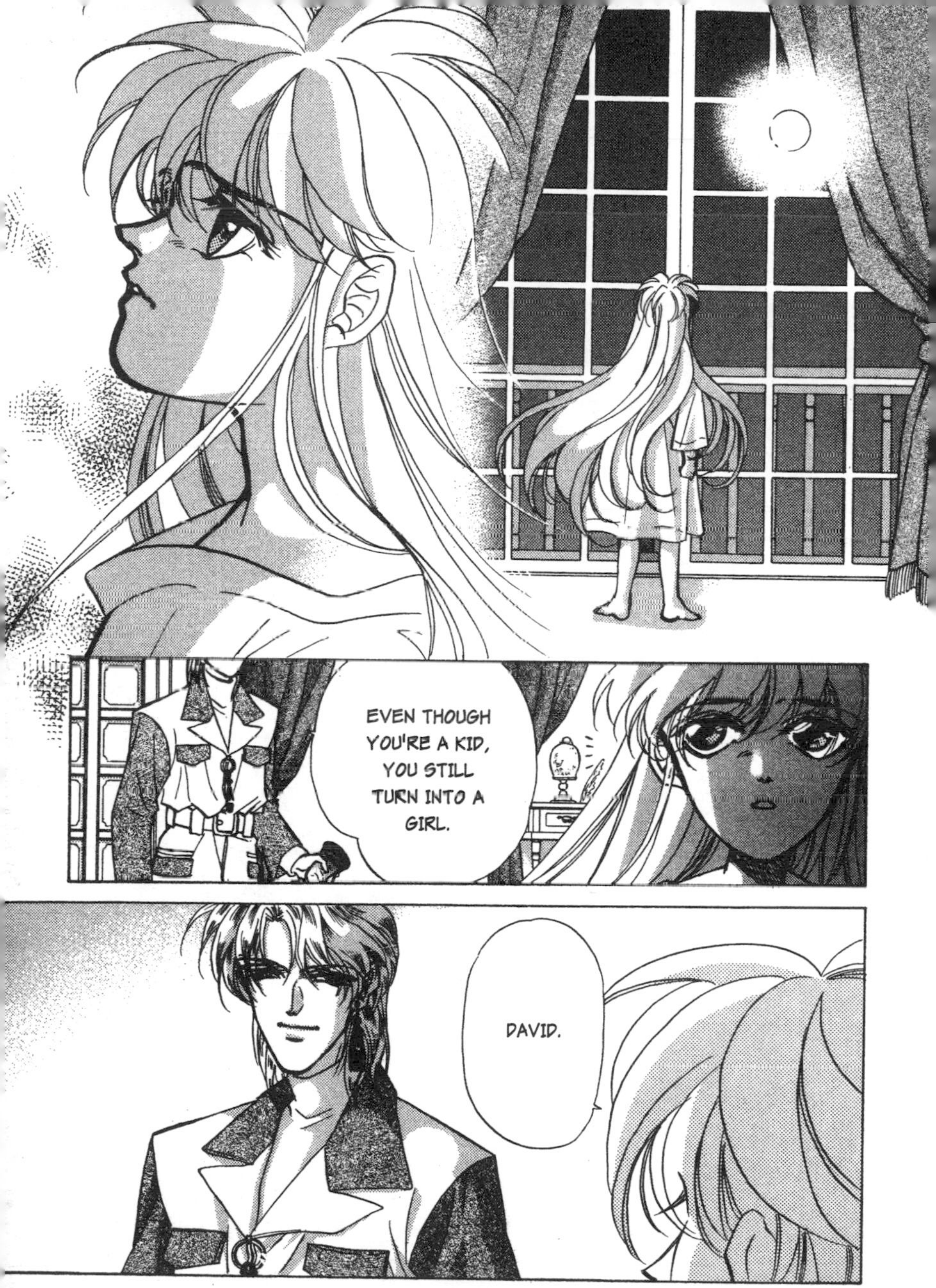
EVEN THOUGH YOU'RE A KID, YOU STILL TURN INTO A GIRL.
DAVID.

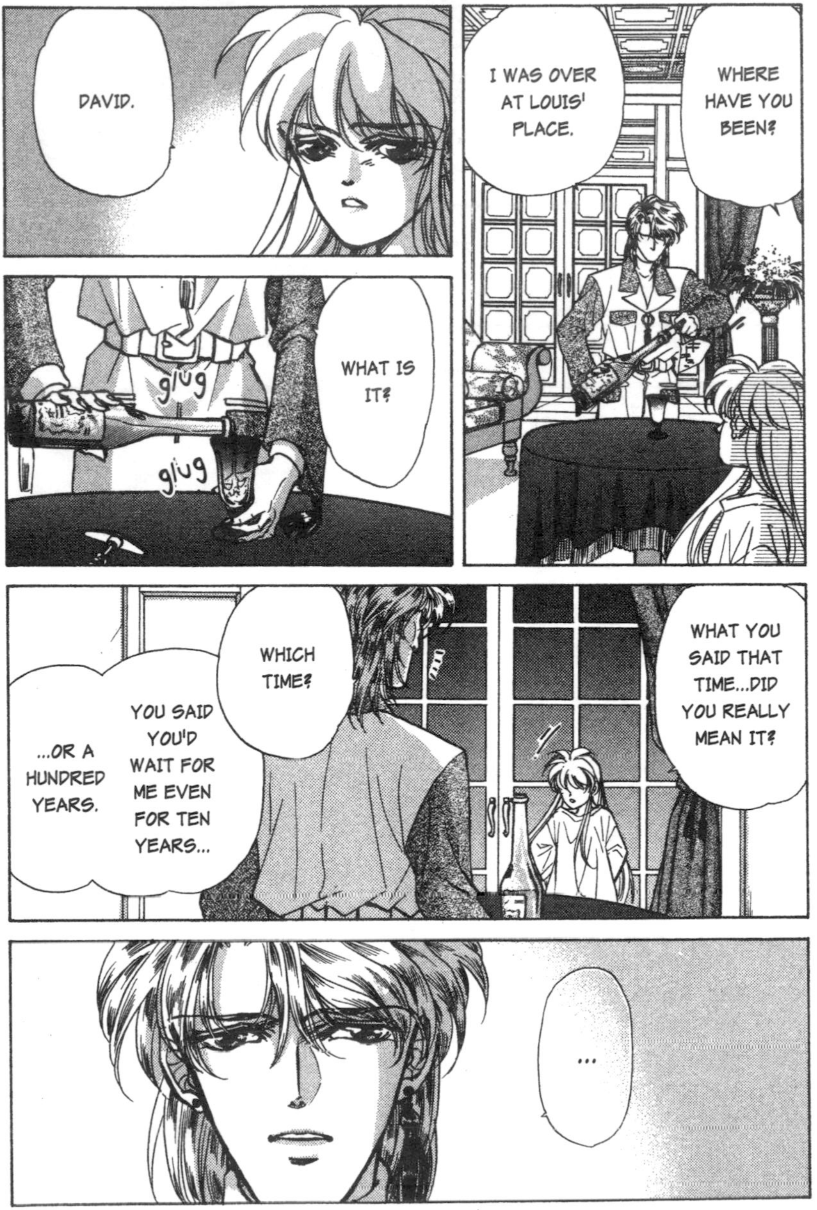
WHERE HAVE YOU BEEN?
I WAS OVER AT LOUIS' PLACE.
DAVID.
WHAT IS IT?
glug
glug
WHAT YOU SAID THAT TIME...DID YOU REALLY MEAN IT?
WHICH TIME?
YOU SAID YOU'D WAIT FOR ME EVEN FOR TEN YEARS...
...OR A HUNDRED YEARS.
...

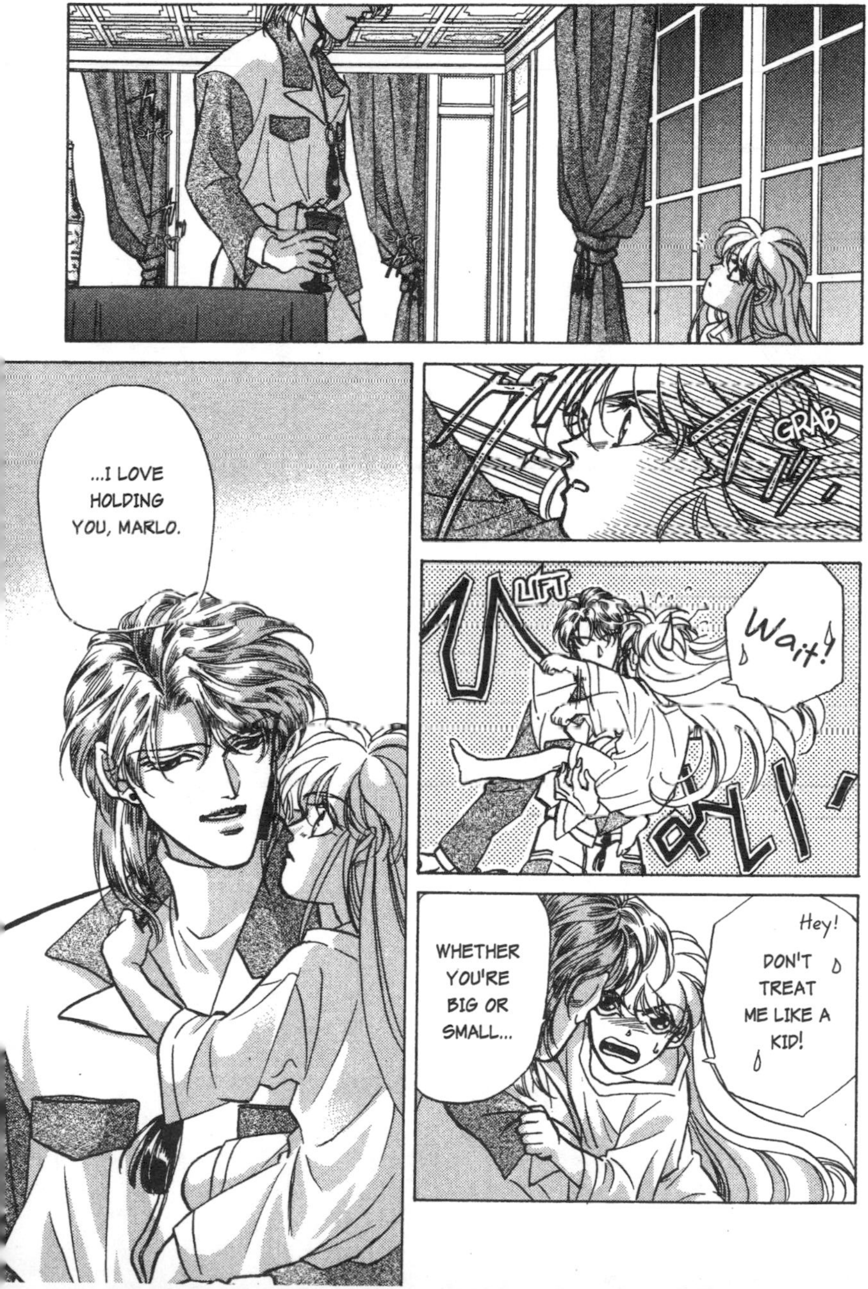
GRAB
LIFT
Wait!
Hey! DON'T TREAT ME LIKE A KID!
WHETHER YOU'RE BIG OR SMALL...
...I LOVE HOLDING YOU, MARLO.

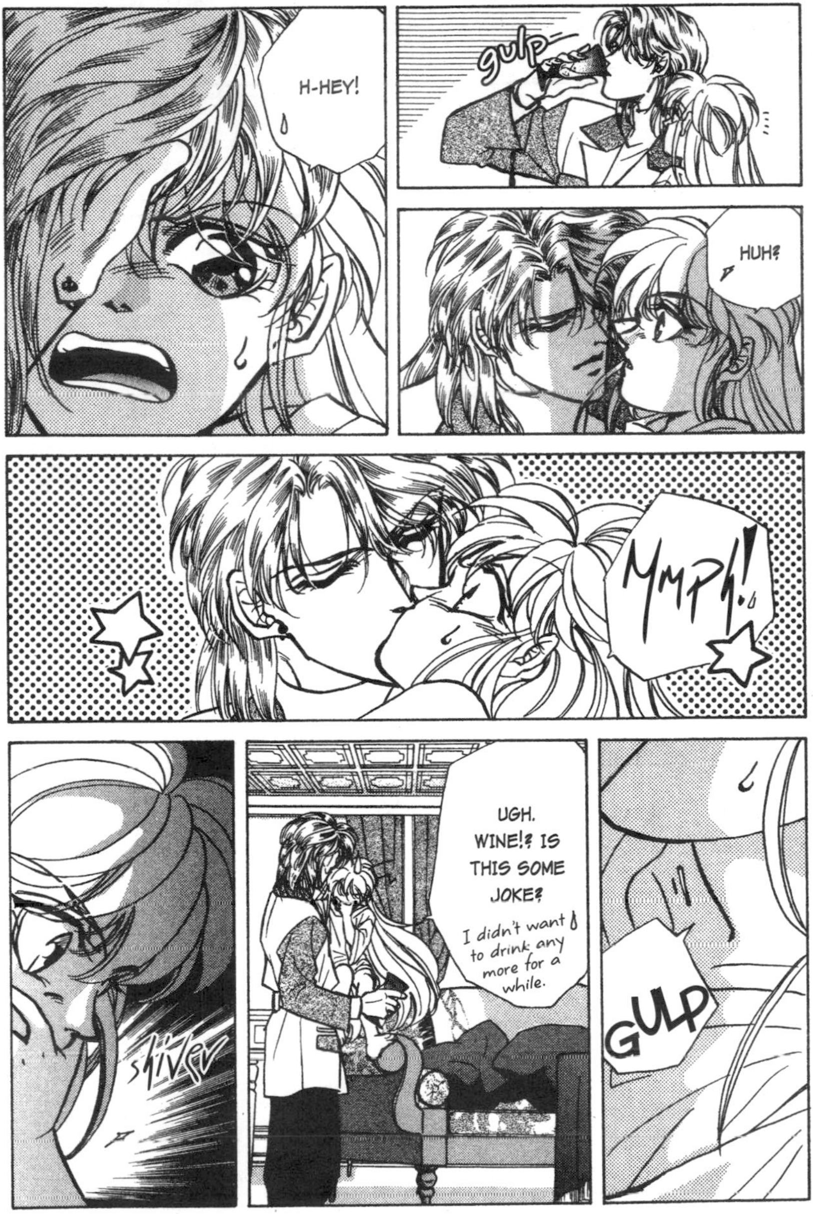
gulp
HUH?
H-HEY!
MMPH!
GULP
UGH. WINE!? IS THIS SOME JOKE?
I didn't want to drink any more for a while.
shiver

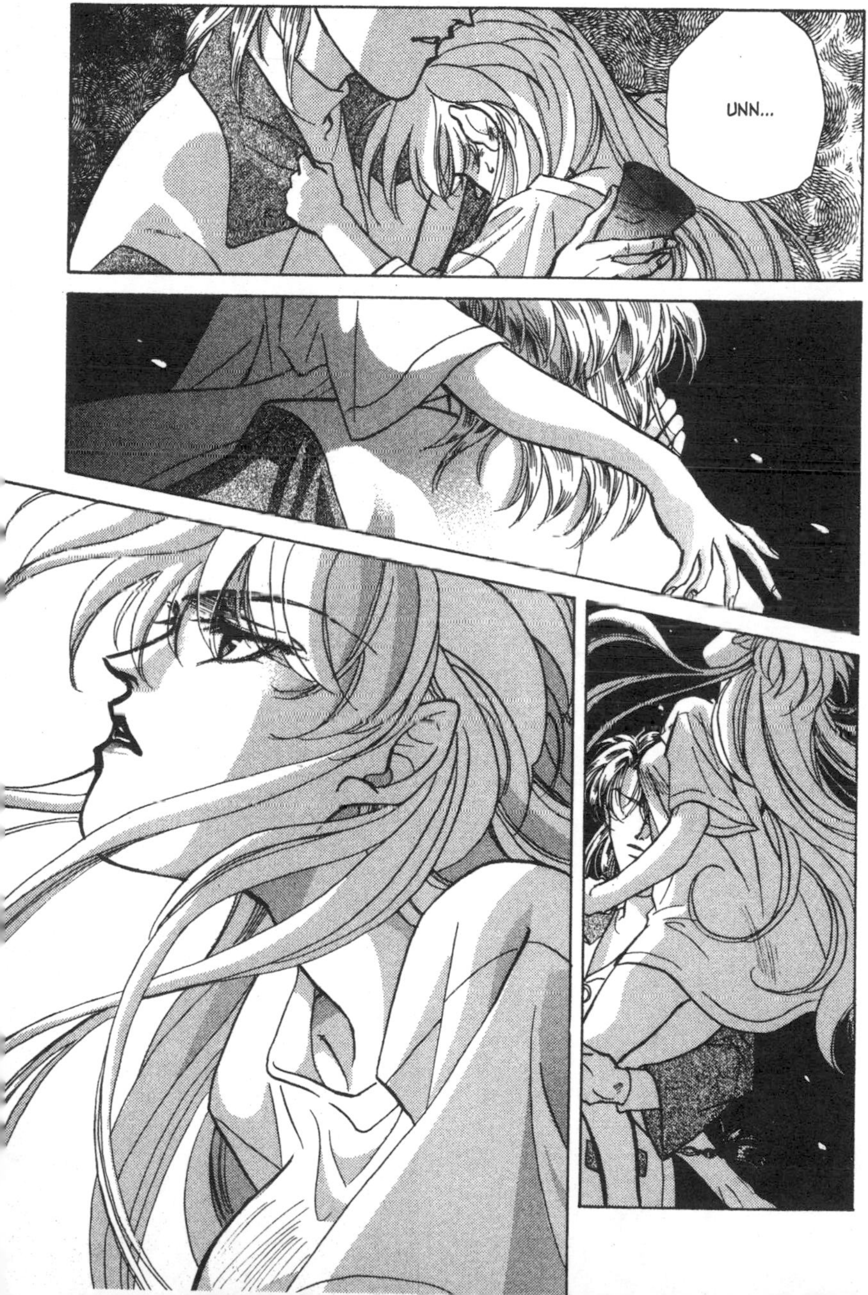
UNN...

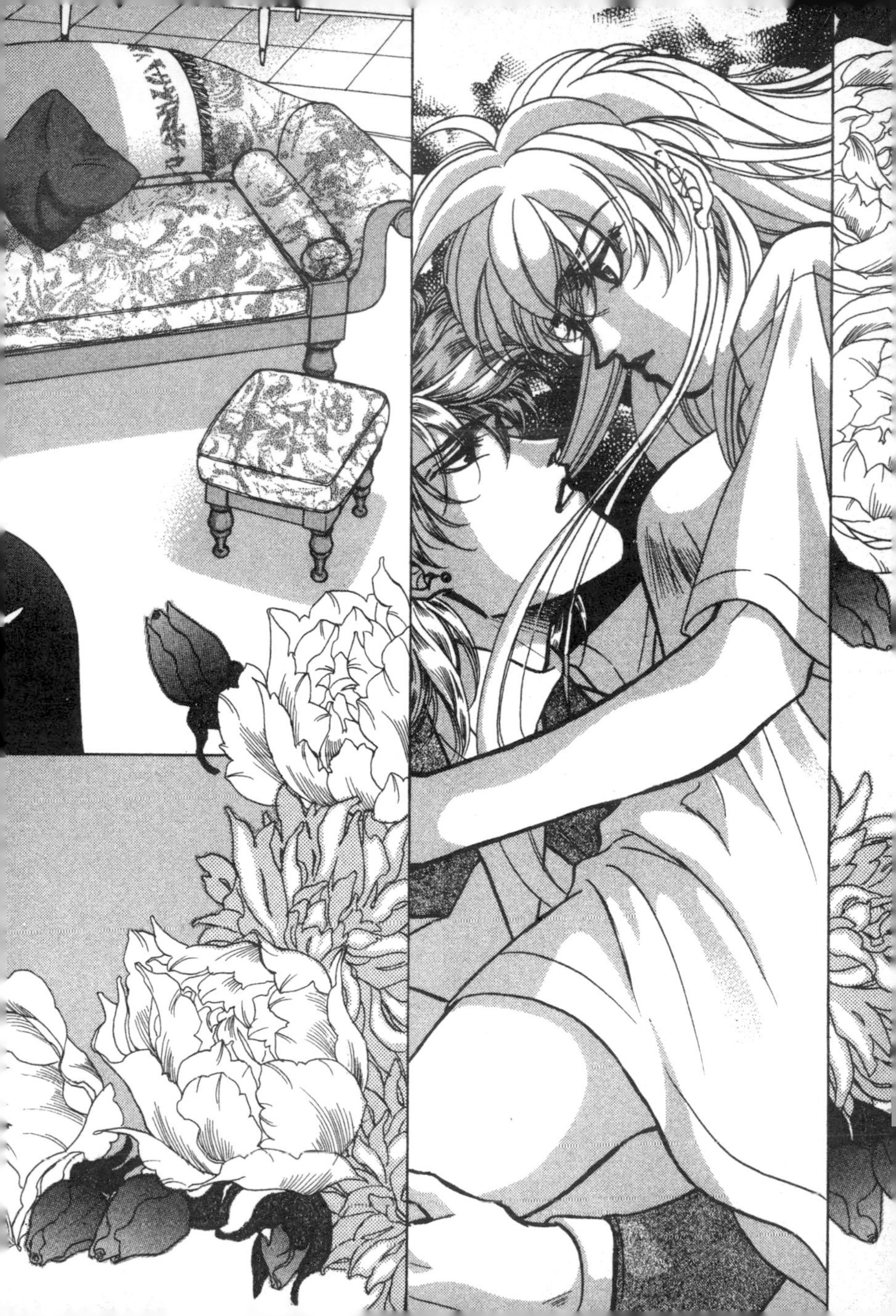

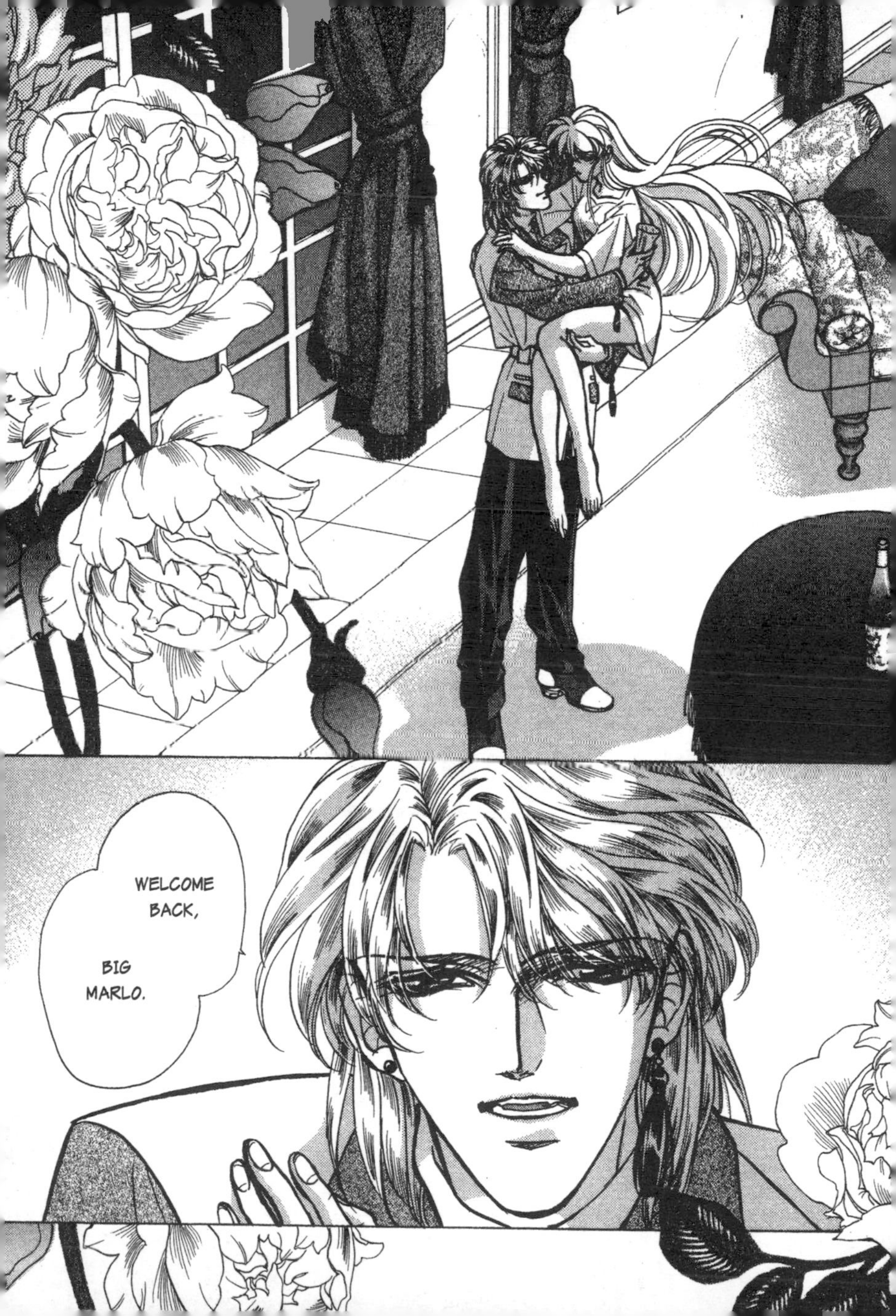
WELCOME BACK, BIG MARLO.

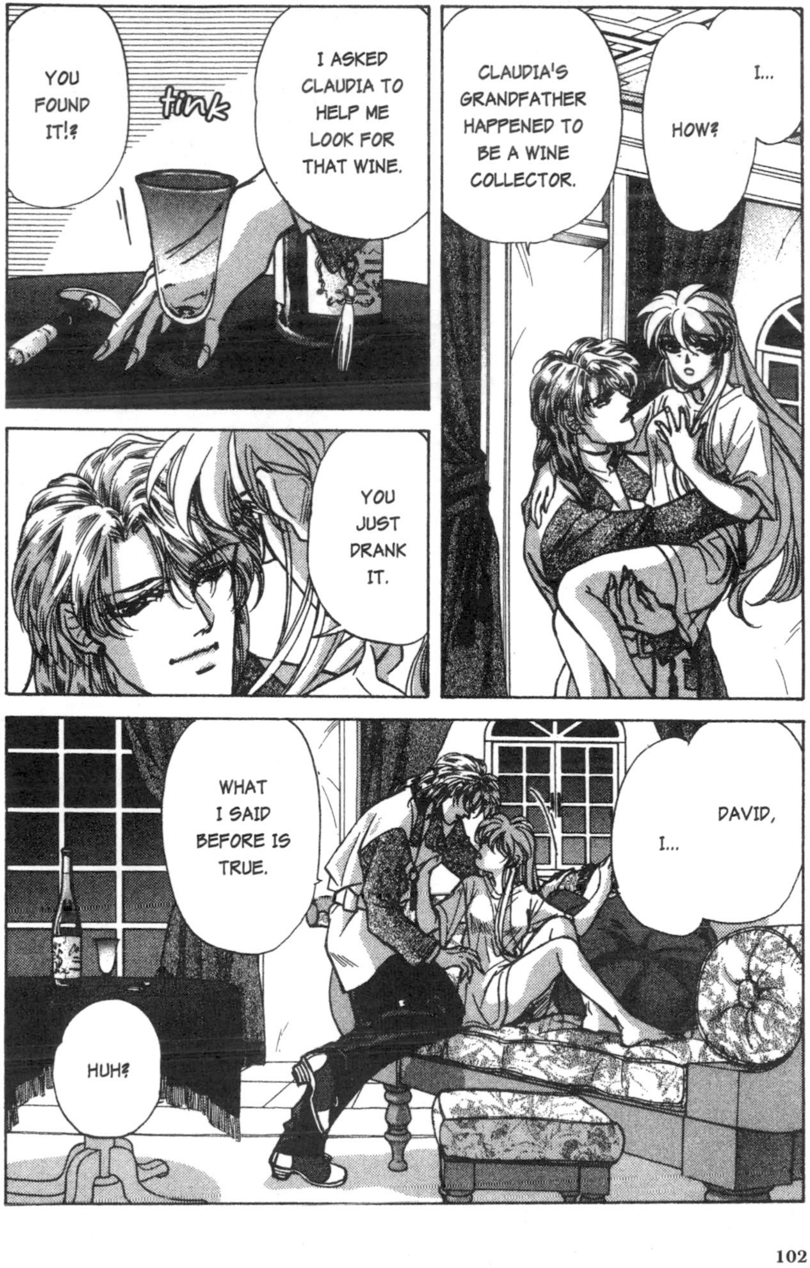
I...
HOW?
CLAUDIA'S GRANDFATHER HAPPENED TO BE A WINE COLLECTOR.
I ASKED CLAUDIA TO HELP ME LOOK FOR THAT WINE.
tink
YOU FOUND IT!?
YOU JUST DRANK IT.
DAVID,
I...
WHAT I SAID BEFORE IS TRUE.
HUH?

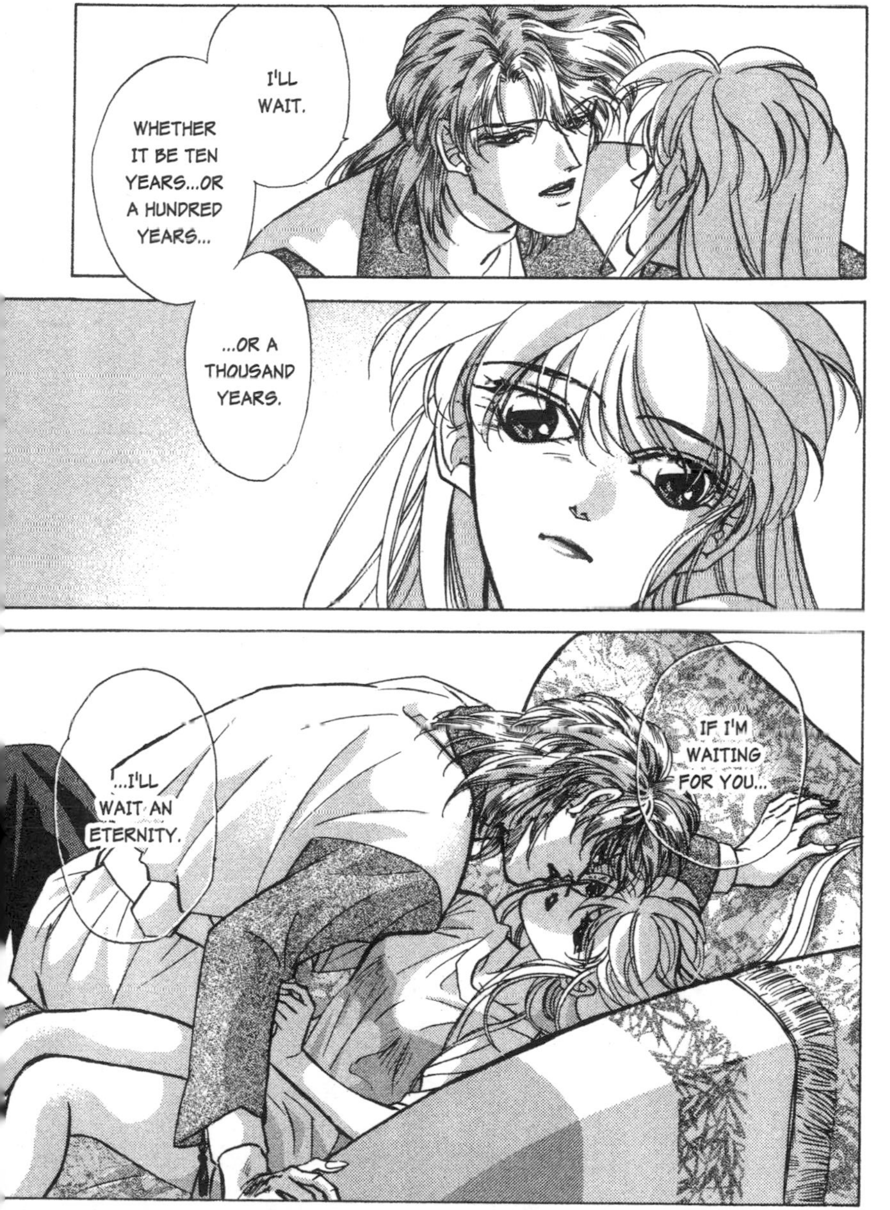
I'LL WAIT.
WHETHER IT BE TEN YEARS...OR A HUNDRED YEARS...
...OR A THOUSAND YEARS.
IF I'M WAITING FOR YOU...
...I'LL WAIT AN ETERNITY.

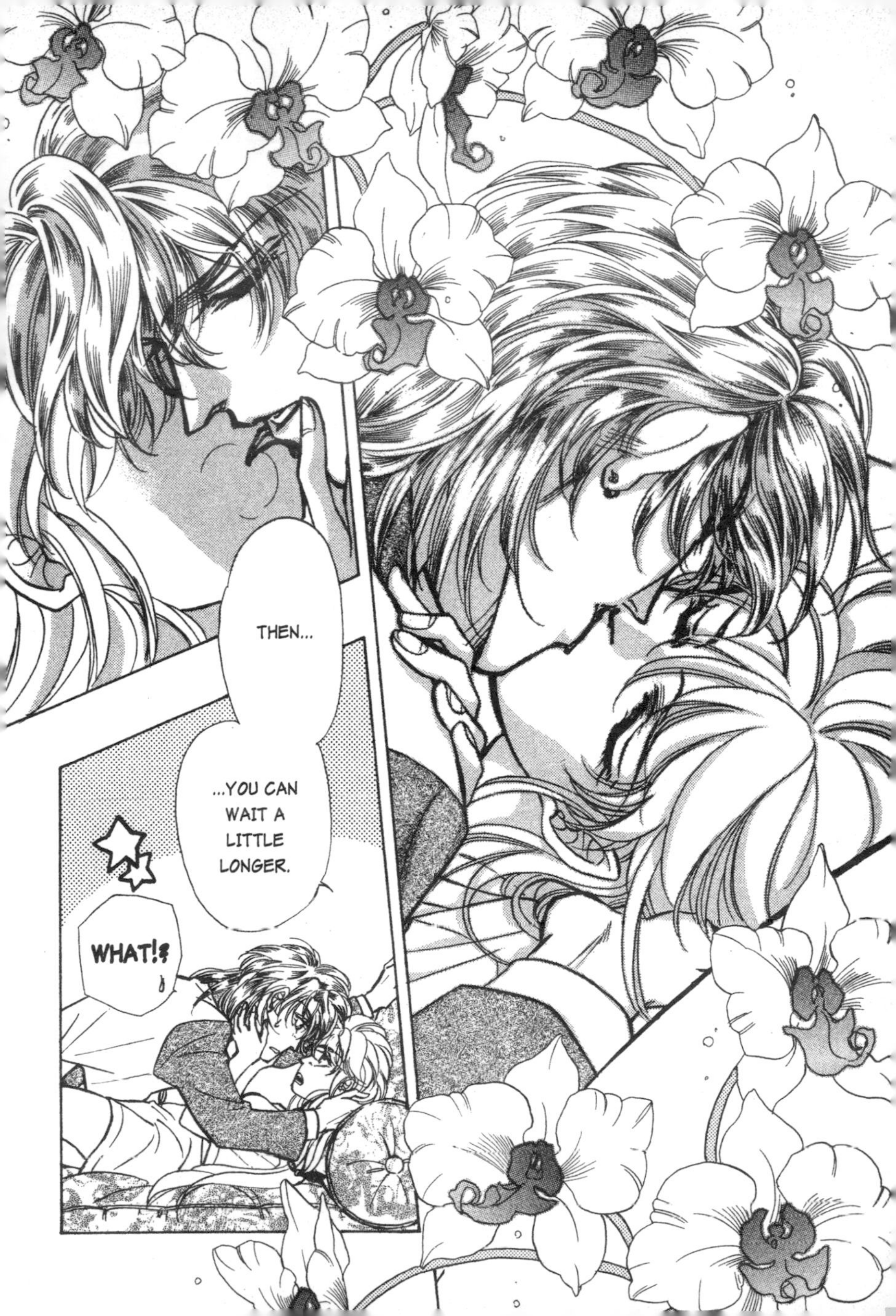
THEN...
...YOU CAN WAIT A LITTLE LONGER.
WHAT!?

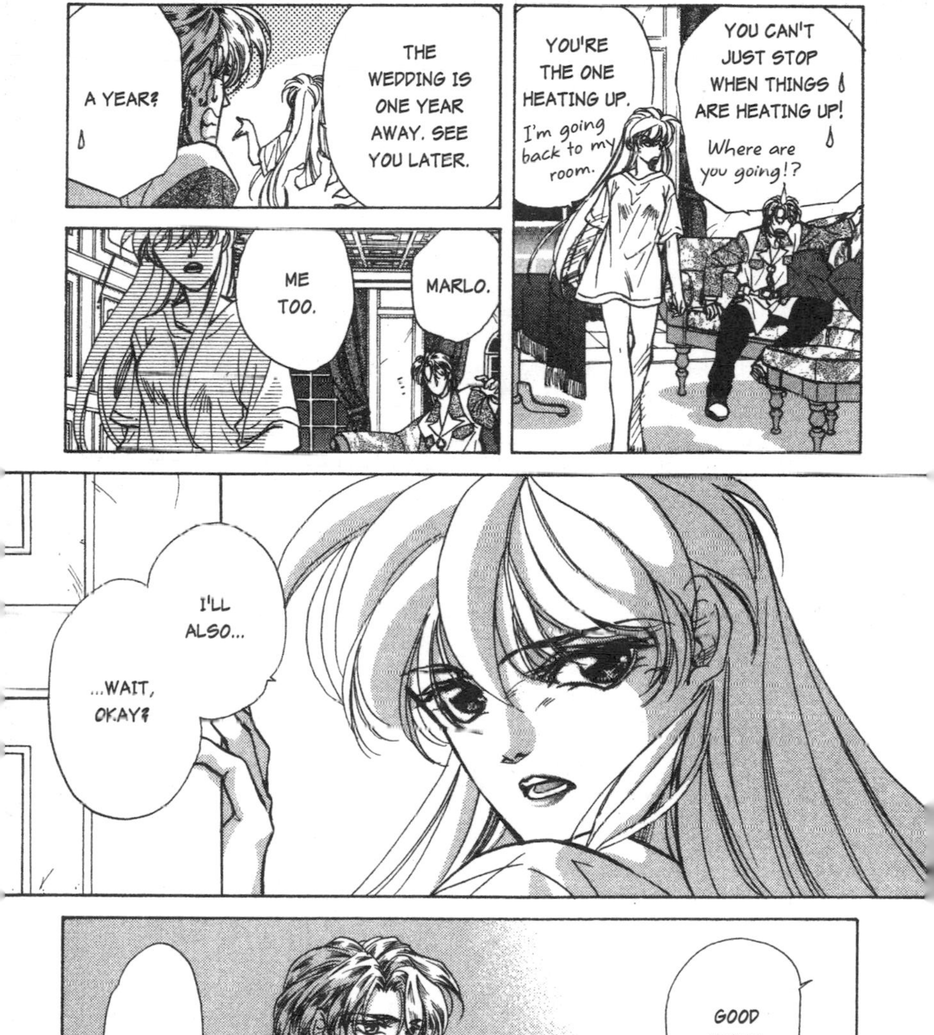
YOU CAN'T JUST STOP WHEN THINGS ARE HEATING UP!
Where are you going!?
YOU'RE THE ONE HEATING UP.
I'm going back to my room.
THE WEDDING IS ONE YEAR AWAY. SEE YOU LATER.
A YEAR?
MARLO.
ME TOO.
I'LL ALSO...
...WAIT, OKAY?
GOOD NIGHT.
click
...

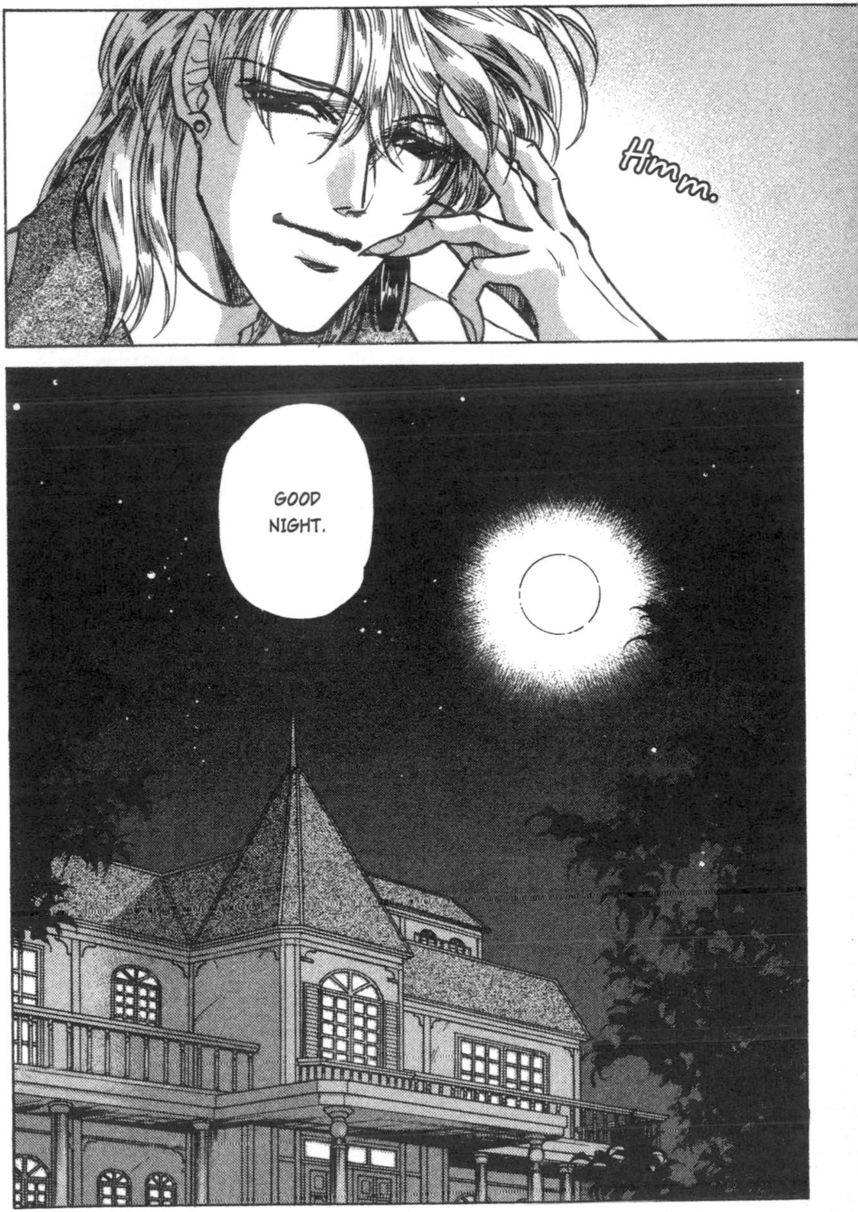
Hmm.
GOOD NIGHT.

Chapter Six End

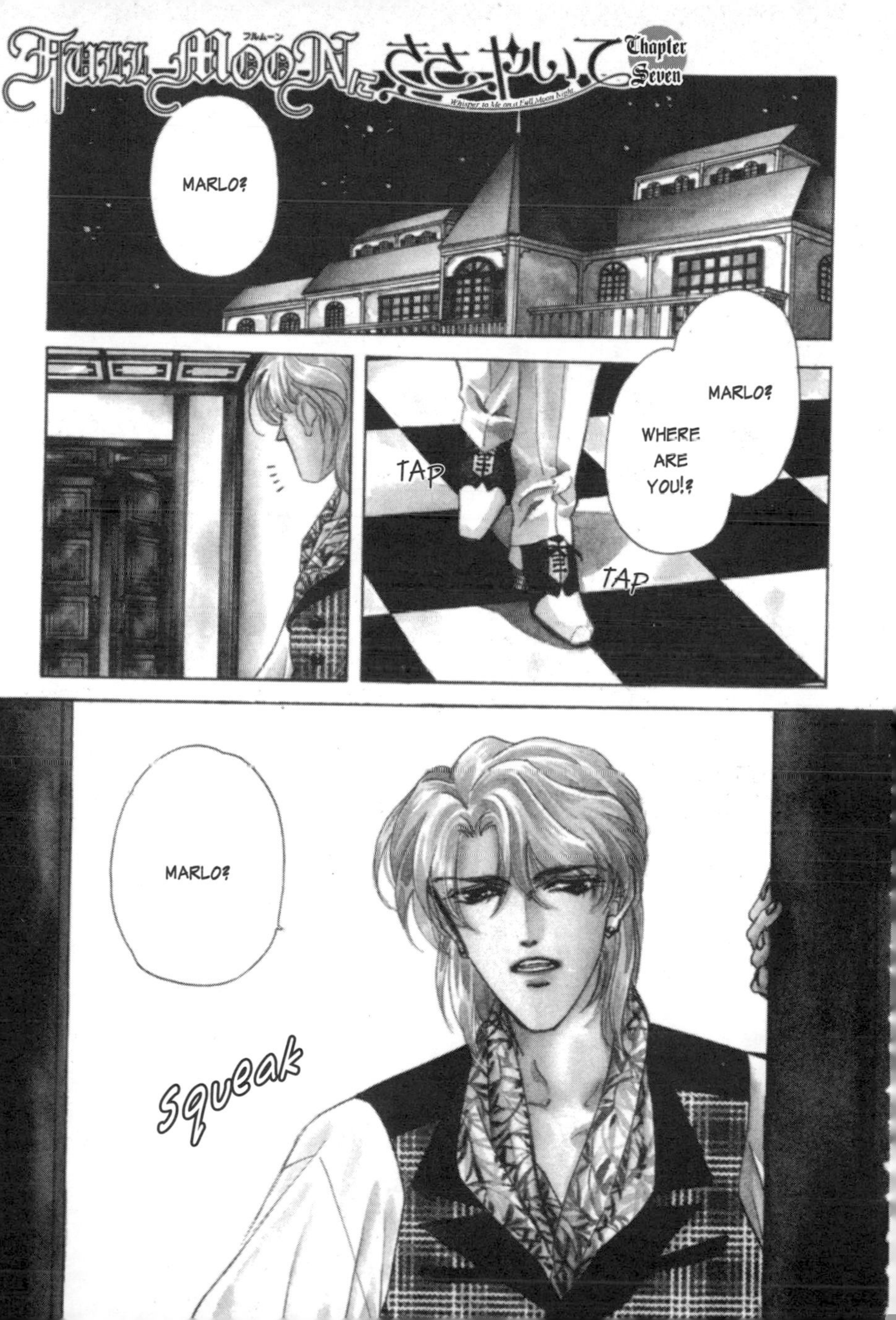
FULL MOON にささやいて
Chapter Seven
Whisper to Me on a Full Moon Night
MARLO?
MARLO?
WHERE ARE YOU!?
TAP
TAP
MARLO?
squeak

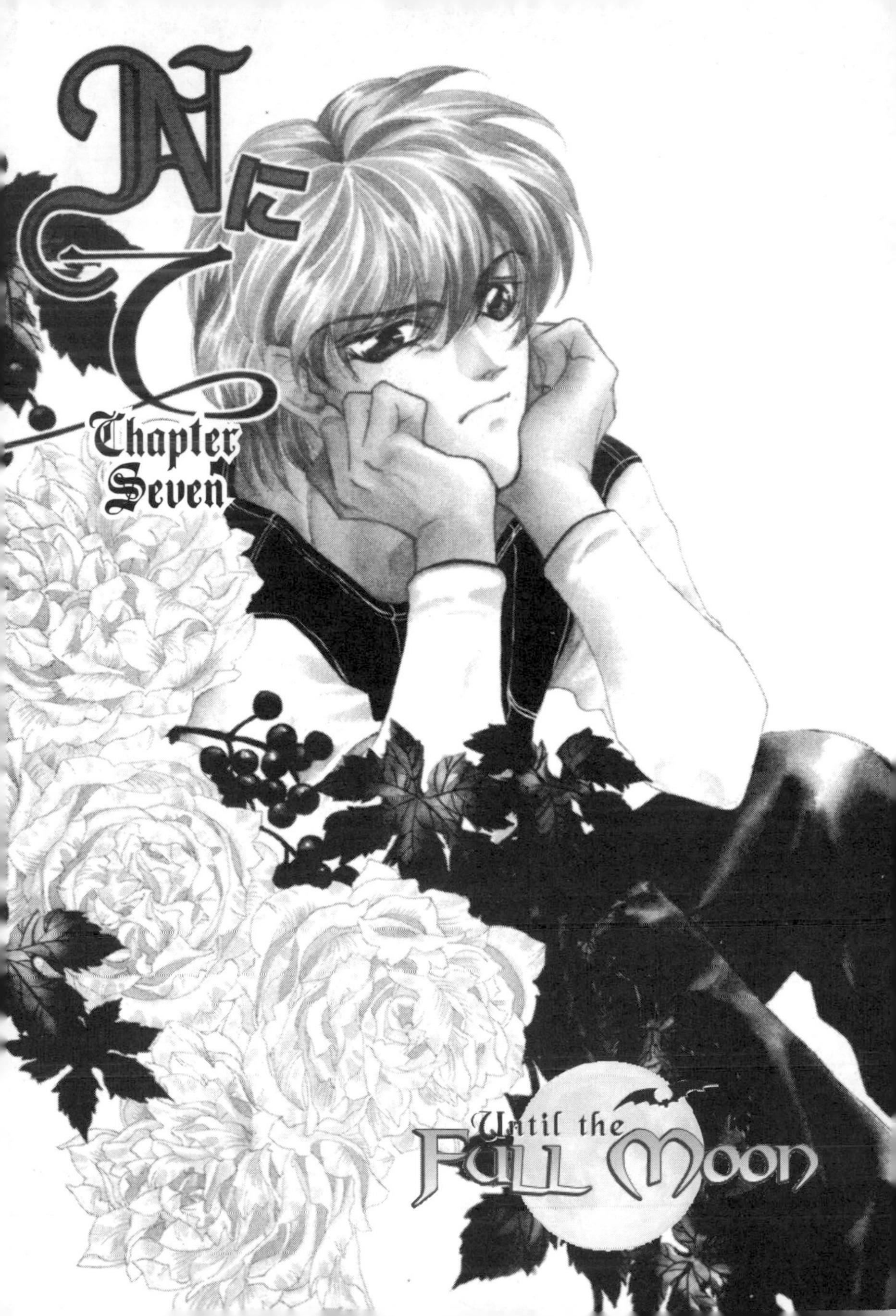
Nにて
Chapter Seven
Until the
Full Moon

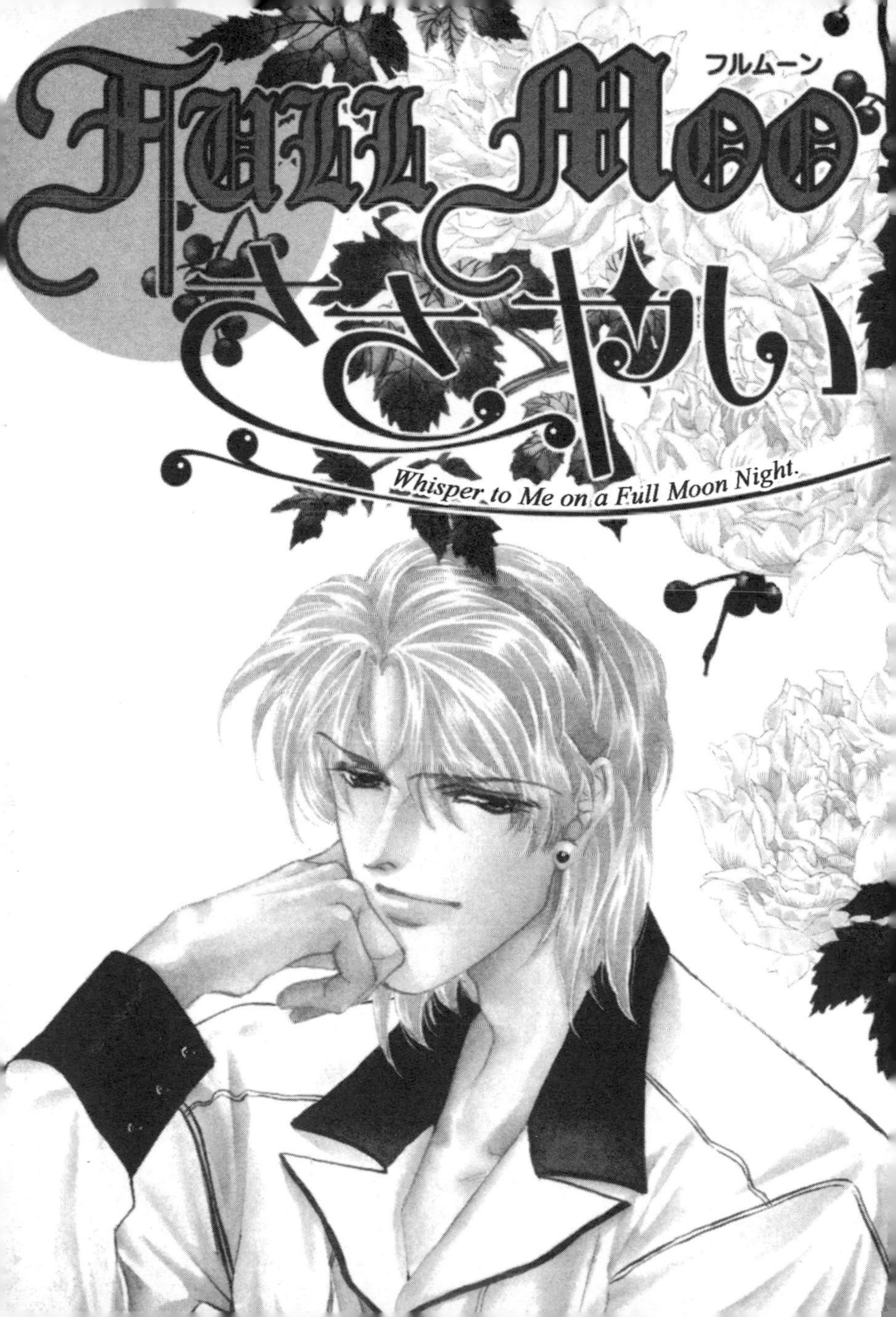
FULL MOO
フルムーン
Whisper to Me on a Full Moon Night.

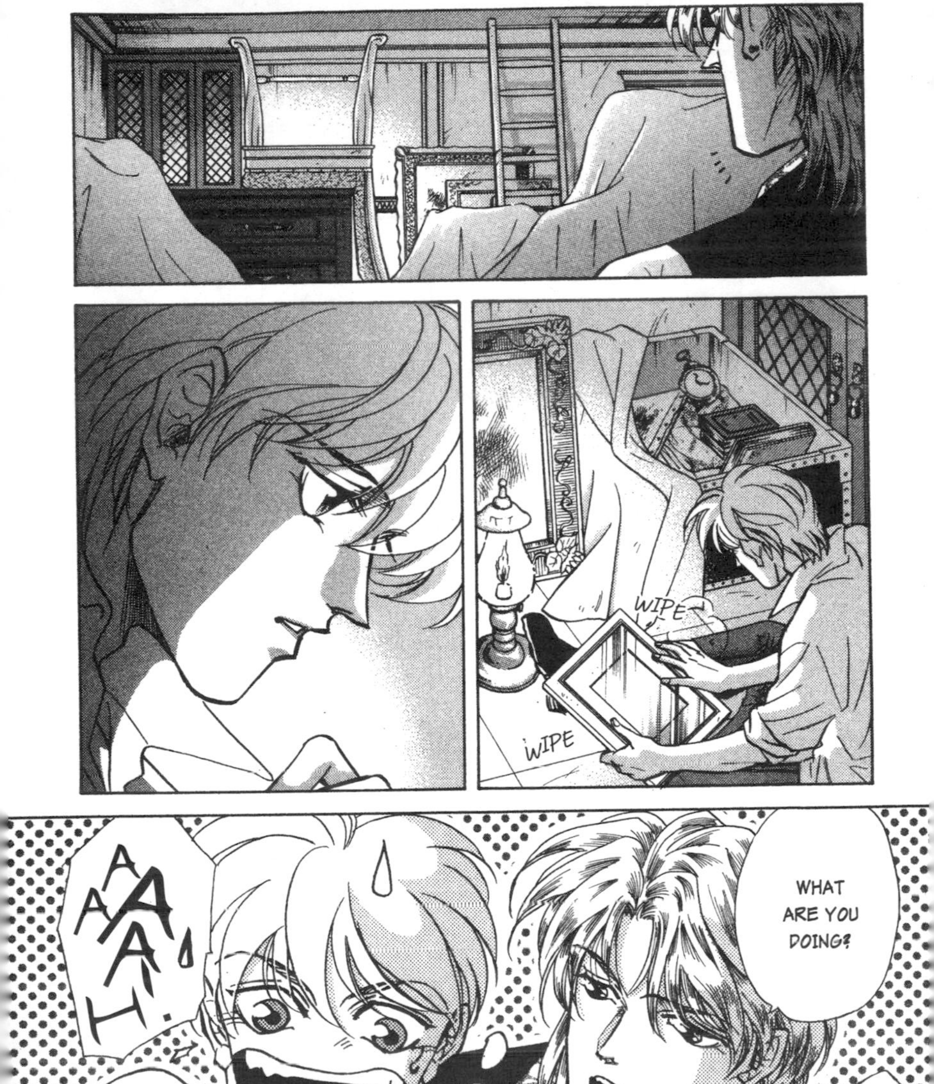
WIPE
WIPE
WHAT ARE YOU DOING?
AAAAAH.
BOO!

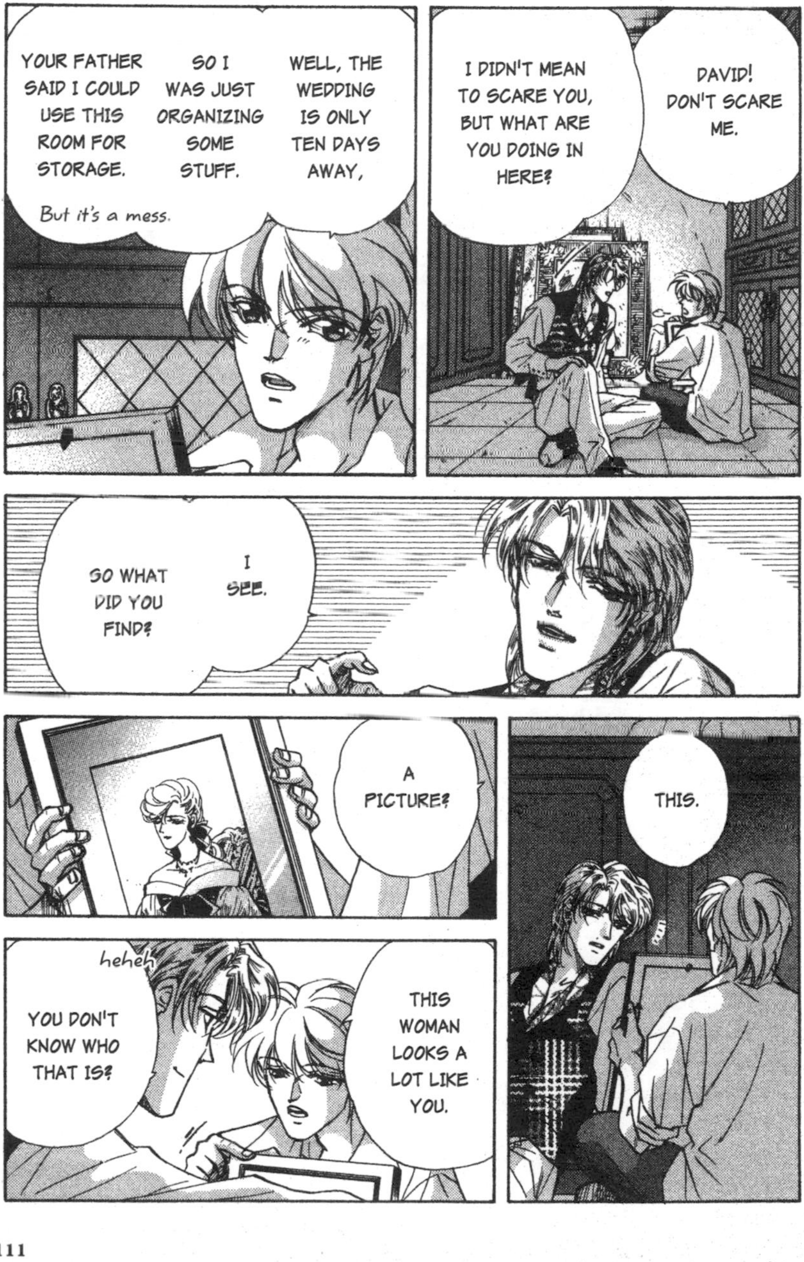

DAVID! DON'T SCARE ME.
I DIDN'T MEAN TO SCARE YOU, BUT WHAT ARE YOU DOING IN HERE?
WELL, THE WEDDING IS ONLY TEN DAYS AWAY,
SO I WAS JUST ORGANIZING SOME STUFF.
YOUR FATHER SAID I COULD USE THIS ROOM FOR STORAGE.
But it's a mess.
I SEE.
SO WHAT DID YOU FIND?
THIS.
A PICTURE?
THIS WOMAN LOOKS A LOT LIKE YOU.
heheh
YOU DON'T KNOW WHO THAT IS?

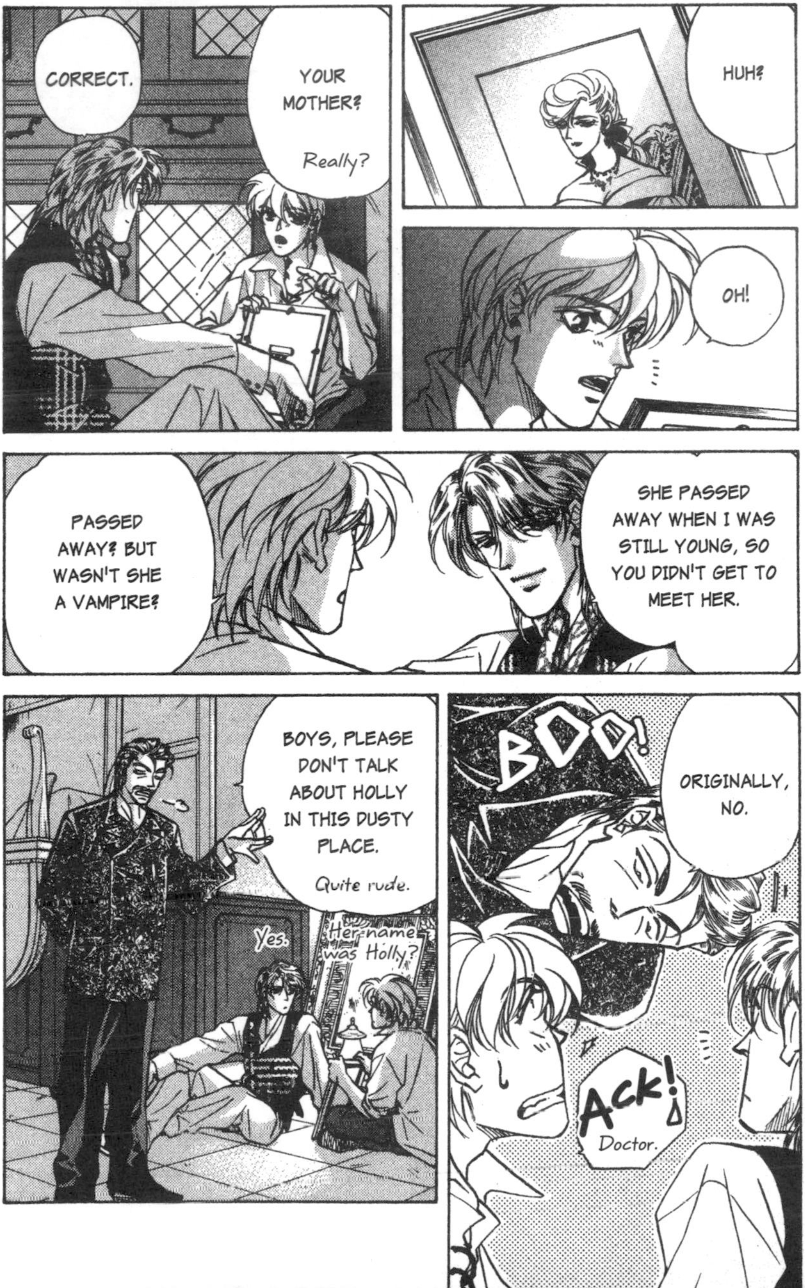
HUH?
OH!
YOUR MOTHER?
Really?
CORRECT.
SHE PASSED AWAY WHEN I WAS STILL YOUNG, SO YOU DIDN'T GET TO MEET HER.
PASSED AWAY? BUT WASN'T SHE A VAMPIRE?
ORIGINALLY, NO.
BOO!
ACK!
Doctor.
BOYS, PLEASE DON'T TALK ABOUT HOLLY IN THIS DUSTY PLACE.
Quite rude.
Her name was Holly?
Yes.

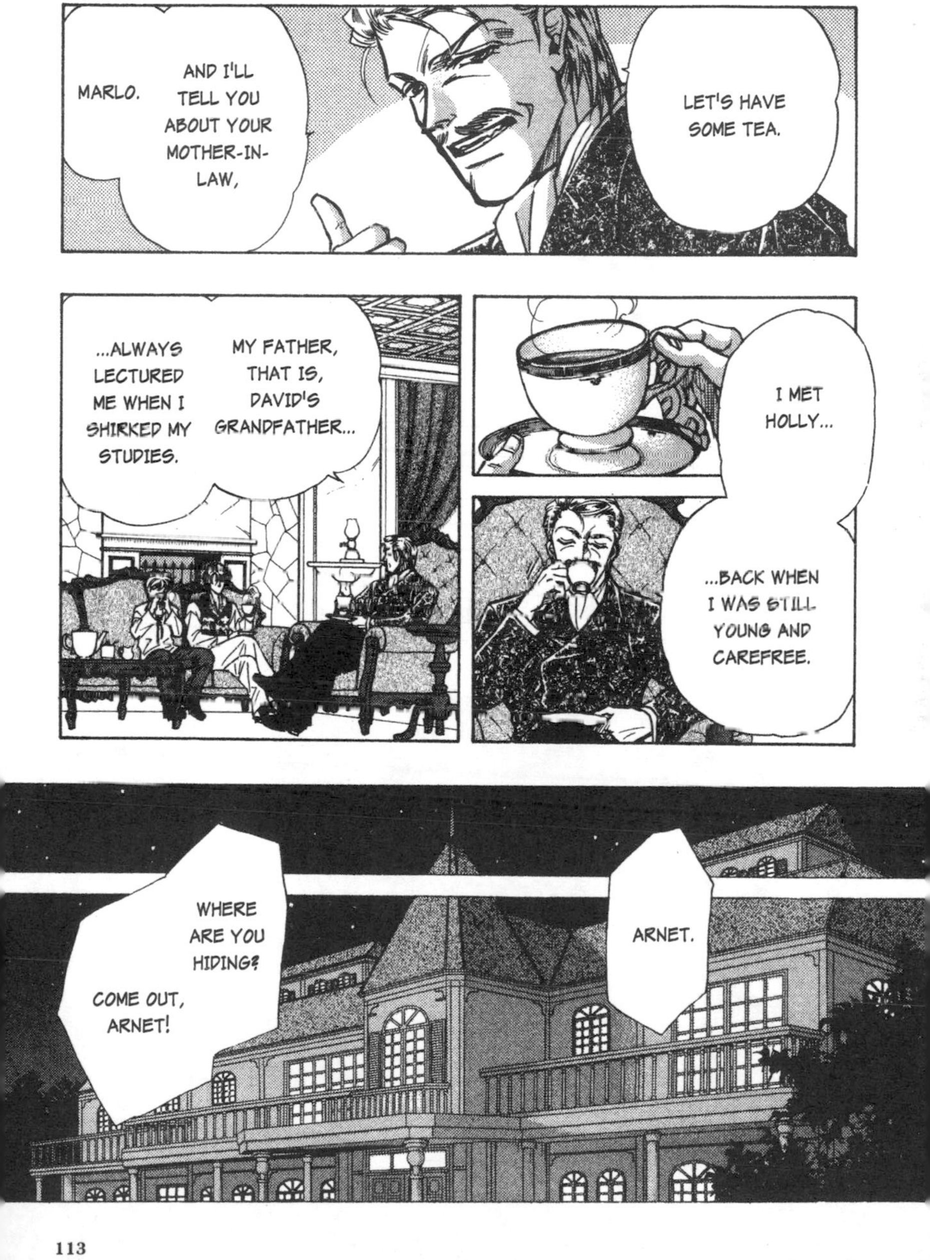
LET'S HAVE SOME TEA.
AND I'LL TELL YOU ABOUT YOUR MOTHER-IN-LAW,
MARLO.
I MET HOLLY...
...BACK WHEN I WAS STILL YOUNG AND CAREFREE.
MY FATHER, THAT IS, DAVID'S GRANDFATHER...
...ALWAYS LECTURED ME WHEN I SHIRKED MY STUDIES.
ARNET.
WHERE ARE YOU HIDING?
COME OUT, ARNET!

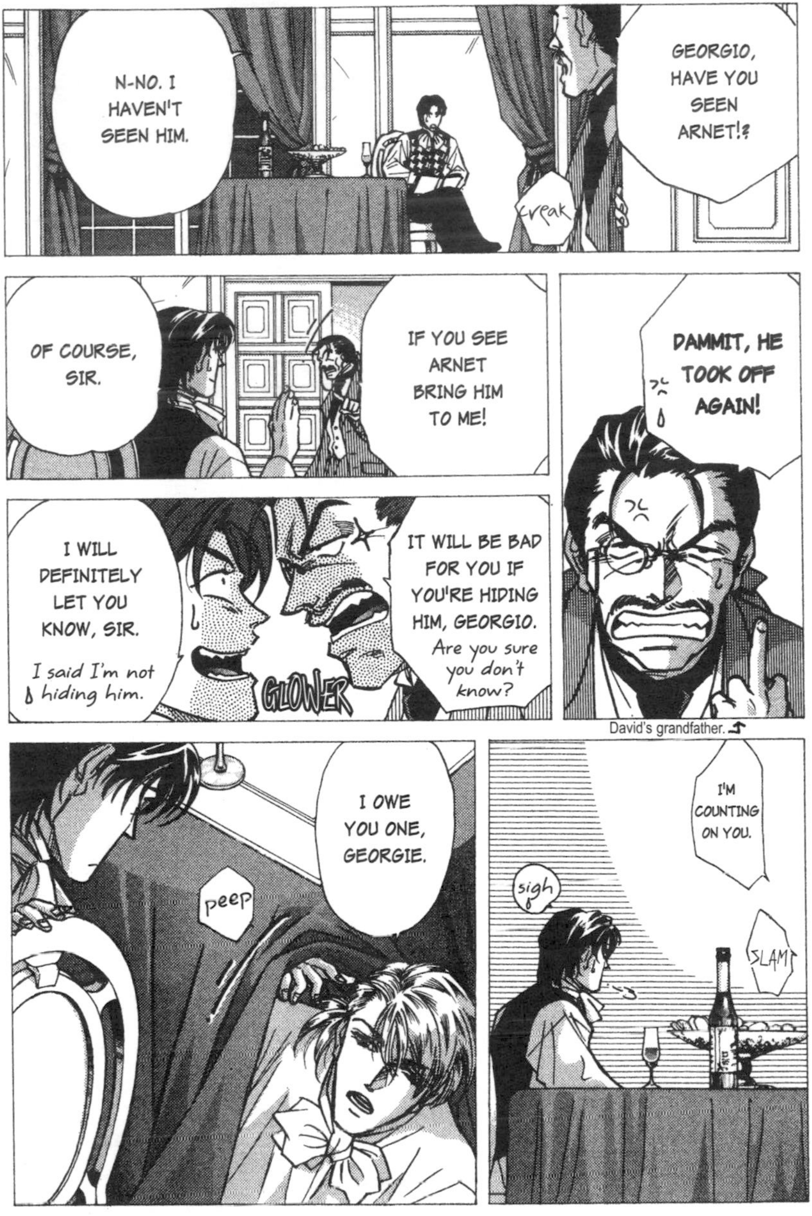
GEORGIO, HAVE YOU SEEN ARNET!?
creak
N-NO. I HAVEN'T SEEN HIM.
DAMMIT, HE TOOK OFF AGAIN!
David's grandfather.
IF YOU SEE ARNET BRING HIM TO ME!
OF COURSE, SIR.
IT WILL BE BAD FOR YOU IF YOU'RE HIDING HIM, GEORGIO.
Are you sure you don't know?
GLOWER
I WILL DEFINITELY LET YOU KNOW, SIR.
I said I'm not hiding him.
I'M COUNTING ON YOU.
SLAM
sigh
I OWE YOU ONE, GEORGIE.
peep

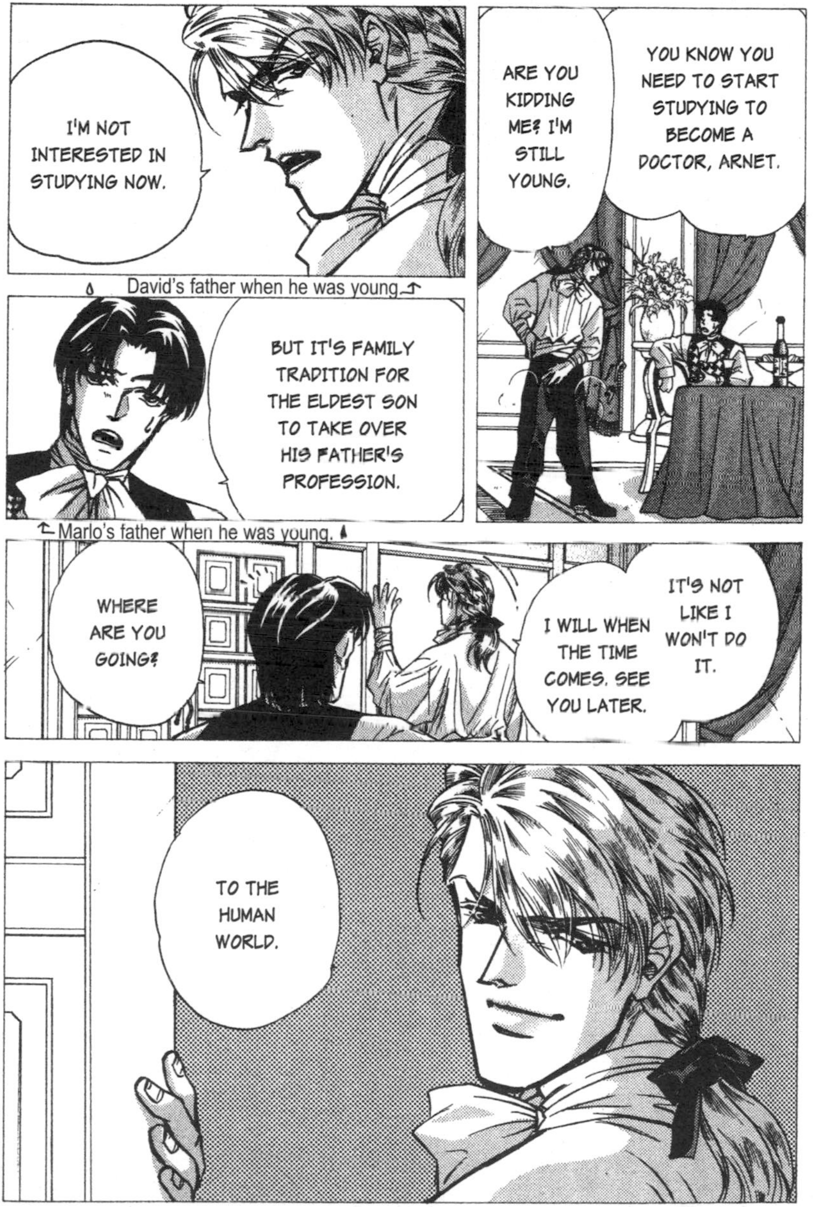
YOU KNOW YOU NEED TO START STUDYING TO BECOME A DOCTOR, ARNET.
ARE YOU KIDDING ME? I'M STILL YOUNG.
I'M NOT INTERESTED IN STUDYING NOW.
David's father when he was young
BUT IT'S FAMILY TRADITION FOR THE ELDEST SON TO TAKE OVER HIS FATHER'S PROFESSION.
Marlo's father when he was young.
IT'S NOT LIKE I WON'T DO IT.
I WILL WHEN THE TIME COMES. SEE YOU LATER.
WHERE ARE YOU GOING?
TO THE HUMAN WORLD.

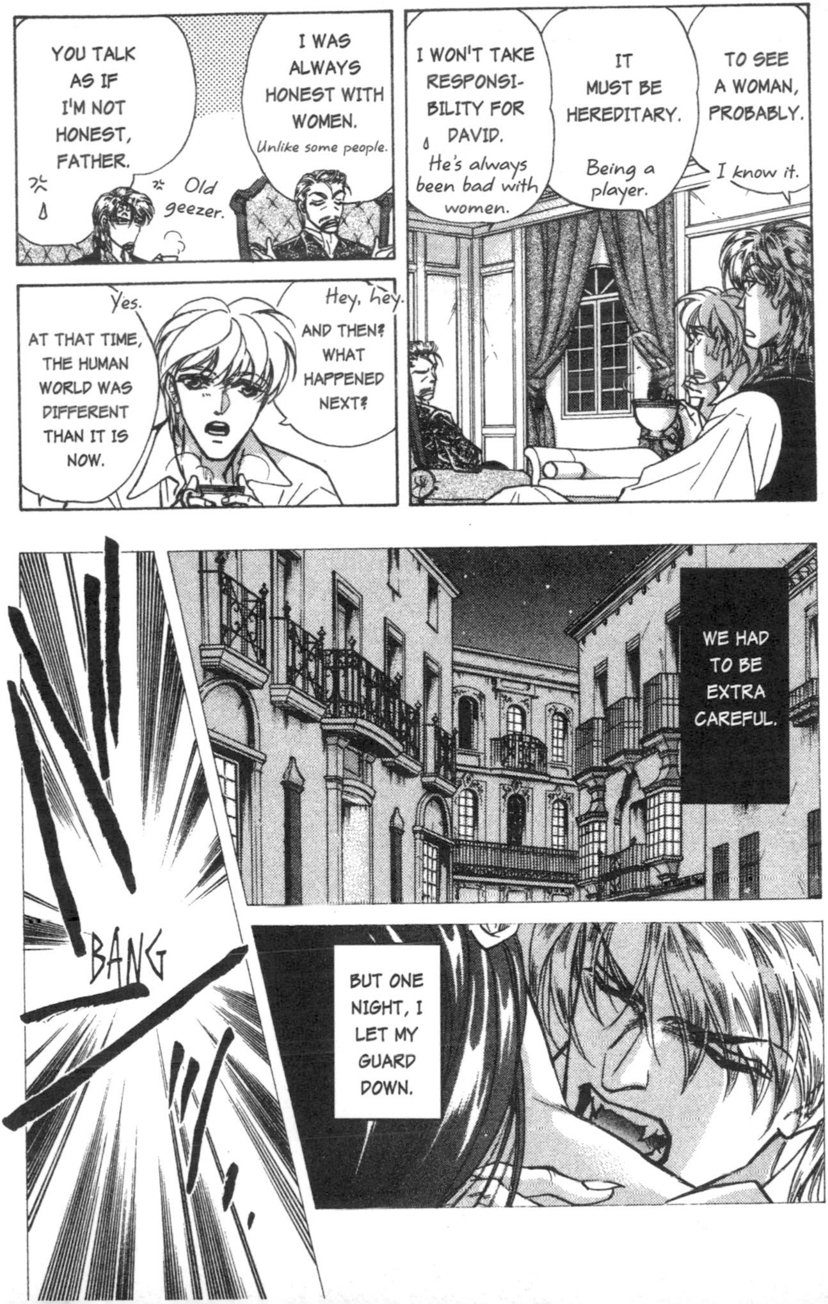
TO SEE A WOMAN, PROBABLY.
I know it.
IT MUST BE HEREDITARY.
Being a player.
I WON'T TAKE RESPONSIBILITY FOR DAVID.
He's always been bad with women.
I WAS ALWAYS HONEST WITH WOMEN.
Unlike some people.
YOU TALK AS IF I'M NOT HONEST, FATHER.
Old geezer.
Hey, hey.
AND THEN? WHAT HAPPENED NEXT?
Yes.
AT THAT TIME, THE HUMAN WORLD WAS DIFFERENT THAN IT IS NOW.
WE HAD TO BE EXTRA CAREFUL.
BUT ONE NIGHT, I LET MY GUARD DOWN.
BANG

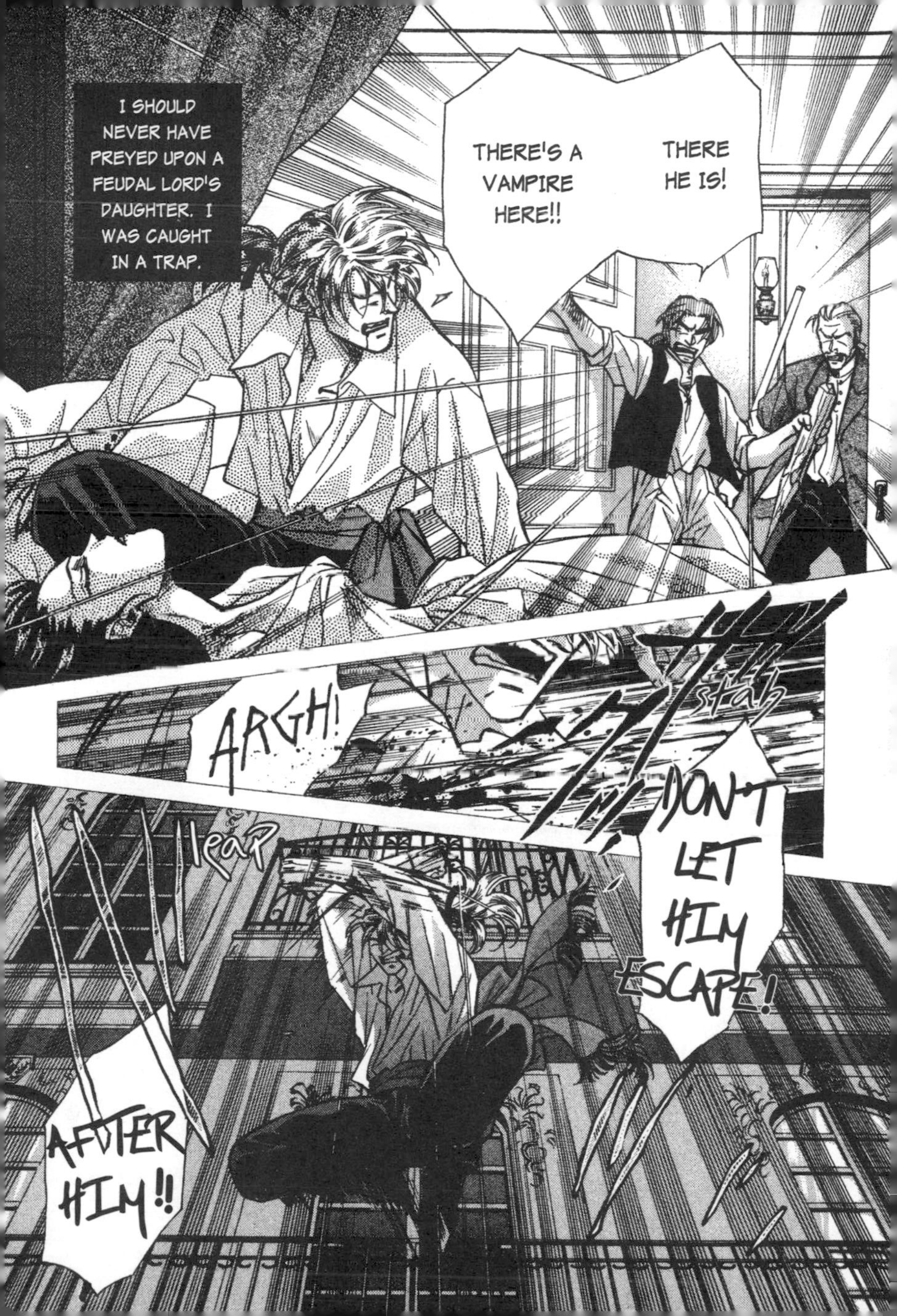
THERE HE IS!
THERE'S A VAMPIRE HERE!!
I SHOULD NEVER HAVE PREYED UPON A FEUDAL LORD'S DAUGHTER. I WAS CAUGHT IN A TRAP.
stab
ARGH!
DON'T LET HIM ESCAPE!
leap
AFTER HIM!!

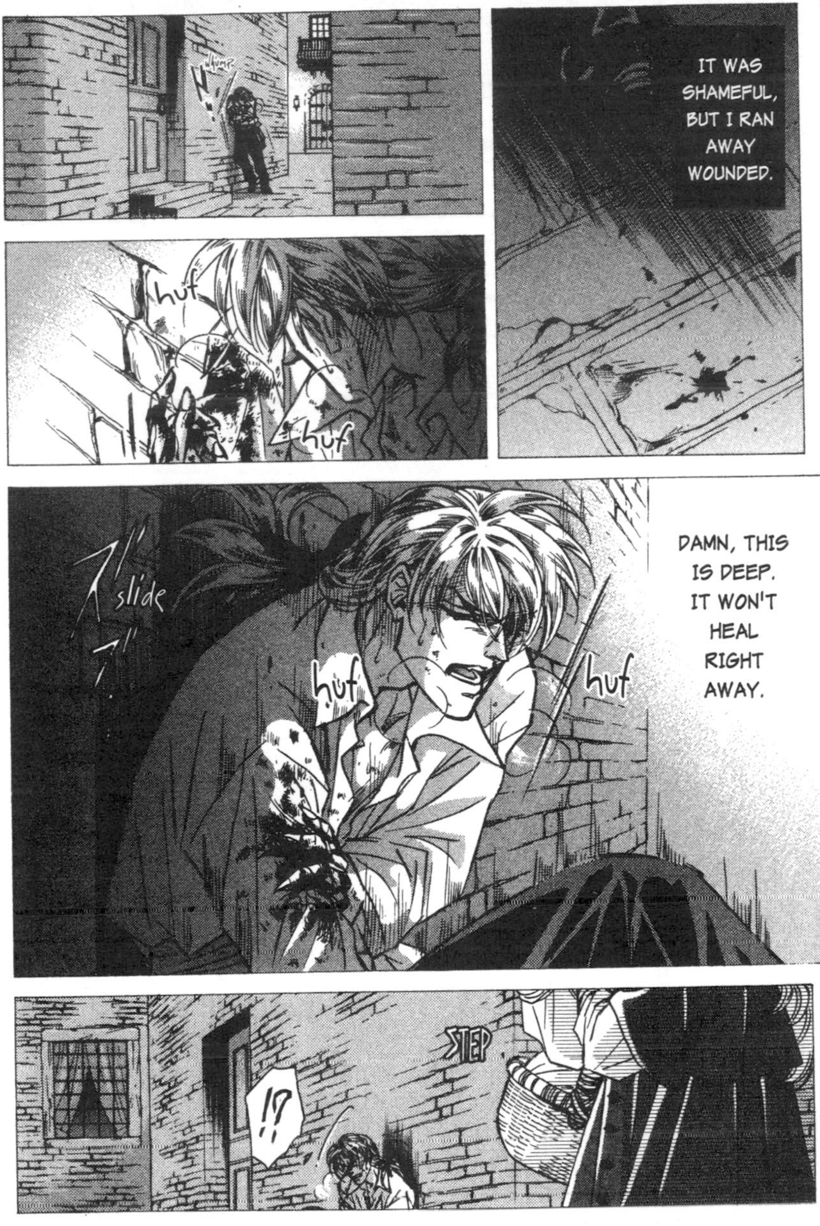
IT WAS SHAMEFUL, BUT I RAN AWAY WOUNDED.
whump
huf
huf
DAMN, THIS IS DEEP. IT WON'T HEAL RIGHT AWAY.
huf
huf
slide
STEP
!?

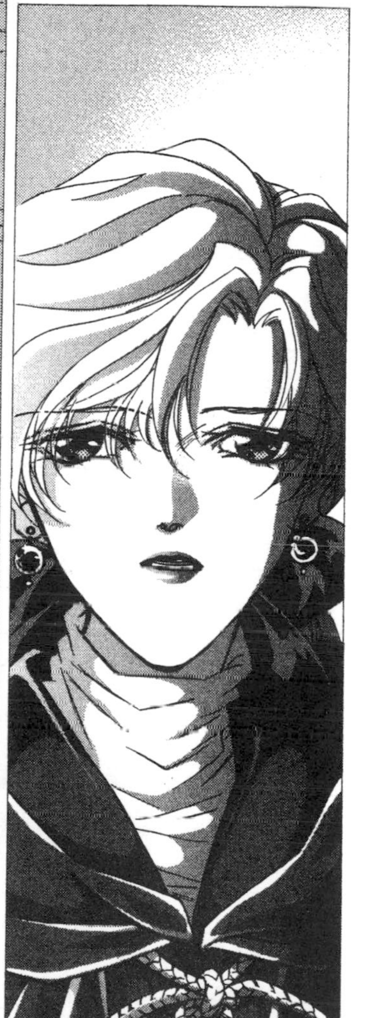
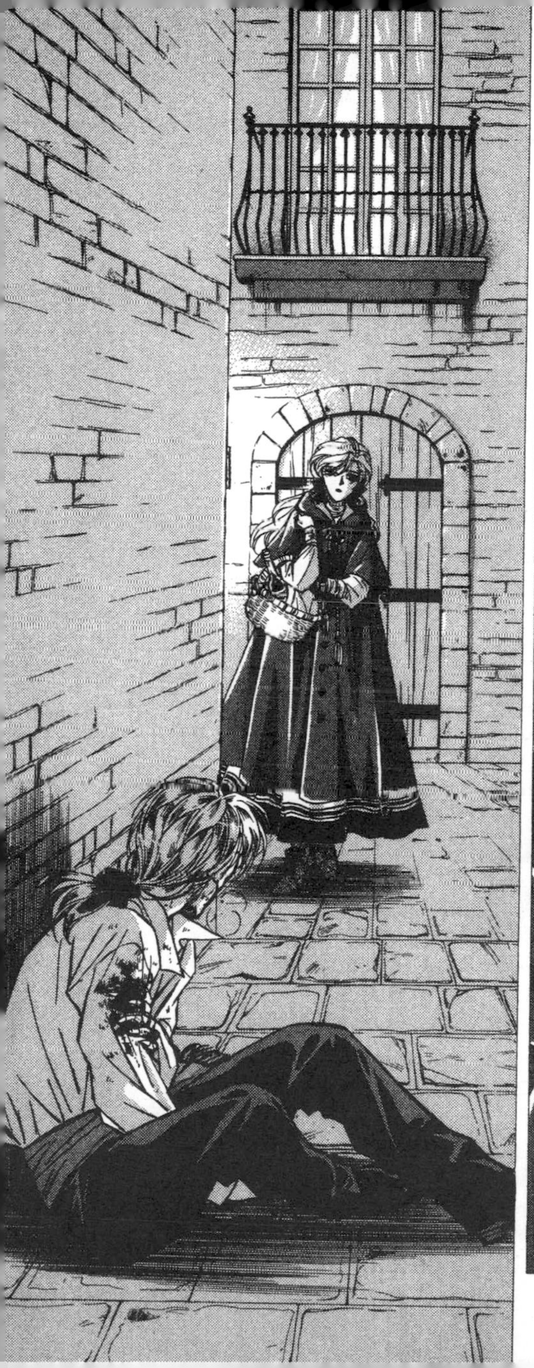

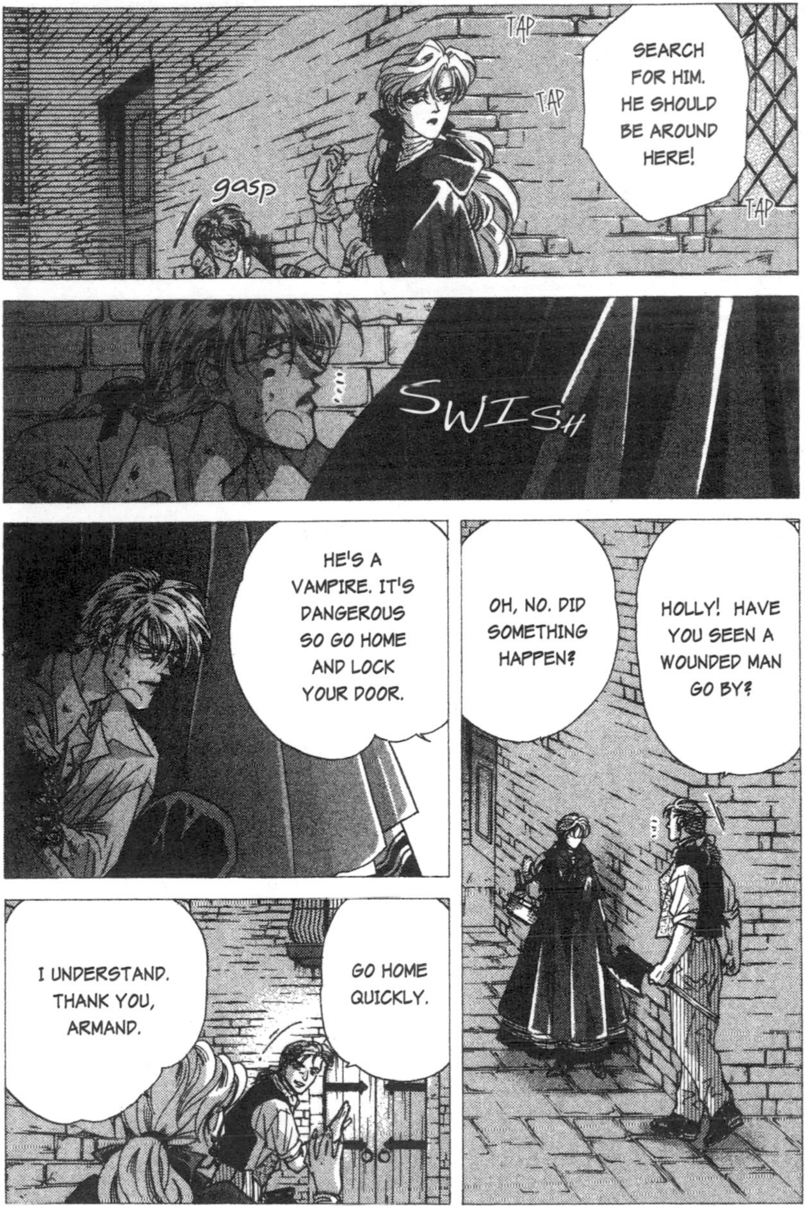
TAP
SEARCH FOR HIM. HE SHOULD BE AROUND HERE!
TAP
TAP
gasp
...
SWISH
HOLLY! HAVE YOU SEEN A WOUNDED MAN GO BY?
OH, NO. DID SOMETHING HAPPEN?
HE'S A VAMPIRE. IT'S DANGEROUS SO GO HOME AND LOCK YOUR DOOR.
GO HOME QUICKLY.
I UNDERSTAND. THANK YOU, ARMAND.

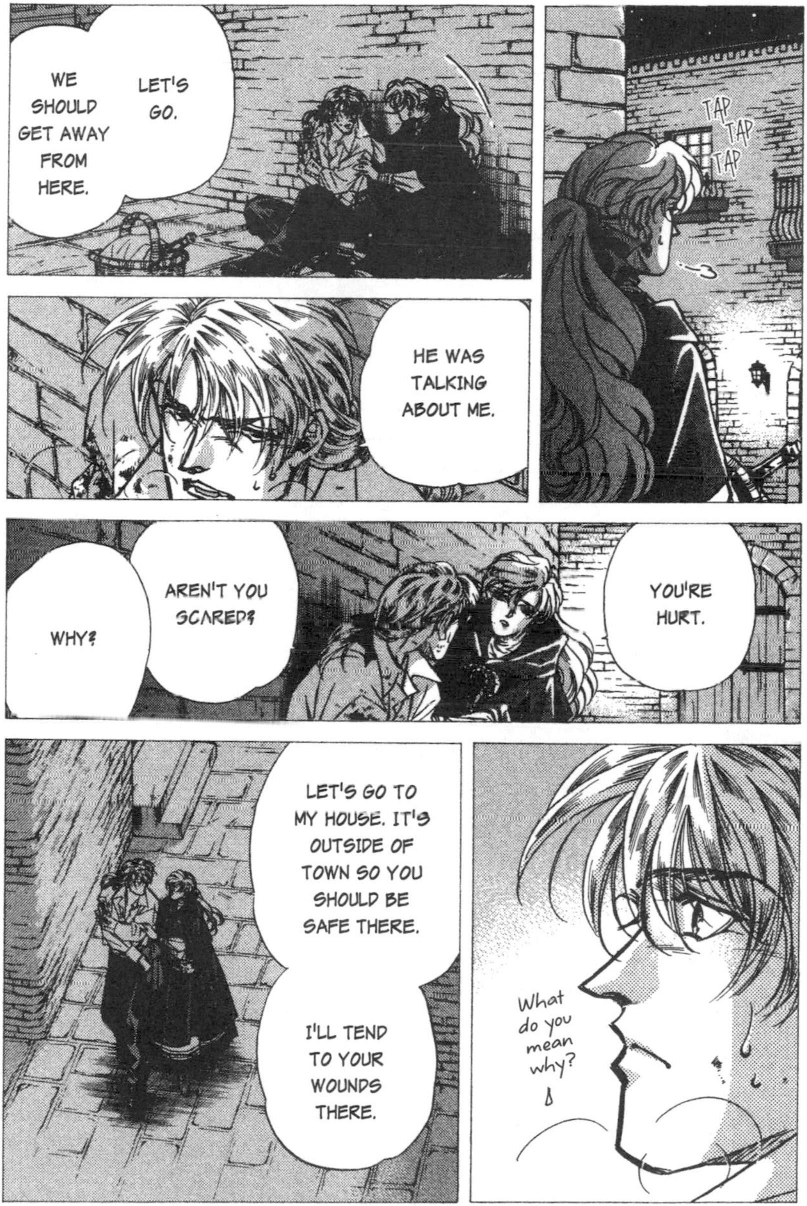
TAP TAP TAP
LET'S GO.
WE SHOULD GET AWAY FROM HERE.
HE WAS TALKING ABOUT ME.
YOU'RE HURT.
AREN'T YOU SCARED?
WHY?
What do you mean why?
LET'S GO TO MY HOUSE. IT'S OUTSIDE OF TOWN SO YOU SHOULD BE SAFE THERE.
I'LL TEND TO YOUR WOUNDS THERE.

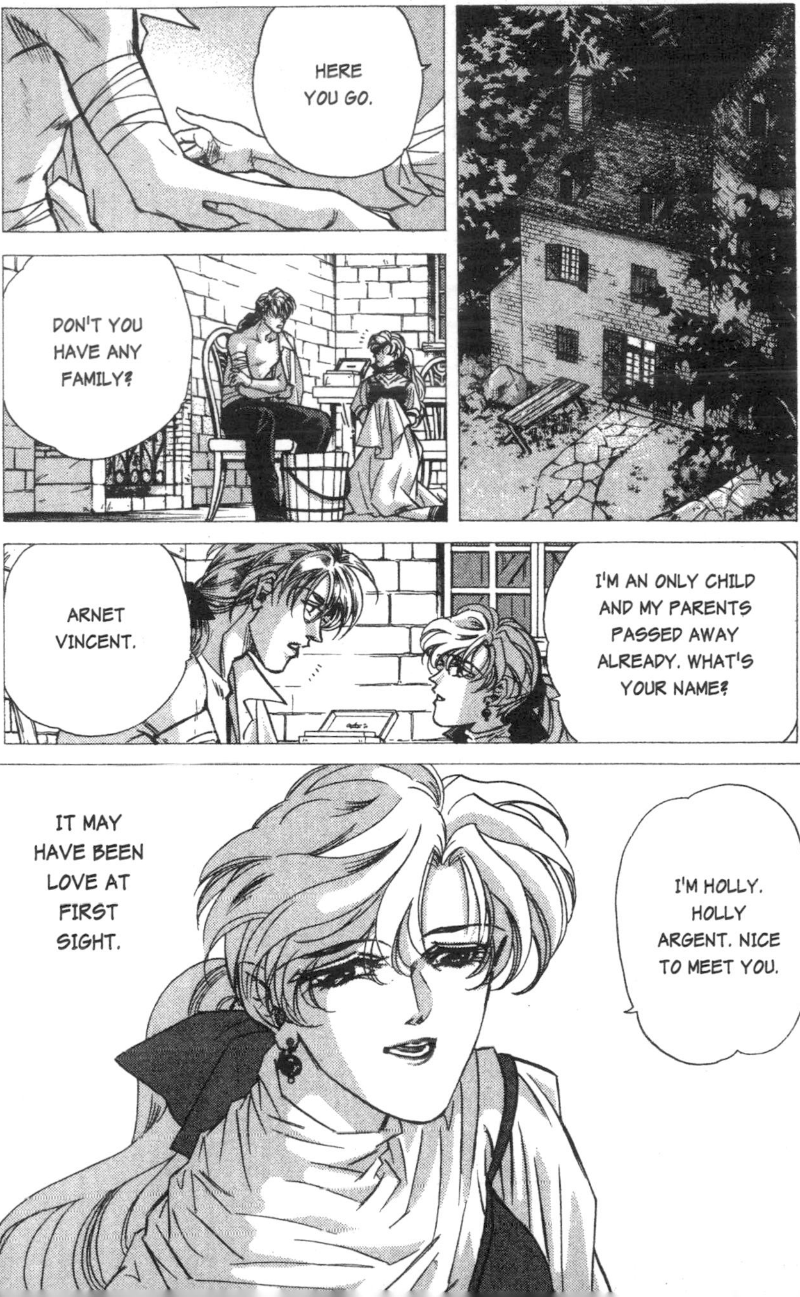
HERE YOU GO.
DON'T YOU HAVE ANY FAMILY?
I'M AN ONLY CHILD AND MY PARENTS PASSED AWAY ALREADY. WHAT'S YOUR NAME?
ARNET VINCENT.
I'M HOLLY. HOLLY ARGENT. NICE TO MEET YOU.
IT MAY HAVE BEEN LOVE AT FIRST SIGHT.

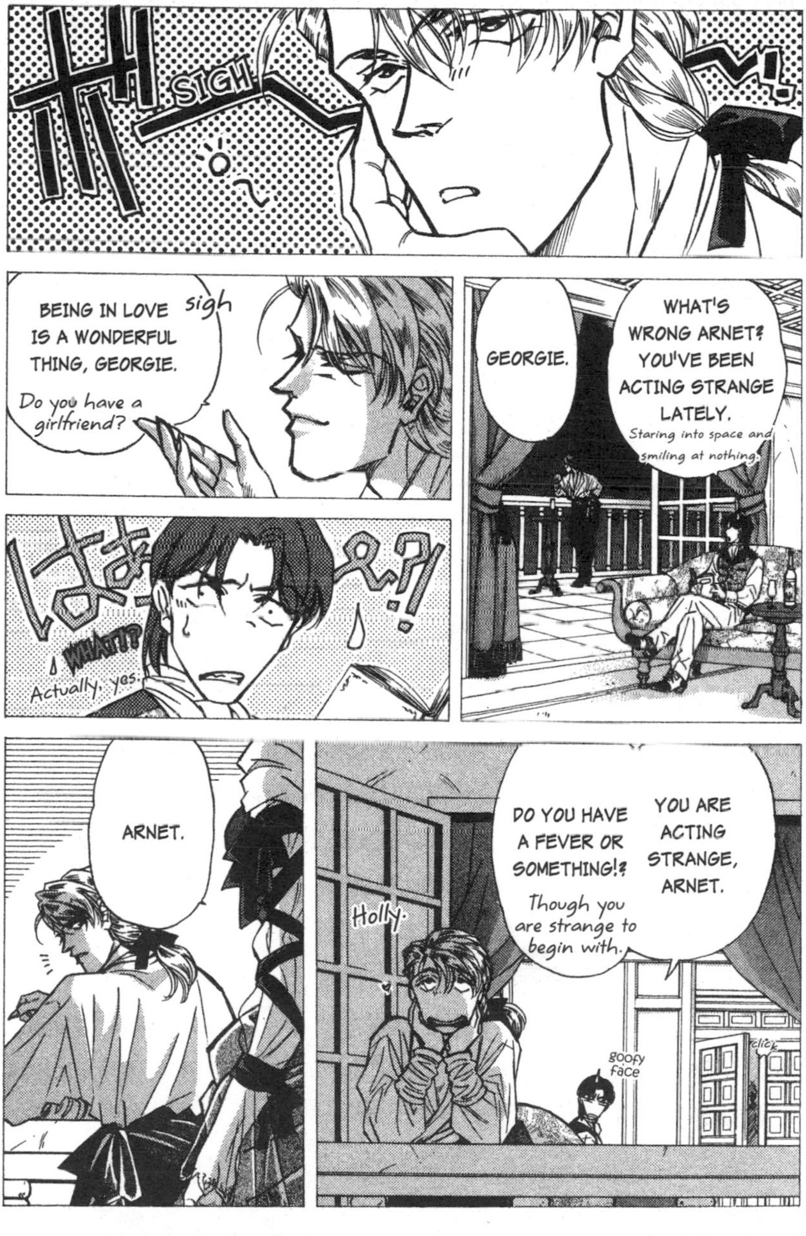
SIGH
WHAT'S WRONG ARNET? YOU'VE BEEN ACTING STRANGE LATELY.
Staring into space and smiling at nothing.
GEORGIE.
BEING IN LOVE IS A WONDERFUL THING, GEORGIE.
sigh
Do you have a girlfriend?
WHAT!?
Actually, yes.
YOU ARE ACTING STRANGE, ARNET.
DO YOU HAVE A FEVER OR SOMETHING!?
Though you are strange to begin with.
Holly.
click
goofy face
ARNET.

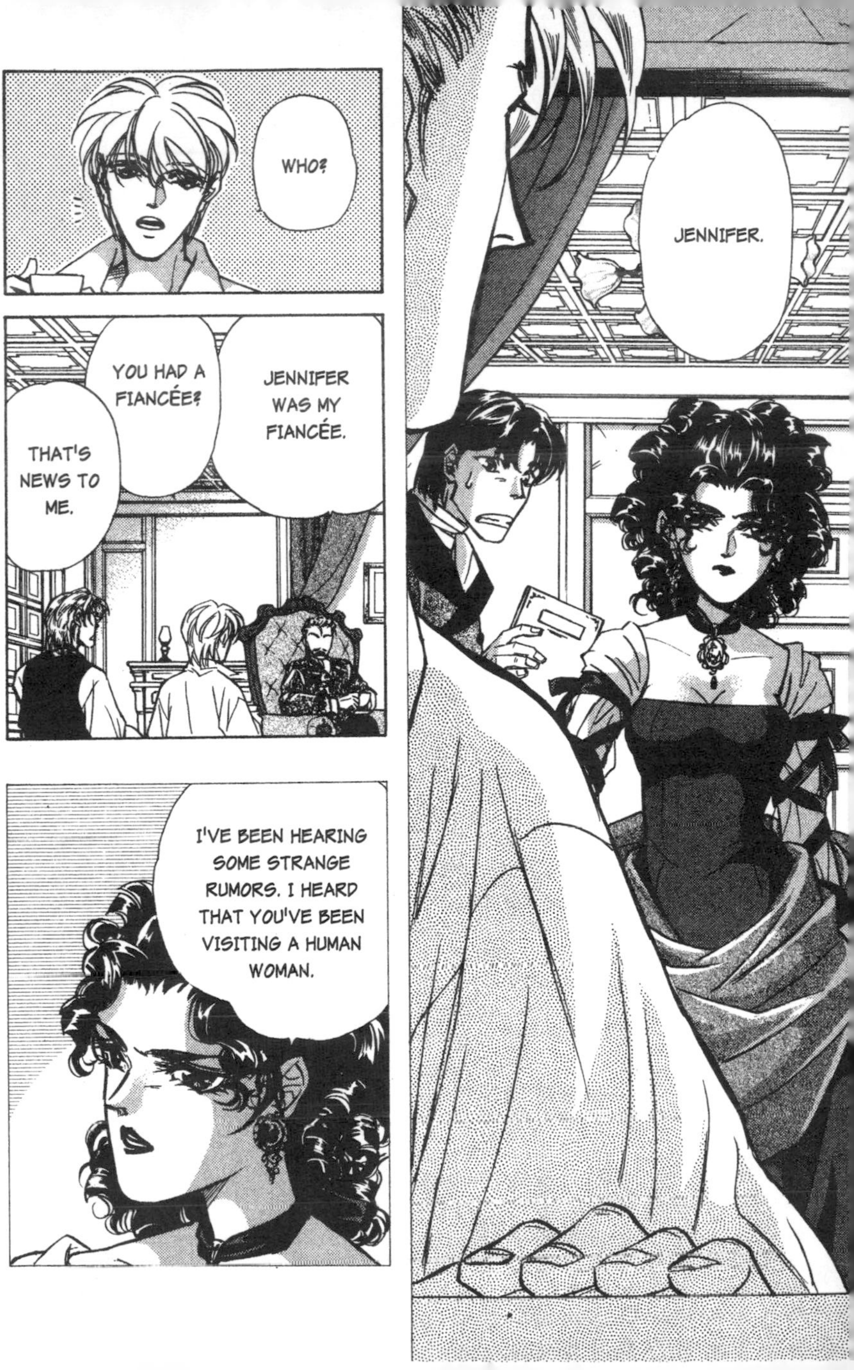
JENNIFER.
WHO?
JENNIFER WAS MY FIANCÉE.
YOU HAD A FIANCÉE?
THAT'S NEWS TO ME.
I'VE BEEN HEARING SOME STRANGE RUMORS. I HEARD THAT YOU'VE BEEN VISITING A HUMAN WOMAN.

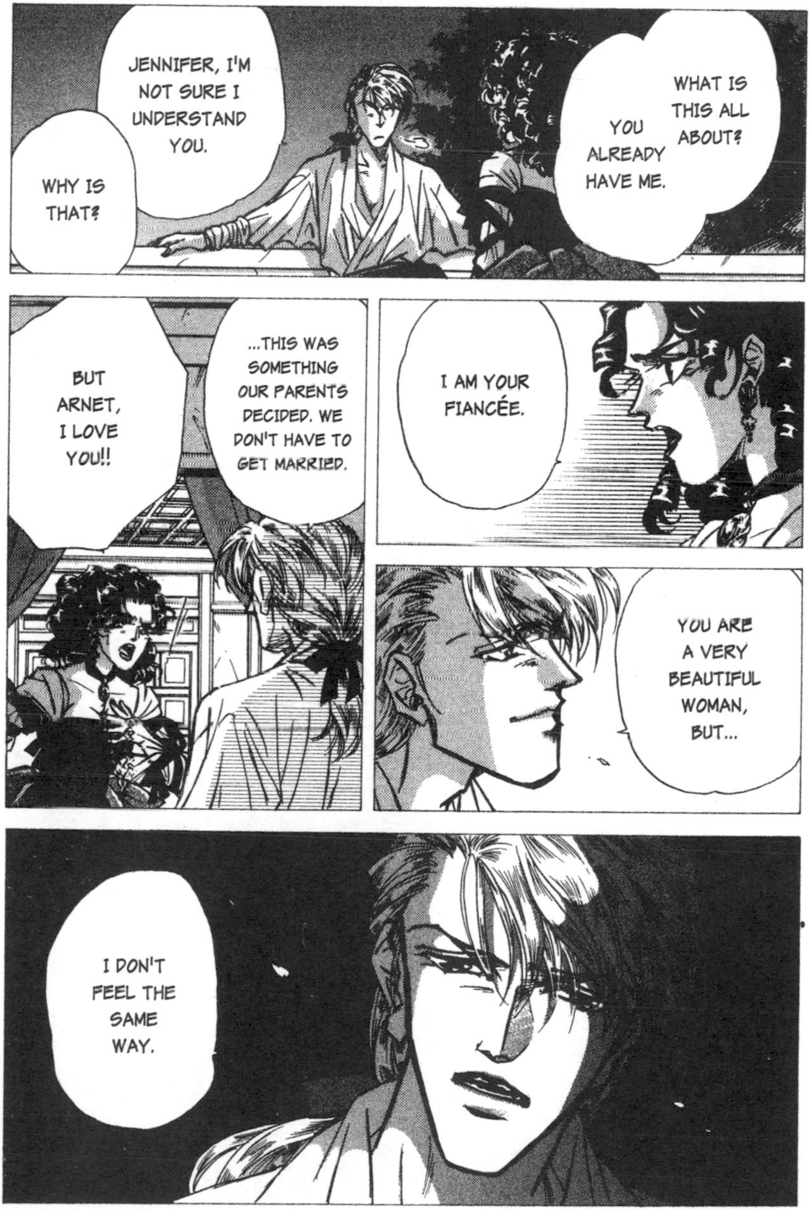
WHAT IS THIS ALL ABOUT?
YOU ALREADY HAVE ME.
JENNIFER, I'M NOT SURE I UNDERSTAND YOU.
WHY IS THAT?
I AM YOUR FIANCÉE.
YOU ARE A VERY BEAUTIFUL WOMAN, BUT...
...THIS WAS SOMETHING OUR PARENTS DECIDED. WE DON'T HAVE TO GET MARRIED.
BUT ARNET, I LOVE YOU!!
I DON'T FEEL THE SAME WAY.

ARNET?
I'M SORRY, JENNIFER.
sniffle
I'LL REMEMBER THIS, ARNET. I'LL MAKE YOU REGRET HURTING ME LIKE THIS!!
DID SHE?
NO, I HAVEN'T SEEN HER SINCE.
WHAT? THAT'S SO COLD-HEARTED.
Cruel.
That wasn't the best way to deal with it.
I TRIED TO SEE HER AGAIN, BUT SHE DIDN'T WANT TO SEE ME.
I felt bad.
THAT ISN'T GOOD.
RATHER HEARTLESS, FATHER.
THAT DOESN'T MATTER NOW. ARE YOU GOING TO LISTEN OR NOT?
Shut up.

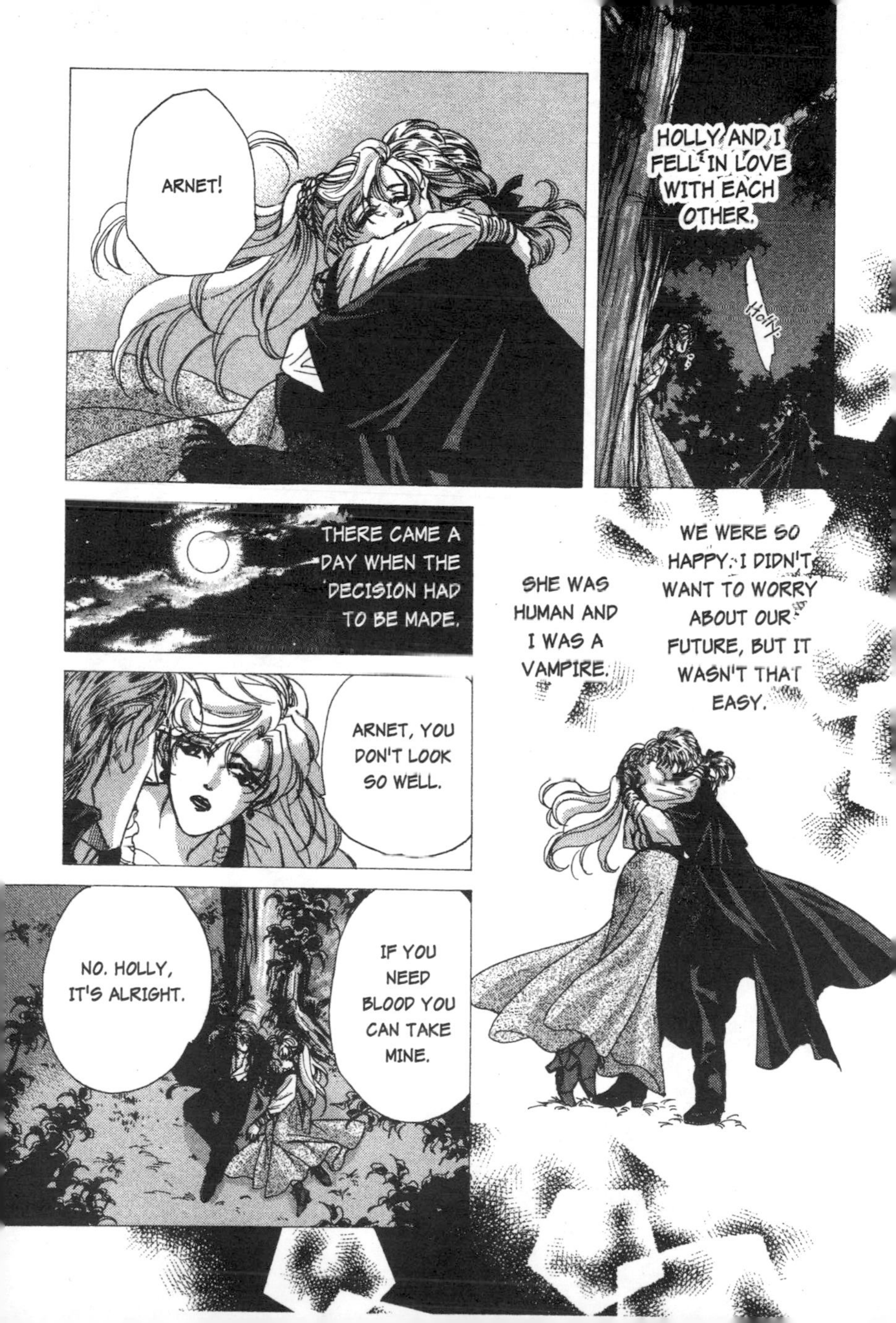
HOLLY AND I FELL IN LOVE WITH EACH OTHER.
Holly
ARNET!
WE WERE SO HAPPY. I DIDN'T WANT TO WORRY ABOUT OUR FUTURE, BUT IT WASN'T THAT EASY.
SHE WAS HUMAN AND I WAS A VAMPIRE.
THERE CAME A DAY WHEN THE DECISION HAD TO BE MADE.
ARNET, YOU DON'T LOOK SO WELL.
IF YOU NEED BLOOD YOU CAN TAKE MINE.
NO. HOLLY, IT'S ALRIGHT.

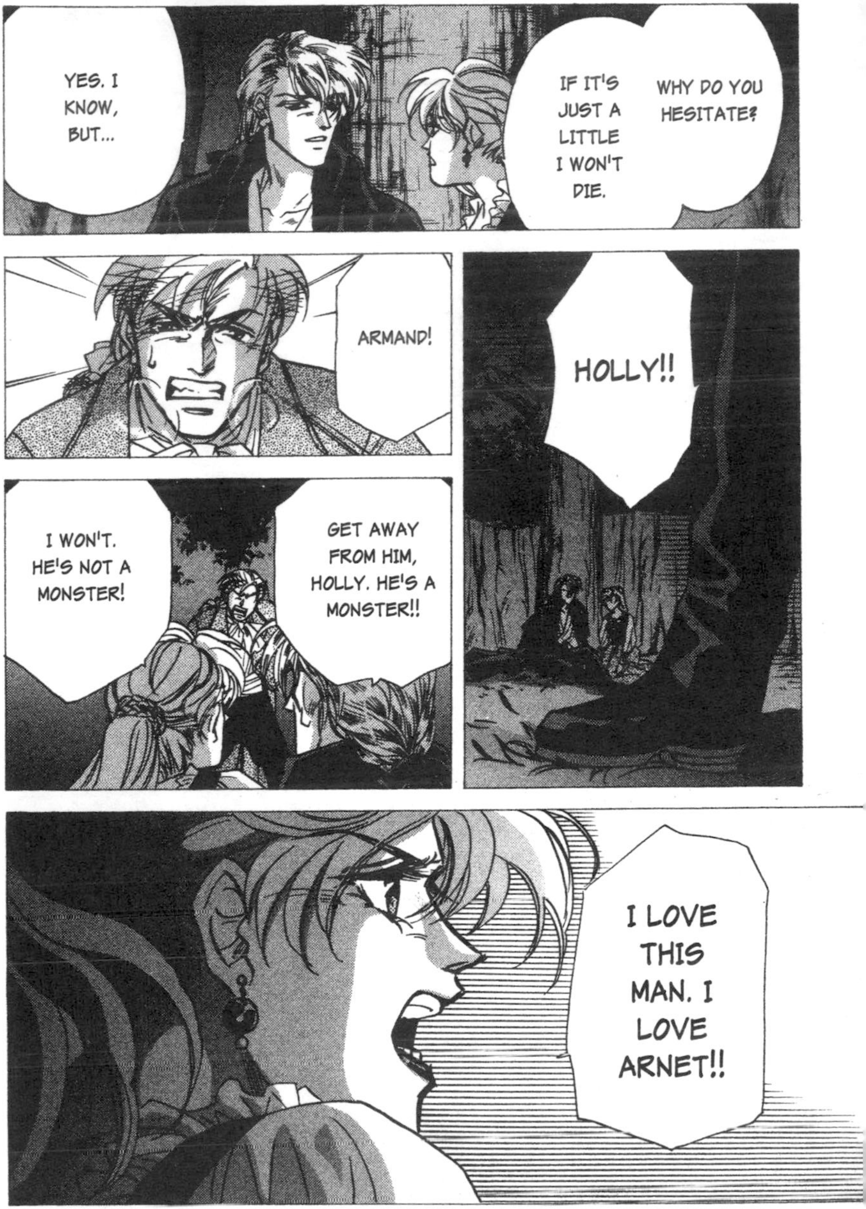
WHY DO YOU HESITATE?
IF IT'S JUST A LITTLE I WON'T DIE.
YES. I KNOW, BUT...
HOLLY!!
ARMAND!
GET AWAY FROM HIM, HOLLY. HE'S A MONSTER!!
I WON'T. HE'S NOT A MONSTER!
I LOVE THIS MAN. I LOVE ARNET!!

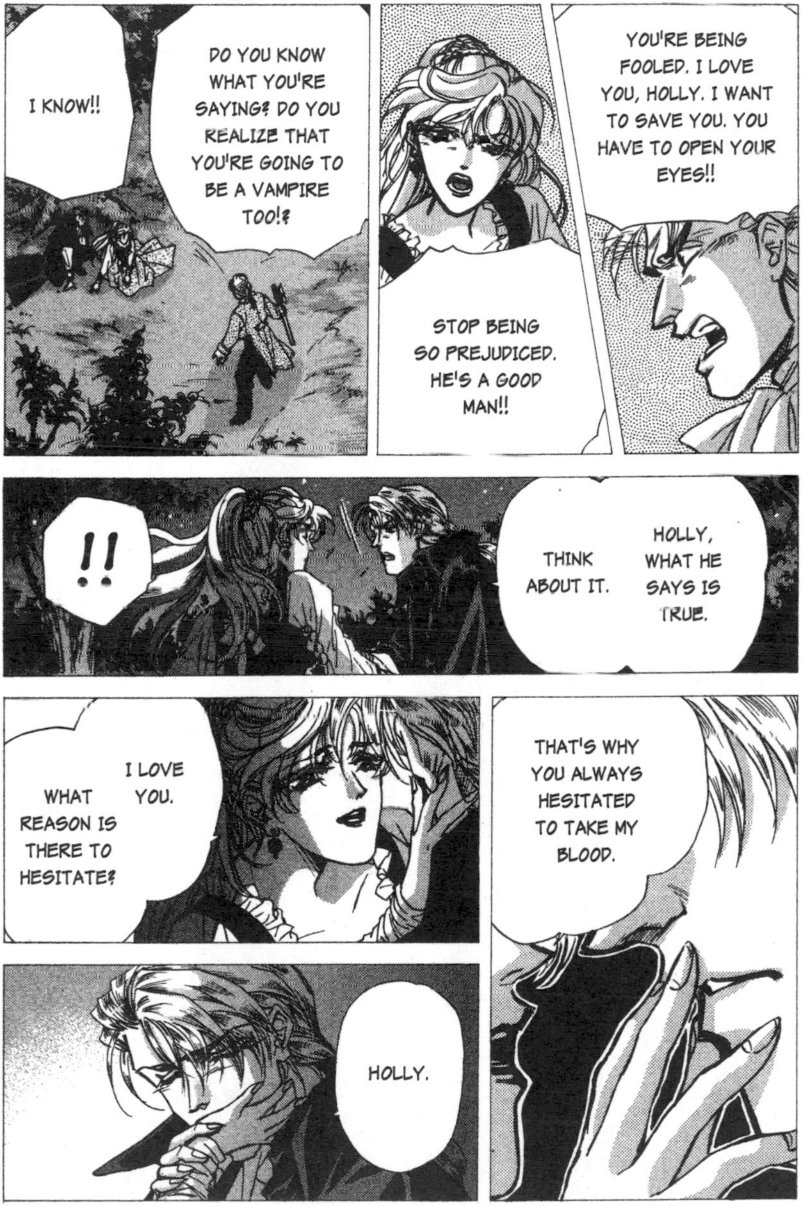
YOU'RE BEING FOOLED. I LOVE YOU, HOLLY. I WANT TO SAVE YOU. YOU HAVE TO OPEN YOUR EYES!!
STOP BEING SO PREJUDICED. HE'S A GOOD MAN!!
DO YOU KNOW WHAT YOU'RE SAYING? DO YOU REALIZE THAT YOU'RE GOING TO BE A VAMPIRE TOO!?
I KNOW!!
HOLLY, WHAT HE SAYS IS TRUE.
THINK ABOUT IT.
!!
THAT'S WHY YOU ALWAYS HESITATED TO TAKE MY BLOOD.
I LOVE YOU.
WHAT REASON IS THERE TO HESITATE?
HOLLY.

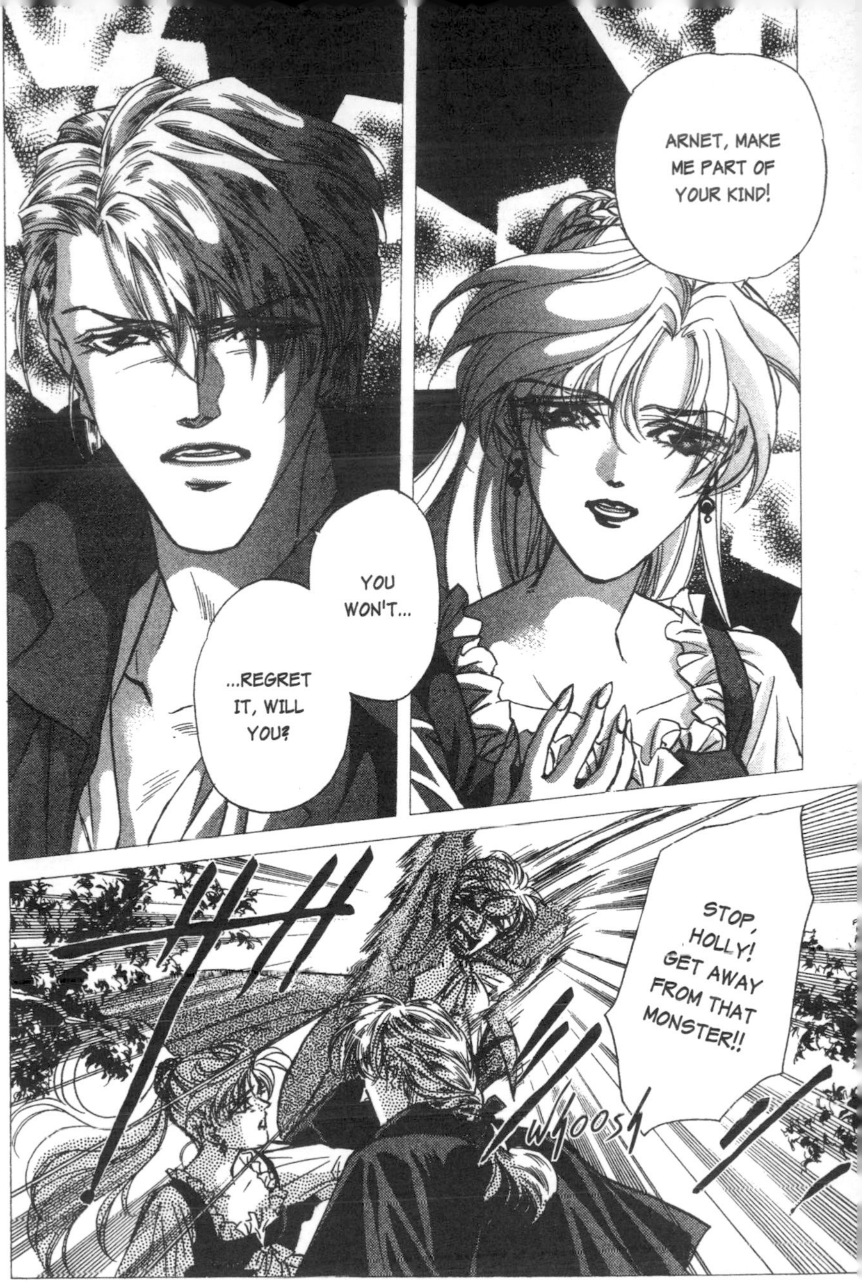
ARNET, MAKE ME PART OF YOUR KIND!
YOU WON'T...
...REGRET IT, WILL YOU?
STOP, HOLLY! GET AWAY FROM THAT MONSTER!!
WHOOSH

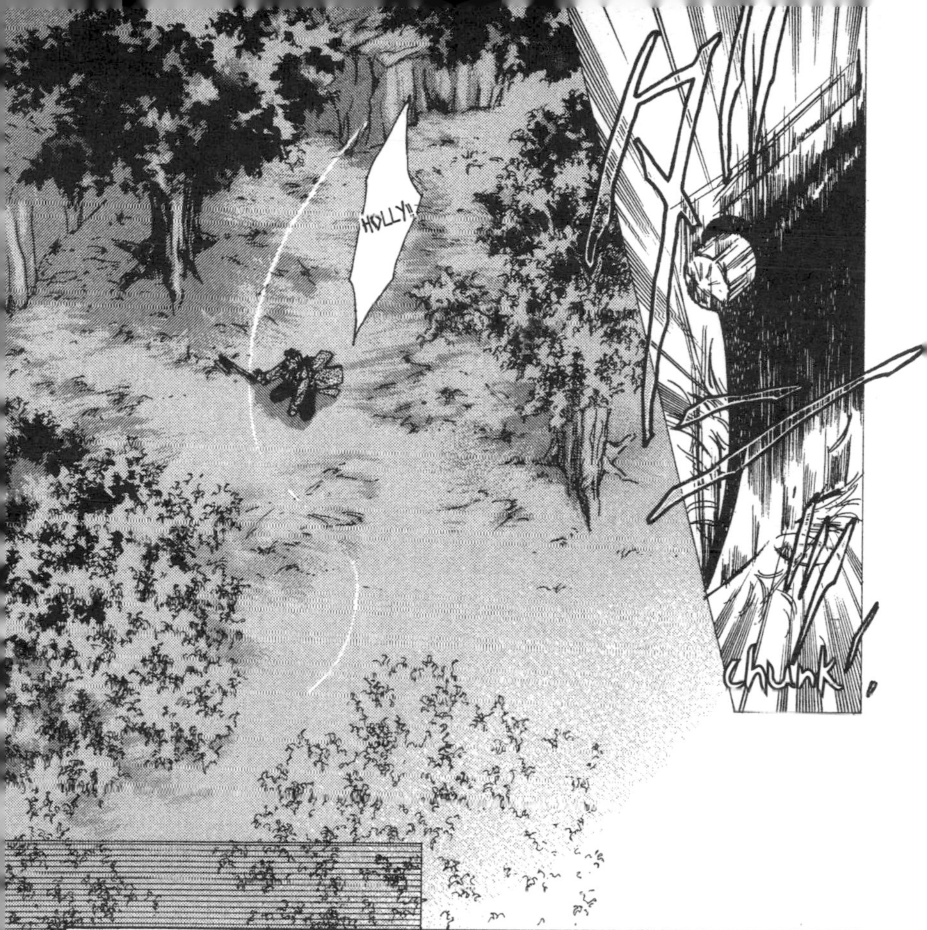

chunk!
HOLLY!!

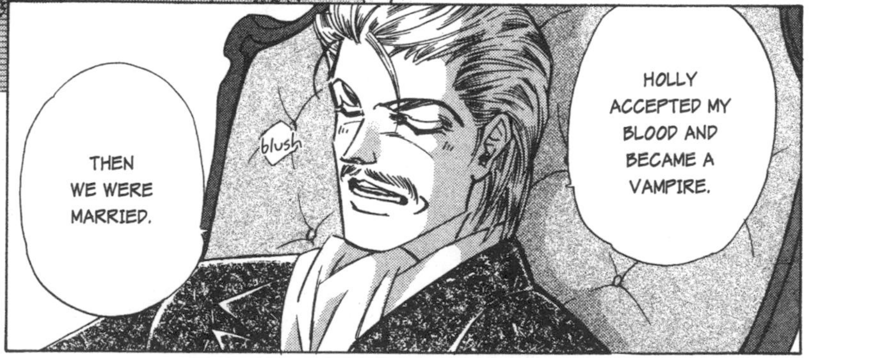

HOLLY ACCEPTED MY BLOOD AND BECAME A VAMPIRE.
blush
THEN WE WERE MARRIED.

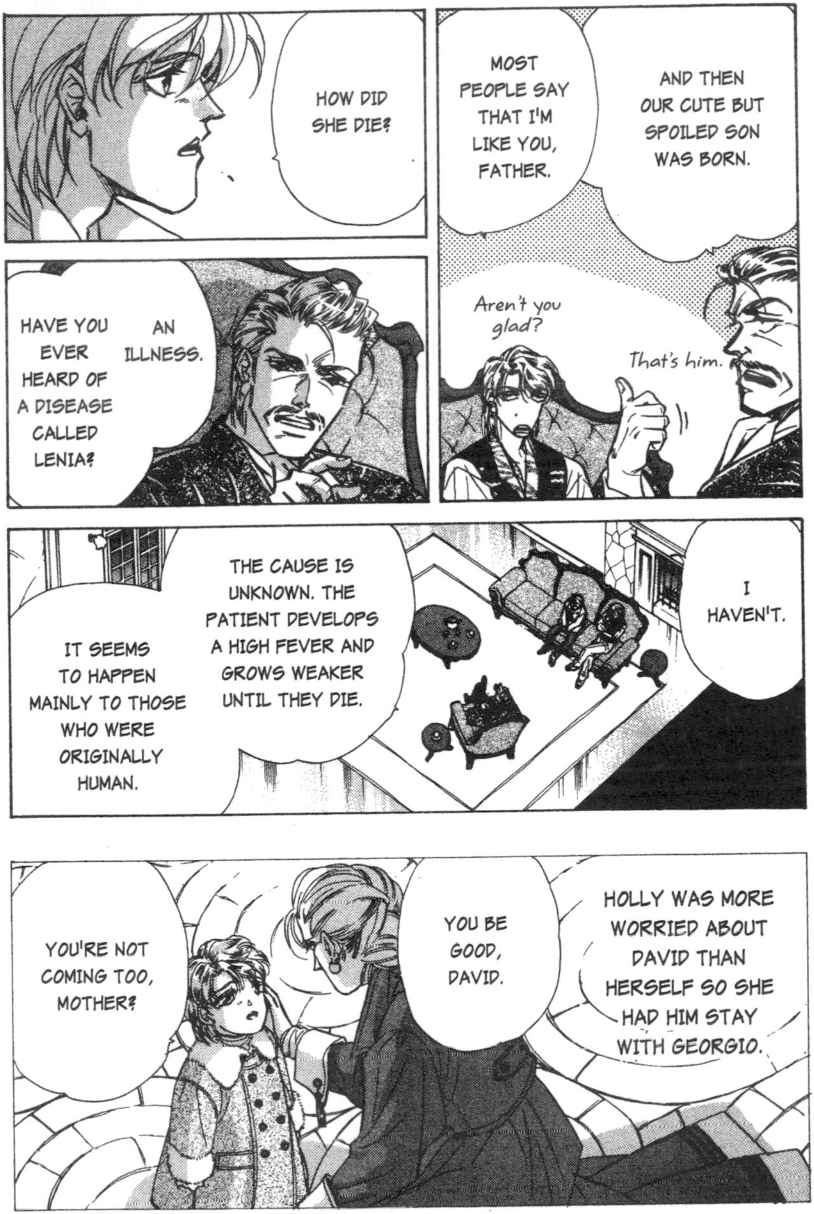
AND THEN OUR CUTE BUT SPOILED SON WAS BORN.
MOST PEOPLE SAY THAT I'M LIKE YOU, FATHER.
That's him.
Aren't you glad?
HOW DID SHE DIE?
AN ILLNESS.
HAVE YOU EVER HEARD OF A DISEASE CALLED LENIA?
I HAVEN'T.
THE CAUSE IS UNKNOWN. THE PATIENT DEVELOPS A HIGH FEVER AND GROWS WEAKER UNTIL THEY DIE.
IT SEEMS TO HAPPEN MAINLY TO THOSE WHO WERE ORIGINALLY HUMAN.
HOLLY WAS MORE WORRIED ABOUT DAVID THAN HERSELF SO SHE HAD HIM STAY WITH GEORGIO.
YOU BE GOOD, DAVID.
YOU'RE NOT COMING TOO, MOTHER?

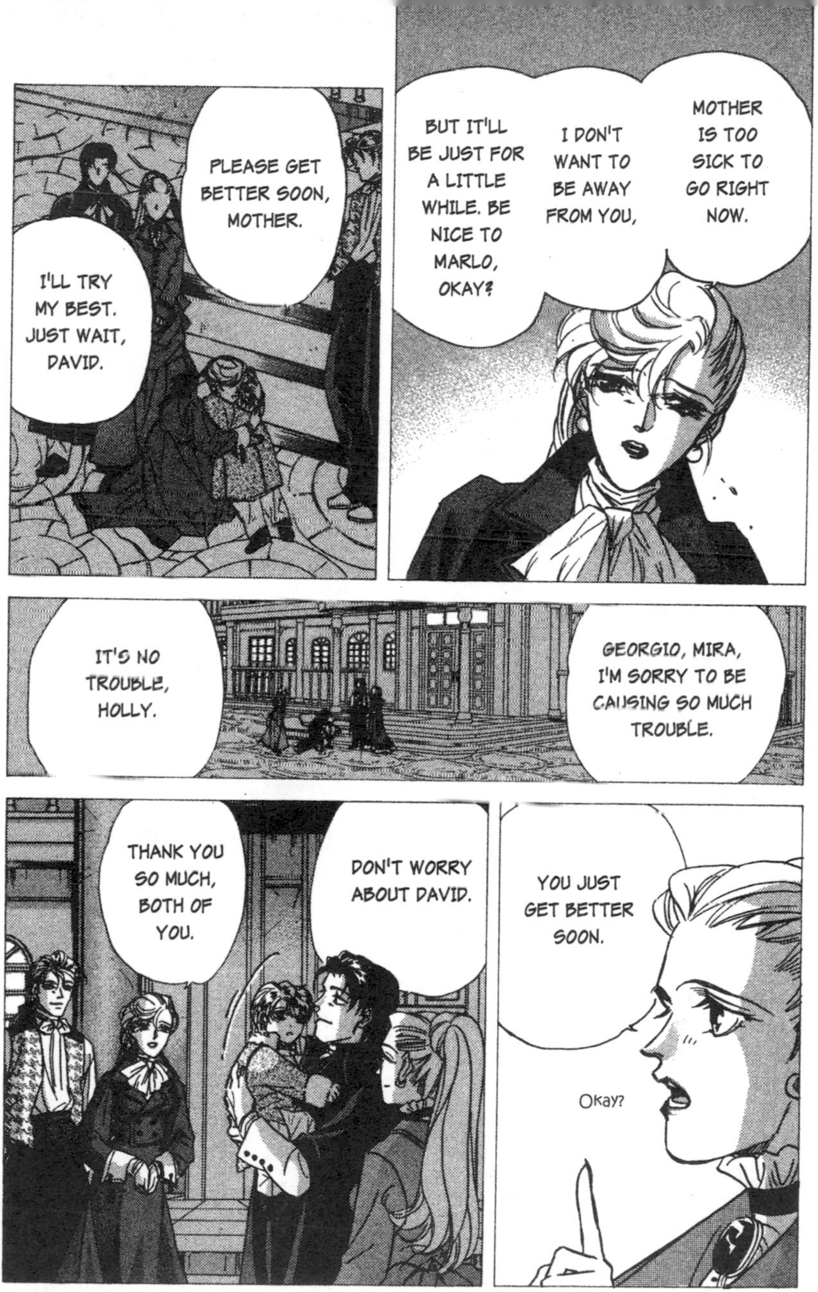
MOTHER IS TOO SICK TO GO RIGHT NOW.
I DON'T WANT TO BE AWAY FROM YOU,
BUT IT'LL BE JUST FOR A LITTLE WHILE. BE NICE TO MARLO, OKAY?
PLEASE GET BETTER SOON, MOTHER.
I'LL TRY MY BEST. JUST WAIT, DAVID.
GEORGIO, MIRA, I'M SORRY TO BE CAUSING SO MUCH TROUBLE.
IT'S NO TROUBLE, HOLLY.
YOU JUST GET BETTER SOON.
Okay?
DON'T WORRY ABOUT DAVID.
THANK YOU SO MUCH, BOTH OF YOU.

Madam Mira when she was younger.

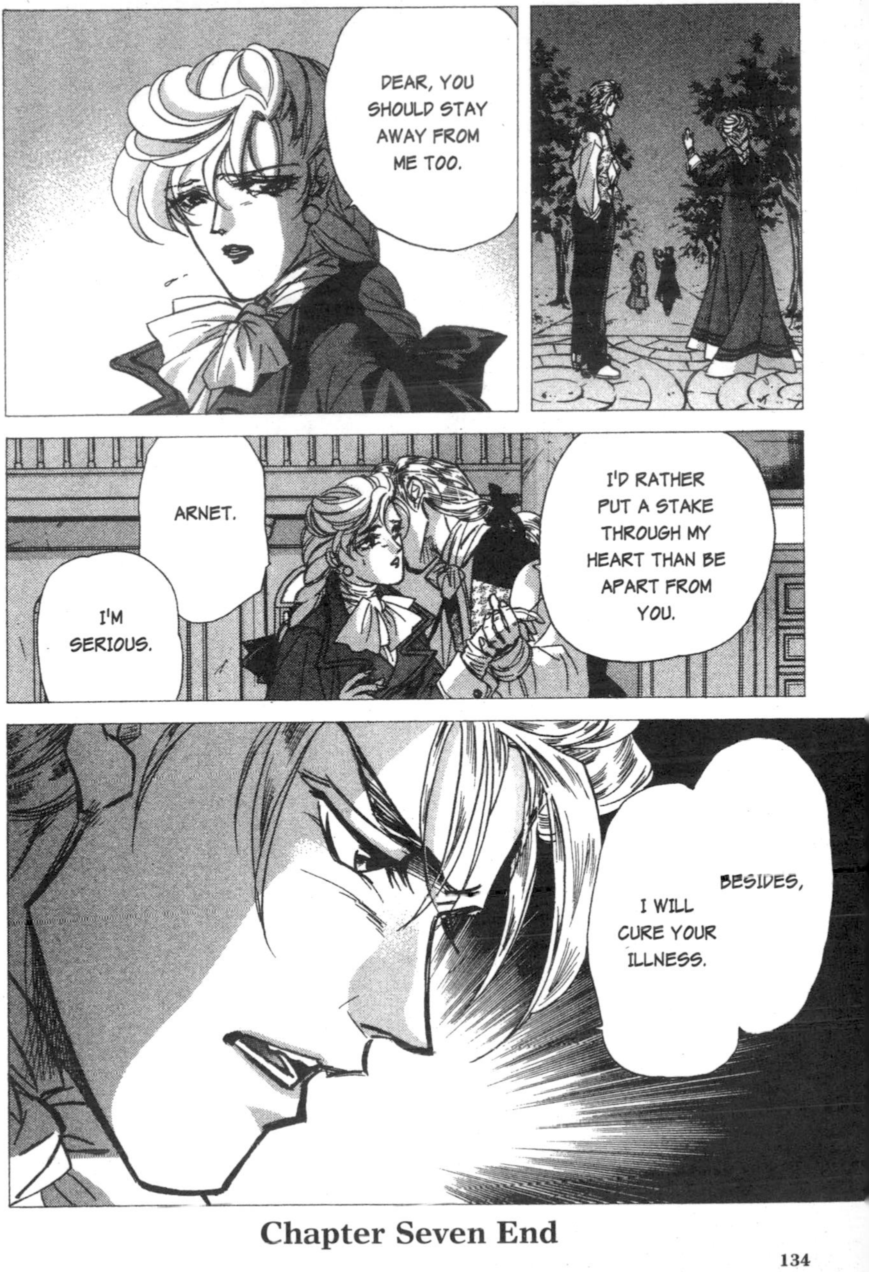
DEAR, YOU SHOULD STAY AWAY FROM ME TOO.
I'D RATHER PUT A STAKE THROUGH MY HEART THAN BE APART FROM YOU.
ARNET.
I'M SERIOUS.
BESIDES, I WILL CURE YOUR ILLNESS.

Chapter Seven End

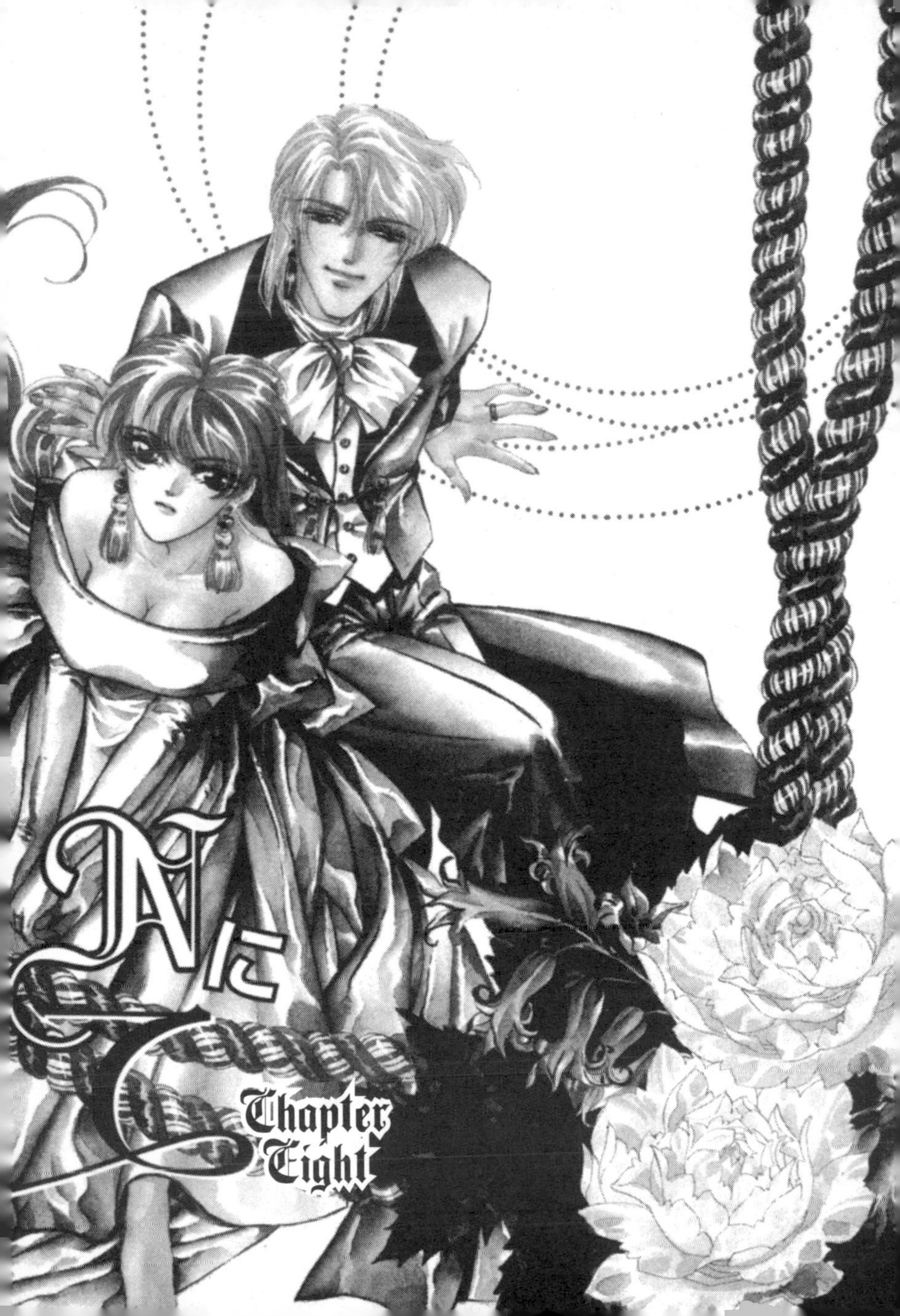
Nに
Chapter Eight

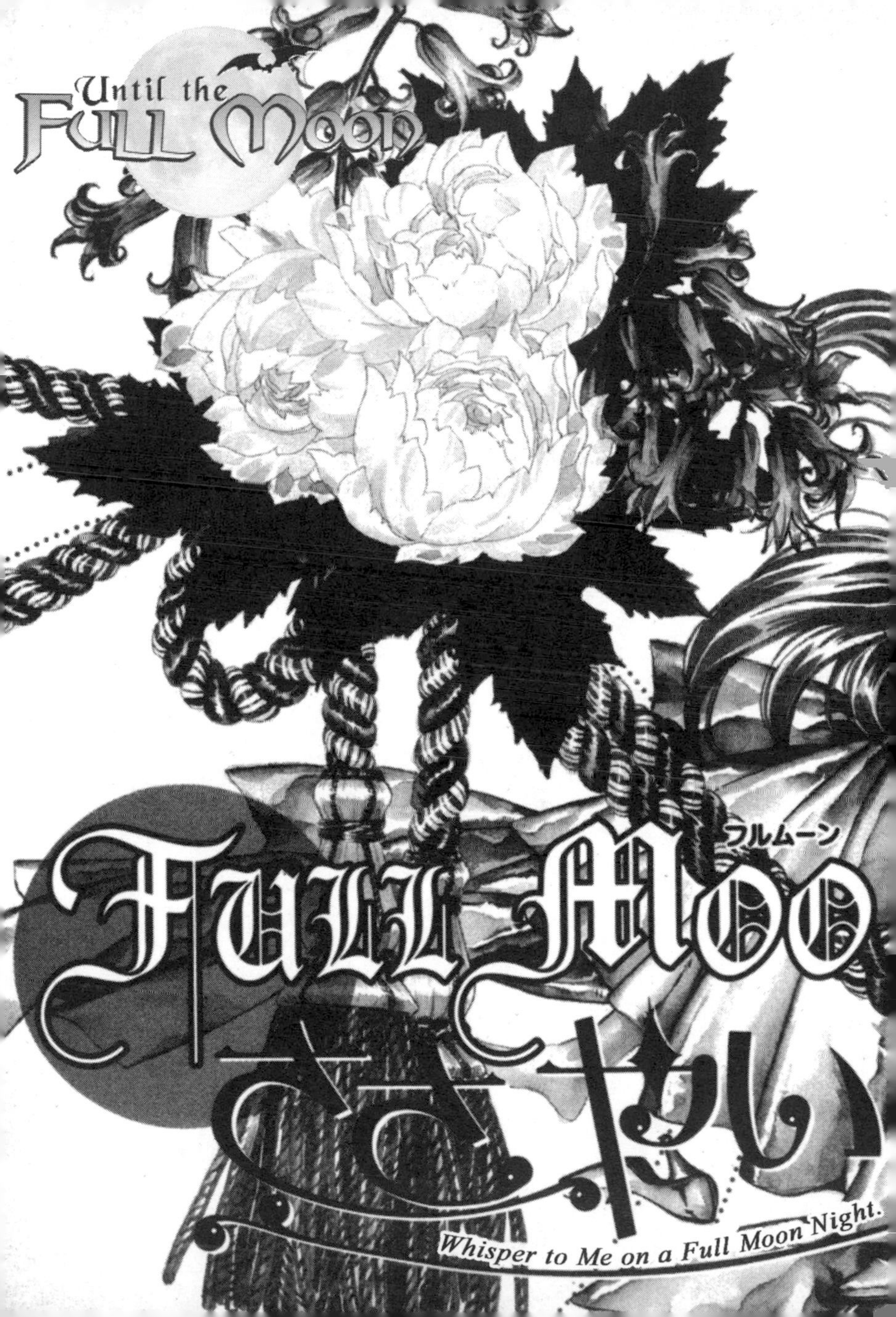
Until the Full Moon
フルムーン
FULL MOO
Whisper to Me on a Full Moon Night.

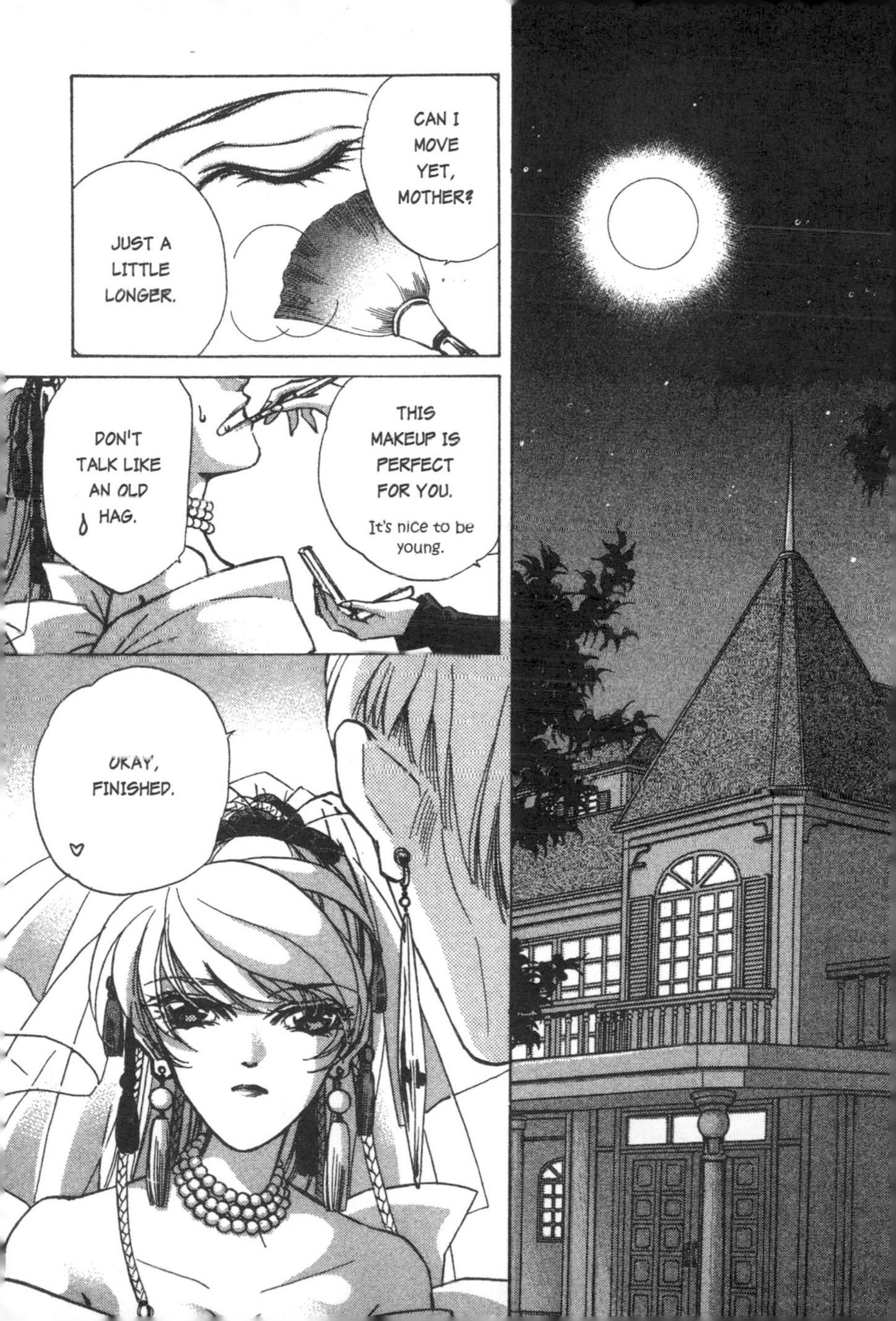
CAN I MOVE YET, MOTHER?
JUST A LITTLE LONGER.
THIS MAKEUP IS PERFECT FOR YOU.
It's nice to be young.
DON'T TALK LIKE AN OLD HAG.
OKAY, FINISHED.

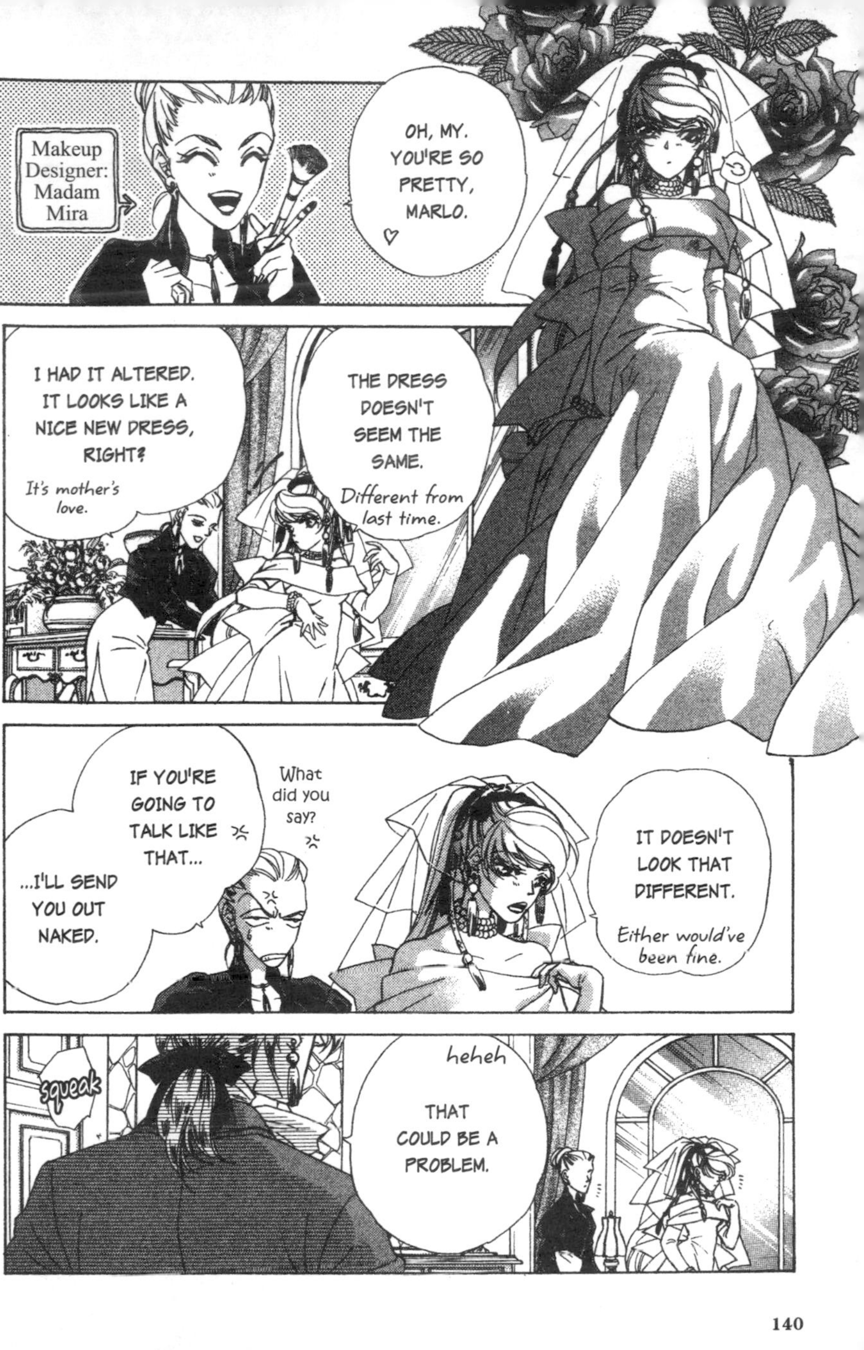
OH, MY. YOU'RE SO PRETTY, MARLO. ♡
Makeup Designer: Madam Mira
THE DRESS DOESN'T SEEM THE SAME.
Different from last time.
I HAD IT ALTERED. IT LOOKS LIKE A NICE NEW DRESS, RIGHT?
It's mother's love.
IT DOESN'T LOOK THAT DIFFERENT.
Either would've been fine.
What did you say?
IF YOU'RE GOING TO TALK LIKE THAT...
...I'LL SEND YOU OUT NAKED.
heheh
THAT COULD BE A PROBLEM.
squeak

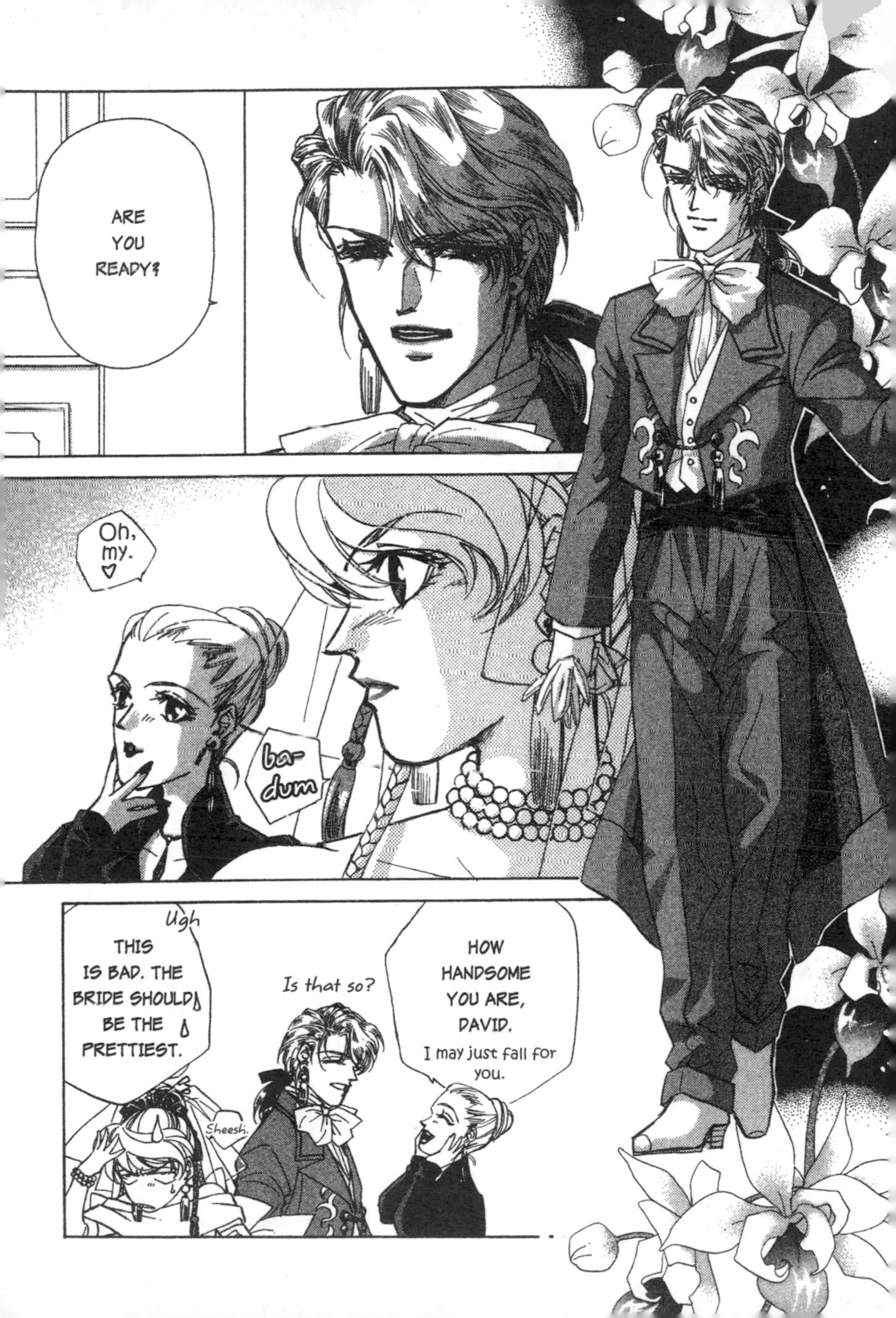
ARE YOU READY?
Oh, my. ♡
ba-dum
HOW HANDSOME YOU ARE, DAVID.
I may just fall for you.
Is that so?
Ugh
THIS IS BAD. THE BRIDE SHOULD BE THE PRETTIEST.
Sheesh.

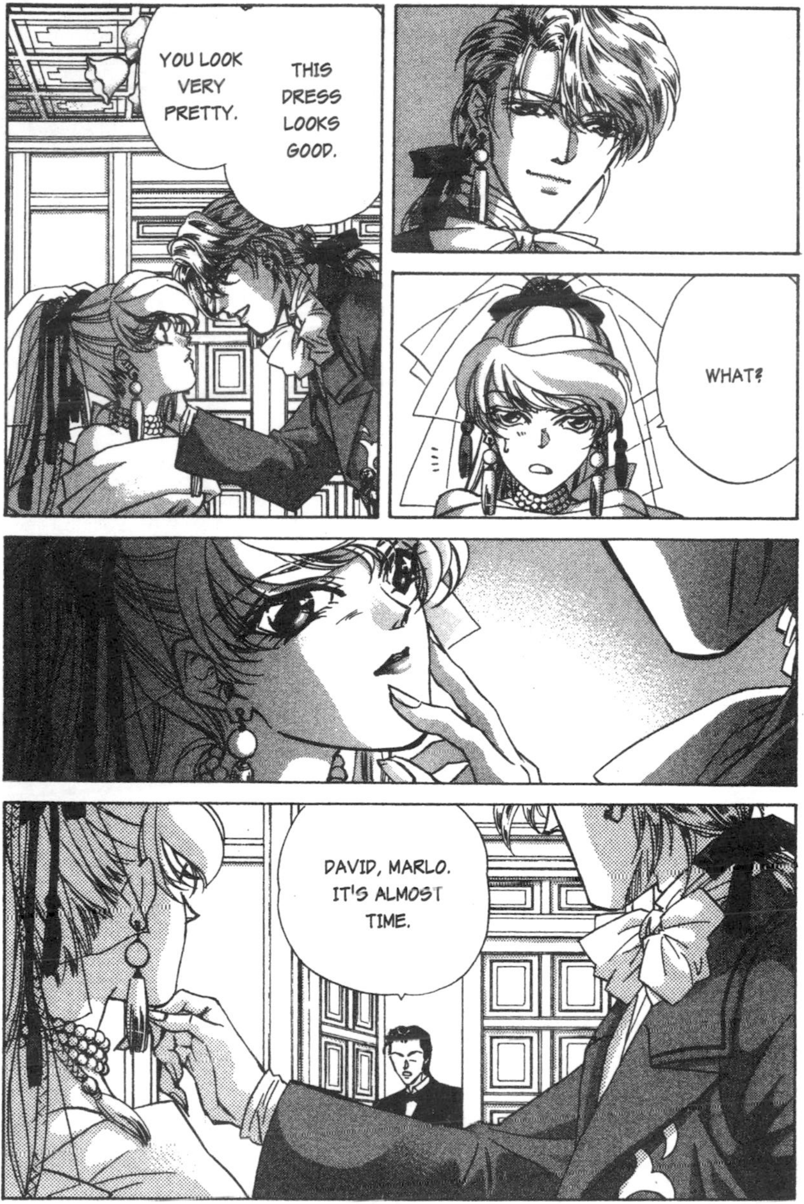
WHAT?
YOU LOOK VERY PRETTY.
THIS DRESS LOOKS GOOD.
DAVID, MARLO. IT'S ALMOST TIME.

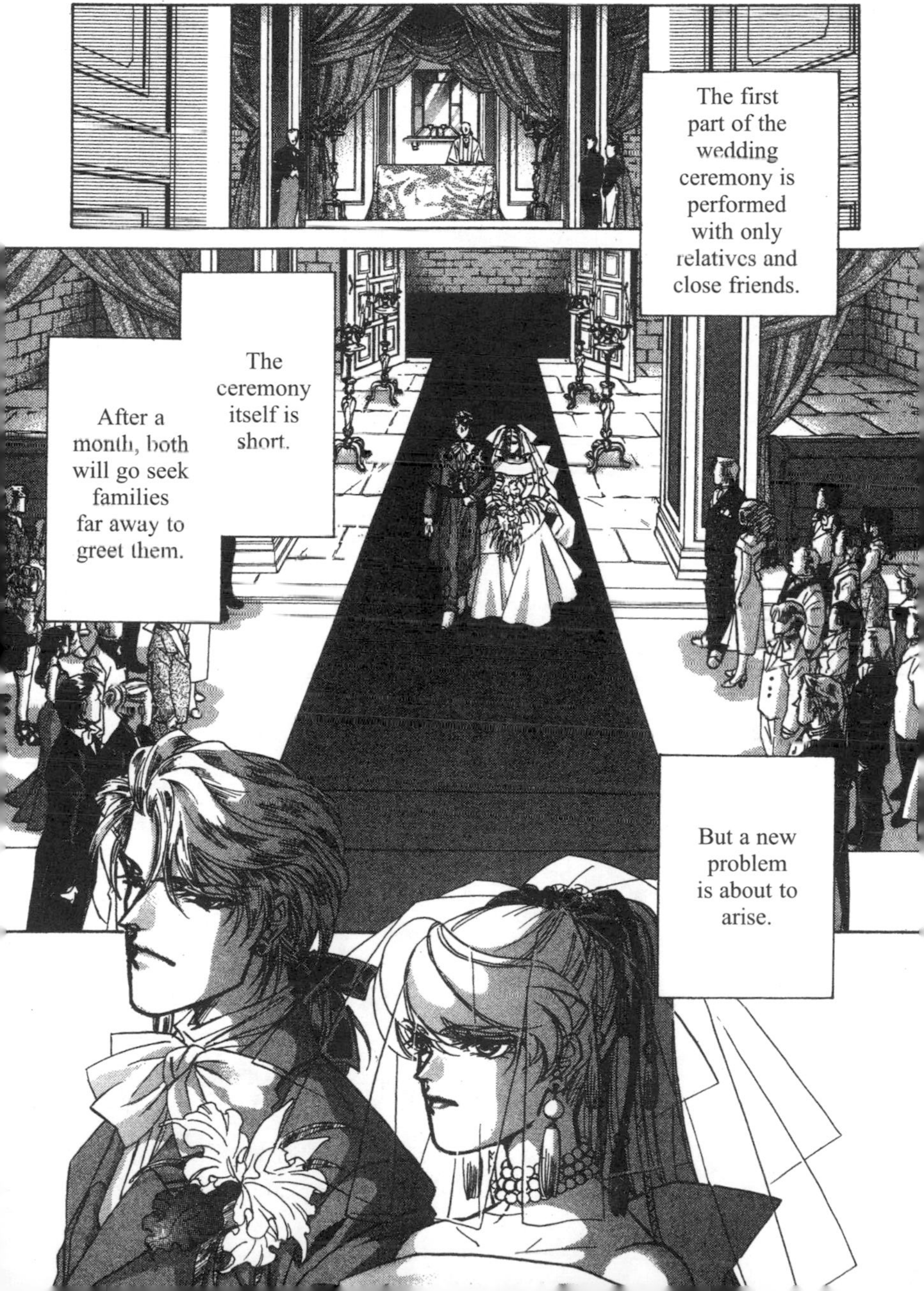
The first part of the wedding ceremony is performed with only relatives and close friends.
The ceremony itself is short.
After a month, both will go seek families far away to greet them.
But a new problem is about to arise.

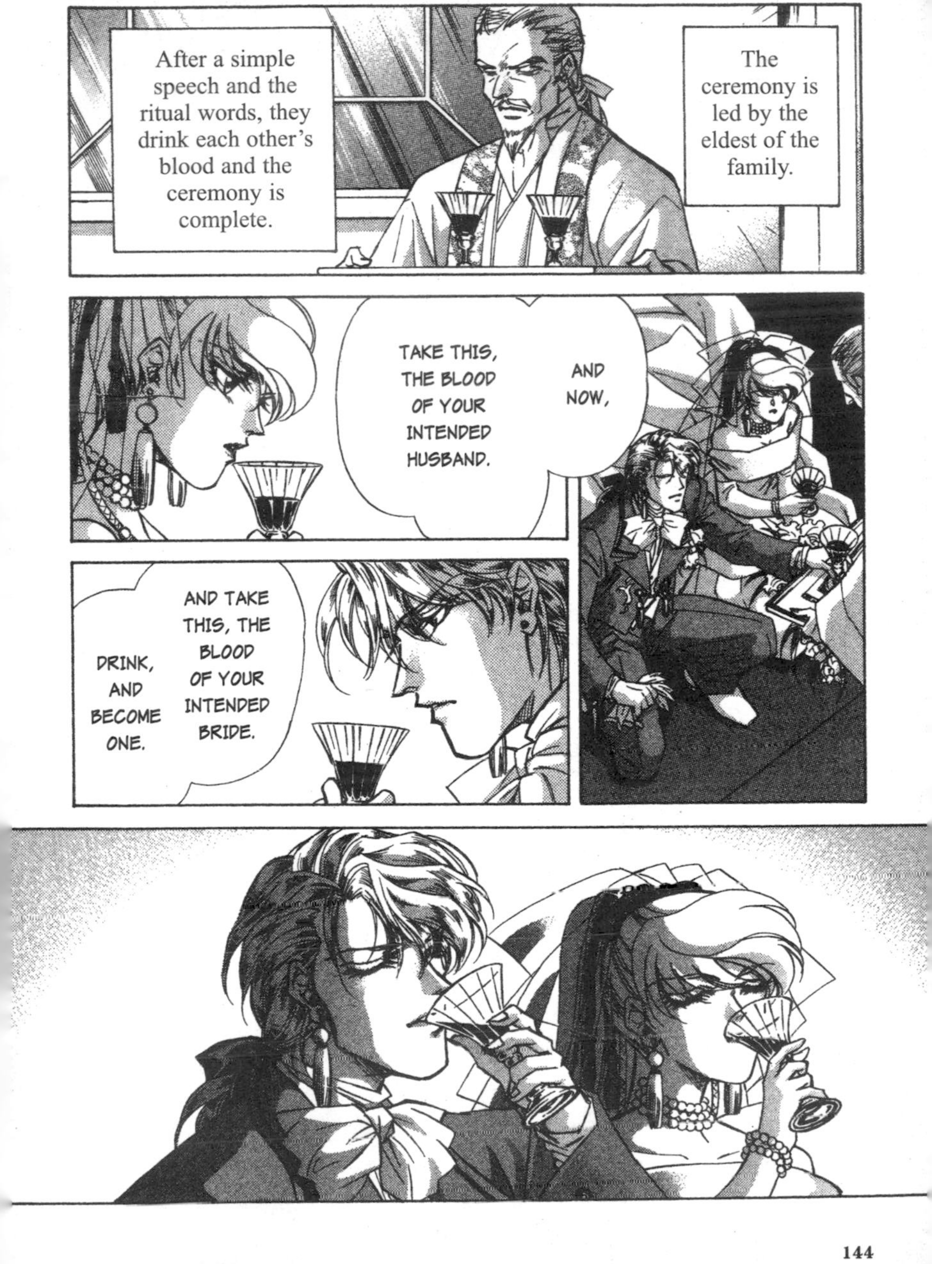

The ceremony is led by the eldest of the family.
After a simple speech and the ritual words, they drink each other's blood and the ceremony is complete.
AND NOW,
TAKE THIS, THE BLOOD OF YOUR INTENDED HUSBAND.
AND TAKE THIS, THE BLOOD OF YOUR INTENDED BRIDE.
DRINK, AND BECOME ONE.

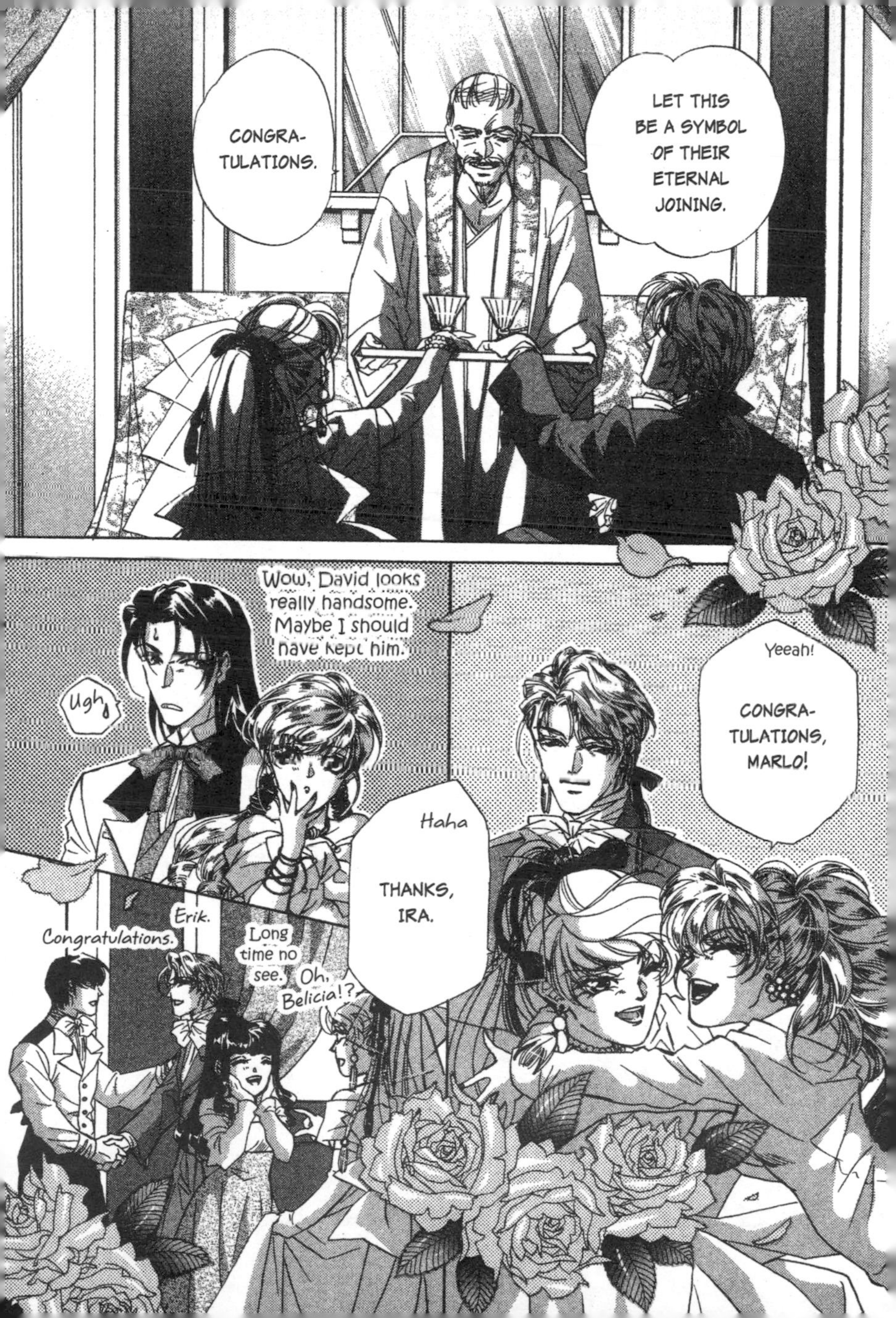
LET THIS BE A SYMBOL OF THEIR ETERNAL JOINING.
CONGRA-TULATIONS.
Yeeah!
CONGRA-TULATIONS, MARLO!
Wow, David looks really handsome. Maybe I should have kept him.
Ugh
Haha
THANKS, IRA.
Long time no see.
Oh, Belicia!?
Erik.
Congratulations.

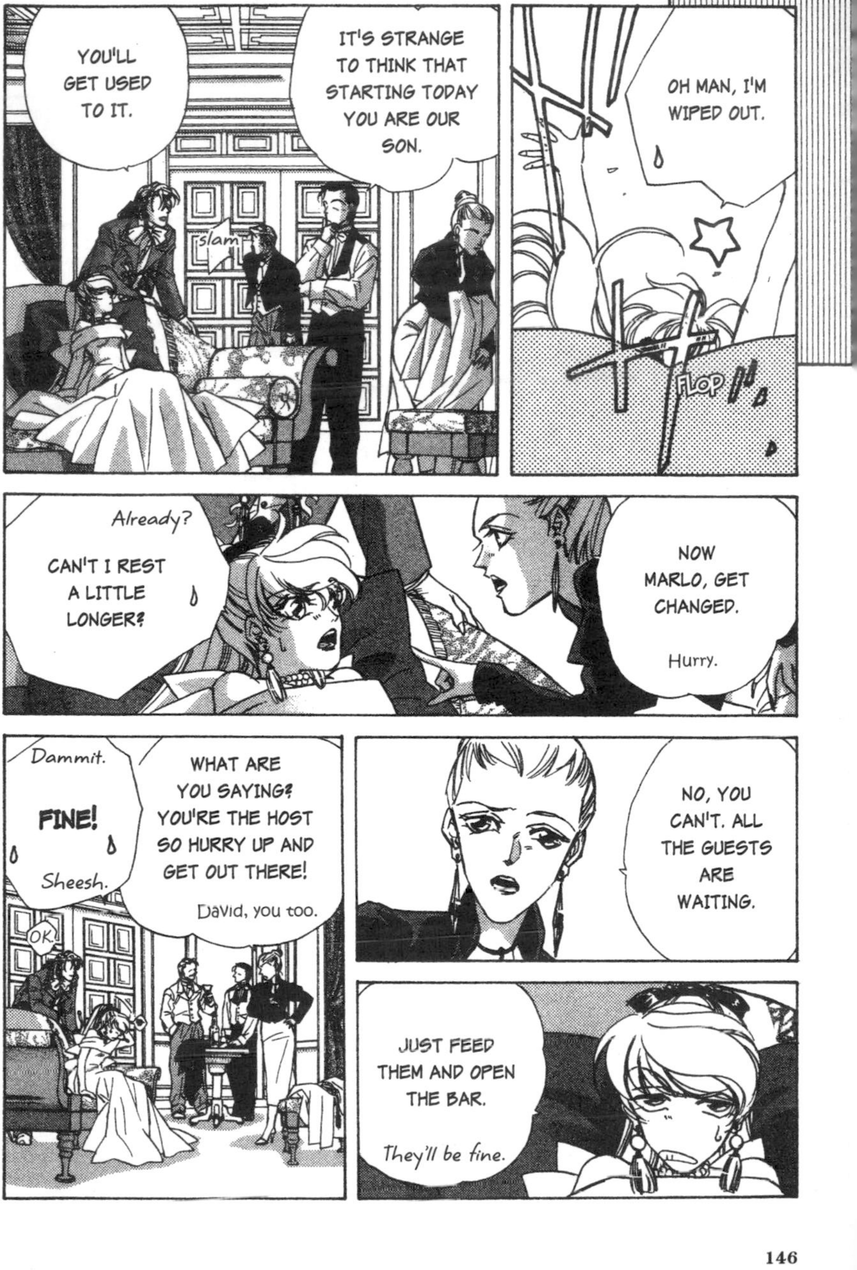
OH MAN, I'M WIPED OUT.
FLOP
IT'S STRANGE TO THINK THAT STARTING TODAY YOU ARE OUR SON.
YOU'LL GET USED TO IT.
slam
NOW MARLO, GET CHANGED.
Hurry.
Already?
CAN'T I REST A LITTLE LONGER?
NO, YOU CAN'T. ALL THE GUESTS ARE WAITING.
JUST FEED THEM AND OPEN THE BAR.
They'll be fine.
WHAT ARE YOU SAYING? YOU'RE THE HOST SO HURRY UP AND GET OUT THERE!
David, you too.
Dammit.
FINE!
Sheesh.
OK.

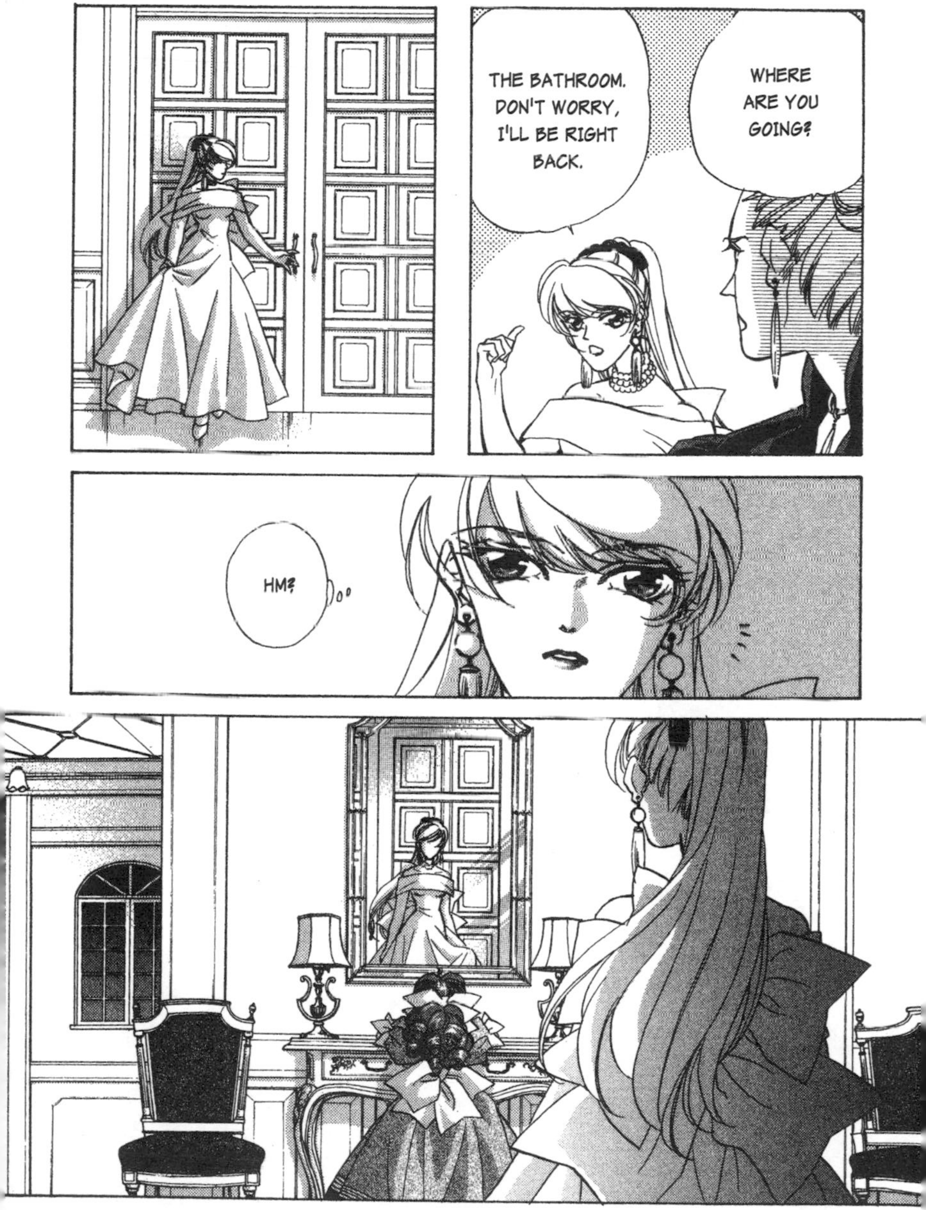
WHERE ARE YOU GOING?
THE BATHROOM. DON'T WORRY, I'LL BE RIGHT BACK.
HM?

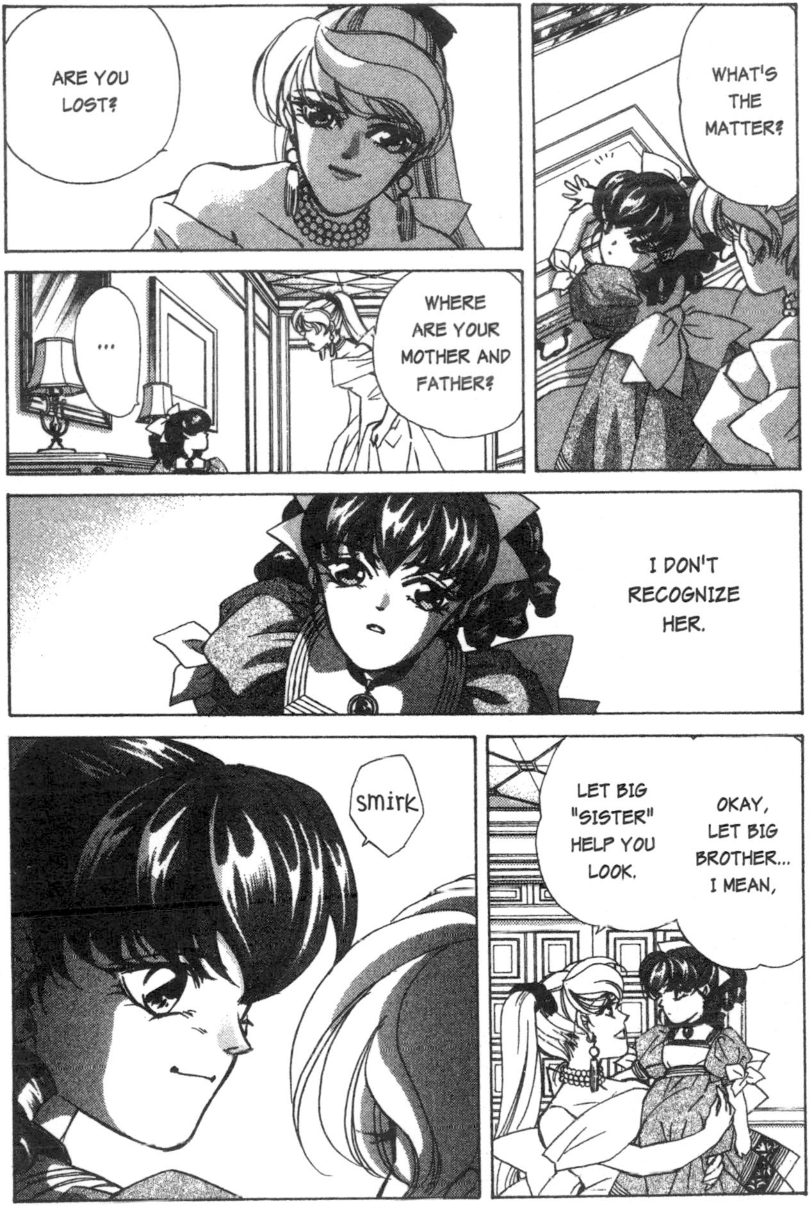
WHAT'S THE MATTER?
ARE YOU LOST?
WHERE ARE YOUR MOTHER AND FATHER?
...
I DON'T RECOGNIZE HER.
OKAY, LET BIG BROTHER... I MEAN,
LET BIG "SISTER" HELP YOU LOOK.
smirk

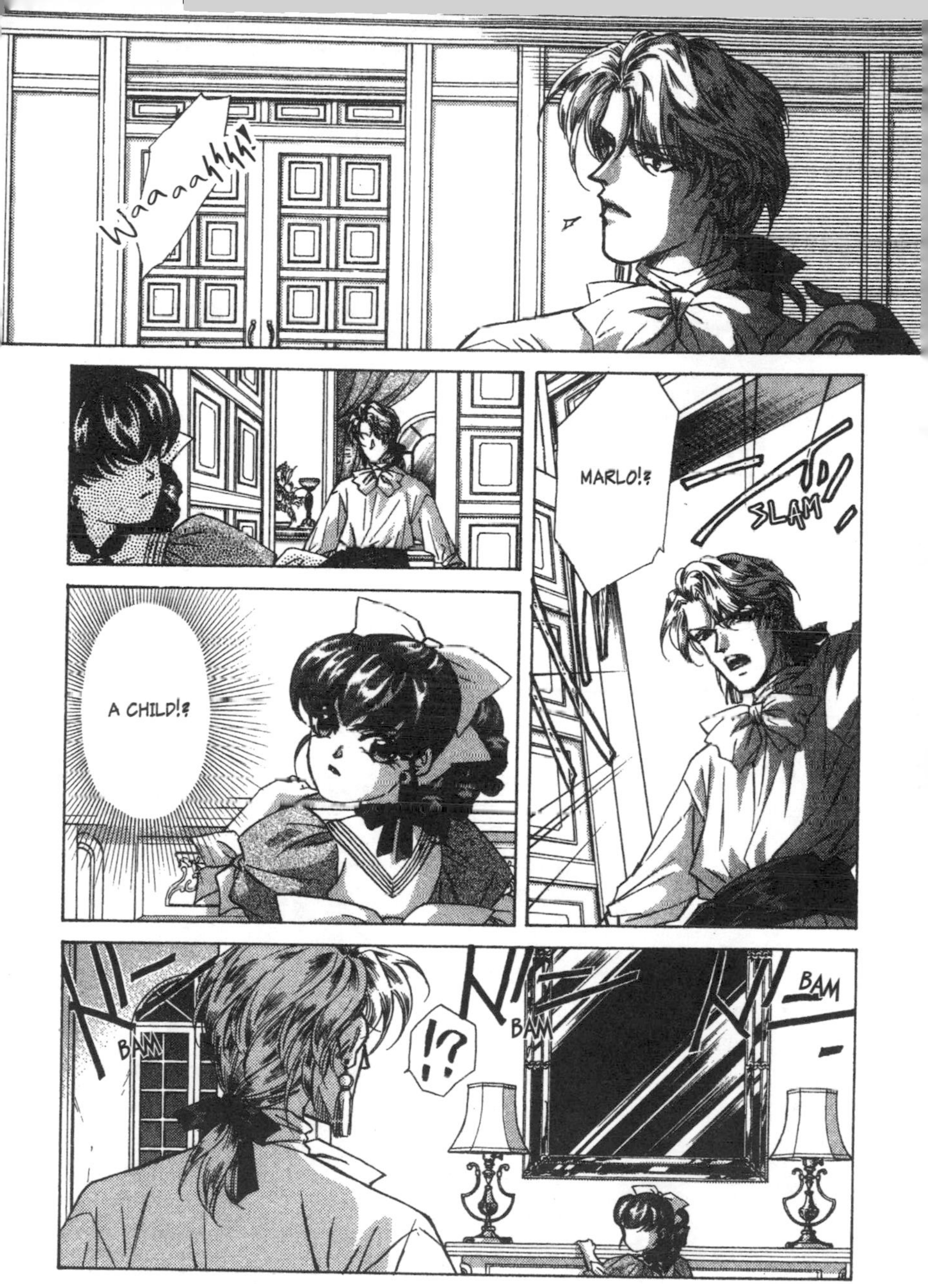
Waaaahhhh!
MARLO!?
SLAM
A CHILD!?
BAM
BAM
!?
BAM

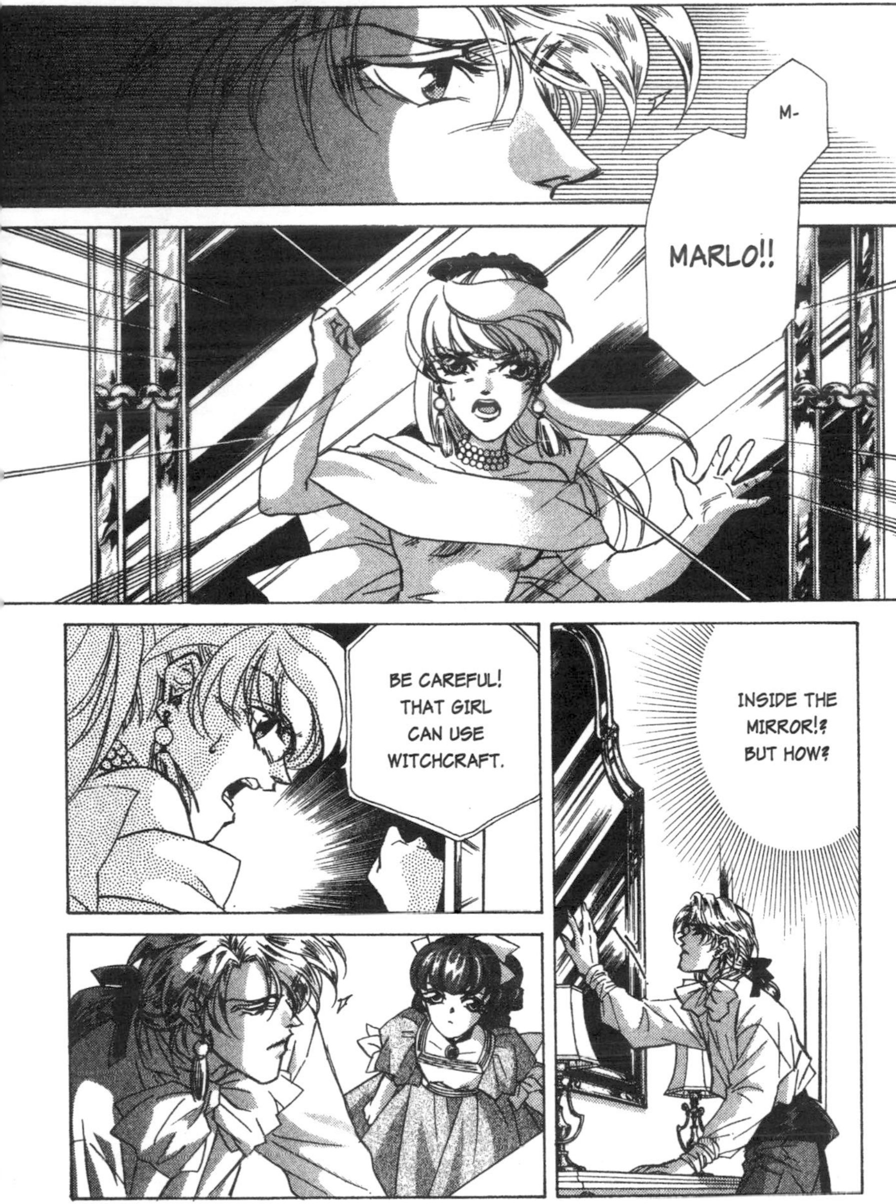
M-
MARLO!!
INSIDE THE MIRROR!? BUT HOW?
BE CAREFUL! THAT GIRL CAN USE WITCHCRAFT.

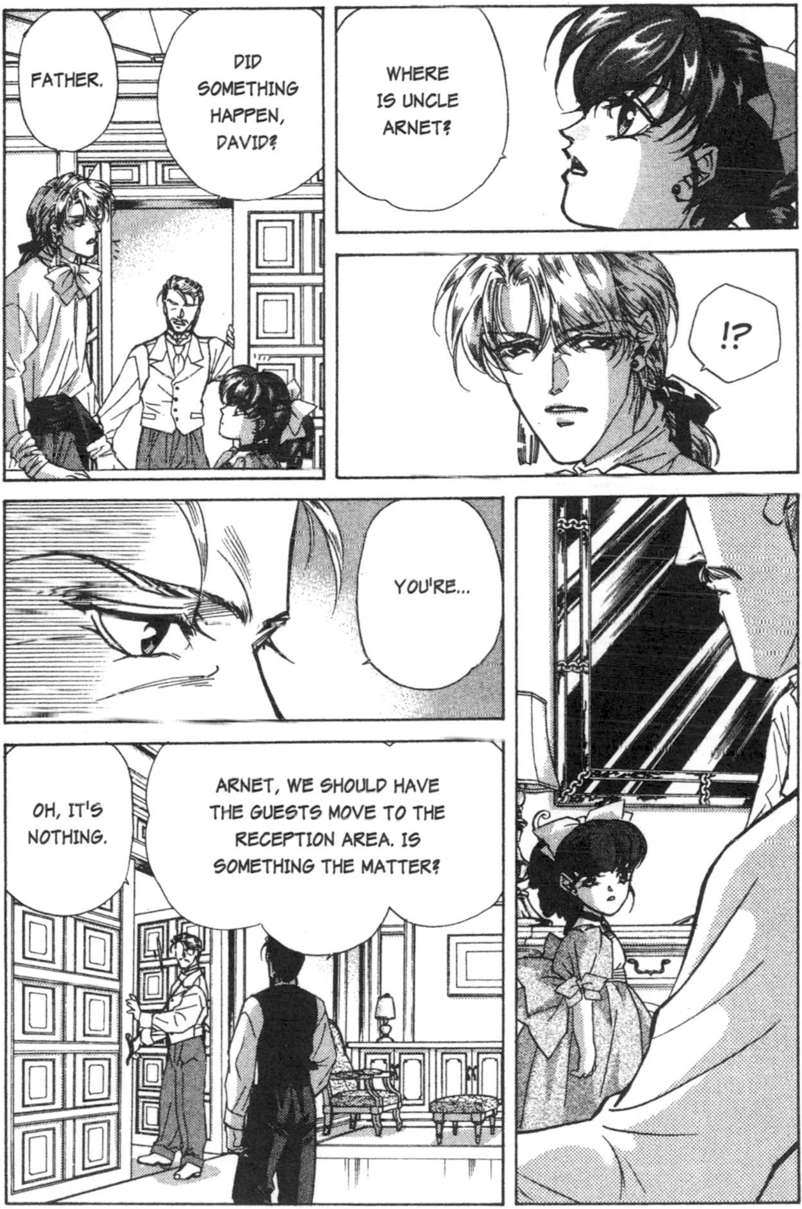
WHERE IS UNCLE ARNET?
!?
DID SOMETHING HAPPEN, DAVID?
FATHER.
YOU'RE...
ARNET, WE SHOULD HAVE THE GUESTS MOVE TO THE RECEPTION AREA. IS SOMETHING THE MATTER?
OH, IT'S NOTHING.

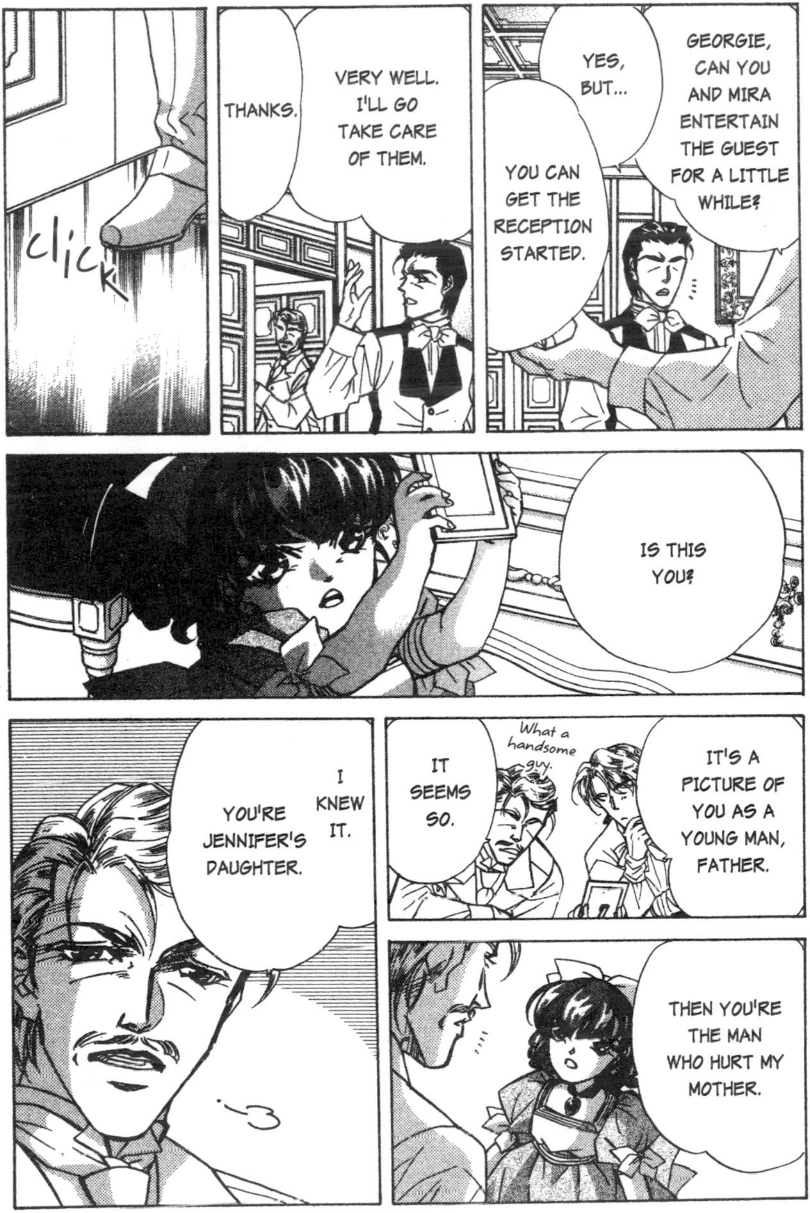
GEORGIE, CAN YOU AND MIRA ENTERTAIN THE GUEST FOR A LITTLE WHILE?
YES, BUT...
YOU CAN GET THE RECEPTION STARTED.
VERY WELL. I'LL GO TAKE CARE OF THEM.
THANKS.
click
IS THIS YOU?
IT'S A PICTURE OF YOU AS A YOUNG MAN, FATHER.
What a handsome guy.
IT SEEMS SO.
THEN YOU'RE THE MAN WHO HURT MY MOTHER.
I KNEW IT.
YOU'RE JENNIFER'S DAUGHTER.

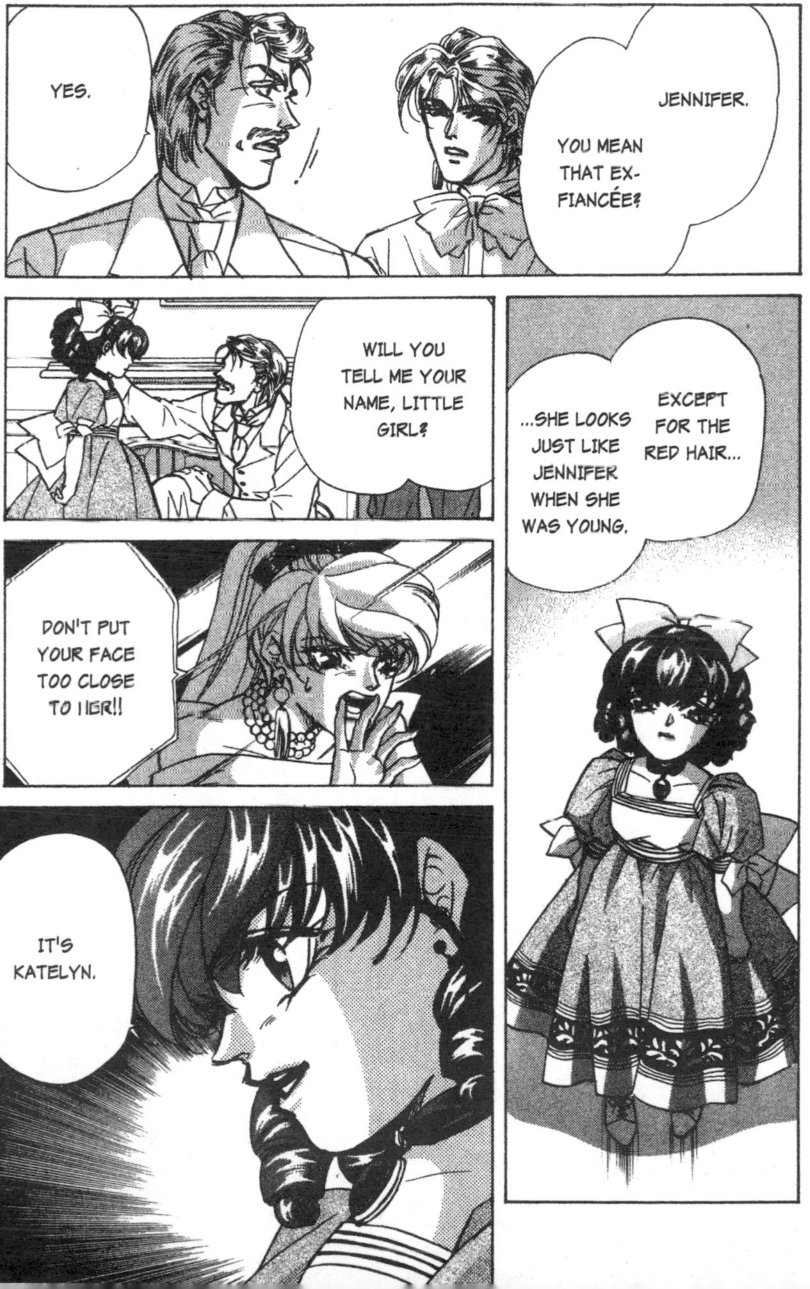
JENNIFER.
YOU MEAN THAT EX-FIANCÉE?
YES.
EXCEPT FOR THE RED HAIR...
...SHE LOOKS JUST LIKE JENNIFER WHEN SHE WAS YOUNG.
WILL YOU TELL ME YOUR NAME, LITTLE GIRL?
DON'T PUT YOUR FACE TOO CLOSE TO HER!!
IT'S KATELYN.

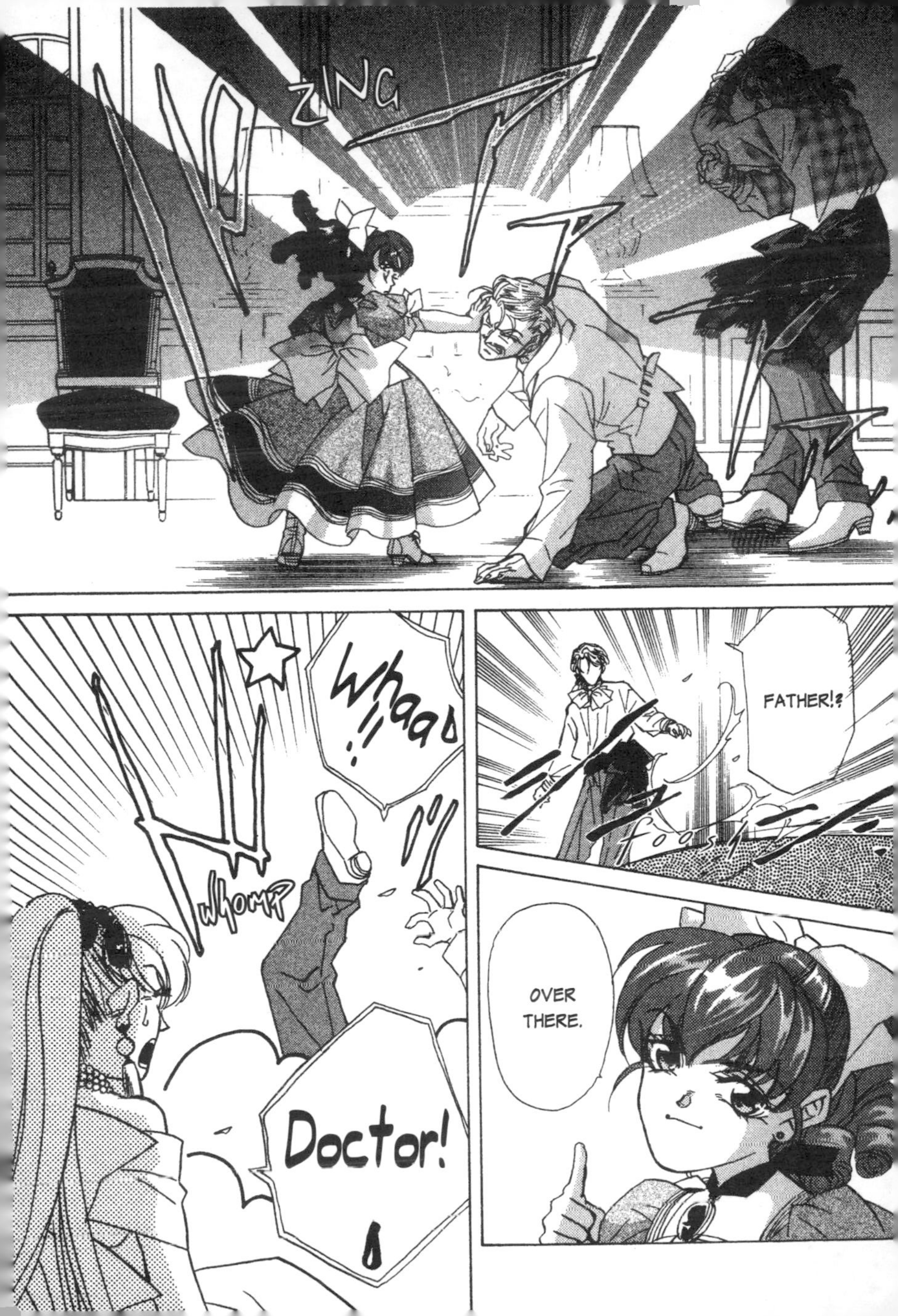
ZING
FATHER!?
foosh
OVER THERE.
Whomp
Whaaa!!
Doctor!

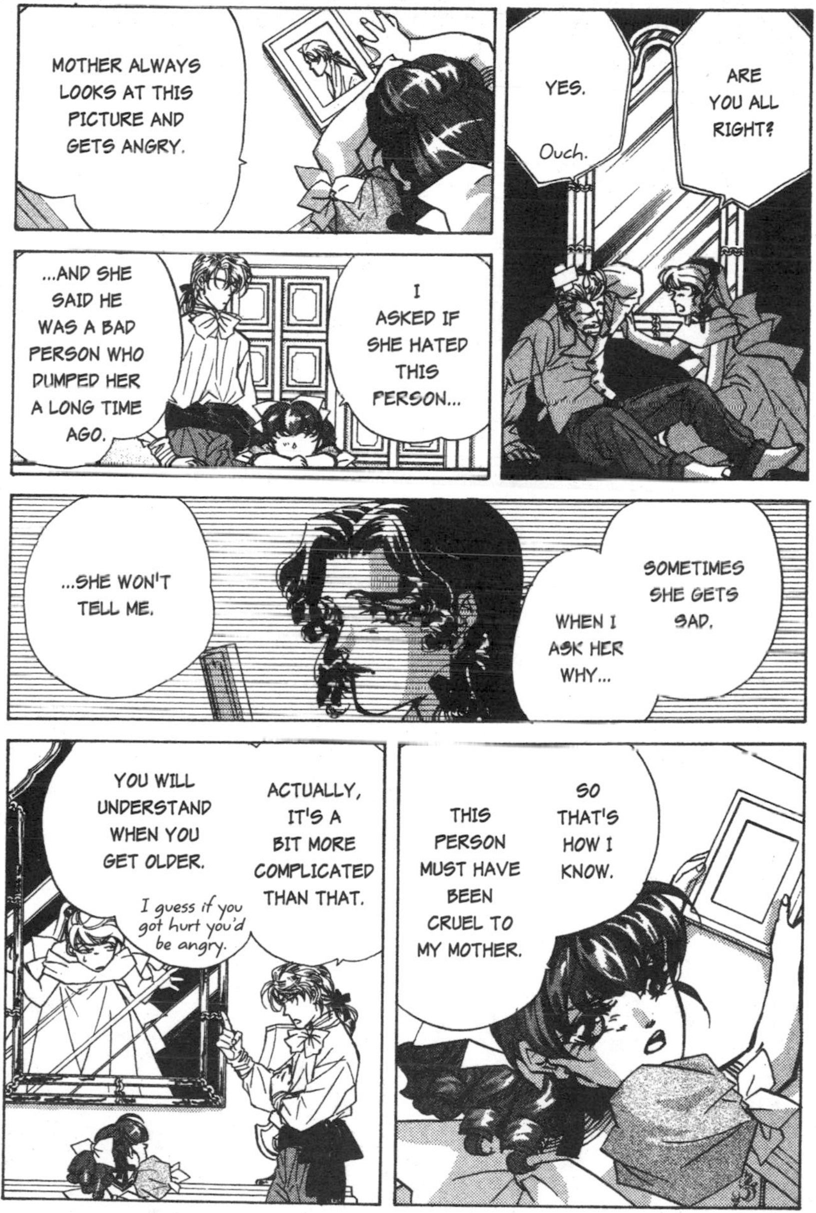
ARE YOU ALL RIGHT?
YES.
Ouch.
MOTHER ALWAYS LOOKS AT THIS PICTURE AND GETS ANGRY.
I ASKED IF SHE HATED THIS PERSON...
...AND SHE SAID HE WAS A BAD PERSON WHO DUMPED HER A LONG TIME AGO.
SOMETIMES SHE GETS SAD.
WHEN I ASK HER WHY...
...SHE WON'T TELL ME.
SO THAT'S HOW I KNOW.
THIS PERSON MUST HAVE BEEN CRUEL TO MY MOTHER.
ACTUALLY, IT'S A BIT MORE COMPLICATED THAN THAT.
YOU WILL UNDERSTAND WHEN YOU GET OLDER.
I guess if you got hurt you'd be angry.

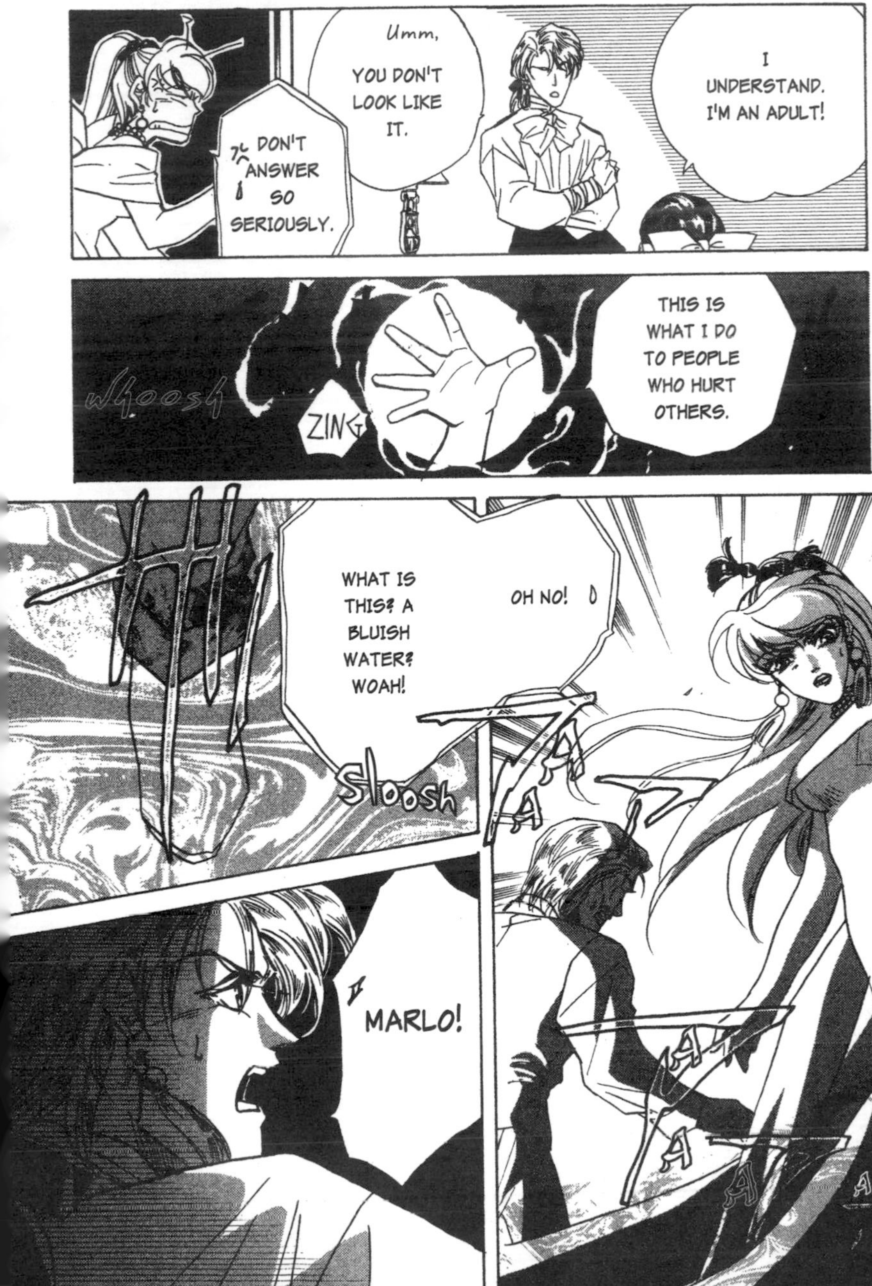
I UNDERSTAND. I'M AN ADULT!
Umm, YOU DON'T LOOK LIKE IT.
DON'T ANSWER SO SERIOUSLY.
THIS IS WHAT I DO TO PEOPLE WHO HURT OTHERS.
ZING
whoosh
OH NO!
WHAT IS THIS? A BLUISH WATER? WOAH!
Sloosh
Aooo
MARLO!

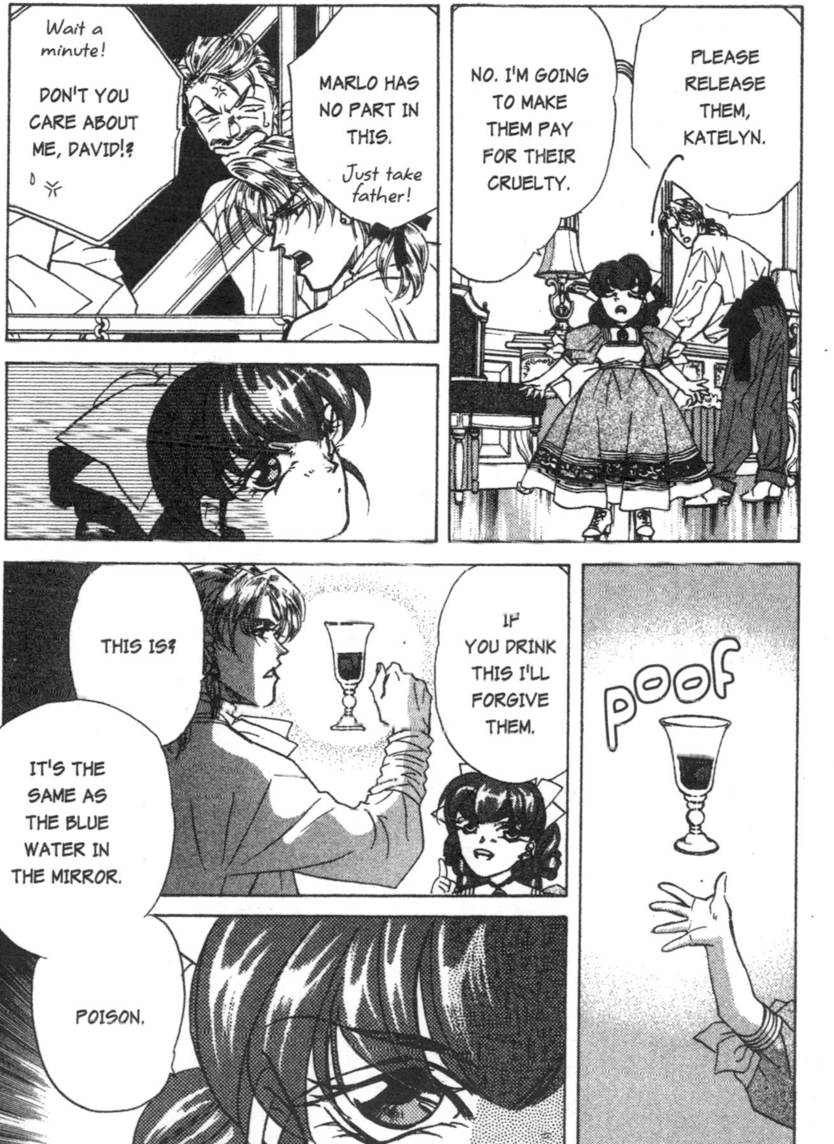
PLEASE RELEASE THEM, KATELYN.
NO. I'M GOING TO MAKE THEM PAY FOR THEIR CRUELTY.
MARLO HAS NO PART IN THIS.
Just take father!
Wait a minute!
DON'T YOU CARE ABOUT ME, DAVID!?
poof
IF YOU DRINK THIS I'LL FORGIVE THEM.
THIS IS?
IT'S THE SAME AS THE BLUE WATER IN THE MIRROR.
POISON.

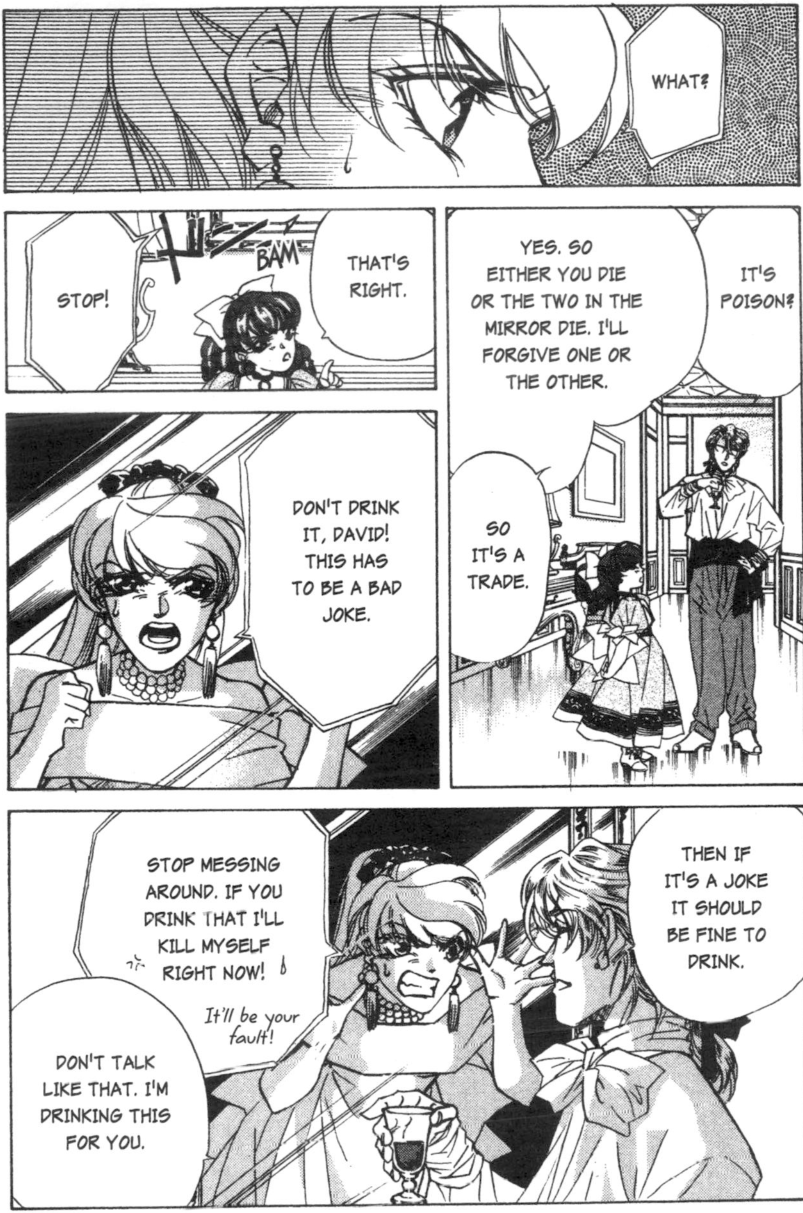
WHAT?
IT'S POISON?
YES. SO EITHER YOU DIE OR THE TWO IN THE MIRROR DIE. I'LL FORGIVE ONE OR THE OTHER.
SO IT'S A TRADE.
THAT'S RIGHT.
BAM
STOP!
DON'T DRINK IT, DAVID! THIS HAS TO BE A BAD JOKE.
THEN IF IT'S A JOKE IT SHOULD BE FINE TO DRINK.
STOP MESSING AROUND. IF YOU DRINK THAT I'LL KILL MYSELF RIGHT NOW!
It'll be your fault!
DON'T TALK LIKE THAT. I'M DRINKING THIS FOR YOU.

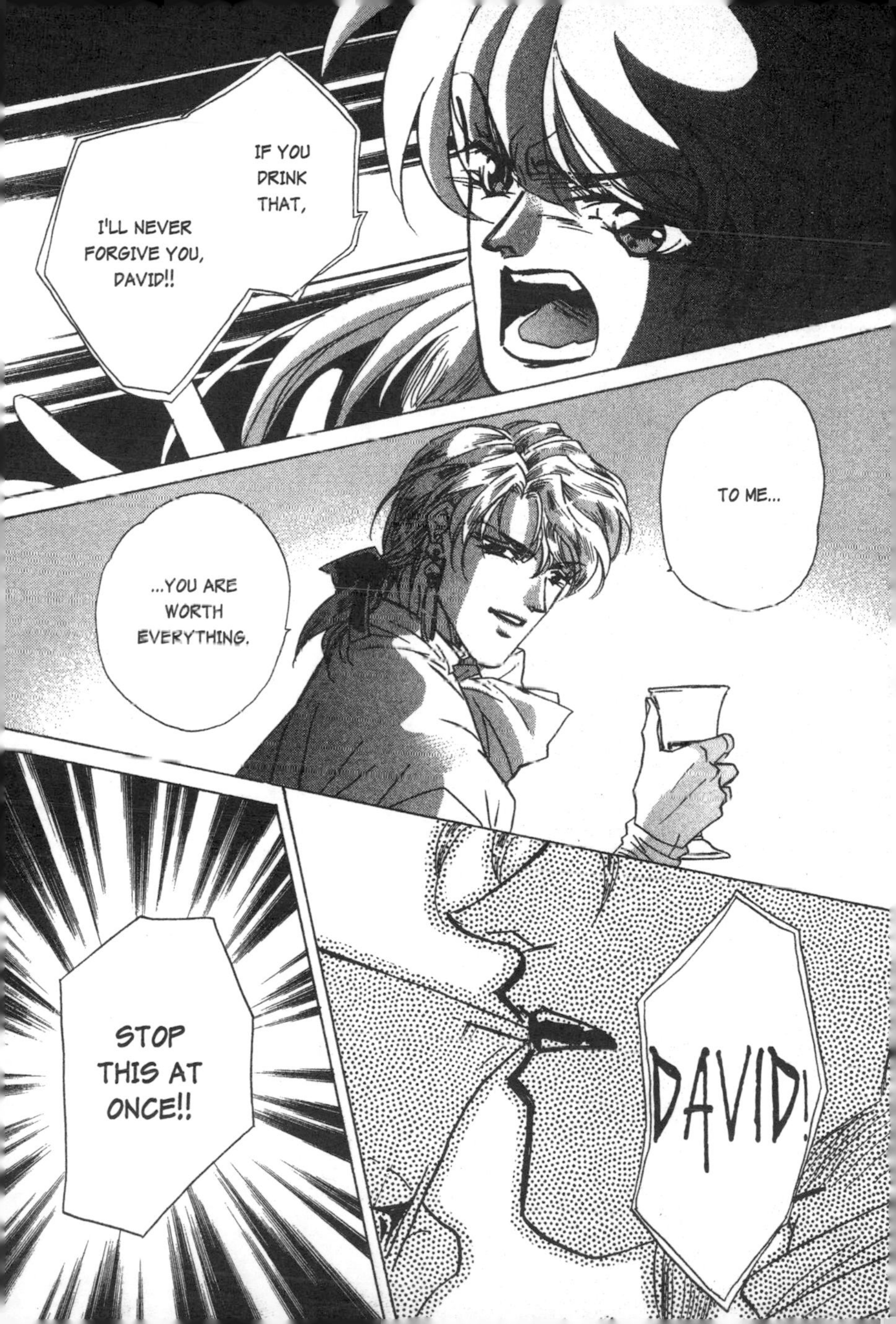
IF YOU DRINK THAT, I'LL NEVER FORGIVE YOU, DAVID!!
TO ME...
...YOU ARE WORTH EVERYTHING.
DAVID!
STOP THIS AT ONCE!!

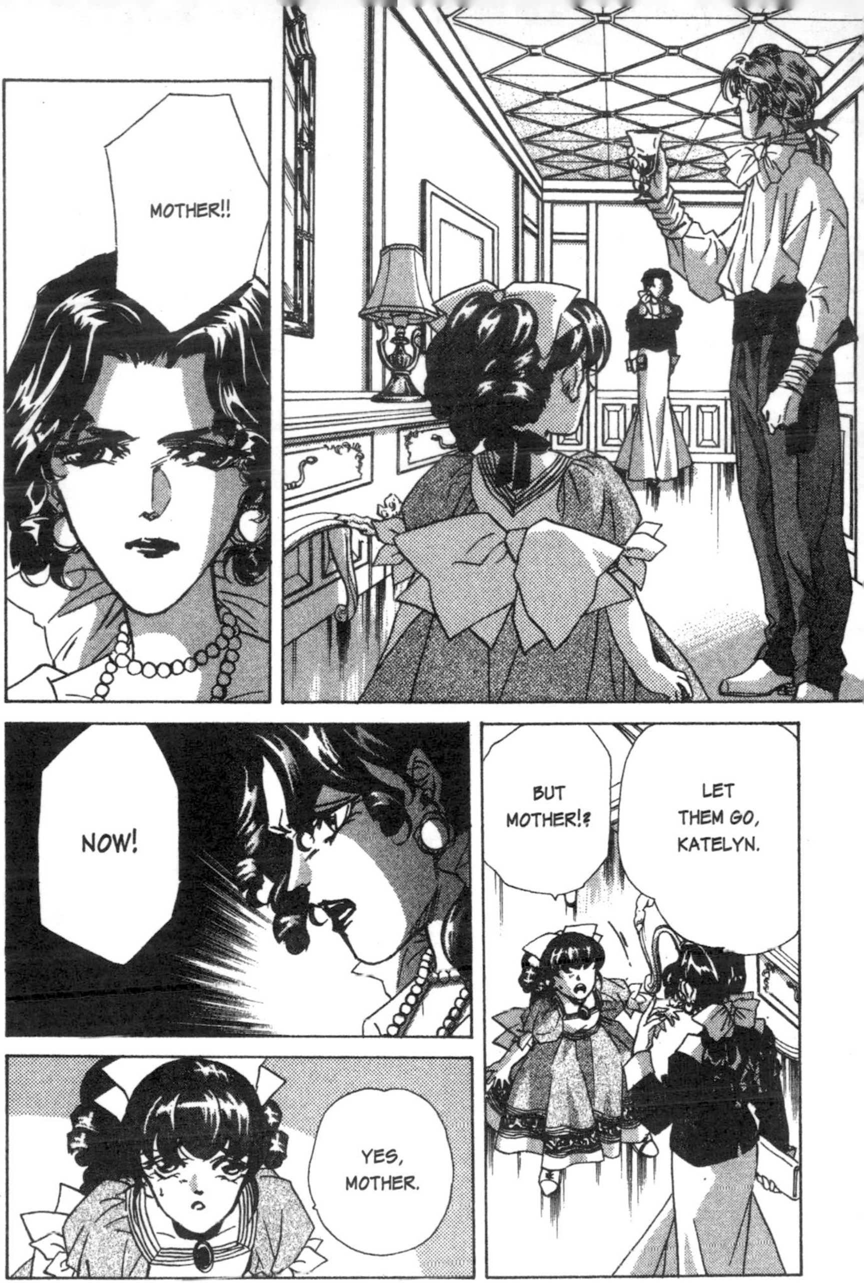
MOTHER!!
LET THEM GO, KATELYN.
BUT MOTHER!?
NOW!
YES, MOTHER.

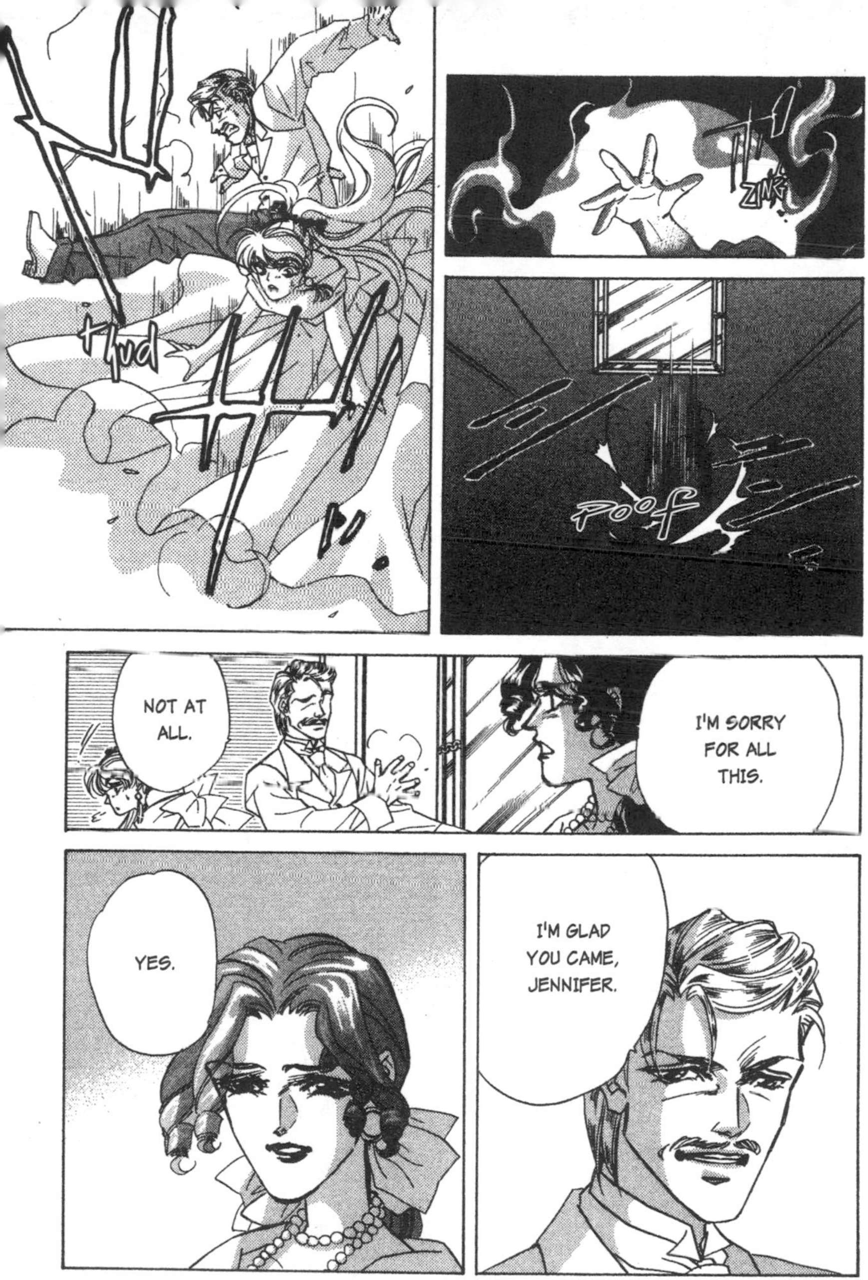
ZING
POOF
thud
I'M SORRY FOR ALL THIS.
NOT AT ALL.
I'M GLAD YOU CAME, JENNIFER.
YES.

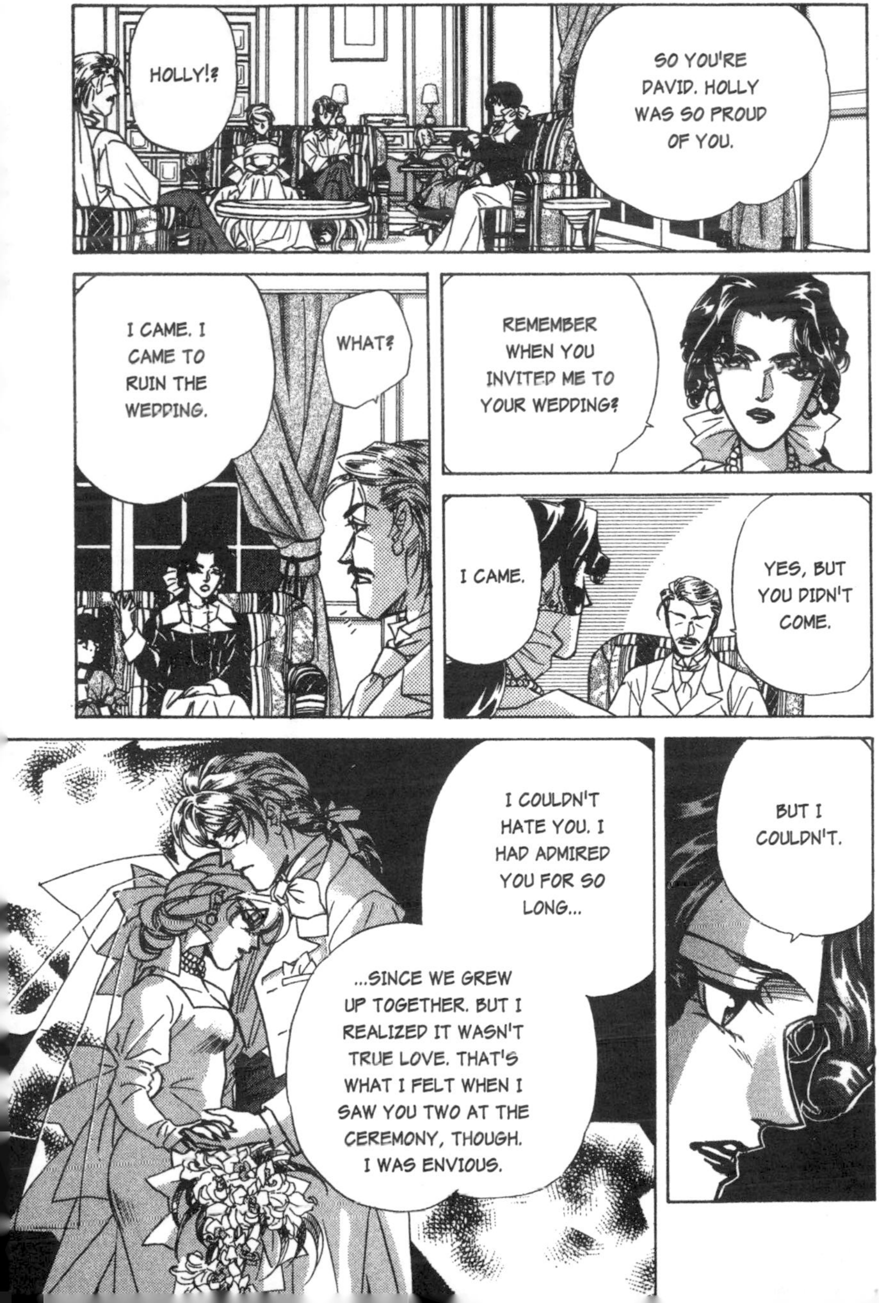
SO YOU'RE DAVID. HOLLY WAS SO PROUD OF YOU.
HOLLY!?
REMEMBER WHEN YOU INVITED ME TO YOUR WEDDING?
YES, BUT YOU DIDN'T COME.
I CAME.
WHAT?
I CAME. I CAME TO RUIN THE WEDDING.
BUT I COULDN'T.
I COULDN'T HATE YOU. I HAD ADMIRED YOU FOR SO LONG...
...SINCE WE GREW UP TOGETHER. BUT I REALIZED IT WASN'T TRUE LOVE. THAT'S WHAT I FELT WHEN I SAW YOU TWO AT THE CEREMONY, THOUGH. I WAS ENVIOUS.

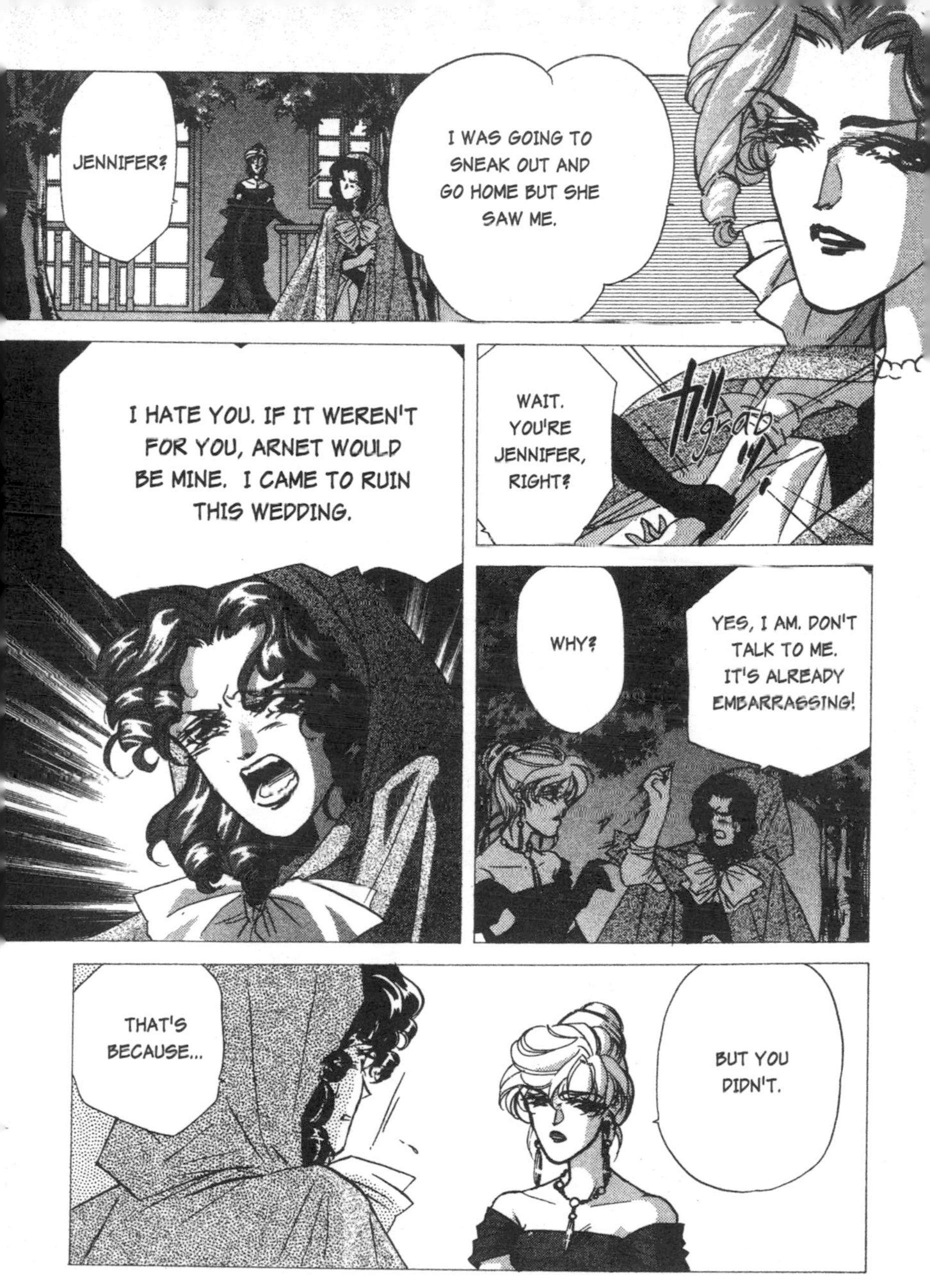
I WAS GOING TO SNEAK OUT AND GO HOME BUT SHE SAW ME.
JENNIFER?
WAIT. YOU'RE JENNIFER, RIGHT?
grab
YES, I AM. DON'T TALK TO ME. IT'S ALREADY EMBARRASSING!
WHY?
I HATE YOU. IF IT WEREN'T FOR YOU, ARNET WOULD BE MINE. I CAME TO RUIN THIS WEDDING.
BUT YOU DIDN'T.
THAT'S BECAUSE...

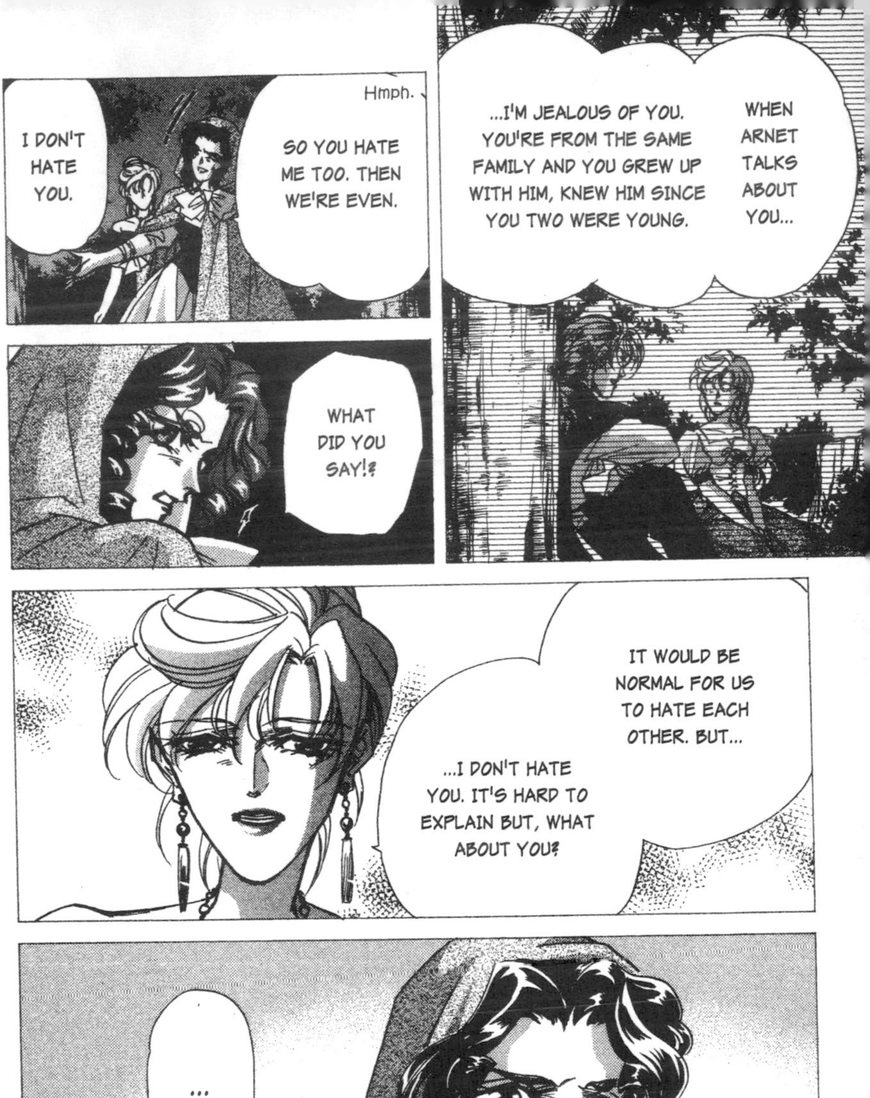
WHEN ARNET TALKS ABOUT YOU...
...I'M JEALOUS OF YOU. YOU'RE FROM THE SAME FAMILY AND YOU GREW UP WITH HIM, KNEW HIM SINCE YOU TWO WERE YOUNG.
Hmph.
SO YOU HATE ME TOO. THEN WE'RE EVEN.
I DON'T HATE YOU.
WHAT DID YOU SAY!?
IT WOULD BE NORMAL FOR US TO HATE EACH OTHER. BUT...
...I DON'T HATE YOU. IT'S HARD TO EXPLAIN BUT, WHAT ABOUT YOU?
...

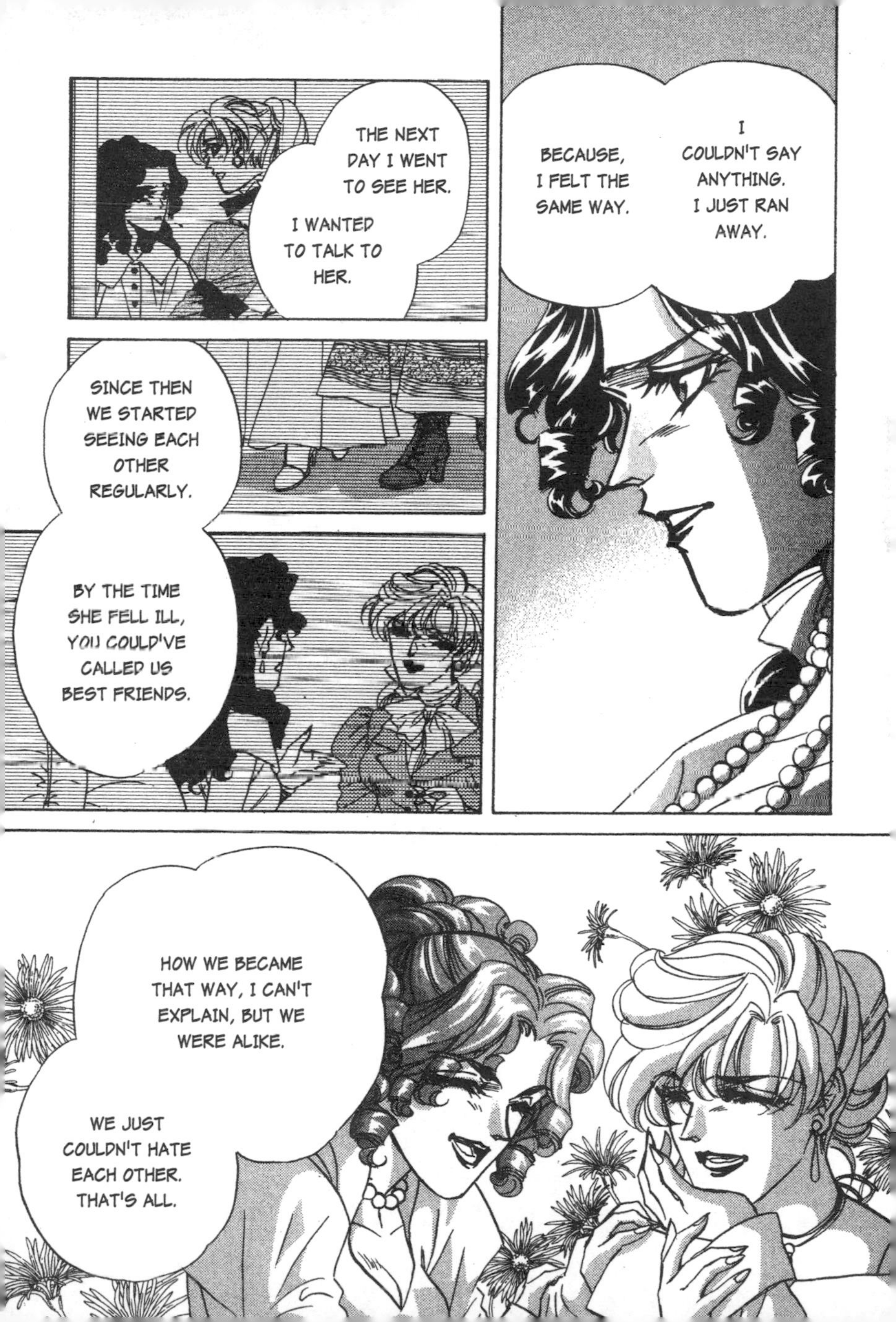
I COULDN'T SAY ANYTHING. I JUST RAN AWAY.
BECAUSE, I FELT THE SAME WAY.
THE NEXT DAY I WENT TO SEE HER.
I WANTED TO TALK TO HER.
SINCE THEN WE STARTED SEEING EACH OTHER REGULARLY.
BY THE TIME SHE FELL ILL, YOU COULD'VE CALLED US BEST FRIENDS.
HOW WE BECAME THAT WAY, I CAN'T EXPLAIN, BUT WE WERE ALIKE.
WE JUST COULDN'T HATE EACH OTHER. THAT'S ALL.

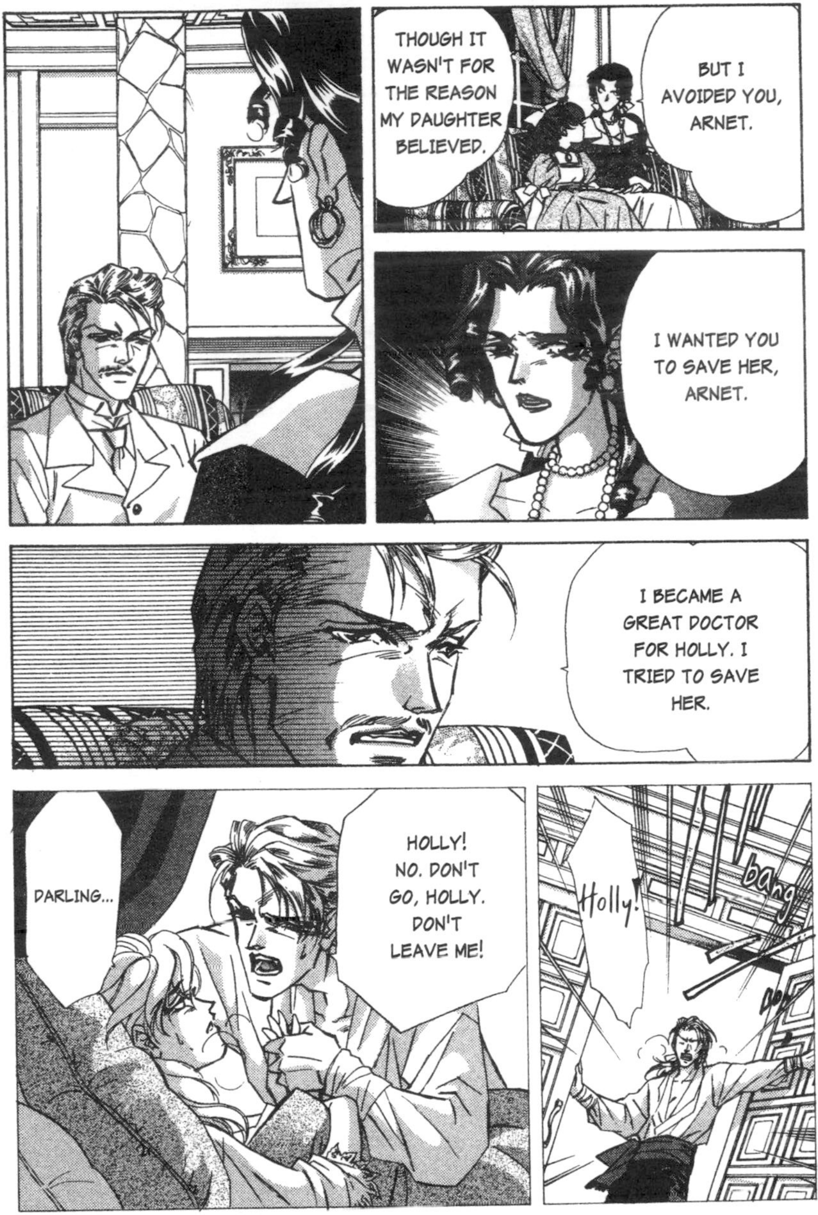

BUT I AVOIDED YOU, ARNET.
THOUGH IT WASN'T FOR THE REASON MY DAUGHTER BELIEVED.
I WANTED YOU TO SAVE HER, ARNET.
I BECAME A GREAT DOCTOR FOR HOLLY. I TRIED TO SAVE HER.
Holly!
bang
HOLLY! NO. DON'T GO, HOLLY. DON'T LEAVE ME!
DARLING...

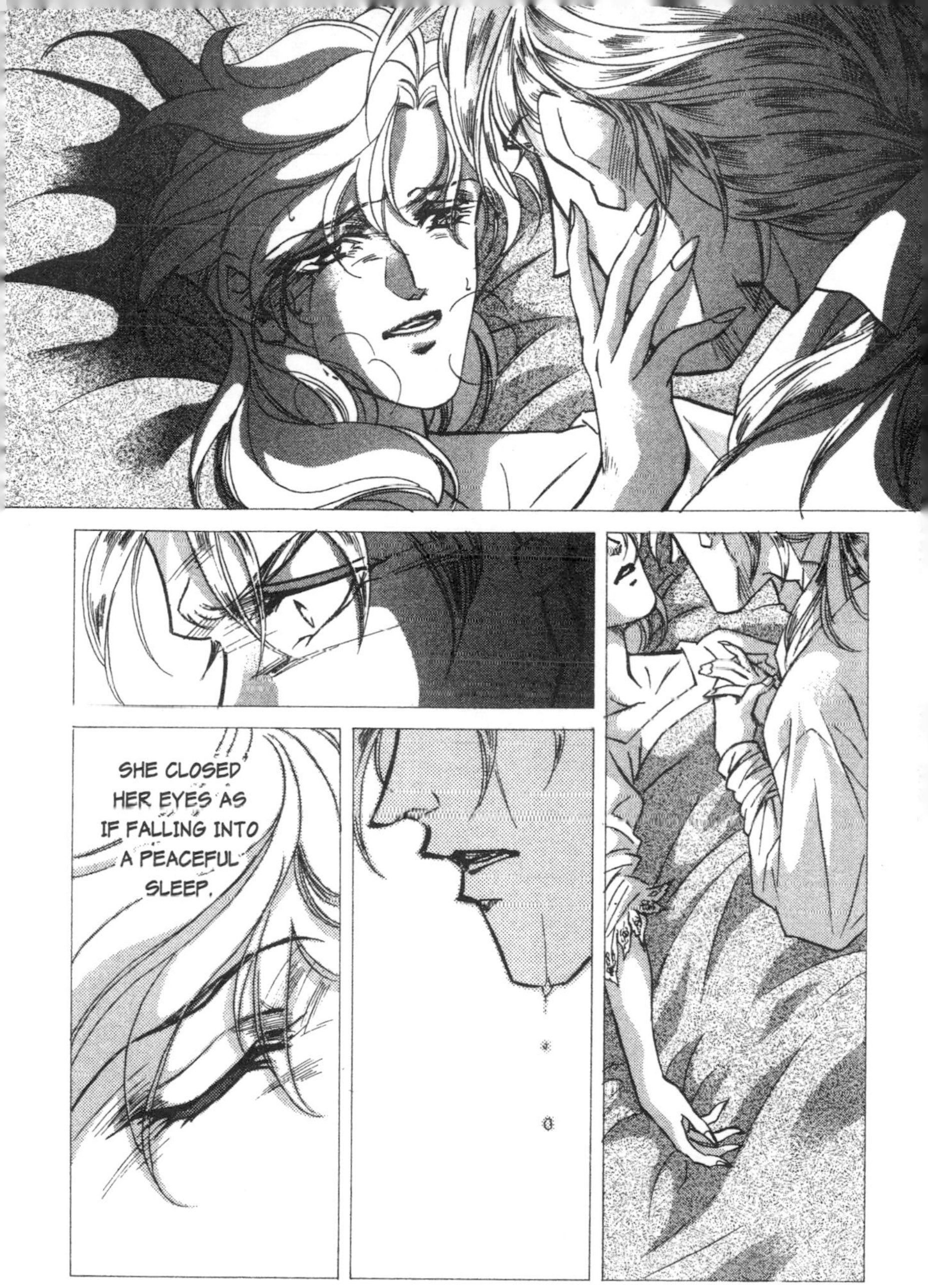
SHE CLOSED HER EYES AS IF FALLING INTO A PEACEFUL SLEEP.

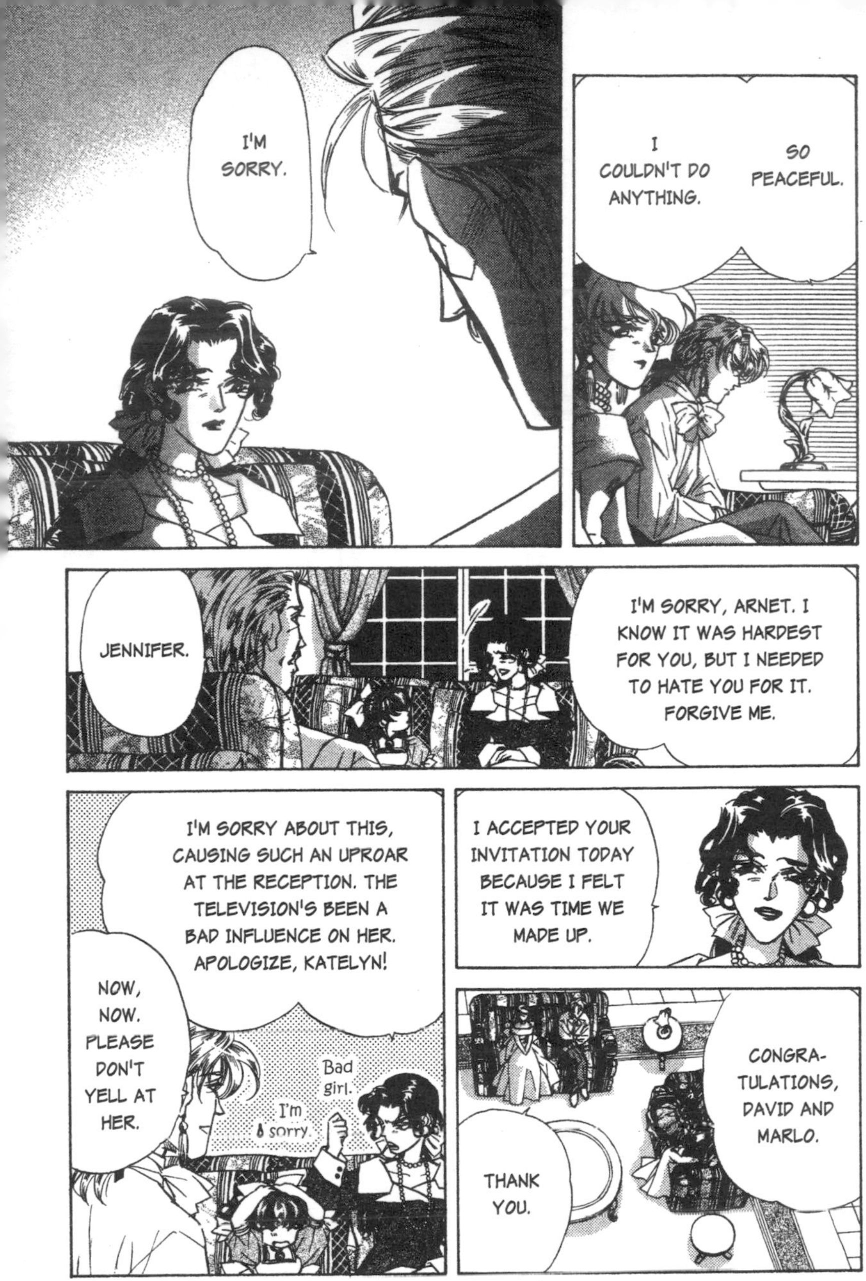
SO PEACEFUL.
I COULDN'T DO ANYTHING.
I'M SORRY.
I'M SORRY, ARNET. I KNOW IT WAS HARDEST FOR YOU, BUT I NEEDED TO HATE YOU FOR IT. FORGIVE ME.
JENNIFER.
I ACCEPTED YOUR INVITATION TODAY BECAUSE I FELT IT WAS TIME WE MADE UP.
CONGRA-TULATIONS, DAVID AND MARLO.
THANK YOU.
I'M SORRY ABOUT THIS, CAUSING SUCH AN UPROAR AT THE RECEPTION. THE TELEVISION'S BEEN A BAD INFLUENCE ON HER. APOLOGIZE, KATELYN!
Bad girl.
I'm sorry.
NOW, NOW. PLEASE DON'T YELL AT HER.

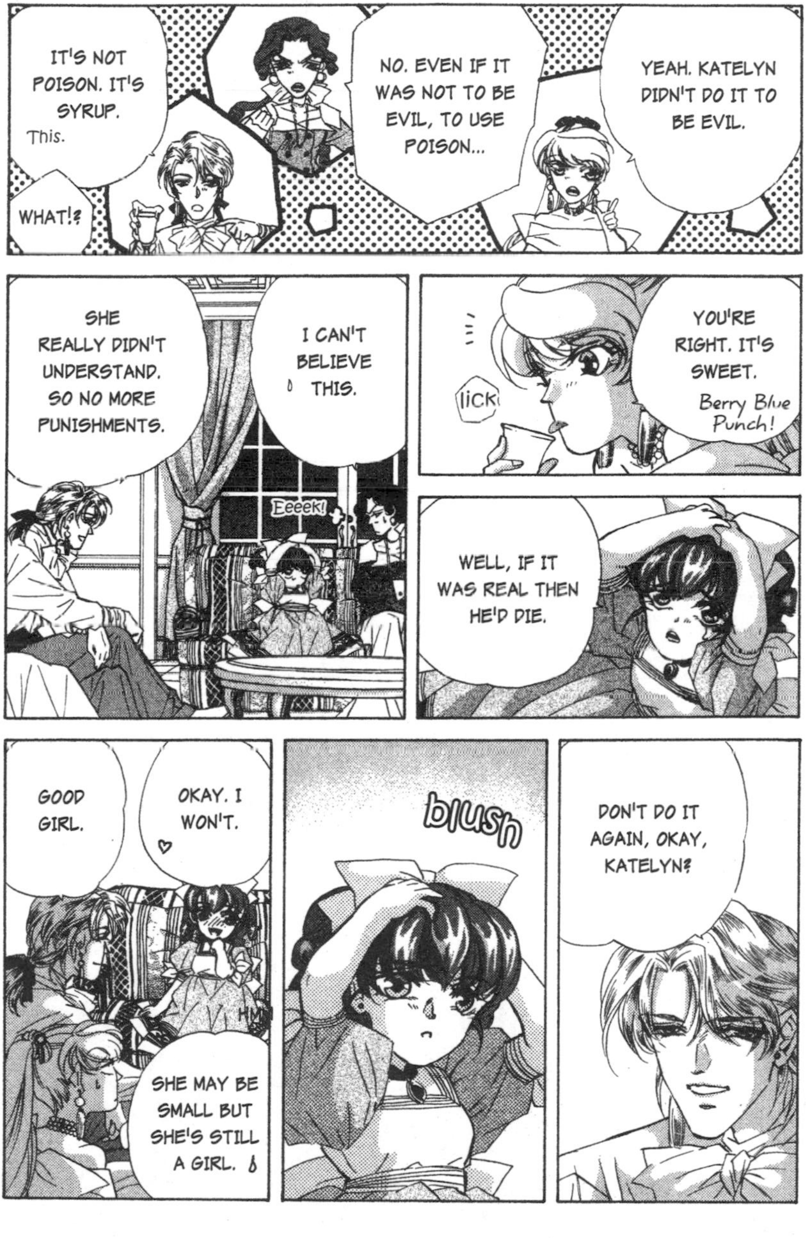
YEAH. KATELYN DIDN'T DO IT TO BE EVIL.
NO. EVEN IF IT WAS NOT TO BE EVIL, TO USE POISON...
IT'S NOT POISON. IT'S SYRUP.
This.
WHAT!?
YOU'RE RIGHT. IT'S SWEET.
Berry Blue Punch!
lick
WELL, IF IT WAS REAL THEN HE'D DIE.
I CAN'T BELIEVE THIS.
SHE REALLY DIDN'T UNDERSTAND. SO NO MORE PUNISHMENTS.
Eeeek!
DON'T DO IT AGAIN, OKAY, KATELYN?
blush
OKAY. I WON'T.
GOOD GIRL.
SHE MAY BE SMALL BUT SHE'S STILL A GIRL.

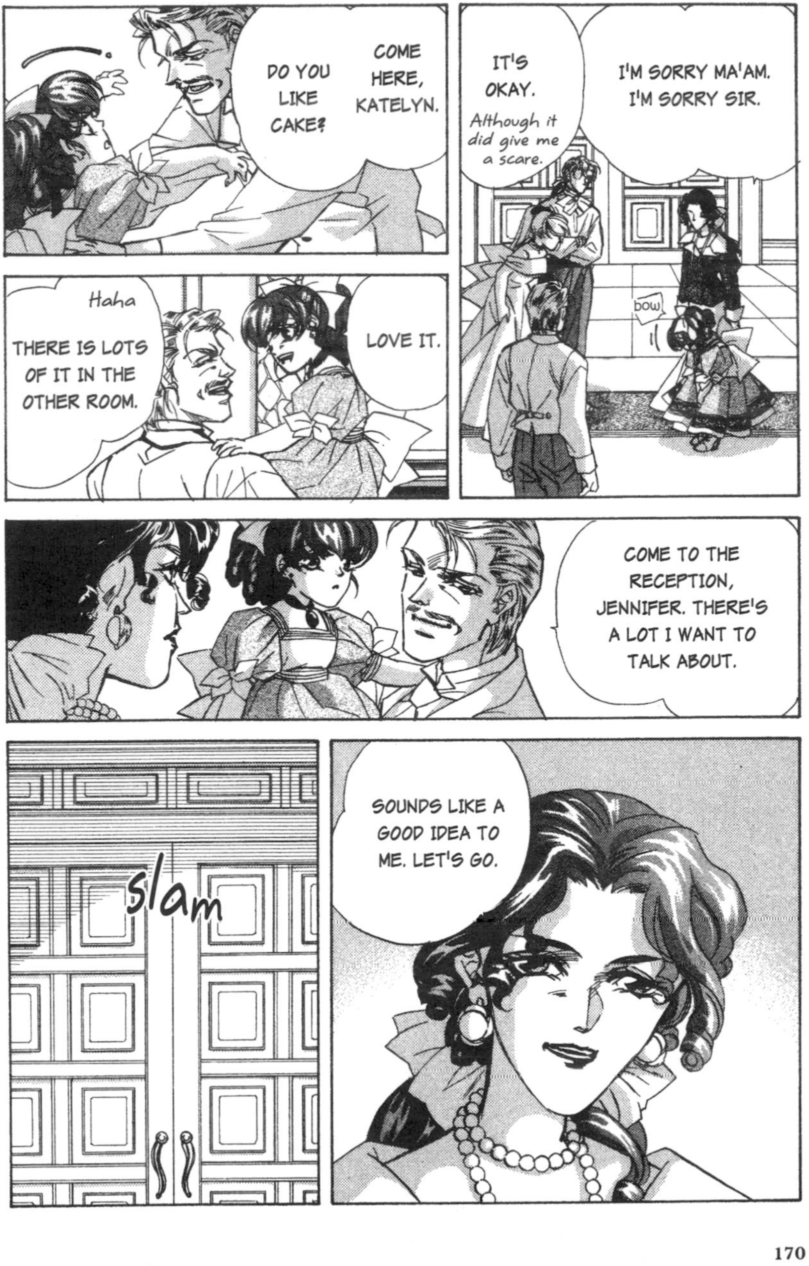
I'M SORRY MA'AM. I'M SORRY SIR.
IT'S OKAY.
Although it did give me a scare.
bow
COME HERE, KATELYN.
DO YOU LIKE CAKE?
LOVE IT.
Haha
THERE IS LOTS OF IT IN THE OTHER ROOM.
COME TO THE RECEPTION, JENNIFER. THERE'S A LOT I WANT TO TALK ABOUT.
SOUNDS LIKE A GOOD IDEA TO ME. LET'S GO.
slam

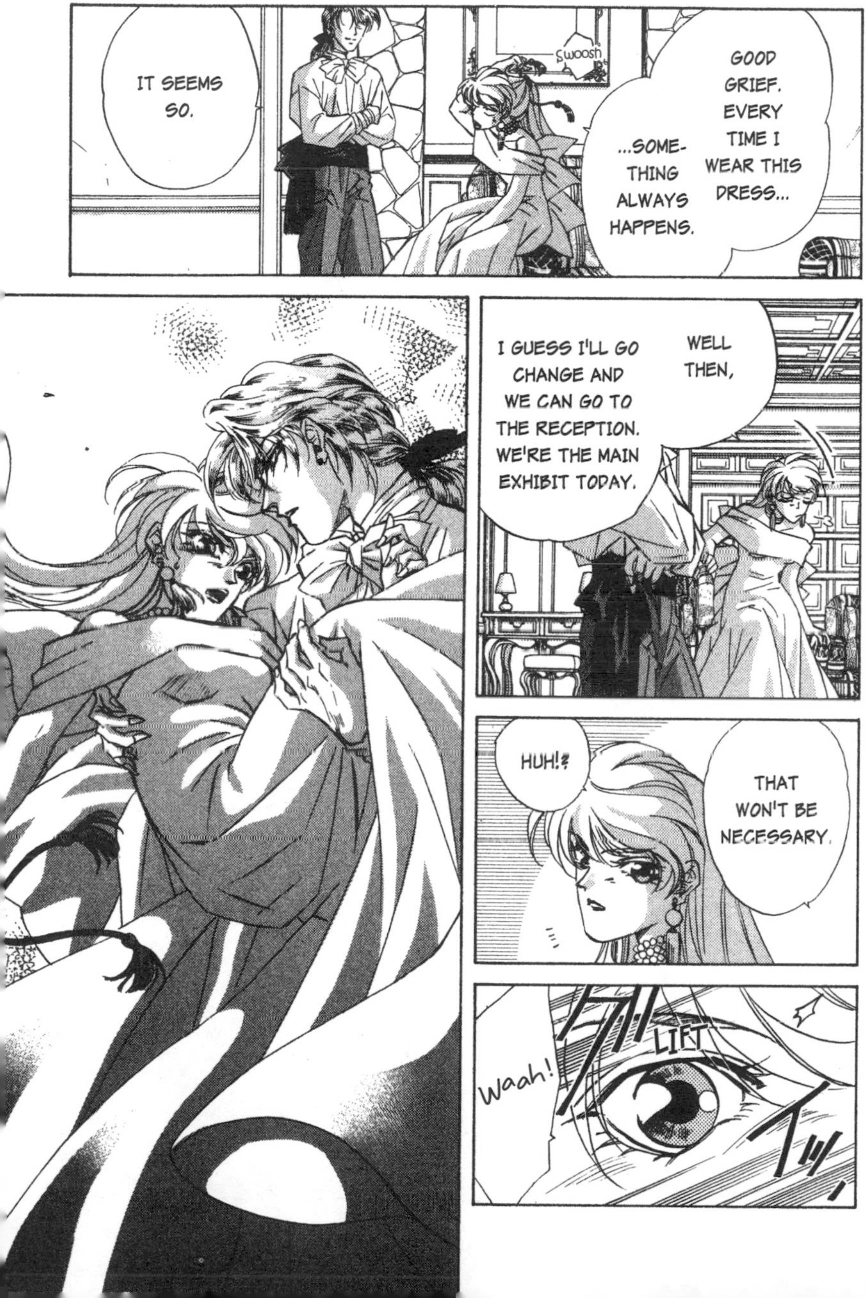
GOOD GRIEF. EVERY TIME I WEAR THIS DRESS...
...SOME-THING ALWAYS HAPPENS.
Swoosh
IT SEEMS SO.
WELL THEN,
I GUESS I'LL GO CHANGE AND WE CAN GO TO THE RECEPTION. WE'RE THE MAIN EXHIBIT TODAY.
THAT WON'T BE NECESSARY.
HUH!?
LIFT
Waah!

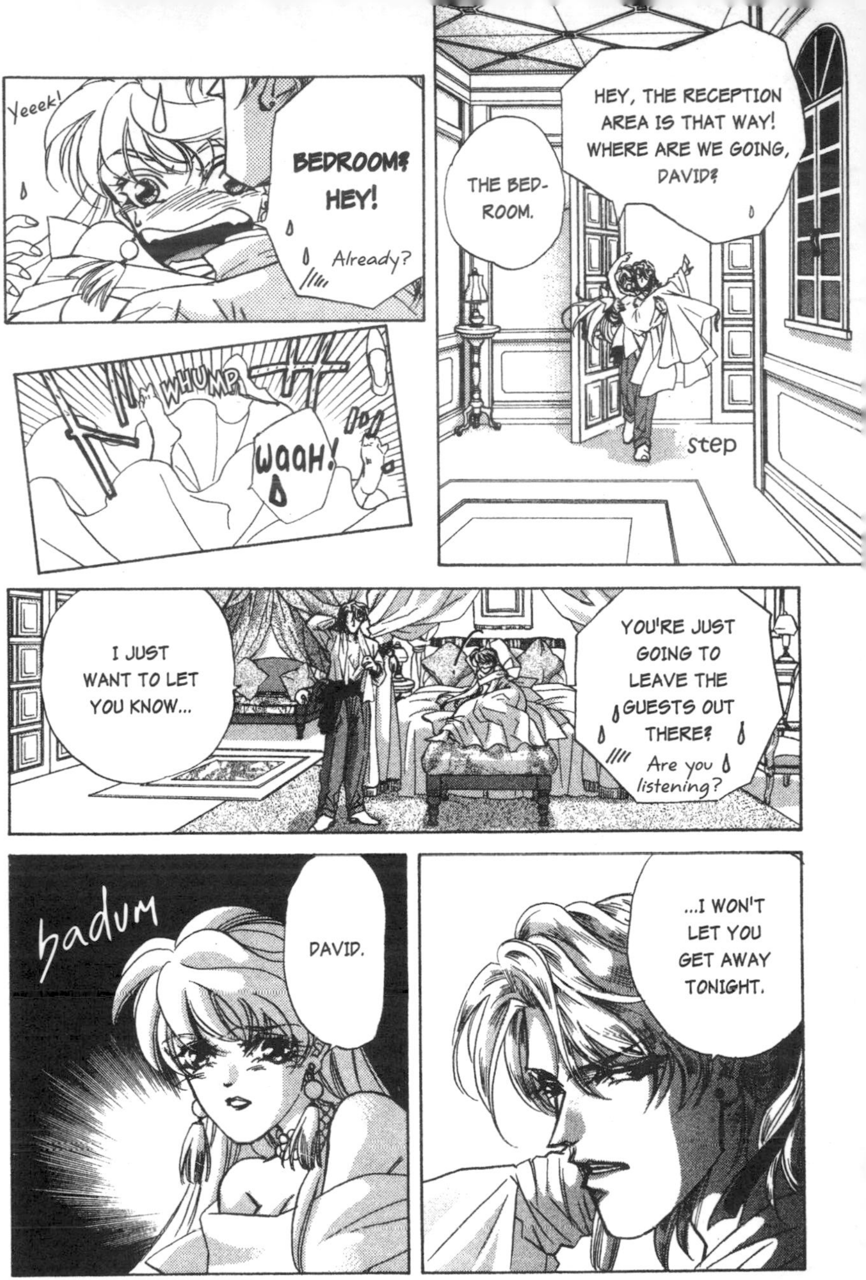
HEY, THE RECEPTION AREA IS THAT WAY! WHERE ARE WE GOING, DAVID?
THE BED-ROOM.
Step
BEDROOM? HEY!
Already?
Yeeek!
WHUMP
WAAH!
YOU'RE JUST GOING TO LEAVE THE GUESTS OUT THERE?
Are you listening?
I JUST WANT TO LET YOU KNOW...
...I WON'T LET YOU GET AWAY TONIGHT.
DAVID.
badum

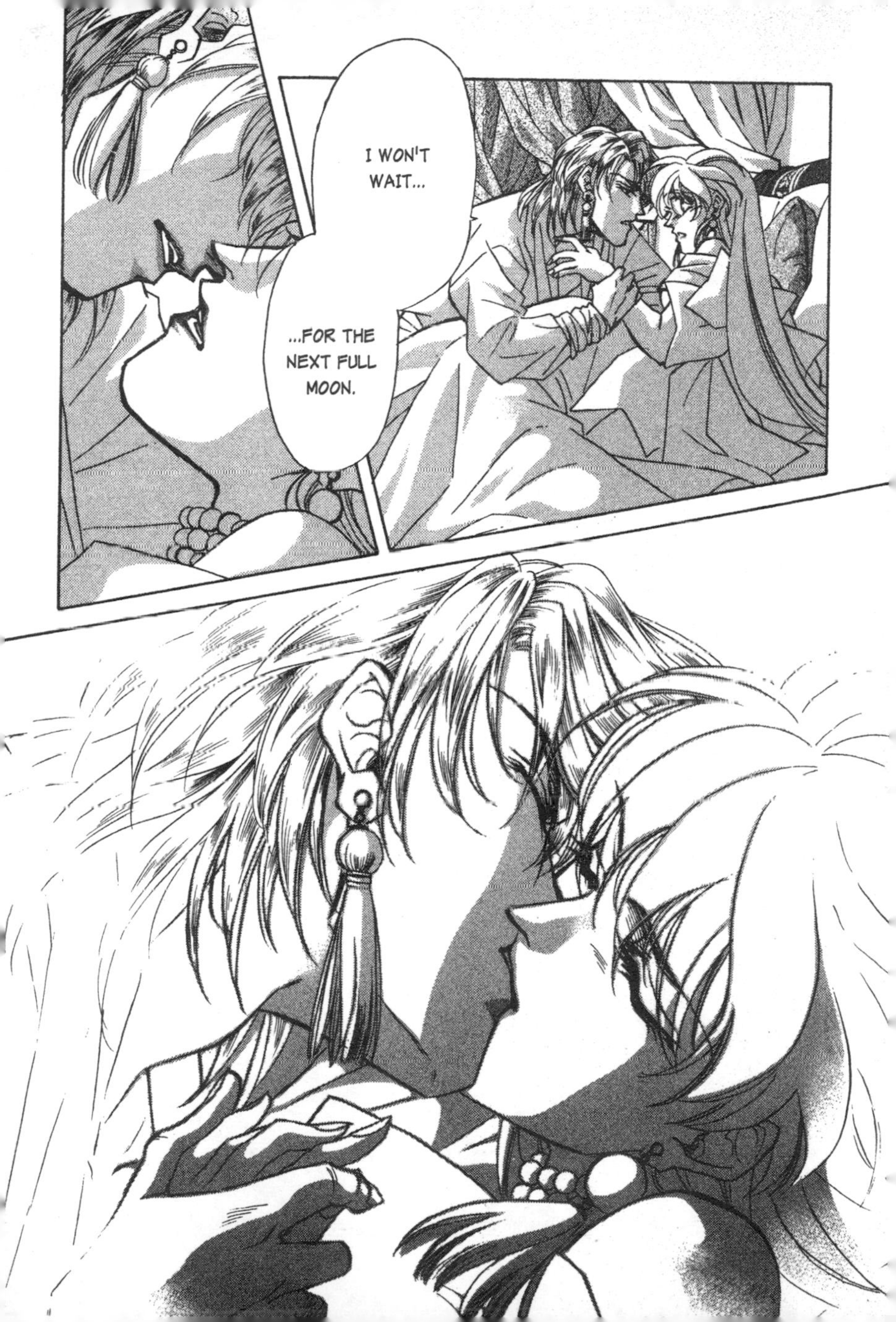
I WON'T WAIT...
...FOR THE NEXT FULL MOON.

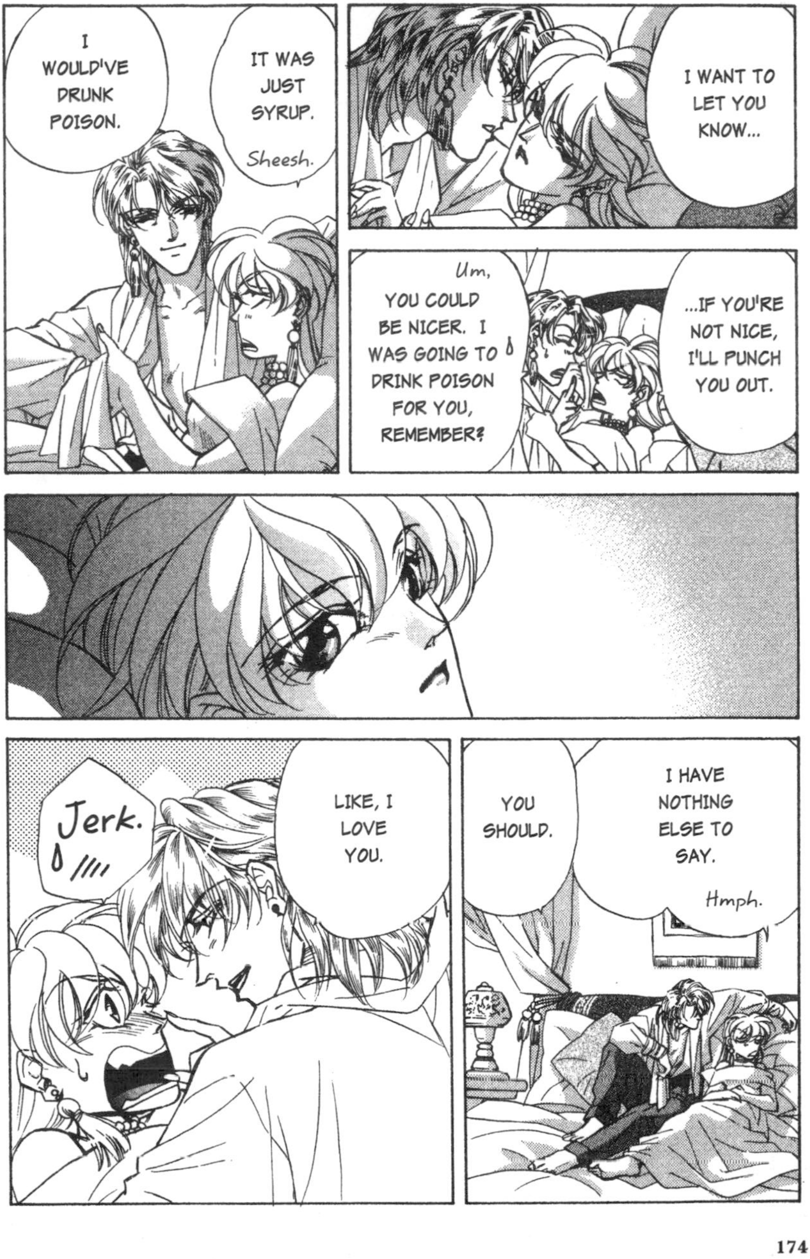
I WANT TO LET YOU KNOW...
...IF YOU'RE NOT NICE, I'LL PUNCH YOU OUT.
Um, YOU COULD BE NICER. I WAS GOING TO DRINK POISON FOR YOU, REMEMBER?
IT WAS JUST SYRUP.
Sheesh.
I WOULD'VE DRUNK POISON.
I HAVE NOTHING ELSE TO SAY.
Hmph.
YOU SHOULD.
LIKE, I LOVE YOU.
Jerk.

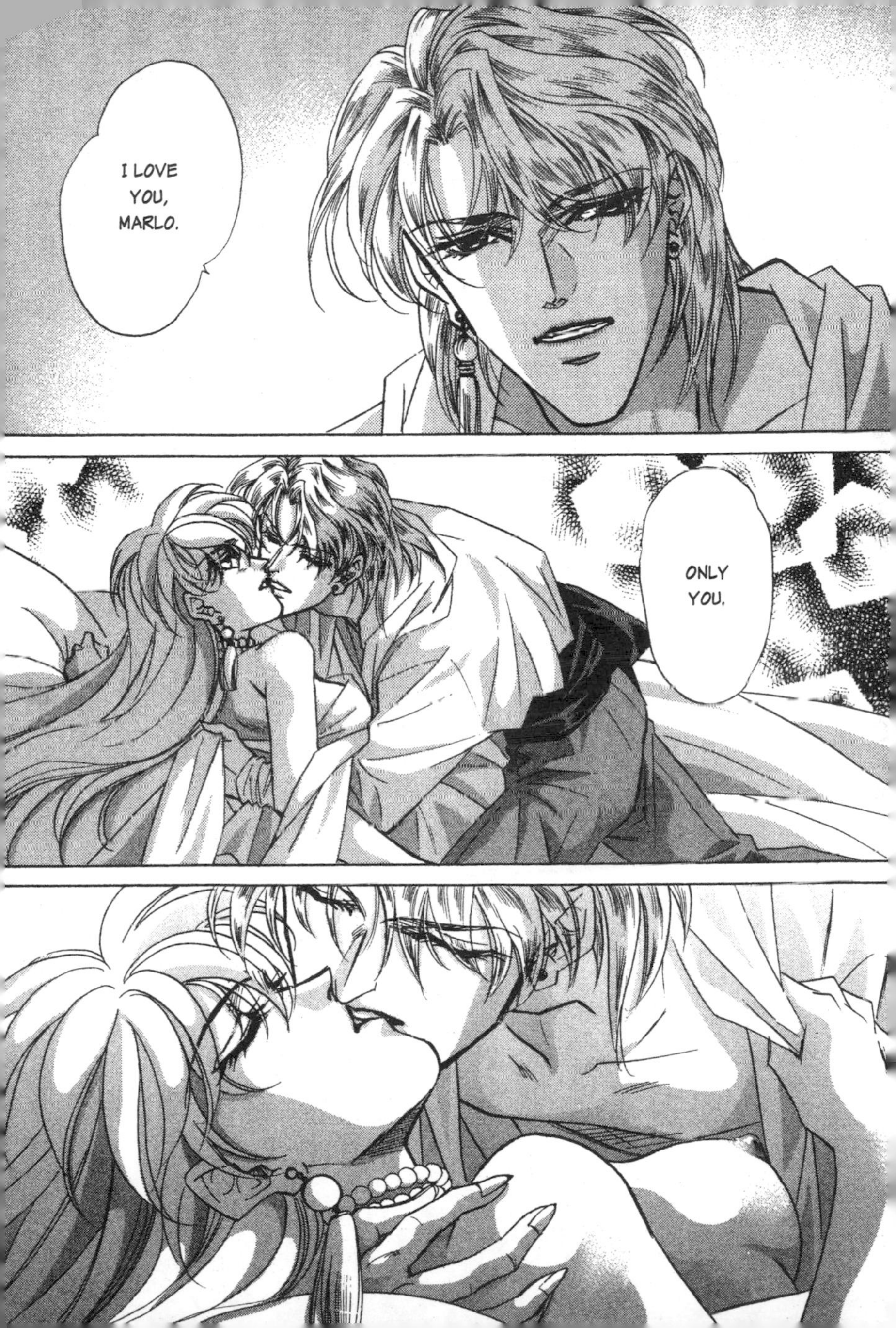
I LOVE YOU, MARLO.
ONLY YOU.

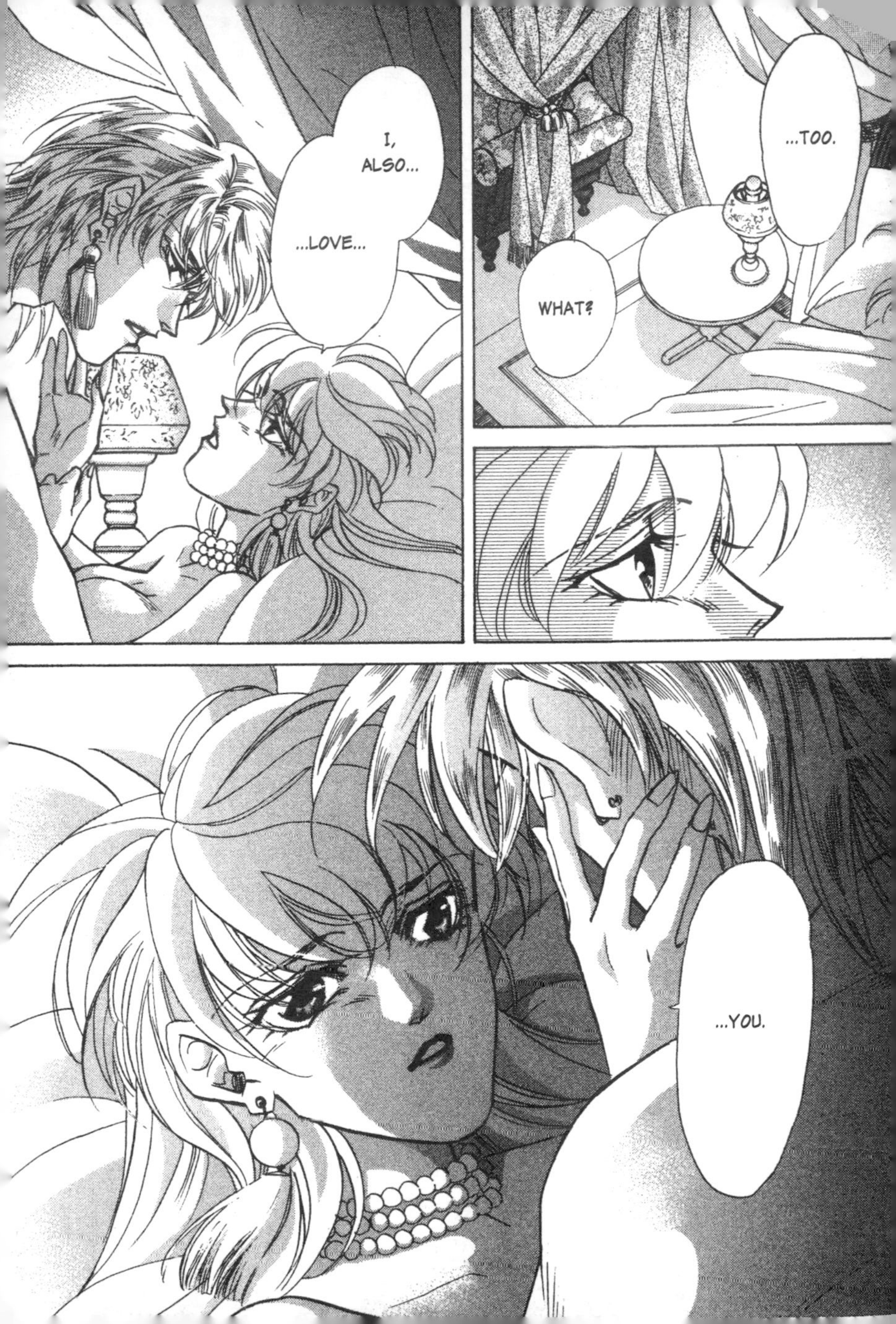
...TOO.
WHAT?
I, ALSO...
...LOVE...
...YOU.

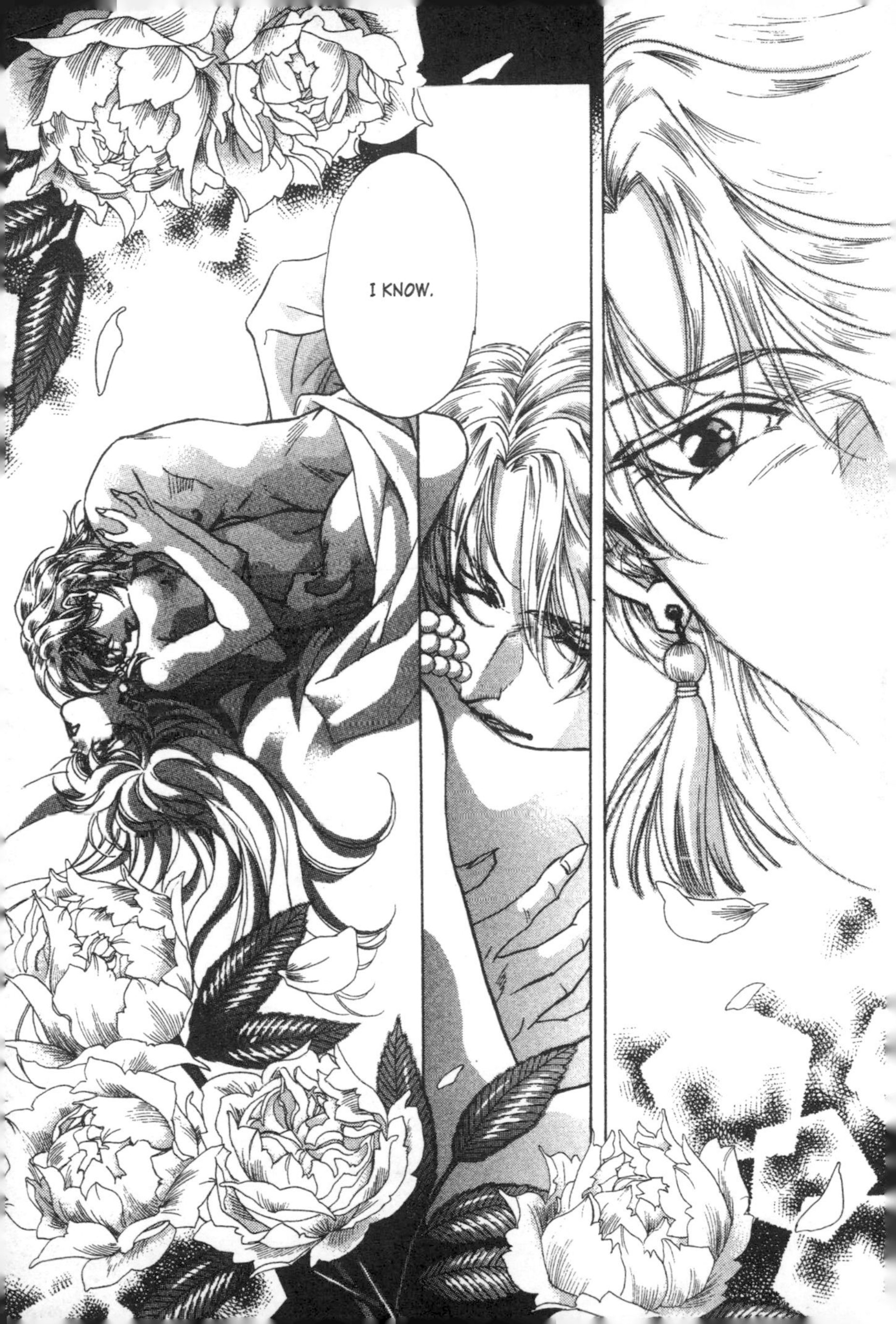
I KNOW.

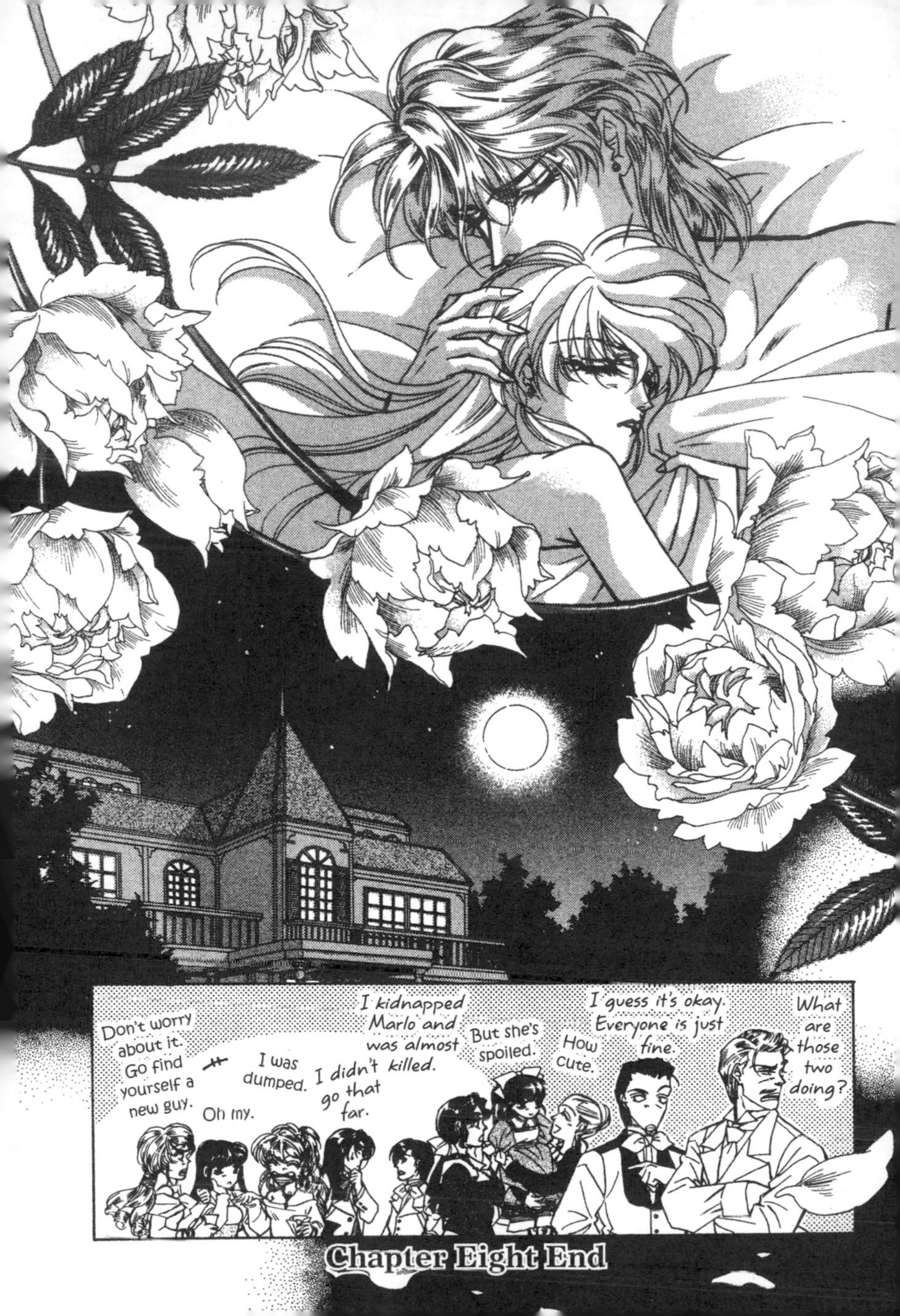
What are those two doing?
I guess it's okay. Everyone is just fine.
How cute.
But she's spoiled.
I kidnapped Marlo and was almost killed.
I didn't go that far.
I was dumped.
Oh my.
Don't worry about it. Go find yourself a new guy.
Chapter Eight End

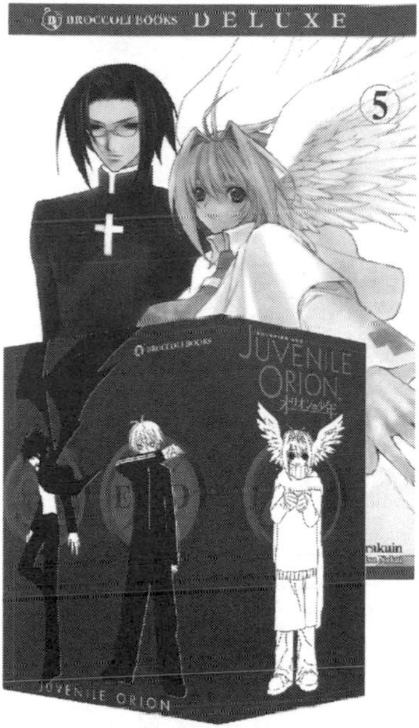
BROCCOLI BOOKS DELUXE
5
BROCCOLI BOOKS
JUVENILE ORION
オリオンの少年
JUVENILE ORION

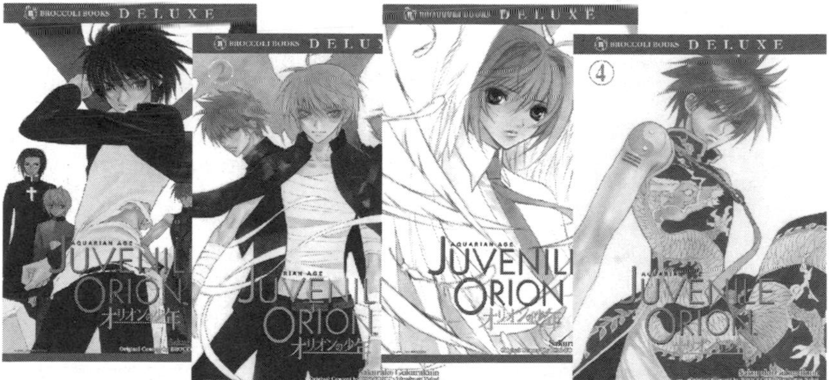
BROCCOLI BOOKS DELUXE
JUVENILE ORION
オリオンの少年
BROCCOLI BOOKS DELUXE
2
JUVENILE ORION
オリオンの少年
BROCCOLI BOOKS DELUXE
JUVENILE ORION
BROCCOLI BOOKS DELUXE
4
JUVENILE ORION

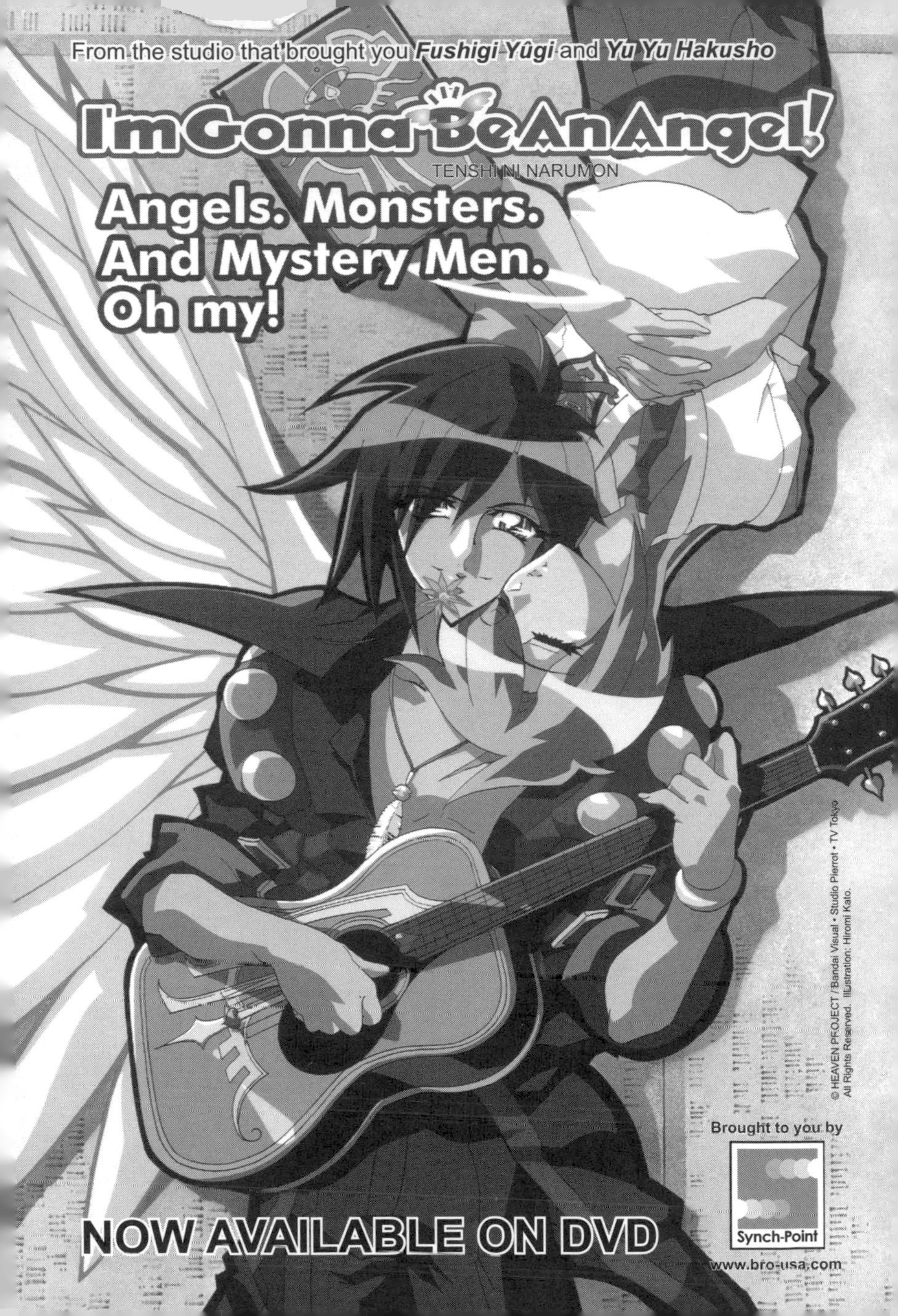
From the studio that brought you Fushigi Yûgi and Yu Yu Hakusho
I'm Gonna Be An Angel!
TENSHI NI NARUMON
Angels. Monsters.
And Mystery Men.
Oh my!
© HEAVEN PROJECT / Bandai Visual • Studio Pierrot • TV Tokyo
All Rights Reserved. Illustration: Hiromi Kato.
Brought to you by
Synch-Point
NOW AVAILABLE ON DVD
www.bro-usa.com

DI GI CHARAT THEATER™

Leave it to Piyoko!™

PLANET ANALOGUE WILL BE RICH!!
やんや

DELUXE
Di Gi CHARAT
Leave it to Piyoko!
1

Join the celebration!
Di Gi Charat Theater - Leave it to Piyoko!, starring none other than Pyocola-sama, is coming out!

Support us, the Black Gema Gema Gang, and our mission to save Planet Analogue by buying the manga!!

Available in book stores now!

brought to you by
BROCCOLI BOOKS
www.bro-usa.com

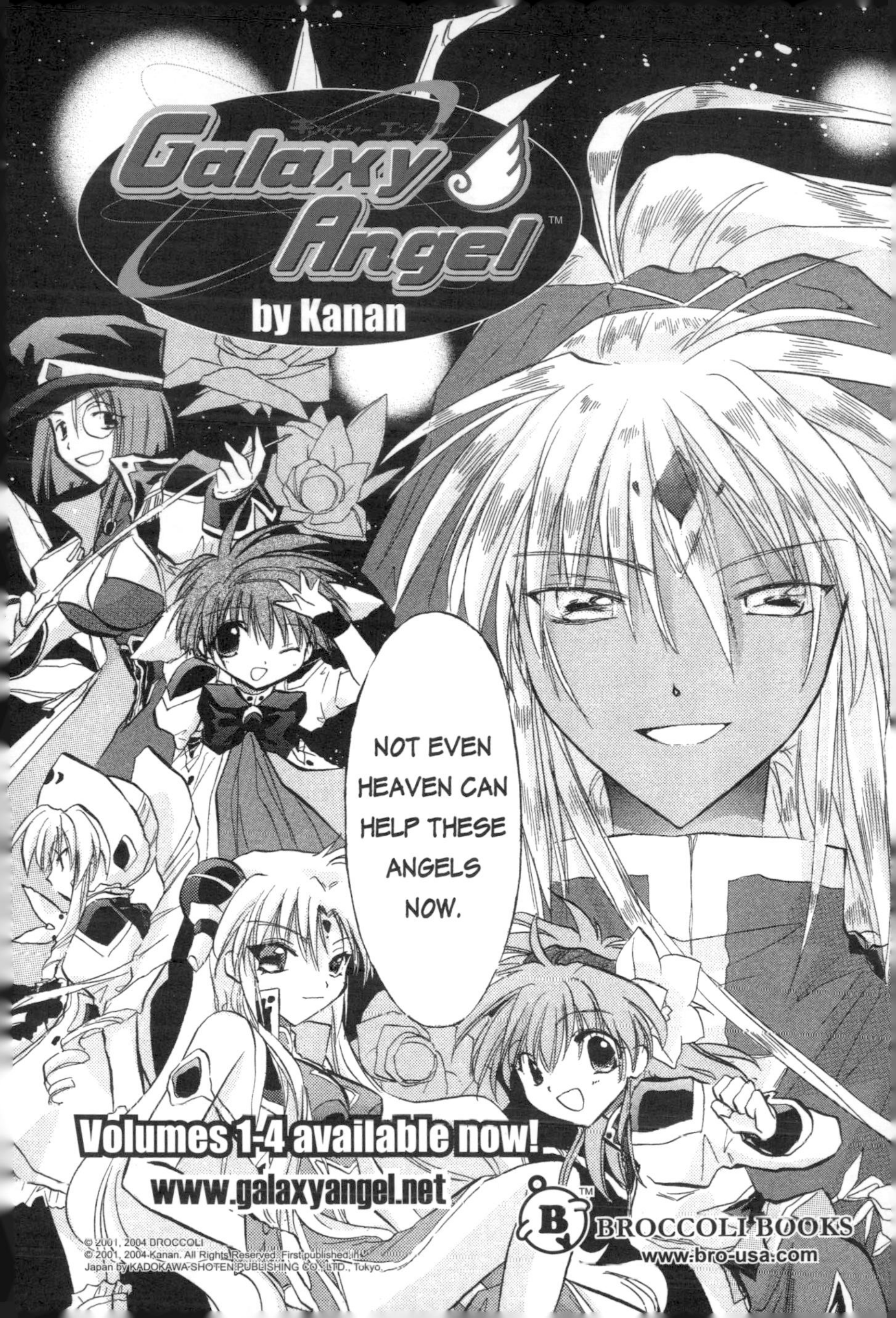
Galaxy Angel™
by Kanan
NOT EVEN HEAVEN CAN HELP THESE ANGELS NOW.
Volumes 1-4 available now!
www.galaxyangel.net
BROCCOLI BOOKS
www.bro-usa.com
© 2001, 2004 BROCCOLI
© 2001, 2004 Kanan. All Rights Reserved. First published in Japan by KADOKAWA SHOTEN PUBLISHING CO., LTD., Tokyo.

BROCCOLI BOOKS

READ: POINT: CLICK.

www.bro-usa.com

After reading some Broccoli Books manga, why not look for more on
the web? Check out the latest news, upcoming releases, character
profiles, synopses, manga previews, production blog and fan art!

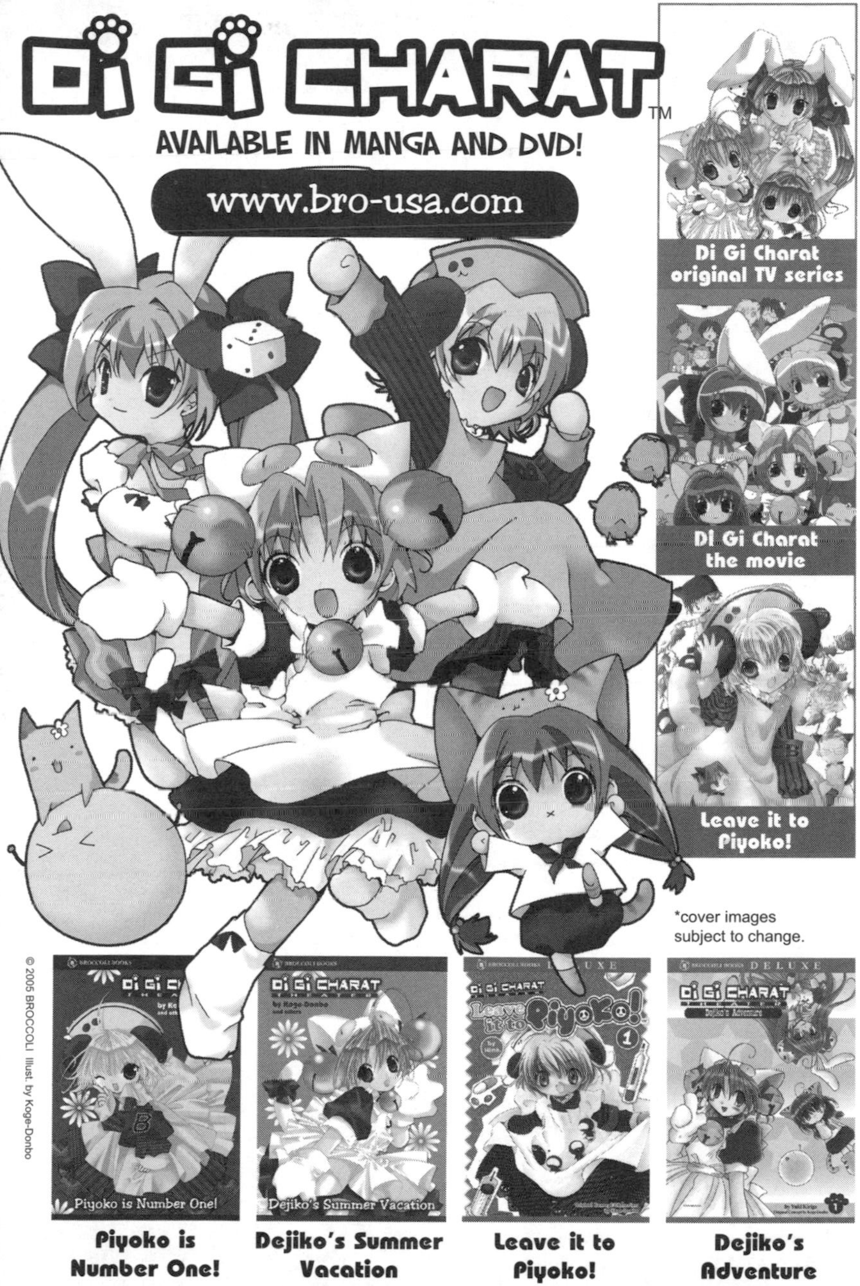

DI GI CHARAT™
AVAILABLE IN MANGA AND DVD!
www.bro-usa.com
Di Gi Charat original TV series
Di Gi Charat the movie
Leave it to Piyoko!
*cover images subject to change.
© 2005 BROCCOLI Illust. by Koge-Donbo
BROCCOLI BOOKS
DI GI CHARAT
Piyoko is Number One!
BROCCOLI BOOKS
DI GI CHARAT
by Koge-Donbo and others
Dejiko's Summer Vacation
BROCCOLI BOOKS DELUXE
DI GI CHARAT
Leave it to Piyoko! 1
BROCCOLI BOOKS DELUXE
DI GI CHARAT
Dejiko's Adventure
Piyoko is Number One!
Dejiko's Summer Vacation
Leave it to Piyoko!
Dejiko's Adventure

STOP!
YOU'RE READING THE WRONG WAY!

This is the end of the book! In Japan, manga is generally read from right to left. All reading starts on the upper right corner, and ends on the lower left. American comics are generally read from left to right, starting on the upper left of each page. In order to preserve the true nature of the work, we printed this book in a right to left fashion. Those who are unfamiliar with manga may find this confusing at first, but once you start getting into the story, you will wonder how you ever read manga any other way!

THIS QUESTIONNAIRE IS REDEEMABLE FOR:

Until the Full Moon Sticker

Broccoli Books Questionnaire

Fill out and return to Broccoli Books to receive an Until the Full Moon sticker!*

PLEASE MAIL THE COMPLETE FORM, ALONG WITH UNUSED UNITED STATES POSTAGE STAMPS WORTH $1.50 ENCLOSED IN THE ENVELOPE TO.**

Broccoli International
Attn: Broccoli Books Sticker Offer
12211 W Washington Blvd #110
Los Angeles, CA 90066

(Please write legibly)

Name: _____

Address: _____

City, State, Zip: _____

E-mail: _____

Gender: ☐ Male ☐ Female **Age:** _____

(If you are under 13 years old, parental consent is required)

Parent/Guardian signature. _____

Occupation: _____

Where did you hear about this title?

☐ Magazine (Please specify): _____

☐ Flyer from: a store convention club other: _____

☐ Website (Please specify): _____

☐ At a store (Please specify): _____

☐ Word of Mouth

☐ Other (Please specify): _____

Where was this title purchased? (If known)

_____

Why did you buy this title?

_____
_____
_____

CUT ALONG HERE

6-26-14

How would you rate the following features of this manga?

	Excellent	Good	Satisfactory	Poor
Translation	☐	☐	☐	☐
Art quality	☐	☐	☐	☐
Cover	☐	☐	☐	☐
Extra/Bonus Material	☐	☐	☐	☐

What would you like to see improved in Broccoli Books manga?

____

Would you recommend this manga to someone else? ☐ Yes ☐ No

What related products would you be interested in?

☐ Posters ☐ Apparel Other: ______________________

Which magazines do you read on a regular basis?

____

What manga titles would you like to see in English?

____

Favorite manga titles: ______________________

Favorite manga artists: ______________________

Vhat race/ethnicity do you consider yourself? (Please check one)

☐ Asian/Pacific Islander ☐ Native American/Alaskan Native
☐ Black/African American ☐ White/Caucasian
☐ Hispanic/Latino ☐ Other: ______________________

al comments about this manga:

____

____

____

CUT ALONG

Thank you!

* While supplies last.
** For residents of Canada, please send an International Reply Coupon (IRC) of $3.00 US made out to "Broccoli International."